GW00994567

A Family
DIVIDED

For our Dear Friend, Robert
Bowman

With fond and warm personal
regards on the occasion of his
first visit to Pittsburgh.
Next time bring Michelle!

Michael Ireland
April 18, 2013

Robert Mendelson

A Family
DIVIDED

A Divorced Father's
Struggle with the Child
Custody Industry

Prometheus Books
59 John Glenn Drive
Amherst, New York 14228-2197

Published 1997 by Prometheus Books

01 00 99 98 97   5 4 3 2 1

Library of Congress Cataloging-in-Publication Data

Mendelson, Robert.
  A family divided : a divorced father's struggle with the child custody industry / by Robert Mendelson.
      p.   cm.
  ISBN 1–57392–151–3 (cloth : alk. paper)
  1. Nieland, Michael L.—Trials, litigation, etc. 2. Trials (Custody of children)—Pennsylvania—Pittsburgh. 3. Custody of children—United States. I. Title.
KF228.N54M46   1997
346.7301'73'0269—dc21   97–14239
                                                                     CIP

Printed in the United States of America on acid-free paper

Acknowledgments

This book could not have been written without the generous cooperation of Michael Nieland. For nearly two years he subjected himself to my persistent interrogation in the hope that other divorced fathers and their children would be spared the ordeal of exploitation by the family court system that he and his children endured.

I am also grateful to Steven L. Mitchell, the editor-in-chief of Prometheus Books, for reading my manuscript with an open mind and concluding that, indeed, Dr. Nieland's story needed to be told. I am also indebted to Steven and to Prometheus's Kathy Deyell whose individual talents as editors enabled them to dissect my manuscript and put it back together better than before.

Certainly, I would be remiss not to thank my wife, Debra, and our two children, Lauren and Jesse, for their love and understanding while I spent many long days, nights, and weekends writing about another father's living nightmare.

Lastly, I want to acknowledge the millions upon millions of Michael Nielands out there who suddenly found themselves excluded from their children's lives simply because they were no longer married to their former spouses. It is my wish that this book will shed some light on this injustice.

Contents

8   A FAMILY DIVIDED

Foreword

I went to court to divorce my wife—not my children. My wife seemed to have other ideas.

At first, I wasn't too concerned. I assumed the courts would act swiftly and decisively to find the truth and to put an end to aberrant behavior from any quarter. After all, this is America. . . . Justice for all!

It never occurred to me that the judicial system would act in any way other than with extreme prudence, especially when making decisions that forever impact innocent children and parents. I fully expected my family's custody hearing to be free of gender prejudice and to distinguish the truth from innuendo or outright lies. I was wrong.

I witnessed firsthand how the principals in the Family Division of the court system fail to seek the truth. No one seems to pay attention to the ethical codes or the laws pertaining to custody issues—certainly not the judges or the court-appointed psychiatrists and psychologists. Consequently, gender stereotypes are perpetu-

ated, unfounded accusations become evidence, and custody schedules are ignored—with disastrous consequences to the children.
The indifference of those in charge not only damages families already entangled in the system, but sets a precedent that undoubtedly deters many other parents from ever setting foot in family
courts in order to assert their parental rights. All too often, loving
fathers or mothers are maneuvered from their children's lives forever by an ex-spouse.

The repercussions are significant. More and more, politicians,
religious leaders, behavioral experts, and informed observers blame
the lapse of law and order in our society on the breakdown of the
family. Invariably, a dysfunctional adult's background reveals an
aborted relationship with one or both parents. It seems nearly every
malefactor in the news comes from a broken home.

I believe that the courts should do everything possible to keep
both parents involved with their children after divorce. It is my contention, however, that today's family courts are fostering family
breakdown by their unenlightened, assembly-line, careless, and un-
feeling approach to child custody issues.

My education on these issues has come at great cost. What my
children and I have been forced to endure has been a horror. I wish
that what we had to confront was unique. Sadly, it isn't. Bits and
pieces of custody cases that illustrate the destructiveness of such
disputes to the families involved and to society as a whole are regularly reported in the media.

These cases only begin to tell the story. With a reported 50 percent of marriages now ending in divorce and 50 percent of such
marriages involving children, the problem is enormous. The injustices—perpetrated by ex-spouses in complicity with negligent
family courts—should not be allowed to continue unchecked.

I hope that by publicizing the ethical squalor my family has
faced there will be a greater awareness of this problem. Changes
need to be made in the laws in order to preserve the vital bonds between children and their parents. At a minimum, statutes already

on the books must be enforced so that judges, mental-health professionals, and attorneys are held accountable to the ethical rules of their professions.

Otherwise, countless children will continue to grow up without the influence and guidance of their own mothers and fathers. It takes nothing more than common sense to understand that this is very much not *in the best interests of the child, the parents, or society.*

—Michael L. Nieland, M.D.
Sometime Plaintiff, Sometime Defendant, Full-time Dad

Michael Nieland never thought of himself as a hero . . . or a villain . . . or a victim. But divorce proceedings seem to have a way of thrusting respectful, law-abiding citizens into starring roles in a drama that can be stranger than fiction, especially when young children are involved. Battle lines form. Winners emerge, but at what cost to the children?

Sometimes, as in Michael's case, the defeated fight back. It isn't easy. The odds can be overwhelming, the cost prohibitive, the system itself seemingly corrupt. At one point or another—despite the apparent injustice of it all—many finally give up. Exhausted. Forlorn. Beaten.

This true story is about one parent under siege who refused to give up.

1. Irretrievably Broken

You just don't end a marriage; it's not that easy to do.

—*Michael L. Nieland, M.D.*
Husband, Dad

The year was 1968. Michael Nieland, a twenty-nine-year-old physician, made a decision that would alter his life in a way he would never have anticipated. He accepted a research fellowship in dermatology at the Johns Hopkins Hospital in Baltimore—another important step in his developing medical career.

He had graduated *cum laude* from Harvard University in 1960 which paved the way for his admission to Harvard Medical School, from which he graduated in 1964. Next, he was off to Chapel Hill, where he spent two years as a medical intern and resident at the University of North Carolina Memorial Hospital. Then, duty called. During the Vietnam

13

era Michael served two years in the U.S. Public Health Service with the rank of surgeon (the equivalent of lieutenant commander in the navy). Because of his interest in tropical medicine, he worked as a research associate in the Laboratory of Parasitic Diseases at the National Institutes of Health in Bethesda, Maryland.

He anticipated that his dedication to a life in medicine and medical research would continue at Johns Hopkins, as would another one of his lifelong pursuits—music. He had grown up with music. His father was a highly regarded teacher and cellist in the world-renowned Boston Symphony and Boston Pops. His mother, as a young woman, sang in the Philadelphia Grand Opera Company, where she met Michael's father.

Their legacy of music was passed on to their only son—although it wasn't altogether voluntary. Michael began taking violin lessons, because his parents said so, at age nine. By the time he was a teenager, music practice had turned from drudgery into a pleasure. The results were apparent. In high school, while attending the Boston Latin School,* he became concertmaster of its symphony orchestra and later concertmaster of the Boston Public School Symphony Orchestra comprised of musicians from the city's entire school system. And, as further acknowledgment of his musical talent, he served two years as concertmaster of the Massachusetts All-State Symphony Orchestra.

Thoughts of being a professional musician did cross Michael's mind on more than one occasion, but medicine ultimately won out. Nonetheless, he didn't abandon his music despite the academic rigors required to develop into an accomplished physician. Throughout his Harvard University

---

*A public magnet school that has among other alumni Leonard Bernstein and Arthur Fiedler, not to mention Benjamin Franklin and John Hancock.

days he played in the Harvard Bach Society Orchestra and studied with famed violin soloist Ruth Posselt. When he relocated to Chapel Hill to continue his medical training, he played in the Duke University Symphony Orchestra and he furthered his training with Giorgio Ciompi, a professor of violin at Duke and a former member of the world-famous Albeneri Trio. A short time after his arrival at the Bethesda-based National Institutes of Health in 1968 he was accepted as a student of the esteemed violinist Berl Senofsky, a professor at Peabody Conservatory in Baltimore.

Now, as Michael began his tenure at Johns Hopkins, he was able to continue his violin studies with Senofsky minus the sixty-minute commute on the Baltimore-Washington Parkway he had been making previously.

It's obvious that the essence of Michael's life can be defined by two words: medicine and music.

Working hard at both pursuits left him little time for a social life. He had a date with a nurse here, a music student there, but nobody captured his heart, which was just as well, because there wasn't time to really get to know anyone. When he finished his day's work at the hospital and caught up on his medical reading, he spent the little time left either practicing his violin or attending concerts. Then it was back to the hospital—engrossed in his medical research with the electron microscope as a research fellow along with fulfilling the patient-care responsibilities of a resident in dermatology.

Before too long Michael found himself getting to know the half-dozen or so other residents. The youthful doctors shared a few laughs and gripes amid the hard work. A camaraderie developed.

During the second year of their fellowships an attractive young doctor arrived on the scene. Dr. Nancy Wanger, twenty-eight, had just completed a one-year dermatology program at the University of West Virginia, where she also attended medical school. She was accepted at Johns Hopkins to complete her residency in dermatology.

Michael found Nancy to be bright, ambitious, funny, . . . and married—with two little girls.

So much for romance. Michael, the only bachelor among the residents, sometimes wondered if there were any unmarried women left. Although disappointed at the lack of a romantic possibility, he became friends with Nancy. So did the other residents. She became one of the gang. The medical training, the laughs, the camaraderie continued. The months flew by.

With Christmas of 1969 approaching Nancy invited the residents and their spouses to her house for a holiday gathering. At the get-together Michael met Nancy's husband, Alex. They exchanged pleasantries and, in the process, Michael found out that Alex was also a physician—a resident in obstetrics and gynecology in the navy.

To Michael, Alex seemed to be a nice-enough guy. Nonetheless, he couldn't help noticing something very odd —the Wangers ignored each other. During the previous months Nancy had hinted all was not well at home. At the party it was obvious to Michael, and most likely to everyone else, that Nancy and Alex were having marital problems.

A few days later Nancy confided to Michael that her marriage had crumbled, that she and Alex were actually separated, that her husband had no interest in their two little girls, that she was unhappy and worried about what the future held for her and her children.

Michael wasn't sure what to say. He was somewhat surprised at Nancy's candor and unflattering portrayal of Alex. But, this was no time to ask her probing questions. Instead, he tried to comfort his friend.

Days passed. Nancy continued to rely on her handsome, unmarried colleague for moral support. Finally, the inevitable occurred. On a cold wintry evening, at the New Year's Eve celebration of one of the other residents, Nancy and Michael found themselves talking well into the night. When the party broke up he suggested they go for coffee somewhere. She proposed they go back to his Charles Street apartment so she could see for herself the view he often touted—overlooking Wyman Park and the Baltimore Museum of Art.

With the declared breakup of Nancy's marriage, Michael found his gentle, soft-spoken friend more and more irresistible. He and she both seemed to realize that their platonic relationship was coming to an end.

Love bloomed.

However, their careers came first. By the summer of 1970 they had nearly completed their residencies. The time came to move on. Michael had won the prestigious Earl D. Osborne Fellowship in Dermatopathology, which entitled him to spend the final year of his training with the renowned Dr. Elson B. Helwig at the Armed Forces Institute of Pathology in Washington, D.C. Meanwhile, Nancy accepted a research fellowship position in electron microscopy at the University of Tennessee College of Medicine under the tutelage of the well-known specialist Dr. Ken Hashimoto. Michael returned to the Washington area and Nancy moved to Memphis with six-year-old Brita and five-year-old Sarah, but without her husband.

Except for a few weekends, there were no ongoing junkets between cities during the next year. Nancy and Michael were too busy completing their fellowships. While there were no specific long-term commitments, Michael hoped to join Nancy in Memphis after they completed the final steps of their medical training.

Naturally, there were telephone calls. And there was mail. Michael didn't throw away a single letter Nancy sent him.

He liked very much what she had to say. She eloquently expressed her love for him over and over again.

But these weren't merely love letters. They were snippets from Nancy's life—what was and what would be.

She talked about her childhood years which were spent on a dairy farm in West Virginia. She believed the rural setting made her independent and self-sufficient, but also somewhat of a loner. When she eventually left the farm to attend Marshall University in Huntington, West Virginia, she was by her own admission a terribly shy and self-conscious freshman. For her sophomore year she transferred to Shepherd College, where she would complete her undergraduate studies while commuting from home. As she alluded to those years in a letter to Michael, she confided that, except for her eight brothers and sisters and a few friends, she didn't really talk to anyone very much—and never really wanted to—until she met him.

What about Alex Wanger, her husband of nine years, whom she had left behind in Maryland? Nancy didn't portray Alex in a particularly flattering light. She mentioned in one letter that he wanted her to consider reconciliation. She told him there was no chance.

She wasn't happy with Brita and Sarah spending time with Alex, either. In one instance she wrote that the children returned to her very distressed after visiting their father. On another occasion, when Alex had flown to Memphis for the weekend to be with the children, Nancy expressed great relief that he departed prior to a birthday party for Sarah. She explained to Michael that Brita and Sarah would have been very uncomfortable with all the other children asking who he was.

Although Nancy did convey concern to Michael about her children having only one parent, she also claimed that Brita and Sarah had never had a "real" father and that they seldom mentioned Alex. According to Nancy, he never was very much a part of the family. Indeed, four months after they moved to Memphis, she reported that Alex had not called or written Brita and Sarah even once. She also told Michael that although Brita particularly felt spurned by her father, Sarah had no feelings one way or the other about him.

Nancy admitted to Michael that she wished her husband would just miraculously readjust to his new life, settle down, have his own children, and leave her and the girls alone. A few months later Nancy got her wish. She gleefully reported that Alex had a fiancée and had accepted a two-year naval assignment in Guam.

In obvious contrast to Alex, there was nothing that Nancy said she wanted to change about Michael. In many letters she spoke warmly about his sensitivity, his kindness, his wit, his masculinity, his intellect, his thoughtfulness, his understanding, his passion for music, and his religion, Judaism. She ended one letter with the Hebrew word for good-bye: Shalom. And, when it became more and more apparent that they would exchange wedding vows in the not-too-distant future, Nancy decided she and the children should convert to Judaism. Why not? She had informed Michael that her father was Jewish although as a child she went to a Christian Sunday school rather than a Jewish one. On the family farm she didn't recollect observance of any religious ceremonies, and by the time she reached high school she said that religion had become less believable and less important to her. Not any more, though. She stated in another letter that she had no reservations or inner conflicts about becoming Jewish. She could convert wholeheartedly. And that is exactly what she and the children would do. She began to meet regularly with Rabbi Wax at Temple Israel in Memphis.

Nancy, Brita, and Sarah also seemed to acquire Michael's taste for classical music. Nancy wrote to him how she wished she could hear him play the violin, how she would watch the

Boston Pops on television and hopefully catch a glimpse of his father, how Sarah wanted to take piano lessons, how Brita and Sarah enjoyed their first concert, how she too enjoyed classical music, and how she looked forward to partaking in that aspect of his life.

Music aside, Nancy also continued to allay concerns Michael had about Brita and Sarah. Nancy asserted that she felt after they were married there would be few, if any, awkward moments for Brita and Sarah once the girls witnessed the natural, happy relationship between their mom and the new man of the house. In fact, Nancy declared that during one of his visits to Memphis Michael was more like a father to the girls than anyone had been previously. She assured him that the girls loved him too and that they hoped their mom would marry him.

She lovingly reconfirmed in nearly every letter that certainly it was her wish to marry him. In one introspective passage she did mention that she sometimes worried how he perceived her—as though he might someday feel he had been given a misleading bill of sale. However, on the heels of that particular note came a follow-up which related how fortunate she was that he loved her and how she looked forward to making him as happy as possible.

Obviously, all went well with Michael and Nancy during their year apart. Their love survived the test of time, and Brita and Sarah were prepared to have Michael adopt them and be their new father—since Alex's parental role had been diminished. Also, Nancy had completed her conversion to Judaism. So had the girls—who would continue their schooling at the Memphis Hebrew Academy. And, Nancy had given her enthusiastic support to Michael's involvement in music.

On a professional level, Michael and Nancy—after years and years of studying medicine—had finally completed their training. With the real world beckoning, Nancy decided to continue her affiliation with the University of Tennessee College of Medicine as an instructor in medicine (dermatology).

Michael would be busy, too. He received a three-year Veterans Administration Career Development Award. His options were numerous, but only one made sense: Dr. Hashimoto approved Michael's grant application and Michael accepted a clinical investigatorship position at the Veterans Administration Hospital in Memphis. In addition, he accepted the position of assistant professor of medicine (dermatology) at the University of Tennessee College of Medicine. He and Nancy would be together again.

They had separate homes in Memphis. But not for long. On August 29, 1971, a few months after Nancy's and Alex's divorce became final, Michael and Nancy were married at the Washington Hebrew Congregation in Washington, D.C., in the presence of Brita and Sarah and a few family members.

There was no honeymoon. They didn't want to traumatize the girls by immediately going off without them. So, the married couple and Nancy's two little girls flew back to Memphis the next day. Happy. In love "'til death do us part."

Nearly sixteen years later, as Michael relaxed on his flight home from a medical meeting in Charleston, South Carolina, he wondered what had gone wrong.

By the time the flight touched down at the Greater Pittsburgh International Airport, he had thought about this over and over again. He and his bride seemed so in love. But, in the end, love wasn't enough. He and Nancy were just too different. They had incompatible definitions of marriage and family. To Michael marriage meant sharing everything: love, chores, parenting, decision making, and the essential material resource—money.

Yet, from the very beginning, the Nielands never truly shared their income. In the early days there was no significant income to share. And with little money there was little strife— no "His Way" or "Her Way." But, then came money. With the bigger and bigger paychecks came more and more disagreements. There was no sharing, no compromising. Common ground on practically any subject became nonexistent.

Michael knows Nancy blames him for their mutual isolation. She apparently thought that all he cared about was money and that all the other supposed disputes were just a diversion. In turn, Michael blames Nancy. By not discussing major expenditures they were operating as two families under one roof. He can't understand why they couldn't agree on this fundamental issue. Conceivably, he theorizes, the scars of her first marriage prevented her from permitting her second husband to become her partner both financially and emotionally.

Perhaps, he speculates, it goes back even earlier—possibly to her childhood. In the nearly eighteen years they spent together she rarely talked to him about her formative years, other than acknowledging that she and her eight siblings were raised on her parents' dairy farm in the eastern panhandle of West Virginia and that things weren't always easy. There is simply no way to identify conclusively the source of Nancy's refusal to pool their incomes or to share household responsibilities or to confer on child-rearing matters. Whatever the motivation, the end result, in Michael's eyes, did irreparable harm to the marriage.

It is true that when Nancy didn't see the need for the newlyweds to deposit both their incomes in one bank account he didn't object—initially. He didn't want her to think he wasn't a modern man who fully embraced the equality of women. He understood that she didn't work for him. And, when she bestowed gift after gift on Brita and Sarah he didn't voice his disapproval, even though he expected eventually to become their father through adoption. She was the children's mother long before he came on the scene, so he reasoned that when it came to parenting, she must have known what she was doing. As for Nancy's reliance on domestic help to maintain the household, he was in no position to offer an alternative. Each parent was trying to establish a career. And, in regard to the limited amounts of time together, he again concluded it was the price dual-career families had to pay. What mattered most was that he loved her and she loved him, or so he thought.

But as the honeymoon aura wore off, Michael started to question many of Nancy's viewpoints. In retrospect, he concludes, the marriage may very well have begun to disintegrate the moment they failed to consolidate their incomes, as sparse as they were in those early days. A level of trust between husband and wife hadn't been established and, sadly, never would be established. While waiting for his luggage in the airport baggage area, he replayed in his head his version of the step-by-step demise of the Nieland marriage.

Because Michael's new wife was always too busy to discuss finances, he did what he had to do—he paid all the bills with his paycheck. He even made payments on Nancy's medical school loans (loans that he didn't recall her mentioning prior to their marriage). He accepted the responsibility. After all, they were a family. And—owing to his career development award—Michael earned $25,000 annually, nearly $15,000 more than Nancy's annual compensation.

Before long, however, things started to change.

In 1972, opportunity beckoned the one-year-old family to Pittsburgh. Nancy accepted a part-time academic position at the University of Pittsburgh and became the director of the Out-Patient Dermatology Clinic at the Pitt-affiliated Falk

Clinic. In addition, several excellent possibilities existed for joining an established private practice in the community—one of her primary interests. She soon joined the private practice of the university's dermatology division director.

The move to Pittsburgh also served Michael's career well. He became an assistant professor of medicine (in dermatology) at Pitt's medical school, where he was able to continue his three-year Career Development Award position as clinical investigator at the VA hospital that adjoined the University of Pittsburgh campus.

While the new positions offered great potential for both of them, their income level didn't change appreciably. Money was still tight and their expenses were escalating. They were now contending with a mortgage payment for a home they purchased in Squirrel Hill, one of Pittsburgh's more affluent neighborhoods. There were the ever-increasing costs for a daily sitter/housekeeper and for items such as clothing and gifts for the children. And, there was a new Nieland offspring, too—Jennie, born on May 13, 1972, just a few weeks before the move to Pittsburgh. Even with all of the added expenses the bulk of the bills continued to be paid by Michael and the Nielands continued to be a somewhat financially strapped but loving family.

One Saturday morning in 1973 Michael found himself with some free time on his hands. The kids were outside doing their own thing and Nancy had office hours until noon. Somewhat bored, he decided to do some cleaning—starting with the bedroom closets. As he made his way into an area that never saw the light of day, he discovered empty boxes. Lots of them. All kinds—from department stores, clothing stores, shoe stores. . . . He was quite surprised, but presumed that Nancy had been on some private shopping sprees. Without further thought he threw out the mini-mountain of trash. In a few hours Nancy came home. After they exchanged the usual husband and wife pleasantries he asked her about the boxes. Her reaction wasn't exactly nonchalant. She ignited into a rage, accusing him of invading her privacy. The rage didn't end with words. She punched him!

Michael was caught completely off guard. A few more roundhouse swings followed from the 110-pound doctor. He was in no real danger. Still, he had to protect himself. He shrank into a human cocoon, not unlike the defensive technique boxer Mohammed Ali would make famous. Eventually, Nancy was spent. The couple headed to neutral corners. Michael was in a state of disbelief at what had just taken place. He didn't know whether to laugh or cry. He wondered why what he did was so wrong. He knew one thing for sure—he would never talk about the boxes again. Ever!

Life went on in the Nieland household although, since the closet episode, Michael and Nancy were perhaps a little wary of each other, a little less trusting. Quite possibly, at that point Nancy made a conscious—or subconscious—decision that she must never fully reveal her income to Michael out of fear he would try to place limitations on her spending.

As the closet incident faded from memory they returned to being husband and wife in the bedroom and out. Together they went to movies, dined out, attended concerts, went antiquing, and traveled to cities such as London, New York, Chicago, and Washington for medical meetings.

Pittsburgh had begun to feel like home. They were both working very hard, but they were also making friends and Michael was becoming very involved with the musical community. He no longer took private violin lessons because of time constraints, but he still participated in occasional string quartet evenings at home with members of the Pittsburgh Symphony. And he accepted an invitation to become a member of the McKeesport Symphony Orchestra (based in McKeesport, a city bordering Pittsburgh) for the upcoming 1973–74 season.

The happy couple decided the time had come for Michael to adopt Brita and Sarah. Michael expected the procedure to be routine. After all, Nancy had told him (and had written to him) repeatedly that Alex had abandoned the children. And —since their marriage—there had been minimal contact between Alex and Nancy (although he was stationed in Guam). Michael expected to do little more than sign a few papers.

They filed the petition for adoption on November 4, 1974. It contained, in part, the following allegation:

> ... H. Alexander Wanger failed to make any effort to see the said Adoptees from November 1971 to January 1973, and only after notification to him of the interest and desire of Your Petitioner to adopt the Adoptees, did he request to see them. Further, that he did maintain minimal communication with the Adoptees since January 1973 to the present time, and has not paid any money for their support from June 1973 to the present time.

Michael was stunned by what unfolded. Alex planned to dispute the allegation. He claimed he wanted to be a father to the children, but—instead—he had been denied access by Nancy.

A hearing was held March 25 and 26, 1975, before the Honorable Hugh C. Boyle, Judge of the Orphans' Court Division of the Allegheny County Court of Common Pleas. The hearing contained accusations and counteraccusations.

The Nielands' attorney, B. Mark Chernoff, in his brief submitted to the court, argued that Michael should be permitted to adopt Brita and Sarah because Dr. Wanger had voluntarily separated himself from his children in November 1971 by moving 8,000 miles away. In three and a half years he had corresponded with his children by writing only two letters, one postcard, and two cards accompanying birthday and

Christmas gifts for the years 1971 and 1972. In that same time period Dr. Wanger was said to have talked to his children by telephone on only three or four occasions and he never saw the children. He also allegedly failed to pay any child support for nearly three years.

Based on the brief filed by Dr. Wanger's attorney, William S. Smith, it is clear that Dr. Wanger viewed the relationship with his children altogether differently. Mr. Smith asserted that Wanger did everything he was supposed to do as a father prior to his naval assignment in Guam. Once stationed there, he received no responses from his daughters after sending them Christmas presents and letters (even after he wrote to them again and asked the children to write to him and let him know if they had received their presents). He ceased further correspondence because he suspected they were not receiving his mailings.

Smith further stated that during Alex Wanger's tenure in Guam he did ask Nancy Nieland to permit his daughters to visit him, but she never responded. Dr. Wanger also returned to West Virginia for several weeks during the summer of 1973 to see his children. Two days prior to the scheduled visit it was canceled by his older daughter, who preferred to accept an invitation to visit her teacher's farm. When Dr. and Mrs. Wanger (Linda, his new wife) returned to the United States permanently in July 1974 he asked to see his children both that summer and at Christmas time, but Nancy Nieland informed him each time that, if he wanted to see them, he would first be required to consent to their adoption by Michael Nieland. Dr. Wanger refused.

As for the child support payments, Smith said that they were discontinued on the advice of counsel in an effort to elicit some response to his previous communications. Any plans to visit with his children were either ignored or some reason was given to Dr. Wanger as to why he could not spend time with them. Even though Nancy Nieland's husband was the petitioner, Smith concluded that the real "finger pointer" was Nancy Nieland. According to Mr. Smith it was Wanger's belief that Nancy Nieland had consistently thwarted his efforts to have a relationship with his children.

The court—after reviewing all of the testimony and the briefs—must have found Alex's defense compelling. The ruling was in his favor. Michael's petition for adoption was denied.

Just as in the closet episode, Michael was dumbfounded at the whole sequence of events. During the past few years he had taken a back seat in Nancy's dealings with Alex. He couldn't really say for sure what occurred between them with regard to the girls. He thought he had known. He had believed what Nancy told him and had written to him in the Memphis letters, that Alex never was very much a part of the family. In fact, from what Nancy had described time and again Michael never even contemplated any relationship with Brita and Sarah other than being their father. Now, he wondered if Nancy had been completely truthful with him about Alex not caring for his little girls . . . and what kind of paternal arrangement would be implemented . . . and how his family would be affected. . . .

Michael's wondering soon came to an abrupt halt. Nancy, despite the court ruling, had convinced Alex somehow to permit Michael to adopt the children. How did she do it? Michael wasn't sure, so he posed the question to his wife. When an explanation wasn't forthcoming he had pangs of concern over their lack of communication, but he let the matter drop. He didn't want the girls to feel like bouncing balls. He became their dad, accepting the parenting role. Alex was apparently out of the picture forever.

Still, the proceedings had left one question unanswered for Michael. Were there going to be further surprises in their marriage? He recalled a passage from one of Nancy's letters to him during their year of separation, in which she mused as to whether Michael, after their marriage, would feel he had been given a misleading bill of sale. He hoped not. He wanted to trust his wife. So, not unlike his reaction to the closet incident, he tried to forget about Nancy's apparently inaccurate portrayal of Alex.

As for being the girls' dad, nothing changed. He continued to do all the parental things—taking the girls to ballet and music lessons, to school and Hebrew school, helping them with their homework, and all the other things normally expected of a father. But, what he didn't do was to continue to agree with all of Nancy's notions of parenting such as bestowing gift after gift upon Brita, Sarah, and toddler Jennie. The two older girls didn't understand that his protests were lodged because he cared, not out of disapproval. Nancy didn't understand either. Problems were definitely developing.

By the end of 1975 Nancy had firmly established a private practice with Drs. Esther Farney and Peggy Heinz. Her career focus away from academics enhanced her income—which approached $50,000 annually—surpassing her husband's academic salary. Although their earnings were climbing, their debts were, too.

Michael couldn't figure out where the money was going. He concluded that the time had come to combine their incomes in order to have some semblance of a monthly budget so they could pay their bills and save for each child's education. It was time to sit down and discuss the specifics. But, just as Nancy never communicated to Michael why Alex gave up Brita and Sarah for adoption, Michael couldn't pin her down to discuss money matters. She never had time to discuss the problem. Instead, she became a master at finding errands that needed to be run, phone calls that needed to be returned, shopping that needed to be done. The time was never quite right for working out a household budget.

Michael tried to be understanding. He deduced that she was extremely wary of any financial constraints now that she had disposable income for perhaps the first time in her life. Maybe she viewed her income as her money and hers only and she would do with it what she wanted. While he was not happy with her obstinacy, he acquiesced. Michael was sure she would come around to his way of thinking eventually, but in the meantime the atmosphere had become ripe for resentment, mistrust, and hostility.

In the wake of this breakdown of communication the marriage moved on. The Nielands still seemed in love. They socialized with friends and their ongoing travels to various medical meetings served conveniently as romantic getaways.

But each knew little about the other's spending. Since they filed joint tax returns, each knew the other's annual income, though. For the year 1977 Michael earned close to $50,000 for his academic pursuits at the VA hospital and at the University of Pittsburgh School of Medicine. Nancy, focusing almost exclusively on her private practice, made close to $100,000.

Michael decided the time had come to curtail his academic activities in order to begin his own private laboratory practice. He established the Pittsburgh Skin Pathology Laboratory, P. C., and recruited Alan Silverman, a dermatologist just out of training, to join him as his partner. They also began a private clinical office practice.

Michael suggested to Nancy that she join them. She accepted a limited role because she didn't want to affect her thriving private practice in another part of the city. So the group practice of Drs. Nieland, Silverman, and Nieland was born—each an equal shareholder in the Pittsburgh Skin and Cancer Clinic, P. C.

The projected added income from the new practices would be put to good use. About a year earlier the Nielands had moved to an elegant stone house in Murdoch Farms, an exclusive section of Squirrel Hill. They then embarked on an extensive restoration of their 1920s home at a total cost that exceeded six figures.

While they agreed on purchasing and renovating the stately residence, they didn't agree on anything else financially. Michael continued to pay the bulk of the bills. Again and again he tried to create a Nieland financial plan. He established a separate house account, but Nancy paid no attention to it, other than making sporadic deposits and withdrawals. The account was almost always underfunded, with Michael making up the difference. Michael attempted to reason with her, but her reaction to the mere mention of money worsened over time, from her previous avoidance of the issue to changing the subject abruptly and harshly. Nancy criticized what she perceived to be his increasingly strict attitude with Brita and Sarah and nagged him about his violin practice time.

Resentment, mistrust, and hostility permeated the Nieland home. Sides were forming.

Michael no longer blindly accepted Nancy's "experienced" child-rearing judgment. His paternal instincts with preschooler Jennie were proving to be more than adequate. He often put her to bed with impromptu nighttime stories that made her laugh, or he whisked her to a fast-food restaurant for a special lunch together.

Brita and Sarah seemed much more wary of their adoptive father. Michael conceded he had relied on Nancy's "better judgment" for far too long. She had her way completely the first few years in Pittsburgh. Most notably, she decided to transfer the girls from a Jewish day school in Pittsburgh to a private girls' school—the Ellis School. He quietly assented even though they had been going to Jewish day schools since their attendance at the Memphis Hebrew Academy. He decided to be passive no longer. He was the children's father and he wanted his voice to be heard.

It wasn't. He had no say in the deluge of toys and clothes Nancy constantly purchased for Brita, Sarah, and Jennie. He vehemently disapproved—as much on principle as on the basis of his concern that the children were growing up in an environment that was only take, take, take. The older girls rarely helped clear the table after meals, they didn't make their beds, and, in general, they did whatever they wanted most of the time. Yet, he might not have minded so much if he'd received some acknowledgment from the girls and Nancy that his opinions mattered. But, he didn't.

Just as in choosing their schools, Nancy denied him any part of the decision-making process involving the kids. If Dad said, "No skipping Sunday school," Mom whispered something to the children and they ended up not going.* All the concessions, all the presents seemed to be from Mom. All the rules and all the concerns about spoiling the children seemed to come from Dad.

Michael's pleas for a greater parental role were to no avail. Instead, Nancy countered by continuing to criticize the hour or so he tried to squeeze in each day to practice the violin. Her extravagant spending on the children continued. Clearly, two sides were established. It shouldn't be too hard to figure out which side teenaged Brita and Sarah chose. Michael began to feel more and more isolated. Talking with Nancy just seemed futile.

Matters got worse. Nancy announced one day while the family was congregated in the kitchen that Sarah had ceased taking her violin lessons because, like most children her age,

---

*The majority of Jewish children who attend religious instruction do so on Sunday mornings (although the Jewish sabbath falls from dusk on Friday to dusk on Saturday, Jewish law precludes any kind of work or instruction on the Sabbath). Jewish children may also attend Hebrew school, which usually takes place on a weekday afternoon, but this is not equivalent to Sunday school.

she hated practicing. Michael seethed. For two solid years he had not only offered his daughter encouragement, but he had taken her devotedly to her Saturday morning lessons. Now it was all over and he hadn't had any say in the matter. He told Nancy privately, in no uncertain terms, that as her father he had a right to have been consulted. Evidently, she didn't agree. Not long afterward he received another similar jolt from Nancy: Brita, following Sarah's precedent, had ended her cello lessons. Once again, he seethed. This time he said nothing. What was the point?

A decision-making trend had been established. In 1979 he came home on Brita's sixteenth birthday to find Nancy's present to her parked in the driveway. He was as surprised as Brita. Or did Brita expect the used Volvo? An angry discussion ensued. Michael demanded to know why he was kept in the dark. The argument culminated with Nancy saying accusingly, "You're screaming at me."

"I'm not screaming at you," he responded, "I'm just telling you the truth and it sounds like I'm screaming at you."

Nancy was incensed. Was she going to throw another punch? Cooler heads prevailed. Brita kept her car. Needless to say, nothing was resolved.

A year later, after Sarah's sixteenth birthday—and after she had totaled a family car in a one-car accident—another surprise car appeared in the driveway with the salesperson impatiently waiting for a signature and Sarah impatiently waiting for the keys. Was this Nancy's way of giving Michael input into family decisions? Sarah got her car—a used Ford Mustang V6. After dinner another doctor-to-doctor discussion ensued. Nothing was resolved.

The next year, to Michael's surprise, he came home one day to learn that an underground lawn sprinkling system costing several thousand dollars had been installed. More high-octane words were bandied about. Again, nothing was resolved. Then, to his ongoing surprise, came the refurbishing of Sarah's charming and fully functional bathroom. Gone were the valuable antique fixtures and tub. This time no voices were raised. But, if looks could kill. ... Yet again, nothing was resolved.

Time passed, and Brita attended Bowdoin College in Brunswick, Maine. She returned home during summer vacation with her own surprise—a boyfriend who was going to help the contractor enclose the porch to the tune of $40,000 and, oh, by the way, live with the Nielands. What porch enclosure? What boyfriend? Another parental confrontation. Nancy had known about both the boyfriend and the porch, but continued to make major expensive decisions as if Michael didn't exist. Nothing was resolved.

And, on a regular basis, there were "routine" purchases using credit cards that precipitated a revolving monthly debt that usually totaled about $23,000! Michael had no way of knowing whether or not they could afford to pay their bills. Verbal altercations were now monthly, sometimes weekly, sometimes daily. Nothing was resolved.

On and on it went.

But, the vows stated "for better or worse." Michael continued to hold out hope that the "better" would surface soon, although he was beginning to wonder if he were kidding himself.

The surprises weren't over. The Nieland family grew. Michael and Nancy had always hoped to have more children after Jennie. And, despite their compounding problems, their sex life never suffered. Sometimes, the problems may even have made it better. Yet, no more children arrived until Nathaniel, born October 15, 1980, and Ariel, born June 14, 1982. Michael was overjoyed. It was almost as though he and Nancy were being given a second chance. But their lives didn't change. He and Nancy didn't cut back on their office hours. Their financial lives remained separate. The round-the-clock household help expanded dramatically. And the heated discussions resumed. Michael wasn't happy with Nancy.

Nancy didn't appear to be happy, period. Perhaps it was attributable to postpartum depression, which isn't uncommon among women who have recently given birth. She started seeing Dr. Albert Corrado, a psychiatrist. She urged Michael to attend a few of the sessions. He agreed—he would try anything. But it didn't seem to help their relationship. The bickering and nagging and accusations didn't go away. For example, their difficulties resolving financial matters generated bitter discussion in Dr. Corrado's office. After much debate, Michael suggested that they simply divide up all the fifteen or so charge accounts and each be responsible for paying his or her accounts instead of Michael paying all the bills and trying to get Nancy to help. (Dr. Corrado thought this was a good idea, but Michael thought sitting down together and communicating about financial matters on a regular basis was a better solution.) Nancy agreed to the plan and the couple's credit cards were divided up essentially equally, based on their outstanding balances, although Nancy earned far more than her husband. Michael took solace in the fact that all future charges Nancy made would be her responsibility. Because of the disparity in income, he thought the agreement was more than fair on his part, although he sensed that Nancy believed he had somehow taken advantage of her. Michael noticed that she seemed even more resentful toward him.

Finally, on July 19, 1983, the inevitable happened. The 11:00 news had ended. Michael had gone to bed. Johnny Carson blared on the bedroom TV. Michael was about to fall asleep when he heard what sounded like distraught voices. It sounded like Nancy and Brita—home from school for summer vacation. He couldn't quite make out what they were saying except that Brita seemed upset. Suddenly, there was silence. Then, the master bedroom door flew open and a white pump came hurtling at Michael, who was flat on his back. Nancy's designer shoe whizzed by, barely missing his head. He had dodged the first bullet, but the onslaught was far from over. Nancy came barreling at her supine husband. She flailed away while spewing out allegations that he had looked at Brita's checkbook. (He had done so because Nancy refused to tell him how much money she was giving their daughter monthly.) Michael tried to use his forearms as shields to block most of the blows. Suddenly, her yelling stopped and was replaced by a shriek of pain. Michael opened his eyes. Apparently, Nancy had hurt her arm while using him as a punching bag. Michael suppressed his anger. He sprang into action, dressing quickly so he could take his wife to the hospital. Off they went to the emergency room of nearby Presbyterian University Hospital. X-rays were taken. She had an ulnar fracture of the right forearm. Out of embarrassment, they concocted a story about Nancy tripping on some steps at home. End of story, for now.

Michael was astounded at the escalation of violence in their relationship. Without question he felt bad about her arm injury. Yet, just as in the closet skirmish, he knew in his heart he had done nothing wrong. He also knew he couldn't continue living in this bizarre household. It wasn't safe for anyone—and it was not the way life was meant to be lived. There needed to be changes. It was time for both of them to spend more time being husband and wife and father and mother rather than being two stressed-out workaholics who passed in the night. They had to reduce their office hours.

Naturally, a mutual work reduction would mean less income. It shouldn't be too painful a sacrifice, however. Families don't need $500,000 annually to survive, Michael reasoned. He was confident they could find a way to scrimp by on something like $300,000 a year! Of course, that would mean establishing the infamous family budget which would have to reflect the projected loss of income. It would also mean less time in the office for each doctor, which should translate into less work-related stress for each of them, more time for their kids, reduced time for the omnipresent house-keepers, and more time for the two of them to pursue mutual and separate interests.

Lately, everything Nancy did seemed to be work-related, which Michael guessed may have been one of the reasons she started slugging him. She had no other outlet. He, on the other hand, had music. Since Ariel was born he had resumed quarterly violin lessons with celebrated violinist Sidney Harth, a Pittsburgh resident. In addition, he had become executive vice president and a member of the board of directors of the Pittsburgh Youth Symphony Orchestra, and he also served on the boards of several other musical organizations.

This proposed schedule and priority revamping should give Nancy a chance to cultivate her own outside interests. He would be more than happy to accompany her in whatever activities she chose, if he were welcome. Otherwise, he would give Nancy her space. It didn't matter to him. He would not be insulted either way. He just wanted to end the frustration in the Nieland household. He didn't want a sequel to the broken-arm trauma. Reduced office hours and an overall budget were the components of the only plan that made sense.

How could she be upset about the prospect of working less? If they truly pooled their incomes, they would still be awash in money. He would offer as proof the fact that he had put himself on a budget starting in 1978 and she hadn't even noticed. Yet, he had saved enough money so that they could purchase a condominium for an ailing aunt and so that they could join Alan Silverman in acquiring an office building for the dermatopathology laboratory and a satellite clinical office. (Even though Michael used his own savings, the investments were in the names of both Nielands.)

It's not as if a budget would mean no purchasing of an occasional extravagance. Michael himself had proven that to be the case. Because Nancy had her own retirement fund, he had reinvested his own VA retirement fund in a violin he long coveted. But he did so only after he made sure it would not create any hardship debt, and he knew there would be no hardship because he knew how much money of his own he had coming in and going out.

Nancy wanted no part of Michael's plan, whether it included extravagances or not. In fact, she didn't even want to discuss it with him. She remained unhappy. She continued to see Dr. Corrado and insisted that Michael continue to attend the sessions. He would, but he wasn't hopeful of any kind of miraculous resolution. Their problem was basic: a total lack of communication. The cure was just as basic: trusting each other. Still, he went yet another time to the doctor's office.

He was stunned by what he heard. She accused him, in front of the psychiatrist, of breaking her arm. To Michael, Nancy's accusation was incomprehensible. What good could come out of this when the truth wasn't discussed? He got ready to walk out.

But she wasn't finished yet. She threw out the word "divorce." He was devastated further, if that were possible. Despite all of their problems—and he realized they were significant—he had never really contemplated divorce. How could she? Didn't she love him any more? Could her profound unhappiness have been attributable to postpartum depression as much as two years after Ariel's birth? Or was there something more?

In the coming weeks and months the word "divorce" kept coming up again and again from Nancy, but more as an insult than a threat or a promise. Needless to say, the Nielands' problems weren't going away. It depressed Michael, who had hung on through thirteen years of marriage.

There was no family budget. No talk of reducing office hours. Michael worried that Nancy had become obsessed with building the size of her practice. He knew that she was a capable physician and mother, but there are only so many hours in a day. No wonder she always seemed so stressed out by the end of the day—that is, when he even saw her. She never seemed to be home. And when she was, and it was time for bed, there was less intimacy. Often, she tucked Nathaniel and Ariel into the queen-sized bed she and Michael shared or she stayed up late dictating letters to referring physicians into a tape recorder.

With no wife to speak of and with an entourage of housekeepers orchestrating the meals and practically running the household, Michael sometimes felt like a visitor in his own home. He didn't fully enjoy his time with his children, especially with the housekeepers' youngsters almost always hovering about. He found himself seeking refuge in the library practicing his violin more and more.

Nancy's long hours were paying off financially. Her practice was booming. She knew how to market herself. Frequently, she appeared on television or radio giving advice on dermatology problems. Michael and his partner had also built a solid private practice in clinical dermatology and dermatopathology that included evaluating all of Nancy's patients' biopsies. Because the nature of Nancy's practice focused exclusively on seeing patient after patient rather than time-intensive laboratory work, she had begun to out-earn her husband rather substantially, surpassing a two-to-one ratio, even though Michael's 1983 income was $185,025—exceeding the national average for physicians. Clearly, there was more than enough money to go around—or should have been. Including Nancy's $381,878 paycheck for 1983, the combined Nieland income was well over $500,000.

Yet, incredibly enough, there were some months Michael had trouble paying all the bills. On paper they were wallowing in money, but in real life it was nowhere to be found. Where was it all going? He didn't know because their income was never really combined. And not only was the financial secrecy causing severe marital strife, Michael discovered it was penalizing him financially. Because the Nieland accountant recommended they file joint income tax returns, the IRS viewed the Nielands' incomes as one. For 1983, Michael had had 56 percent of his income withheld, Nancy 46 percent. The disparity penalized Michael by depriving him of disposable income, and it gave Nancy tens of thousands of dollars of additional spending money. True to form, he had no input into how she spent her inequitable windfall. He asked her only to do what was fair. If she refused to combine their incomes, she needed at least to alter her withholding tax. She refused without providing any explanation. Michael just couldn't get her to sit down with him to discuss the matter.

Like a groggy prizefighter entering the final rounds of battle, Michael held out hope that at some point establishing a budget and merging their incomes would make sense to Nancy out of love and fairness. By knowing their expenses there wouldn't be a need for excessive earnings. They would be able to modify their work schedules so there could be more time for family life. There would still be plenty of money.

Michael wanted to believe changes were imminent. He didn't want to contemplate divorce. He wanted to make his marriage work. But nothing changed.

One late afternoon he was home with the children, the housekeepers, and no Nancy. (Nothing unusual.) He noticed that everybody was doing his and her own thing, except for

Jennie. He seized the opportunity, asking her if she would care to join him in the living room for an impromptu recital.

Jennie had the makings of an excellent pianist, but, like most kids her age, she hated to practice and, just as with Brita and Sarah, that was fine with Nancy. Michael had somewhat resigned himself to the fact that Jennie, too, would soon give up the piano.

He actually expected Jennie to decline his request, but she didn't. They adjourned to the living room and soon the sounds of a violin and piano filtered through the home. In the background, a door could be heard opening. It was Nancy. She was home. She walked into the living room and immediately asked Jennie if she would like to go shopping. The music stopped. Michael was infuriated, but he was weary of confronting his wife. In a few moments mother and daughter were gone. Michael put his violin away.

The marriage was falling apart at the seams.

By the mid-1980s, their combined annual income had surpassed the $600,000 plateau. Nancy continued to out-earn Michael on approximately a two-to-one basis. But, to Michael, it shouldn't have been *his* money or *her* money. It should have been *their* money. If their incomes were combined Nancy would be making the greater financial contribution to their marriage, but Michael wouldn't be contributing a paltry amount, unless an annual paycheck in the $150,000 to $200,000 range is considered meager. Contributions to family life cannot be measured purely in dollars and cents. But all this was academic because there was no combining of income.

Communication between the two, though never ideal, had become all but nonexistent. They continued to meet regularly with Dr. Corrado, but it wasn't helping. In many of the sessions Nancy dwelled on what she called his incessant violin playing. He responded that he practiced no more than an hour a day three or four times a week. Dr. Corrado told Michael privately that it wouldn't matter if he practiced for five minutes or for three hours, it would always seem like three hours to Nancy because she just didn't approve. Michael couldn't understand why there was such resentment. He thought back to her Memphis letters and how Nancy had written that she was looking forward to sharing his passion for music and how she hoped he found the time to practice his violin because she knew that helped him relax.

Michael tried not to let the marital woes interfere with being a father. With Nancy often busy doing whatever it was she was always doing, even on weekends, he began to take five-year-old Nathaniel and three-year-old Ariel out to breakfast every Sunday, followed by a stroll to a little park nearby where they often played hide-and-seek. The kids seemed to love the time with their dad and he certainly relished the chance to be a father without competing with housekeepers, babysitters, and their children.

There were no Sunday rituals that included Brita and Sarah. They wanted nothing to do with their dad. He didn't know what he could do to rectify the situation. He attended all of their milestone events such as debutante balls and school graduations, but, other than that, he rarely saw them any more. Both were away at school, Brita in medical school and Sarah in college. They were home only in the summers, and when they were home he realized he was no longer welcome in their lives. Probably, he never had been. So, he did the only thing he could do, he gave up. He did so with a profound sense of frustration, sadness, and disappointment. He had tried to act with the best intentions by adopting two little girls who Nancy said had been abandoned by their natural father—and adopt them he did, even though it was far from a routine adoption. Now, after years of emotional investment, his two daughters treated him as if he got in their way.

He held his wife largely responsible because she perpetually denied him a meaningful role in their lives.

He vowed to himself it wouldn't be the same for Jennie, Nathaniel, or Ariel. Or would it? He perceived the same pattern being established all over again. That realization dawned on him during a sunny Saturday afternoon in 1986. He wanted to take advantage of the weather and take the kids to the park. Nancy, as usual, wasn't home, but a babysitter was on duty. Michael told her she could leave. She said that was impossible. Nathaniel had a hair appointment at 2:30 P.M. (at Nancy's chic Walnut Street salon). Afterward, she had orders to take Nathaniel and Ariel to her house for the evening so that Nancy could take Sarah and Jennie out to dinner. Michael told the babysitter he would take care of the younger ones after the hair appointment. She responded by saying, "You're putting me in a very difficult position." He couldn't believe what he was hearing. "Look," he remembers saying, "this is my house, these are my kids, please take the rest of the day off." She did, but when Nancy returned home around 9 P.M. with the older children, she was furious that he had adjusted her plans.

It was happening all over again. The schedules that didn't include Michael, the incessant shopping sprees, the full-time help in the house, the ongoing income schism. He couldn't let history repeat itself, but he didn't know how to stop any of it. So, he called his attorney, Mark Chernoff. Mark suggested that Michael meet with Paul Leventon, an experienced and highly regarded attorney who included domestic litigation in his practice.

Michael met with Leventon and told him everything he believed to be true:

He lived in a day-care center. His wife had become a workaholic, earmarking nearly all of her time to her dermatology practice. He also worked hard, but he knew when to turn out the lights. There were other things to do in life than just make money. When it came to earnings, he wanted to combine their incomes in order to have some semblance of a monthly budget so they could pay their bills. Wasn't that commonplace among married couples? As for family life, he wanted more time together. He wanted the chance to instill in the still impressionable six-year-old Nathaniel and five-year-old Ariel foundations in cultural and ethical pursuits such as music and religion. The Nieland household had no family intimacy. Instead, it overflowed with a steady stream of babysitters and housekeepers who filled in while mom worked nearly nonstop and dad—uncomfortable with so many different "helpers" milling about—sought refuge in the library after his own long day at the office. When mom did make it home she spoiled the kids, perhaps out of guilt, with endless shopping excursions that often amounted to piles of unused toys and clothing costing hundreds and sometimes thousands of dollars. He had tried to put his foot down on all of it, including the costly designer clothes, the cars for their sixteenth birthdays . . . but Nancy not only ignored his pleas, she became incensed at his interference in how she wanted to raise "her" kids. And she accused him of being no better a parent than she, with his "twenty-four-hour, seven-day-a-week violin playing," which in all actuality, amounted to a few hours each week, and which he had been doing since their courtship days. In any event, with Brita now twenty-three, and Sarah twenty-two, he conceded that it was probably too late to be instilling core parental values. They had essentially disowned him. But it wasn't too late for Jennie, Nathaniel, and Ariel. And if having a normal family life meant divorcing Nancy, it was a sacrifice he was now prepared to make, but one he hoped he didn't have to.

Leventon suggested that Michael discuss the idea of divorce with Nancy before filing any papers. Maybe the finality of the word "divorce" coming now from Michael would make her more receptive to making changes. In a *personal and confidential* letter to the attorney dated August 20, 1986, concerning the suggestion, Michael described both Nancy's reaction and his own:

> I was able finally to discuss with Nancy on August 15 the fact that I consulted you. It's difficult to talk with the housekeepers always around and about. Nancy's reaction seemed to be one of shock and dismay, a surprise to me since she had frequently urged a separation and divorce herself over a two- to three-year period. The pain for her has been evident all week and this has certainly not made things easier for me. Unfortunately, she has not been able to grasp what has led me to take this step. As of the moment she has not consulted an attorney, as far as I know. In fact, last night she told me she couldn't afford an attorney! I am baffled about her finances as I explained to you. The other day when I asked her to share a $900 bill for the roof she started sobbing and said she couldn't. . . . Yet, [the IRS tax return] indicates her take-home pay last month was $19,000 (plus bonuses)! . . .
>
> I know I don't have to describe for you the deep pain I feel about all this. I have made many difficult decisions over the years, but this is the toughest problem I've ever had to face. Her anguished reaction doesn't make it any easier. . . .

Somehow, during the next few weeks, Nancy found a way to earmark some of her income for an attorney. Yet, contrary to the belief that lawyers turn into sharks when confronted with a potentially lucrative divorce case, Leventon made a sensible and responsible recommendation. It was agreeable to Michael. A few days later, Nancy's attorney, Harry Gruener, received a letter dated September 16, 1986,

outlining Michael's concerns. Leventon informed Gruener
that Michael would seek a divorce from Nancy unless she
would agree to end the constant bickering; stop hiring
babysitters during family time; eliminate living by the creed
"What I earn is mine and what you earn is yours"; cut back
on their working hours so there would be more family time;
and end the allegations of "financial malfeasance." Furthermore, Michael wanted to make sure Nancy understood that
Nathaniel and Ariel were to sleep in their own beds, not in
their parents' bed, and that Nancy would grant Michael limited private time to practice the violin.

Leventon also acknowledged to Gruener that he realized
there are always two sides to every story and that his client
would consider any changes or behavior modification requests sought by Nancy.

Michael received no response from Nancy, nor did Paul
from Harry. Finally, on a typical discordant telephone call between the Nieland medical offices, this time concerning au-
tomobile insurance, Michael remembers asking out of frustration: "What about responding to the letter my attorney
sent you?"

He was jolted by her response. In order to demonstrate to
Paul the level of hostility that existed he immediately jotted
down her reply: "That ridiculous letter! My reaction to that
letter was that you had a total and complete lapse of psychiatric proportions."

A short while later Michael found a letter left out in the
open that Nancy had started to write to him but evidently
never finished. He was amazed and heartbroken by its content, which was so very different from the tone of her letters
from Memphis.

Nancy wrote that she felt Michael had an intense dislike
for her. She claimed that they could no longer have a conversation that didn't leave her in tears and Michael furiously is-

suing a new set of accusations and ultimatums. He wanted to make all the rules, she said, and that as his wife she had no rights, privileges, or feelings. She called Michael a monster who hurt her in every possible way and claimed that it was very clear in the past year and a half that he was disinterested in her. She wondered if every time he looked at her he saw nothing but dollar signs. As proof, she challenged him to recall the last time they spoke about anything in which the discussion didn't revolve around money. She couldn't remember such a conversation, except for the times he launched verbal attacks at her about anything including the supposed glut of housekeepers, alleged greasy meals, and the long hours she kept. She pointed out that he, on the other hand, didn't answer to anyone about what he did all day every day. She accused him of coming and going without ever letting her know his plans or inviting her to join him. The very idea of him divorcing her because she hadn't done enough to please him would have been hilarious, she thought, if it weren't so tragic. In conclusion, she questioned why she kept taking care of him, trying to help him, chasing after him. Her only explanation was that she still loved him. Yet, she couldn't understand why she loved him when she considered the enormous amount of time he spent with his violin, his records, his attorney, his meetings, and his financial calculations.

There was no signature at the end of the letter, but Michael knew the handwriting well. Why, he wondered, did it have to come to this? Why couldn't they have been a family? Was it really too late? All these questions ran through Michael's mind after he read the unsigned letter. He pondered his next move. How about dinner? An old-fashioned family dinner. No arguing about money, no nagging about violin playing, just good food and a little family conversation. He made his request to Nancy as they headed for work. She didn't commit one way or the other. Still, he was optimistic. He thought about it between patients and on the way home.

Dinnertime finally arrived. Michael came downstairs. He saw Nathaniel and Ariel on the porch already eating with a neighborhood boy and the housekeeper's four-year-old child. Michael, disappointed, walked into the dining room only to be greeted by Jennie and a girlfriend, but not an invitation to stay. So, he headed to the kitchen, where at the table he found Nancy and his elderly Aunt Minnie, whom he learned Nancy invited for dinner. Michael sat. The housekeeper served the threesome. The family dinner had begun. There was no conversation. If there had been, their voices would have been competing against screaming kids running about, kitchen cabinet doors slamming, and the housekeeper loading the dishwasher. Michael barely touched his dinner. The family dinner ended. Michael had some answers to his earlier questions.

It became official. On January 12, 1987, he filed for divorce. Michael became a plaintiff. Nancy became a defendant. They separated, except neither one moved out. She wanted the house. So did he. For the time being Michael moved into Brita's unused bedroom.

Michael refused to relinquish his claim on the house because he viewed it as a type of an anchor. It was the only home Nathaniel and Ariel had ever known and the only home Jennie could really remember. As long as he kept the family home he kept a valuable tie to his children. That was important to him because he worried that a mighty struggle concerning custody might take place. His fear stemmed in part from a few remarks he recalled Nancy making about her first husband, Alex, when she wrote from Memphis that she hoped to completely sever every association with the Wangers as soon as possible and that she wanted to limit any time Alex might try to spend with Brita and Sarah.

Neither Michael nor Nancy budged on the house issue. It was lawyer time. They began in earnest to dismantle the marriage. It started to get ugly. The housekeepers had become totally unresponsive to Michael's requests that they leave when he was home with the children. They told him Nancy had given them instructions that they weren't to pay attention to anything he said.

It got uglier. He asked Nathaniel and Ariel if they wanted to go see the movie *Aristocats*, but Ariel replied, "Mom made me promise not to go anywhere with you." Nathaniel also declined his offer: "Mom said not to go anywhere with you. She can buy me more toys than you can because she has more money."

Meanwhile, the attorneys had no progress to report on any issues. Michael had had enough. He worried about his relationship with his children being undermined further by Nancy. He contacted his attorney, hoping to underscore the urgency of the situation. Michael felt it would be better to compose his thoughts in a letter that Leventon could read at his convenience rather than interrupt his busy attorney who, Michael realized, had many cases to juggle. Besides, Michael didn't want to forget any of the points he needed to make. He also knew that attorney-client communications cost money—they are timed and billed accordingly—and letters tend to be a faster mode of relaying information.

The attorneys continued their posturing while the awkward living arrangement continued. Incident after incident occurred. As they began their fifth month of separate bedrooms, something happened that was so ridiculous Michael almost found it humorous:

He returned home from work to find a familiar sight—a housekeeper making dinner. It smelled good. A rib roast was in the oven. He told the housekeeper he could take over from here and she could go home. She said she couldn't. He stuffed a check into her pocket and showed her the door. About an hour later, around 5:30 P.M., he heard Nancy's car pull into the driveway. Next, he heard what sounded like some kind of commotion. Michael looked out the window. Nancy had whisked all the children into her car. He had no idea what she was doing, at least not for a moment. Then, while Michael watched in silence, Nancy dashed into the kitchen, opened the oven door and took out a cooking casserole. In her haste, the glass top fell off and shattered on the floor. Nancy didn't change her expression or clean up. She was on a mission. She hurriedly, and this time adroitly, secured the rib roast from the oven. In a few seconds the roast and casserole were packed into her car. Off went Nancy, the children, and dinner, leaving nothing but the aroma behind. They returned hours later—with no explanation and no leftovers. Michael found the whole scene appalling.

Clearly something had to give, and it did.

Through the attorneys Nancy offered Michael a huge cash settlement basically to give up the house and relinquish the children. This time Michael was outraged. In a four-page letter he drafted to Leventon on May 10, 1987, Michael considered the offer not only insulting, but "almost a bribe, as though I would sell out [my children] for pieces of eight."

He reflected further that perhaps he should consider seeking sole custody of the children, although he really just wanted what is fair—to share them: "Maybe if we go for 100 percent we can at least get half?" However, if he were awarded sole custody he had no doubts he could handle it by making some changes in his schedule. He could work out of his home much of the time because all he really needed to interpret his patients' biopsy slides was a microscope: "In terms of 100 percent custody . . . I can be home practically 100 percent of the time. . . . [T]he laboratory I can run by remote control—my presence is not required but for a couple hours every other day. . . . I believe I could take a leave of absence from the downtown practice or work there in a limited way. . . ."

The next morning, as Michael prepared to leave for work, he noticed something very strange. When he retrieved the letter from his briefcase in order to drop it in the mail he observed that it apparently had been opened and resealed. Michael had a very short list of suspects, but he wasn't overly concerned. Maybe, through the letter's contents, Nancy would appreciate his sincerity and resolve in trying to reach an amicable agreement on all aspects of their settlement?

Apparently, she did. Michael received word from his attorney that Nancy would let him keep the house. She would move out once she found another home, which would probably take another three months—until around Labor Day. This development was agreeable to Michael. The negotiating could now focus on the crucial custody arrangement and then move on to the more mundane matters, such as dividing up the household goods. Perhaps Michael's fear of a monumental struggle had no real basis? As he prepared to leave for a five-day medical meeting in Charleston, South Carolina, it seemed as though the divorce proceedings were on track for a fair resolution. He hoped so.

Michael had done enough contemplating about his marriage for one day. Weary after his flight back to Pittsburgh from the medical meeting, he retrieved his luggage from baggage claim, took the shuttle to the parking lot, got in his car, and started the drive home. But he couldn't get the looming divorce out of his mind. He should have felt comforted that the end of the marriage would also mean the end all of the strife. Yet, for the sake of the children, he would have considered stopping the proceedings if only Nancy would permit him to take his rightful place in the family. Or would he? He wasn't sure. He thought he would. Maybe, just maybe, he still loved Nancy? It was possible. There had been so much turmoil and bickering during the last few years, it was as though a wall existed between the two of them and it had become impossible for him to discern what feelings—if any—remained for his wife of more than fifteen years. He did concede that despite all the adversity the passion somehow never deserted their sex life until just prior to the separation. There was no other woman and—to the best of his knowledge—there was no other man. Maybe he did still love her? Maybe she did still love him? Maybe the prospect of divorce on the horizon would finally open up a line of communication between them? Maybe there was an outside chance that the marriage could still be saved?

He turned into the driveway of their Inverness Avenue residence. Thanks to Nancy's underground watering system, the lawn sparkled green in the bright June afternoon. Michael was eager to receive his upcoming hugs from Jennie, Nathaniel, and little Ariel. Somehow their love and warmth always seemed to make this gigantic mess go away, at least for a little while. As he approached the entrance he noticed a note taped to the door. He peeled it off and read the words in Nancy's handwriting:

Michael,

I took your advice and that of my attorney and moved out. Contact your attorney.

Nancy

He couldn't believe what he read. She had moved out? Where were the kids? Weren't they working out an agreement? For the sake of the children, there were to have been no more surprises.

He read the note again. And again. But Nancy didn't include an explanation. He fumbled for his key and went inside, hoping to find that it was all a cruel joke. It was not. He wandered around forlornly. The house had been emptied almost completely.

Except for another note.

Michael picked it up off the kitchen counter. It began with his favorite word in big, bold letters:

Dad

He read the note:

Daddy,

Don't be mad at me, please. I had no involvement with the move—it's only between you and Mom. Custody will be worked out and I'm planning on spending time with both of you.
   I love you!

Jennie

Michael, note in hand, didn't move. The urgency to resume wandering around and surveying the magnitude of his loss had suddenly passed. With Jennie's note, he knew how much he had lost.

He just stood, a solitary figure in a beautiful house that no longer felt like a home. He didn't know whether to cry, scream, or laugh at the stealth and absurdity of Nancy's clandestine maneuver.

Nancy wasn't bashful in what she had taken: oriental rugs, sofas, nearly all the bedroom furniture, paintings, valuable antique pieces, almost everything in the dining room, all but one television, even his Steinway grand piano.

And the children.

Where were his children? There was not one remnant remaining that would suggest children had ever lived there. No clothes, no toys, no books, nothing.

A call to his attorney found Paul astonished. He didn't recall Nancy's attorney giving any indication whatsoever that Nancy was contemplating such a move. But before ending the telephone conversation with his client, Leventon told him not to worry. He believed everything would now be resolved expediently and fairly.

After hanging up, a feeling of exhaustion swept over Michael. He wanted to lie down, but his bed was gone. So he curled up in a corner, telling himself that better days were ahead.

How wrong he was.

2. Order of the Court

To conceive a child there has to be a mother and a father. The premise that there is such a thing as a primary parent goes against nature. But what if the outlandish were true—that although the primary parent notion is false biologically, it is somehow a law of nature psychologically? Even if that were miraculously the case, how could mental health professionals—pressed by judicial time constraints and armed only with data skewed by an emotional and adversarial environment—identify beyond a shadow of a doubt who is a primary parent and who is a secondary parent? They might just as well flip a coin and send the bill.

—Michael L. Nieland, M.D.
Separated Husband, Separated Dad

Michael strained to think rationally as his footsteps echoed through the empty home. Jennie, Nathaniel, and Ariel must be in Pittsburgh—safe and sound. He knew his wife when it came to her career. She would never abandon her established, and very lucrative, medical practice. He was sure it was only a matter of time until his family surfaced and he was again reading the kids a bedtime story. Over and over Michael kept repeating to himself the logic he prayed was true: that the children were okay and close by.

They were. Within twenty-four hours Leventon had located Nancy, the children, and the contents of the Nieland home. Nancy had rented a house situated just a mile or so from the Inverness Avenue house. Michael anticipated being swiftly reunited with his children and possibly even some of his belongings.

Through the efforts of his attorney, Michael gained prompt access to Jennie, Nathaniel, and Ariel. He was overjoyed at the prospect of having all three children at home without the usual horde of housekeepers. However, his joy was soon tempered by the children's reluctance to return to Inverness with him. He didn't blame them. There was nothing to return to—no toys, no beds, only one fifteen-year-old television. In fact, Nancy had removed more than two-thirds of the seventy or so pieces of furniture purchased during their marriage. Michael immediately embarked on several shopping excursions, but it would take more than a flurry of purchases to replace the belongings that had taken more than fifteen years to accumulate.

Nathaniel and Ariel weren't patient. Less than a week after "The Move," Michael told Leventon: "Nathaniel complained that there were no toys at Inverness when I asked him why he wouldn't come, and he also complained I didn't have as much money as his mother for toys. I'm scrambling as fast as I can to replace TVs, beds, etc." Michael reflected further on how unusual it was that a six-year-old boy had grasped the concept of money so thoroughly.

The emotional setback didn't dampen Michael's determination to protect his right to rear his children, but it made him realize that he had to address the personal property distribution issue quickly. Prior to Nancy's departure he had barely thought about the division of property. Not now. He realized Nancy had to return his fair share of the family possessions (what lawyers humorously call the "pots and pans") in order that the Inverness house would once again have some semblance of "home" to the children.

So, without losing sight of his top priority, the establishment of an equitable custody arrangement, Michael asked Leventon to seek a 50 percent return of the "pots and pans." He made the request hoping Nancy would respond in good faith and the matter would be resolved quickly. The last thing the children needed was to witness their family's plight turned into a three-ring circus.

Leventon appeared optimistic that there would be an expeditious resolution, but Michael wasn't so sure. He recalled that it had taken both sides many months just to reach an informal understanding that he could keep the Inverness Avenue home and, in turn, he wouldn't pursue his share of Nancy's retirement fund (which had a value that more than matched the equity in Inverness). Michael's attorney, on the other hand, had logically assumed that with the two most significant Nieland assets off the bargaining table, the lesser "pots and pans" issues would be settled quickly. In that vein, he wrote Harry Gruener and informed him that he had attempted to calm Michael down by assuring him that surely Nancy's attorney would not have instructed her to remove more than 50 percent of the personal property and that there was no sinister plan for Nancy to secure a disproportionate amount of the property during Michael's absence. In order to remedy the inequity, Leventon enclosed a "voluntary return" list of the items Michael wanted back.

No response to the June 8 letter was forthcoming from

Gruener, so Michael's attorney wrote a follow-up note on June 11. As of June 17 there was still no response. Michael was worried, but Leventon instructed him to remain calm. Another follow-up note was sent to Gruener. It fared no better than its predecessors.

Apparently, Nancy had no sense of urgency to address the personal property issue. After all, she had the goods. Perhaps, too, Gruener had concluded she was justified in stuffing just about anything and everything of value into a fleet of moving vans at the time of "The Move."

At long last, on June 22, came Gruener's eagerly awaited response. He wrote a letter expressing surprise that Leventon's client might feel cheated. He asserted that Michael had stubbornly refused to leave the family home so that the family could remain as intact as possible, that he had declined to accept an outright purchase of the residence in connection with the equitable distribution, that he had undertaken a reign of harassment of the household help, and that he had repeatedly asked his wife to leave the family home. Gruener wrote that he found it hard to believe Dr. Michael Nieland would then have the audacity not only to complain about the personal property selected by his wife, but to submit outrageous inflated values for the property in question—even after being advised that the division was done under the auspices of a qualified appraiser.

Gruener then cited numbers in an effort to validate his assertion. The items Nancy removed from the house, he claimed, were appraised at $54,685. She left behind property valued at $61,595, which didn't even include several musical instruments that would increase the value of the property left behind to $153,595.

To the extent that a $98,910 difference existed in Michael's favor, Gruener closed by notifying Leventon that he would be seeking some adjustments at the time of equitable distribution to compensate Nancy fairly. He then added that he did not wish to spend any additional time on the "personalty" (a legal term referring to personal property) and, hopefully, Michael—in his zeal to wrangle—would turn his attention to the more substantive issues of equitable distribution of the marital property and the divorce itself.

Needless to say, Michael was outraged at the assertions. Evidently, Gruener claimed that there was no understanding between the two sides that Michael would retain Inverness. Furthermore, he asserted that Nancy was justified in taking the family belongings based on a mysterious appraisal that Leventon learned occurred on January 26, 1987 (a day Michael was in New York for a medical meeting).

Michael was stunned. He couldn't believe Nancy conducted an appraisal in their home without notifying him or—at least—his attorney.

For six months, starting in January 1987, their attorneys had supposedly agreed to negotiate in good faith on who would keep the house before moving on to other issues. Yet, while Michael had been relying on the attorneys to make the transition as smooth as possible for the sake of the family, Nancy apparently had been plotting "The Move" in case her soon-to-be ex-husband would be the one to remain at Inverness.

Something else occurred to Michael. For the first time since Nancy's preemptive strike, he realized he hadn't once thought about the finality of losing her as his wife. Perhaps he was afraid he might still harbor some feelings of love? No chance. He couldn't love someone who he believed—in an act of premeditation—stole his family! Her actions demonstrated once again the futility of trying to stay married to her.

He turned his attention back to the attorney's letter. If Nancy's camp wanted to drop bombshells, he was going to retaliate with his own firepower. In a letter to Paul, Michael counterattacked each and every charge leveled against him, particularly that Michael submitted *outrageous inflated values* for the Nieland personal property. Gruener had leveled this charge based on an appraisal (conducted unbeknownst to Michael) by "a qualified appraiser," Robert O. Simon, on January 26, 1987. Nancy must have forgotten that the same Mr. Simon had done an appraisal for insurance purposes nine years earlier, on September 18, 1978. To Michael's good fortune, he still had a copy of the earlier appraisal, and he did some comparisons. Michael commented to Leventon that the earlier appraisal and inventory did not catalog the large number of items *added* in the intervening nine years. The comparisons seem to speak for themselves, especially in light of the fact the value of antiques normally appreciates over time:

1978 appraisal: *One lidded urn, French, late 19th Century* [Old Sevres]
Vase shaped, pink ground, domed foliate lid, waisted neck, flute decorated; lower half with applied scrolled wreath and swag festoons interspersed with gold and white foliate reserves, ending on circular step base with bronze laurel wreath plinth. Height: 17 inches.
$750

1987 appraisal: One French porcelain gold and white decorated vase
$250

1978 appraisal: *One oil painting on board* by Cornelius van Leemputten, 1841–1902 [Listed in *Benizet*]
Landscape, with barn in background with fowl and chicks in foreground, contained in gold leaf frame—8½ inches × 13 inches.
$950

1987 appraisal: One oil painting of fowl contained in a gilded frame.
$350

1978 appraisal: *One honey pot, English, 19th century* [Chamberlains Worcester]
White ground, interior with multi-colored flowerheads, domed lid, gold ring finial, ending on circular fitted stand with applied gold tendrils. Height: 5½ inches.
$300

1987 appraisal: One lidded porcelain jar
$65

With the 1978 appraisal as a guide (and not even taking into account the value appreciation factor) Michael cited nearly one hundred examples of museum-quality items that were either unaccounted for or were significantly undervalued. And, obviously, the examples didn't include the many antiques purchased in the nine years since 1978.

As for the home furnishing necessities—such as furniture, appliances, linen, clothing, housewares—Michael pointed out their homeowner's replacement policy was for $359,100 exclusive of the fine arts, silver, musical instruments, jewelry, etc. The vast majority of these items were taken by Nancy. Yet, according to her attorney's arithmetic, the value of the items Nancy took, including the antiques, amounted to only $54,685!

In regard to Gruener's final assumption about the musical instruments not taken that *would increase the value* of the personalty left at the residence, Michael related the following in his letter to Paul: "Please advise Harry Gruener (his client is already aware of this) that these instruments, with the exception of the violin, are all owned totally by my parents [who asked if they could store them temporarily at my house]. The copies of the instrument appraisals carefully note that all of these items are in my 'possession' only. If I owned them the appraisal would state that they are my 'property.' " And, on a closing note, Michael made the following succinct but passionate summation regarding Gruener's reference concerning Michael's "zeal to wrangle":

> There's very little of value left in this house other than my violin. I was cleaned out. I used to live in a museum and now I'm living in a mausoleum. My kids don't want to come in because they don't recognize anything about the house. You bet I have a zeal to wrangle over issues of equity, truth, decency, and fair play. . . .

In spite of the letter, no amicable resolution was forthcoming on the property issue or the custody issue. In addition, Leventon informed Michael that the courts expect fathers in the throes of divorce to send temporary child support payments until the financial issues are ultimately resolved. Michael wasn't crazy about sending a check every month to someone who had walked off with his kids and belongings. Besides, it wasn't as if she couldn't provide for the children on her own. However, he would take the "high road" and do what was expected of a father. Monthly checks would begin as soon as Leventon deemed it appropriate.

July became August. There was still no progress in any area, just proposals and counterproposals volleying back and forth between the attorneys. The proceedings were getting out of control—exactly what Michael wanted to avoid. Nancy seemed prepared to wage battle on each and every issue no matter what the financial or emotional cost. Michael contemplated the likely "War of the Nielands" that lay ahead. It troubled him, but he never once thought of walking away or giving up. He was a father and nobody could take that role away from him just because he was divorcing his wife.

While Nancy wasn't making life easy for him, at least Jennie, Nathaniel, and Ariel had become more willing to return to the Inverness home. They spent their afternoons with their dad on an informal every-other-day schedule. In the case of the two little ones, Michael attributed his success to a "restocked popsicle supply." With respect to Jennie, there were no significant problems although at times she seemed distant. Could it be the uncertainty of the situation? It had been three months of turmoil, especially for the children. Not only had they had to face the trauma of their parents' increasingly bitter divorce, but they had moved yet again. In early August, Nancy purchased a contemporary house just around the corner from Michael. The warring parties were now neighbors.

To Michael, Nancy's move added to the purposelessness of the fighting. Both sides clearly had enough money to be family providers and share responsibility for the children. Now, Jennie, Nathaniel, and Ariel never had to be more than a block away from either parent. Conceivably, especially when the two younger ones were slightly older, the children could practically come and go from each house as they pleased. In theory, this made sense. In reality, peace didn't appear likely to Michael—only court battles.

Leventon wasn't as pessimistic. He kept telling his client to be patient. Ending a marriage had become less complicated with no-fault divorce, but resolving the issues of custody, property, and support often took time.

There was one happy note in the Nieland family: Brita, in medical school, was getting married at the end of August. Of course, Michael wasn't privy to any of the planning. He even had some reservations about attending the event because of the rancor existing between him and Nancy and the fact that he hadn't been a part of Brita's life for some time. But ultimately he decided that for the occasion he would do his best to rise above the family's turmoil.

As it turned out, his best wasn't needed. *He* wasn't needed. Michael didn't receive an invitation. Apparently, this was the last chapter in his role as the father of Brita and, in all likelihood, Sarah, too. But, there was an astonishing footnote. Michael learned that Alex Wanger—who had relinquished his fathering role more than fourteen years earlier—was not only invited to the wedding, but he was in the wedding procession! Michael could only shake his head at this bizarre turn of events. He was the one who for years Brita and Sarah had called Dad. Michael had no doubts that his exclusion from the wedding was Nancy's way to demonstrate publicly not only that he was about to become her ex-husband, but that he was no longer part of *her* family.

August became September. No progress to report, but plenty of animosity.

It was becoming more and more apparent that for Nancy and Michael to resolve their differences it was going to take a court order. Paul made the first move in regard to his client's most critical concern—custody. In the Court of Common Pleas of Allegheny County he presented an argument for awarding Michael shared physical custody:

> What is determined to be in the *best interests of the child* is the fundamental and controlling determination in all Child Custody Proceedings [*Wesley, J.K., Pa. Super.*, 445 A. 2d 1243 (1982)]. . . .
>
> The Wesley Court details the following guideposts in assisting the lower courts of the Commonwealth in determining the appropriateness of shared physical custody orders:
>
> 1. Both parents must be "fit."

2. Both must be willing and able to provide love and care for the children.
3. Both must demonstrate a desire for a continuing active involvement in their child's life.
4. Although a positive relationship between the parents is preferable, a successful joint custody arrangement requires only that the parents be able to isolate their personal conflicts from their roles as parents and that the children be spared whatever resentments and rancor the parents may harbor.

Michael believes his request for joint custody was fair and just. He wasn't attempting to curtail or sever the relationship between the children and their mother. He was asking only for the same respect in return. After all, does anyone really believe it is in the best interests of a child to have a fit and loving parent pushed aside because of divorce?

Apparently Nancy does. Harry Gruener fired back with a counterclaim that, among other points, stated: "The Defendant [Nancy Nieland] believes . . . that it is in the best interest of the parties' minor children that the Defendant be awarded their permanent care and custody."

The divergent positions seemed to accentuate the dim prospects for an out-of-court settlement. Unfortunately for Michael, court adjudications take time. He could live indefinitely without his personal property, but he could not accept not being with his kids. Michael hoped Nancy wouldn't be totally unreasonable during this drawn-out litigation. Soon came her first test:

With the beginning of a new school year Michael called her in order to make arrangements for transporting the children to school, just as he had done year after year. He didn't believe she would begrudge him this simple pleasure.

Nancy wasn't in a chatty mood. The conversation ended

nearly as soon as it began; Nancy said she had made "other arrangements." Very concerned, Michael met with his attorney, who eased his client's worries. Apparently, Nancy's lawyer hadn't objected in his negotiations with Leventon to Michael taking Jennie, Nathaniel, and Ariel to school. But just to be safe, Michael decided to write Nancy in order that she clearly understood his intentions:

> I want to remind you that for fifteen years, except when they or their friends were old enough to drive, I took Brita, Sarah, Jennie, and Nathaniel to school. Your attempt to exclude me from this contact with my children, particularly now that Ariel is old enough to go to school, is simply intolerable. I insist upon taking all the children to school and I hope you will respond quickly so we can make the necessary arrangements.

This plea to his estranged wife—and the attorneys' informal understanding—were to no avail. On the first day of school Michael and "someone named Joe" arrived in separate cars at Nancy's home to pick up Jennie, Nathaniel, and Ariel. In a letter to Leventon, Michael described the angry confrontation. He said that he arrived at Nancy's house at 7:45 A.M., well ahead of his deadline to get the children to school on time. This shouldn't have created a problem, he pointed out, because there was an agreement between the attorneys that permitted him to take the children to school every day unless Nancy wanted to do it herself. He estimated he waited for five minutes after ringing the bell because no one would open the door. Finally, Nancy came to the door and told him only Nathaniel wanted to go with him. Michael responded by asking about Ariel and Jennie. Nancy, according to Michael, wouldn't give him a direct reply. Instead, she ordered him to get off her property or she would call the police. So, he went down the driveway with Nathaniel and waited to see what would happen next. Moments later Joe showed up and Nancy marched down the driveway with Jennie and a housekeeper who was carrying Ariel. Michael then recalled Jennie saying to him, "I won't go with you. . . . We can go to school with whomever we want" and they got in Joe's car. At that point Michael said he drove away with Nathaniel. Michael concluded his description of the episode by declaring to Leventon that he fully intended to continue showing up every morning because "this is as clear an issue as I can imagine."

Michael was more and more convinced that Nancy might be trying to undermine—or even sever—his relationship with the children. It was only three months prior (during "The Move") that Jennie had left her dad the touching note; now his loving daughter wouldn't even let him take her to school. He speculated that Jennie was subtly being told which side her bread was buttered on—especially in light of the fact that she was less than a year away from getting her driver's license. Michael wondered what kind of conversations might be taking place between mother and daughter. There was no denying something was happening to turn his daughter away from him. And, if a bright fifteen-year-old girl could be swayed, how difficult would it be to influence six-year-old Nathaniel and five-year-old Ariel? Paul had to do something—fast.

Meanwhile, Nancy's attorney had another version of the clashes over custody. Gruener asserted in correspondence to Leventon (dated September 15, 1987) that Michael's visitation with the children "has not worked out. Your client provides my client with short notice."

The accusation had a familiar ring. He thought back, years ago, to the abandonment proceedings brought against Alex Wanger, Brita's and Sarah's biological father. Alex's attorney claimed that Nancy "consistently refused to allow him to see his children evidenced, not by actual words to this effect, but by her actions."

Michael worried that, just as in Alex's case, Nancy would conjure up more and more reasons why he couldn't take the kids to school . . . why they couldn't stay overnight at Inverness . . . and, ultimately, why they didn't want to spend time with their dad.

He couldn't let her excuses disguise what was really happening. He informed Leventon that he didn't give Nancy "short notice" to see his kids. In reality, she was denying him his right to spend time with the children by frequently having them watching a television program or in the middle of playing a game when he came to take them. He stressed to Paul that if this kind of sabotage were permitted to continue there was the real danger he might permanently lose his parental relationship with his children. Not only would that break Michael's heart, it would leave the children with emotional wounds that might never heal.

The custody issue seemed destined to become a lengthy and bitter court battle. So did the property issue. Michael couldn't believe it. Even though the "flea-market nature" of Nancy's secret appraisal had been exposed, she refused to return voluntarily any of the furniture, antiques, appliances, or any of the children's toys and clothing. Instead, her attorney agreed to an independent appraisal that was to be conducted *at Michael's expense* on August 17, in the hope of establishing the fair market value of all the marital assets. However, the appraisal never took place because Nancy refused to permit Michael to accompany the appraiser and herself during the walk-through of her home. Leventon memoed Gruener that Michael "was extremely disturbed over this apparent waste of time and money." A month later, there was still no response from Harry.

Michael couldn't dwell on the property issue right then.

Being a dad to Jennie, Nathaniel, and Ariel was his priority. He wanted his rightful access to them—which included taking them to school. After a battle of nerves and steel wills on both sides, Gruener conceded on this issue. Michael was relieved, but he told Leventon it was not enough. He shouldn't have to fight to be a father. There needed to be a court-ordered shared custody agreement.

The attorneys met in an attempt to establish some ground rules prior to heading into court. At this point Michael was wary of any negotiations outside a court of law, but he grudgingly gave his approval to the mid-September 1987 meeting. Upon its completion, Harry Gruener sent a draft on the topic to Paul Leventon "so that we may discuss it." Michael and Paul reviewed the document:

INTERIM AGREEMENT RE: NATHANIEL AND ARIEL

Week	Sunday	Monday	Tuesday	Wednesday	Thursday	Friday	Saturday
A	Mother	Father 4-7:30 P.M.	Mother	Father 4-7:30 P.M.	Mother	Mother	Father 1 P.M.-6 P.M. (overnight if children desire)
B	Father 9 A.M.-5 P.M.	Mother	Father 4-7:30 P.M.	Mother	Father 4-7:30 P.M.	Mother	Mother
C	Mother	Father 4-7:30 P.M.	Mother	Father 4-7:30 P.M.	Mother	Mother	Father 1 P.M.-6 P.M. (overnight if children desire)
D	Father 9 A.M.-5 P.M.	Mother	Father 4-7:30 P.M.	Mother	Father 4-7:30 P.M.	Mother	Mother

In addition to a custody schedule, several other provisions were suggested, including the following:

- Michael would not enter Nancy's home *at any time.*
- Michael would not interfere with child-care providers "unless they are interfering with his interim rights as provided in this agreement."
- The children would not be forced by either parent to adhere to the custody schedule. Instead, both parties would agree to the appointment of a qualified psychologist to evaluate the matters of immediate concern to the parties.
- Michael would transport the children to school all mornings.
- Nancy would transport the children to Sunday school on the Sundays they are in her custody if, in her judgment, it is practicable.

Michael was far from satisfied with the draft. He strongly believed he was entitled to have the children at least half the time. But, until there was a court-ordered custody schedule, he was willing to accept some of these provisions on a temporary basis. But through his attorney Michael insisted on certain clarifications:

Although he would not compel or force either Nathaniel or Ariel to sleep overnight, he expected both of them routinely to sleep over on alternate Saturday nights. Also, when it was time to pick up or drop off the children, he intended to do so at the front door. Lastly, he would be willing to provide transportation to and from Sunday school every Sunday inasmuch as he considered Nathaniel's and Ariel's attendance at Sunday school very important.

Off to court they went. Michael L. Nieland, Plaintiff. Nancy S. Nieland, Defendant. The end result was what both sides expected:

ORDER OF COURT

And now, to wit, this 23rd day of September, 1987 it is hereby ordered, adjudged, and decreed that Dr. Roland H. Singer, Ph.D., be and hereby is appointed by the Court to conduct psychological evaluations of the parties, the children of the parties and/or other relevant persons, and to make recommendations to the Court regarding the parties' claims to custody and/or shared custody of the minor children. The cost of said evaluations shall be borne equally by the parties.

A Conciliation* is set before the Court on October 20, 1987 at 11:00 A.M. at which time the evaluations, if completed, shall be reviewed by the Court.

BY THE COURT:
Lawrence W. Kaplan [Judge]

Michael wasn't happy with his family's future being placed in the hands of a stranger. He didn't understand why a psychology expert was necessary—Michael was the children's biological father and he felt he should have his children half the time. Why didn't the judge order the attorneys to work out an equitable schedule? Leventon informed him the Family Division didn't operate in that manner. He had to play by the judge's rules now and accept a court-appointed mental health professional who would make recommendations to the court concerning the custody of the children. Faced with no alternatives, Michael accepted Roland Singer. He knew little about the psychologist other than the fact that Dr. Singer was frequently assigned to custody cases by the Family Division. Michael had no idea if that was good, bad, or irrelevant.

---

*A conciliation is an informal procedure generally held in the judge's chambers involving only the judge and the litigants' attorneys. The spouses remain outside.

While thinking about the pending psychological evaluations, Michael tried not to lose track of any developments in
the frustrating "pots and pans" battle. A week earlier, on September 17, Leventon had filed a petition to conduct an on-site
appraisal of marital assets while Michael was present. The
earlier attempt to make such an appraisal failed when Nancy
wouldn't allow him in the house with the appraiser. A ruling
by the court wasn't expected until mid-October.

To Michael, the cliché "making a mountain out of a mole-
hill" seems to describe aptly what was happening in all areas
of the divorce: nothing ever seemed to get settled. Michael
contemplated how he could save his family the upcoming
emotional and financial drain. There might be a way. He and
Leventon formulated a plan to bring the escalating litigation
to a screeching halt. On October 9, 1987, they proposed a final
settlement that included simply an agreement as to the
shared physical and legal custody of Nathaniel and Ariel, the
return by Nancy to Michael of approximately forty *objets
d'art* and eight pieces of furniture, and a fifty/fifty equitable
distribution settlement using June 1, 1987, as the date for
valuation. Leventon stressed to Gruener that Michael was
ready, willing, and able to conclude his case so that both he
and Nancy could get on with their lives and, most importantly, permit the lives of their children to return to a much
greater degree of normalcy.

Just as in the case of the marriage-saving letter Leventon
had sent to Gruener prior to the Nieland separation, there
was no response. It seemed movement toward any resolution
was going to come an inch at a time.

Michael gained an inch, he thought, on the personal property issue. On October 13, despite Gruener's vigorous opposi-
tion, a court order arrived calling for "an on-site inspection
and appraisal by a duly qualified appraiser selected by Plaintiff, Michael L. Nieland with Plaintiff present . . . of all marital

property removed by the Defendant, [Nancy Nieland], from the parties' marital residence." A date was agreed upon: October 25, 1987. Even so, Leventon told his client not to expect any final resolution until after the first of the year. Michael was uneasy about the lag time, but he didn't voice any objections.

His real concern was the custody evaluation. The involvement of Dr. Roland Singer was somewhat confusing. Something didn't seem quite right. Singer seemed to be performing more than a custody evaluation. Michael had expected him to "conduct psychological evaluations of the parties and/or the children of the parties," as Judge Kaplan ordered. Yet, to the best of Michael's knowledge, Singer hadn't begun any psychological testing of any of the Nielands even though he had already served as the court-appointed evaluator for nearly a month. Instead of proceeding within the guidelines of a conventional evaluation as spelled out by the Pennsylvania Bar Institute handbook, including home and office visits with the children, he seemed content to base his evaluation solely on discussions he conducted with Nancy and Michael, in turn, during their regularly scheduled office visits, which had begun in late September 1987. At Michael's sessions Singer kept urging him to "share" the family's problems so that he could "function effectively" in the case. To Michael, it seemed that Singer was behaving more as a therapist than an evaluator.

Even more troublesome to Michael, Singer apparently had also taken upon himself the role of arbitrator by insisting upon implementing the custody schedule Gruener had drafted. Michael found this turn of events extremely upsetting. He had never fully agreed to Gruener's schedule because it had the children spending far more time with their mother than their father (e.g., no confirmed overnights at Michael's home). Michael felt he must acquiesce, though, hoping that it would be only for a few weeks. He dared not object because Singer, as the court-appointed evaluator, might take offense, and that was a risk he couldn't afford to take. Any criticism coming from Michael could prompt the psychologist to portray him in court as an unfit parent and that, in all likelihood, would end Michael's parental rights forever.

Not only was Michael concerned about Singer's multiplying roles, he worried also that Nancy's version of the truth was becoming Singer's version of the truth. He didn't believe the psychologist was making any effort to determine whether or not there was any kind of hidden motivation behind the endless litany of concerns about Michael's parenting that Nancy spouted during her sessions with Singer. Neither she nor Michael was undergoing any psychological testing by Singer—something Michael would have welcomed. Instead, Singer simply interrogated him week after week as if Nancy's complaints were true. Michael's favorite accusation is this: "Michael, why do you allow your six-year-old son to play with knives?"

He knows the origin of this charge. A few weeks prior to the session in which this was discussed, while he was standing at the sink rinsing the dinner dishes, Nathaniel, about to touch a steak knife in the open dishwasher, asked:

"Dad, is this sharp?"

"Of course it's sharp. Don't touch it!"

Good advice. But, boys will be boys. Nathaniel touched the knife anyway. A band-aid sufficiently covered the minor scratch on his forefinger. End of story . . . until Nancy discovered Nathaniel's cut. Michael was practically accused of saying, "Come here, son, I have a present for you—sharp knives."

Michael was troubled that his explanations for such episodes never seemed to satisfy Singer completely. Why did Nancy seem to have more credibility with the psychologist? Michael thought he knew: During the Nielands' 1970–1971 long-distance courtship, Nancy in her letters certainly depicted for him someone who needed sympathy—even rescue—when she wrote that she had rarely talked to anyone other than her brothers and sisters and a few friends during her school years. She also said that while she attended college she considered herself terribly shy and self-conscious and that she didn't really talk to anyone very much, and had never really wanted to, until she met Michael. Additionally, she mentioned that when it came to her estranged first husband she just didn't know how she had ended up in such a difficult situation or how she could get out of it. Michael tried subtly to point out to Singer that Nancy's vulnerable persona might be clouding his judgment, but he dared not be too forceful, as he was extremely wary of the power of the court-appointed evaluator.

Meanwhile, the October 20 date designated in the court order "at which time the evaluations, if completed, shall be reviewed by the Court," had come and gone. Leventon told Michael to remain patient. Was there any other choice?

October became November. Although Singer had been hard at work on the Nieland case, Michael found it curious that he had yet to receive a bill from the psychologist. His main concern, though, was how much longer it would take the psychologist to complete his evaluation. Only then could the court formulate a permanent custody arrangement that would allow the Nielands to get on with their lives.

Finally, Singer announced he was ready for a November 9 conciliation that would consist of the usual participants—the attorneys, a judge, and the evaluator. Leventon told Michael not to have high expectations because conciliations often are nothing more than a progress report. Nonetheless, Michael was pleased the case appeared to be inching forward.

November 9 arrived. The future of the Nieland family was discussed in the office of Judge R. Stanton Wettick, who had taken over the case. (Judges in the Family Division frequently trade cases and orders based in part on who is sitting on the bench on a given day.) Michael and Nancy waited in the hall outside. There was no small talk. No eye contact. Just silence, as though their years together had never occurred.

The conciliation ended. Judging the faces of the participants, Michael was worried. Leventon seemed shaken. Michael was right, his attorney was shaken. Apparently, Singer hadn't been meeting with Nancy and Michael only. Michael's attorney learned behind the closed doors that Singer had been interviewing what were referred to as "ancillary contacts" to discuss Michael's parental abilities. These contacts, all suggested by Nancy, included several of her housekeepers, her personal fitness trainer, and a neighbor. None of these individuals, of course, portrayed him as "Father of the Year." No kidding. Michael asked for more details, but his attorney didn't want to upset his client further.

However, Leventon wanted to know why Michael hadn't told him previously about the "ancillary contacts." But how could Michael have told him? He had had no idea Singer had talked to these people. Singer had never asked him for his verbal or written permission to discuss his case with anyone outside the Nieland family. Wasn't that necessary? Nor had Singer asked Michael for his own list of "ancillary contacts."

Michael was alarmed at his attorney's forlorn demeanor. Didn't Leventon, or Singer himself, comprehend that whatever was stated didn't come from objective sources? Was there any disputing that these individuals—especially employees—had a strong vested interest in reporting what Nancy wanted them to say? The Pennsylvania Bar Institute (PBI) publication no. 1987–378 clearly affirms:

> The [client's] attorney should expect the Mental Health Professional to utilize relevant outside sources for information or corroboration. Which sources are utilized will vary

with the specific case but may include teachers, babysitters, therapists, police, sports coaches, relatives, and friends. *The Evaluator must always be sensitive to how the source obtained the information* (was it first-hand observation or something told to the source by a parent) *and the relationship between the source and each parent.* [Emphasis added.]

In addition, didn't the judge realize that Singer had no written releases from Michael to speak with these individuals?

The ramifications were significant. Testimony that should be considered hearsay and inadmissible in a court of law had been used to undermine Michael's parental abilities. Michael worried that his own attorney might be wondering what kind of "monster" he was representing.

And, because Michael himself didn't know the exact nature of the remarks of the ancillary contacts, he couldn't defend himself. When he later asked Singer for the substance of their stories, the psychologist refused, saying that the nature of their comments was confidential. Michael couldn't understand how testimony given at the conciliation suddenly became confidential.

He was frustrated and angry. A few days later, Singer's first bill for $1,200 arrived at Paul Leventon's office.

Michael wondered if it were merely happenstance that this first bill, which lists Nancy's ancillary contacts, was dated one day after the conciliation, or had Singer deliberately concealed from Michael the fact that he had spoken previously with Nancy's friends and employees? Michael was clearly worried about Singer's impartiality and objectivity.

In the meantime, Singer's work to date, at the expense of mother and father, had been—to Michael—a complete waste of time. To the best of Michael's knowledge, Singer had yet to administer one psychological test even though this is generally accepted as a valuable resource in court-ordered evalua-

tions. Even more unconscionable, he had met with the sub-
jects of the custody dispute—Nathaniel and Ariel—on only
two occasions.

Nothing changed in the subsequent sessions. During the
Nancy-Roland office (or telephone) sessions, Singer evidently loaded up on the latest accusations maligning Michael's
fathering skills. At the Michael-Roland sessions, the accused
then had to defend himself. If nothing else, the list of charges
was creative (although the "playing with sharp knives" complaint is still Michael's favorite):

"Michael feeds the children nothing but pizza . . ." "He
buys them cheap clothing . . ." "He doesn't buy them
toys . . ." "He locks them in closets . . ." "He locks them in the
house . . ." "He locks them out of the house. . . ."

In essence, Michael believed Singer was refereeing a
mud-slinging contest rather than conducting a true psychological analysis of each parent's character, personality
makeup, and motivations. If he had performed any psychological testing, Michael believed the psychologist might have
uncovered a basis for Nancy's unrelenting attack on her
former husband's parenting abilities. Isn't that what a psychological evaluation is all about—to assess motivation?
How else could the psychologist accurately determine if
Michael really was the Big Bad Wolf and Nancy the Fairy
Godmother?

On the other hand, if Singer determined neither parent
was an ogre, then he should testify to that effect before the
court.

Somehow, despite the custody ordeal, Michael was still
spending quality time with the children. He took them to
school on a regular basis and he had custody of the two little
ones basically every other afternoon (when Nancy didn't interfere by making other plans). Nathaniel started to display a
real talent for the cello and Michael saw to it that he had

lessons on a regular basis. Ariel also appeared to be musically inclined. She took piano lessons. As for Sunday school, Michael was doing the best he could to get them both to attend, but it was difficult because he got no support in that area from Nancy.

To Michael, it was nothing short of miraculous that Nathaniel and Ariel seemed generally unperturbed by the tug-of-war between the parents. Jennie was another story. Some days she was very warm toward her dad; on other days he got the cold shoulder. Yet, all in all, Michael concluded that, so far, he and the children had fared well in the midst of such trying circumstances.

Michael's frustration with Dr. Roland Singer carried over into December 1987. Yet, Michael felt powerless to complain because Singer held the key to his future as a father. So, Michael kept his emotions under control and quietly tried to refute the steady attack on his fatherhood in the weekly "She Said-He Said" game.

The defensive posture wasn't working. On December 10, Singer, evidently in his role as self-appointed arbitrator, made changes to the so-called interim custody agreement:

- He crossed out the stipulation: "The children shall be permitted to remain overnight on Saturday, if they desire."
- Ariel's Tuesday and Thursday 4 to 7:30 P.M. time with her father every other week would now begin at 4:30 P.M., "if more comfortable for Ariel."
- In the provision regarding rides to school every morning, Singer added "unless prior arrangements are made. Nancy requested more time to work with Ariel in this

area and one more week work time was granted based on how Nancy structured the situation with Ariel."

- Singer added a provision: "Modifications in visitation arrangements can be made between the parents as long as plans are made clear and each is accorded respect and consideration."
- And, finally, Singer crossed out "Nancy will transport the children to Sunday school on the Sundays they are in her custody if, in her judgment, it is practicable." In its place he wrote, "Nathaniel to attend Sunday school. Problems in this sphere to be worked out between Nathaniel and Michael. Nancy will transport on Sundays she has Nathaniel."

Michael was dumbfounded. Singer was shrinking his time with his children. There was no provision for the children to have overnight stays with their father! Singer had also opened the door for Nancy to sabotage Michael's routine of taking the children to school. This perturbed Michael because he believed these few minutes of daily parental contact were meaningful and demonstrated to the children that they hadn't been abandoned by their father. Now, these innocent trips could come to an end by Nancy's "prior arrangements." And—what about Sunday school? Singer, by not mentioning Ariel in his provision, had failed to address whether or not she must go to religious school.

Michael expressed these concerns to his attorney. Leventon upheld Singer's authority to make the changes, but told Michael not to be too concerned at this point; the custody changes were only temporary. He also informed Michael in a letter dated December 17 that "Dr. Singer will complete his evaluation process by the end of January 1988 and within a few days thereafter issue his critical written recommendation on the issue of general and partial versus shared custody."

Michael took his attorney's advice and decided not to challenge Singer's modifications. After all, they would be in place only until a court order regarding custody was handed down. But, clearly, Michael was not pleased with the turn of events. He intended to note carefully any deviation from the norm. Michael had begun keeping a detailed daily log of his activities with his children in order to respond accurately to Singer's nonstop interrogations based on Nancy's accusations.

Sure enough, Michael's time with his children diminished. According to his log entries, Michael had no overnight time with his children and he took them to school only two out of five mornings the week after Singer's modifications.

December drew to a close. Michael wasn't optimistic about what the New Year would bring. Perhaps his concerns were unfounded. Would 1988 be the year he and Nancy settled their differences? It was the year their marriage officially ended: Their divorce became final on January 7.

The marriage might be over, but the issues remained. In regard to child support Michael had been, since November, sending $1,500 monthly checks to Nancy. A child support hearing was scheduled for March 4. Concerning the custody evaluation, Leventon asked Michael on January 13 to "please advise as to what progress, if any, you perceive has been made with Dr. Singer." Michael had no real progress to report concerning overnights, but at least Nancy didn't seem to be undermining his school transportation routine after all. Michael informed Leventon that in the week following the holiday break he took all three children to school each day. Could Nancy have made some kind of New Year's resolution?

The personal property issue brought everybody back to reality. The results were in from the inspection and appraisal. In a January 27 meeting and an accompanying memo, Leventon revealed to Michael the findings:

When comparing numbered item to numbered item:

	1987 SIMON APPRAISAL	INDEPENDENT APPRAISAL
Value of items in Michael's possession:	$26,345	$ 39,900
Value of items in Nancy's possession:	$55,155	$137,521

Leventon sent a copy of the comparative analysis of personal property to Harry Gruener. Surely now Nancy would agree to a more equitable distribution of what she and Michael had owned together as husband and wife. Gruener didn't respond.

January turned into February. There was no movement on the personal property issue, and on the custody issue there was still no written recommendation forthcoming from Dr. Singer. Just bills. As a result, Paul informed Michael on February 22 that "the March 4, 1988 scheduled Child Support Hearing has been postponed as a result of Dr. Singer's failure to timely provide us with his written recommendation." In a follow-up telephone call Leventon informed Michael that the child support matter probably wouldn't be addressed until after the custody issue was settled.

February became March, then April. Michael was losing whatever patience he had left with Dr. Singer and the court proceedings in general.

And, apparently, Nancy had not made a New Year's resolution concerning the children after all. Instead, Michael's log demonstrates that the undermining of his relationship with the children had resumed:

Sat., Jan. 30, 1988: Came home from the office at 1:30 P.M. Nathaniel had been playing next door with the neighbor's son. He came over to greet me. They continued playing for a while and then they both came in to watch the movie

Ruthless People. Later . . . he told me that he wanted to stay the night. . . . I called Casey [Nancy's babysitter] to tell her that he was going to stay a while with me and I would call her when we got back [from dinner]. We went out for dinner and when we got home he again said he wanted to stay with me. I called Casey to tell her. Casey told me Nancy would be home "late." She asked to speak with Nathaniel who told her he wanted to stay with me. Then Casey called me back and told me Nancy was actually in New York and she wanted Nathaniel home. I reassured her Nathaniel was comfortable and asked her to have Nancy call me. Nancy called about 9:45 and demanded Nathaniel be brought "home." I told her Nathaniel was "at home." She asked to speak with him, but he had fallen asleep. She threatened to call the police and said she was calling from a theatre lobby. I called Paul and left a message for Roland Singer. Roland called back about 10:15 P.M. and suggested he be brought back to Nancy's house, but Nathaniel was still asleep. . . .

Sun., Jan. 31: . . . Gave Nathaniel breakfast (Froot Loops). Before we left for Sunday school Nancy called and demanded to speak with Nathaniel. Said he shouldn't have stayed with me. He told her he wanted to, that he didn't like staying at her house when Casey was there. . . . Stopped then at Nancy's house. Nancy was talking to Casey and Ariel on the telephone—again talked to Nathaniel upstairs. Ariel wouldn't come to Sunday school—said her mother told her she didn't have to go. . . .

Mon., Feb. 8: Took all three children to school. Picked up Nathaniel and Ariel at 4:00. Ariel played outside for a while. . . . When she came in she insisted on having scrambled eggs and toast. . . . Out of the blue she told me "You made Nathaniel stay overnight." I said, "You mean a week ago, why mention that now?" She said, "My mother told me and Nathaniel told me too." I said, "That's not true. Nathaniel wanted to stay here." Ariel said, "You're lying. . . ."

Was Michael the only one who saw what was going on? Before any more damage was done, Singer had to decide whether Michael was a bad parent or whether Nancy was undermining his parental rights. Michael urged his attorney to have the court-appointed evaluator do something other than charge him and Nancy for the weekly sessions. But Singer would not be hurried. Weeks passed. More accusations were directed at Michael.

In one instance the mother of one of Nathaniel's playmates called Singer to complain that her son had gotten some paint in his hair when the boys fixed up an old clubhouse in Michael's backyard. She accused Michael of not supervising the activity. Of course, Michael heard about the charge at his next meeting with Singer. He admitted the boy did end up with some paint in his hair, but somehow Michael believed this wasn't the first time a seven-year-old boy had undergone such a "crisis." Singer said Michael was missing the point. Michael wanted to say, "No, you are missing the point. How do you think the child's mother knew to call you to complain? Did it ever occur to you that Nancy deliberately had her call you?" Michael, though, said nothing. He didn't dare risk offending the evaluator for fear of getting a bad report.

Again, Michael pleaded with his attorney to do something. In a March 1 letter to Leventon, Michael wrote, "I find the repeated delays, mostly because of the need to wait for Roland's report, quite agonizing."

The attorney agreed something more must be done. He met with Gruener and, surprisingly, Nancy's counsel concurred. At both attorneys' urging and after being involved in the Nieland situation for six months, Singer finally released a five-page report in mid-March. Leventon messengered a copy to Michael at his office:

PSYCHOLOGICAL REPORT

[condensed]

This report is a summary of my contacts with Nancy S. Nieland, mother, Michael L. Nieland, father, and the children, Jennie, Nathaniel, and Ariel. The period of time included extends from my first contact 9-28-1987 through 3-2-1988. . . .

Father is Jewish and an only child. Mother is the oldest of nine children; the last three were paternal relatives who were adopted. The father of mother is Jewish and her mother is Christian. Mother was raised as a Christian, but converted to Judaism reputedly to please father.

Michael stopped reading to make sure his eyes hadn't deceived him. Apparently, it was Singer's understanding that Michael had pressured Nancy to convert to Judaism. Michael reflected for a moment on the many letters he had received from Nancy in which she stated her desire to convert. He couldn't fathom the motivations behind Nancy's distortions of the truth. Certainly, they had had their share of problems while married, but none that justified what Michael perceived as Nancy's unrelenting hatred toward him. Yet, he had come to the realization that there was little more he could do to lessen what he believed to be her unfounded animosity. He could accept that. What he couldn't accept is Singer's inability to discern truth from falsehood. Singer had been instructed by the court to conduct psychological evaluations—not merely to repeat endlessly and thereby give credence to unfounded accusations. Michael worried what further distortions of the truth might lie ahead. He resumed reading:

There was considerable marital strife within a few years and each blames the other for the discord. . . . The date of the legal separation is January 1987. Mother had requested that father leave the family home, but he refused. She moved out secretly, as she feared that he would make trouble if she attempted to do so openly and she claims that she divided their possessions fairly. Father maintains that he was grossly cheated in the belongings that mother left behind for him and he remains upset at what she did.

Father maintains that he was grossly cheated? Michael was reminded of the disparities found in the property appraisals. Moreover, what did any of this have to do with a psychological evaluation? Michael read on:

Brita and Sarah have much contempt for their adoptive father and he blames mother for undermining his alleged honorable paternal efforts. . . .

Father feels that mother is attempting to exclude him from the lives of the children as much as possible. Mother maintains that this is not true and the reality of the situation is that father has only recently manifested much interest in the children.

Father has requested a shared custody arrangement as he feels that anything less than this places him at a markedly disadvantaged position in negotiations with mother. It is mother's feeling that father does not handle responsibly the visitation arrangements he has. In her opinion, in the best interests of the children, he should have less time than he does, with his present style of handling the children. She feels that the children are comfortable with her, they are doing well and express little interest in being with their father.

Once again, Michael was reminded of Nancy's letters from Memphis in which she made similar claims against husband Alex. Michael was incensed. Wasn't Singer able to assess that Nancy wanted her second ex-husband not only out of her life, but out of the lives of their children too? He read on:

. . . Father asserts that he is a good parent and tried to be a good husband. He declared that there is no reason why he should not have more time with his children and an increasing opportunity to assume a more active role in their lives. He insists that he is not the monster that mother has portrayed him to be. . . .

Jennie was permitted by the Court to maintain the custody arrangements with which she is comfortable as long as she maintains a mature level of functioning. . . . Recently she has started to spend more time at father's home. Mother perceives this as Jennie's attachment to the family home and feels it has nothing to do with Jennie's working on developing a more positive relationship with father.

The parents are both charming, pleasant, very intelligent, and extremely articulate people. . . . They each have much to contribute to the growth and development of their children. . . . Neither is incompetent in their parental role. . . . The parents wanted to participate in the custody arrangement for the children and not have it forced on them by the Court. It took much hard work with their attorneys to arrive at an interim custody plan. The parents had difficulties with the plan and each complained about parental behavior in implementing the program. We used the plan as a working paper for a custody contract between the parents. . . .

Decisions with respect to visitation were to be made by the parents and the choice was removed from the children. There were to be no overnight visits, but this would be a goal for the future. Plans for Ariel to attend Sunday school were to be discussed. . . . [The parents] agreed . . . that when deadlocked in a conflict, I would act in what I considered to be the best interests of the children. Mother, it appears, sensed that I was contemplating increasing father's time with the children despite her protests that he did not deserve the time he had. I endeavored to assure her that I would be continuing to work with them and see a productive resolution to problems that developed. At this juncture, it was decided to work up a report for the attorneys with my suggestions and recommendations for child custody in the best interests of the children. . . .

It is recommended that with the existing conditions observed in this family system, an equally shared custody arrangement should be attempted, as in the best interests of the children at the current time. . . . The move to a shared custody arrangement will have to be accomplished gradually with the parental strife that exists. A realistic target date for implementation would be the summer of 1988, so that it is well integrated by the 1988–89 school year. I suggest starting out by adding a Friday visit to the Monday, Wednesday week. I encourage overnights to start once a week for a school night and a weekend [on the appropriate custody] days. Concrete planning and when it is to start to be agreed upon by the parents and counselor. . . . This situation will require close monitoring to be helpful to the parents and the children. . . . For the optimal welfare of the children, mother should give father a chance now to have equal parenting time despite their own relationship difficulties with each other.

Roland H. Singer, Ph.D.

Michael was practically in a state of shock. He had found much of the contents of the report to be a gross misrepresentation of the truth. Yet, in the end, Singer recommended what Michael had wanted since the moment he separated from Nancy sixteen months ago: an equally shared custody arrangement. Michael felt vindicated. He told himself the report's finding had made the struggle worthwhile. But he was still not happy with Singer's performance as evaluator. He believed if Singer had really done his job he would have "recognized Nancy's efforts to undermine the children's father from the very beginning."

With the release of the psychological report it seemed logical to assume the custody battle was all but over. Michael found himself eager for the implementation of "equal parenting time," which Nancy had taken away from him ten months earlier when she surreptitiously made "The Move" from Inverness Avenue. Finally, this injustice was to be corrected. Michael wanted it to happen immediately, but he continued to learn that the courts don't work that way.

First, there must be more months of delay because of the crowded court schedule. Evidently the courts no longer placed much emphasis on the old creed, "Justice delayed is justice denied."

Finally on July 7, 1988, more than thirteen months since Nancy took the children from his home, a custody hearing took place before Judge Wettick. Dr. Singer was the star (and only) witness.

The judge began, "I want you to tell me what you think should be in a Court Order [and] should a Court Order be entered today. That is my bottom line."

Already Michael was upset with the proceedings. Wasn't the judge essentially asking Singer to write the custody order rather than discuss the psychological evaluation he had been ordered by the court to perform nearly ten months ago?

It seemed to Michael the judge's questioning should have a different purpose: Are both parents fit? Is there any sign of a character disorder in either parent? Is there any reason one or both parents should not be given shared custody? What procedures were employed to arrive at these conclusions? What was the source for the data? Was the data corroborated by other sources? What is the margin for error in these conclusions? How confident is he in his conclusions? End of testimony. In other words, Michael thinks the psychologist should have acted like a psychologist and the judge should have acted like a judge.

Dr. Singer responded to Judge Wettick's inquiry: "What I

have been attempting to do [for the last nine months] is work with the parents to avoid [going to court over the custody schedule]."

Again, Michael didn't understand why Singer felt bound to "work with the parents" when he was appointed by the court to conduct psychological evaluations. Didn't Judge Wettick realize the court-appointed evaluator had been functioning more as an arbitrator and family therapist than as an evaluator? Apparently not. The judge didn't interrupt. Nor did the attorneys. Singer's testimony rambled on:

> The bottom line today is that *mother is feeling* that she has given a great deal from her position in terms of how *she feels* father would handle the children competently. . . . And *mother feels* that what father has at this time is approximately half of the waking hours of the children, although it is not actually half time. . . .
>
> So at this point *mother feels* that father should be satisfied with what he has. . . .
>
> It is even more than *she really feels* he should have. . . .
> [Emphasis added.]

What does this have to do with a psychological evaluation? Michael thought Dr. Singer sounded more like a spokesman for his former wife than a psychologist or independent evaluator. Michael was upset further by the fact that the words to the effect "father feels" had yet to occur in one of Singer's sentences. Finally, Michael heard how *he* feels:

> DR. SINGER: Father is very upset with [the current interim schedule] and feels that he should have the children half time.
>
> JUDGE: Okay. What makes sense for the children?
>
> DR. SINGER: It is very difficult. I have met with the children, and these are bright, articulate children, but very, very sen-

sitive to the stress in the family situation. I think the children enjoy both homes. I do think that they perceive the father more as a playmate and I think that the father at least communicates that he is very gun-shy in setting limits with the children because, if they are unhappy, they would call and want to go *home*. . . . [Emphasis added.]

Michael scribbled a note to his attorney objecting to the use of the word "home." It seemed to imply that Nancy's residence was the children's home and Michael's residence was a place to visit. Meanwhile, Singer's testimony continued:

. . . and there has been telephoning when the children get angry at each other or get angry at Dad. He doesn't limit it. He is not happy they call Nancy's home, preferring to try to work it out between the children and himself, but the children do call when they are unhappy or when something goes on.

JUDGE: You don't see her undermining the schedule?

DR. SINGER: I think that there may be some subtle bits of this, but I truly feel that she is attempting to work it out.

JUDGE: You are saying it is not intentional?

DR. SINGER: No, I don't think. . . .

Isn't intentional? Michael couldn't believe what he was hearing. Just a few weeks earlier (at the end of June) Michael had written to Singer providing him with an overview of Nancy's documented failure to adhere to agreed-upon modifications in the interim custody schedule. He had reminded Singer that six months earlier the psychologist had been ready to let him have more time with his children, but Nancy balked. Three months after that Singer had recommended to the attorneys that Michael have an equally shared custody arrangement with a phasing-in period, but once more, according to Michael, Nancy continued to resist. Then, after another three months, Michael pointed out that there still was almost no movement toward implementing Singer's recommendations.

He pleaded with Dr. Singer not to allow "Nancy's endless litany of silly, unsubstantiated, trivial, petty, and inaccurate complaints to obscure the fact that she in essence refused to abide by what had been agreed to." The "endless stalling, delaying, foot-dragging . . . cannot be condoned no matter how charmingly, concernedly, and sincerely it is packaged," he added.

Yet, based on what he had just heard Michael could only assume that Singer believed the preposterous notion that one parent depriving the other of custody time with their offspring didn't constitute intentional undermining. He hoped Judge Wettick delved into the undermining factor before changing the subject, but he was disappointed. The judge asked, "Prior to the parties' separation, who was the primary caretaker?" and Singer replied, "I think [the] mother."

The subject had changed and, in Michael's opinion, not for the better. He vehemently disagrees with the logic behind the primary caretaker concept. He does agree that one parent usually does assume the responsibility for routine activities such as making dentist appointments, but does that mean that the other parent is incapable of dialing the dental office's telephone number? In most families Michael would bet a "nonprimary parent" had to assume the responsibility of earning income to ensure that his or her spouse and children would have a roof over their heads and food on their table—not to mention providing the funds to pay for the dentist appointments. However, after a divorce, Michael contends, a so-called nonprimary parent would be more than willing to assume day-to-day responsibilities in order to have shared custody of his or her children.

Aside from Michael's philosophical objection to the "primary caretaker" theory, he objects to Dr. Singer giving Nancy credit for fulfilling that role. There had never been a primary caretaker in the Nieland home in Michael's estimation, just a small army of housekeepers whom he tried to eliminate.

Michael could only imagine what inane question might be next.

JUDGE: [To whom] do the children have stronger attachments?

DR. SINGER: I don't know that. I know the mother has been the primary caretaker although father maintains that I don't get the true story.

JUDGE: From your dealing with the children—

DR. SINGER: From my dealings with the children, father appears to be the primary caretaker.

Michael was startled. Maybe Singer had finally understood the situation.

JUDGE: The mother?

DR. SINGER: I mean the mother.

So much for Singer's sagacious analysis. More bothersome to Michael, though, was Judge Wettick's immediate response to Singer's confusion. He practically placed the word "mother" in the psychologist's mouth. Was it so farfetched for Judge Wettick to conceive of a father being a primary parent?

JUDGE: You have no doubts about that?

DR. SINGER: No. I think part of that has been that the mother makes the arrangements for most of the things that are scheduled in their lives, except for Nathaniel's cello lessons.

JUDGE: I gather she has done that always?

DR. SINGER: Yes. Although father maintains that he was locked out of that and would very much like to do that. Mother maintains she would have been happy to have him working with her, if they could [have done] it in harmony.

JUDGE: Is there anything about the schedule that is inconsistent with the children's best interest?

DR. SINGER: No, I don't think so.

JUDGE: Is there a plan you would think would be more consistent with the children's best interest?

DR. SINGER: I think that what would be consistent with their best interest would be to have more time with the father—to work toward half time with the father. . . . I think there ought to be additional time with the father with some monitoring.

The inclusion of the monitoring restriction disgusted Michael. Hadn't everyone made enough money off the Nielands? He had, already, his suspicions about who the court-appointed monitor would be.

Dr. Singer's testimony shifted to the father's portion of the custody schedule, but the emphasis repeatedly seemed to distance Michael from the children. Singer's frequent use of the word "visit" seemed to make Michael's rights sound more like that of an uncle or family friend than a parent. Michael steadfastly maintains his children don't *visit* him—they live with him a portion of the time. It may seem like a minor quibble, but to a father it is further evidence of an ingrained prejudice against his rightful standing with his children.

Judge Wettick was finished, momentarily, with his questioning of Roland Singer. The psychologist didn't leave the witness stand, however. Michael's attorney began a direct examination:

LEVENTON: In the past nine months, have you found any scintilla of evidence to indicate that father is not very genuine in his desire to have shared physical custody of his children?

DR. SINGER: I do feel he is sincere in wanting this.

LEVENTON: Is Michael not a good parent also?

DR. SINGER: He is a good parent, but there are different kinds of parents, and I think the motivation is questioned, too. Nancy feels that she deep down is basically a good parent and that Michael is deep down so self-centered that he can't be a good parent.

LEVENTON: This is what Nancy believes and you conclude otherwise at that point?

DR. SINGER: In the almost ten months I have worked with them, this is not what I have seen.

LEVENTON: Fine. I have no further questions, Your Honor.

Neither should anyone else, Michael reasoned. What more needed to be said? For the past nine months, he had faced a relentless barrage of complaints and innuendo that had challenged his capabilities as a father. Yet, Dr. Singer had testified under oath that Michael was a good parent. Why should there be any doubts about awarding him equally shared custody? Hadn't the time come to work out and *implement* a shared custody arrangement so the Nieland family could get out of court once and for all?

Apparently not. There were more questions. Nancy's attorney cross-examined Singer:

GRUENER: We had a conciliation with Judge Wettick on November 9, 1987, did we not?

DR. SINGER: November 9th, yes.

GRUENER: You reached certain conclusions that I would like to ask you about.

LEVENTON: Objection. I don't think that is relevant here. We are talking about right after when Dr. Singer was [appointed]—

JUDGE: I think if he has changed his position, then we are entitled to know why. Overruled. Proceed Mr. Gruener.

GRUENER: Do you recall at that time telling Judge Wettick that you regarded Dr. Michael Nieland as having no parenting skills at that time?

DR. SINGER: I don't know whether I said no parenting skills, but there was no question that he was all thumbs.

On what basis did the psychologist draw these conclusions? He didn't make any in-home visits; there were no office visits with both parents and the children present; there was no psychological testing of either the parents or children; and he spent almost no time alone with the children. It was only logical to expect these approaches would have been followed by Dr. Singer during the course of a psychological evaluation, according to the Pennsylvania Bar Institute handbook and to common sense. The "all thumbs" conclusion wasn't based on data derived from traditional means because none of the accepted procedures had been followed. Instead, it must have come from office visit after office visit where, in Michael's case, he spent nearly the entire session refuting the accusations Nancy had apparently made at her prior session. Evidently, that was Singer's method of conducting an evaluation, along with the ancillary contacts—the only deviation from his office visit norm.

The ancillary contacts' comments had been a complete surprise to Michael. He had had no idea Dr. Singer talked to these people concerning his case; he was never asked to sign (nor would he have signed) a release giving the psychologist permission to talk to these people, and he was never asked to provide his own list of contacts. Yet, nine months later, Michael still found his parental ability questioned as a result of comments from sources he believed any rational person would construe as extremely biased.

GRUENER: You interviewed the two older adopted daughters who used to live in the household who, I believe, indicated in your report that they had nothing kind to say about their father. Basically, is that correct?

DR. SINGER: They mentioned some positive things, but their current feelings about him are very negative.

GRUENER: You wrote in your report that they have much contempt for their adoptive father, is that right?

DR. SINGER: The two oldest. I don't think I would include Jennie.

GRUENER: Taking you forward to the meeting of April 21, 1988, in Mr. Leventon's office . . . did you not reiterate that although the father's parenting skills had improved they were still far below standard?

DR. SINGER: I don't know whether I said "below standard," but they were surely not what I would be comfortable [with] not to have some monitoring.

GRUENER: And it was also at that meeting, less than 90 days ago, that you indicated clearly that the primary custodial parent should be Nancy, isn't that right?

DR. SINGER: At that time I did feel that way.

GRUENER: And, as a matter of fact, you told me that two days ago on the telephone, didn't you?

Michael was offended by all of Singer's responses. Moreover, why would Singer have agreed to talk privately with Nancy's attorney about the case, especially two days prior to testifying? Hadn't he been appointed by the court to be an independent evaluator? Is this kind of communication allowed? Not according to the Rules of Professional Conduct adopted by Order of the Supreme Court of Pennsylvania effective April 1, 1988. Michael knew his own attorney had always refused to have any discussions with Roland Singer or any other individuals associated with the case to which Gruener was not privy or in which he did not participate. Furthermore, wasn't Singer an *official* of the court—the court's witness, not either party's witness?

Michael wished that Leventon would jump up and object to Gruener's private contact with the court-appointed evaluator. Gruener's disclosure reminded Michael of another occasion when he related to Leventon a comment by Dr. Singer that he had worked with Gruener on many cases. Could Singer be influenced by their past association? Leventon, putting his faith in Singer's and Gruener's professionalism, gave them the benefit of the doubt.

Michael thought he understood Leventon's desire to avoid the issue of ill-advised, inappropriate conduct. Leventon and Gruener had other clients and the two of them would undoubtedly be negotiating many other divorce settlements, appearing before the same judges, and using many of the same court-appointed psychologists. Leventon could not afford to destroy his working relationships with individuals who work in the Family Division.

In the meantime, Gruener's cross-examination continued uninterrupted. Michael dreaded what form of collusion Singer's responses might contain:

DR. SINGER: I told you that . . . I do think that Nancy is the best parent. Yes, I do feel that way, best in terms of certain standards. If I had to rate on a scale of zero to ten, there's no question Nancy would get higher ratings.

Michael found this assertion odious. What standard was he talking about? Again, how could Singer tell who is the so-called better parent from an evaluation that was just an endless interrogation in regard to the unsubstantiated accusations from Nancy and the ancillary contacts?

And, if it were true that Nancy was the better parent—which Michael was positive she wasn't—did that mean the father deserved to be banished from his children's lives? Michael was relieved when his attorney objected:

LEVENTON: Your Honor, objection. I don't think this is a relevant inquiry.

JUDGE: I have no problem with the question. Overruled.

GRUENER: And you told us at that April meeting, did you not, that a Court Order of shared physical custody in your opinion would not be in the best interest of the children? Do you remember saying that at that meeting?

DR. SINGER: I don't remember saying that, in fact.

Michael found it amazing how Gruener recalled so many comments that Singer didn't remember uttering.

GRUENER: Whether you said that emphatically, do you recall concluding that [shared custody would not be advisable] in the sense of equalizing the time?

DR. SINGER: I was uncomfortable to do that without some additional monitoring, based on the concerns the mother has.

Did this mean after nine months he hadn't been able to figure out whether or not "the concerns the mother has" were valid or a subtle way for a hostile parent to undermine the children's relationship with the other parent? Singer had already testified earlier that "there may be some subtle bits of this." Michael wondered if justice was going to be served.

Gruener turned his attention to the custody schedule. Weekends, weekdays, overnights, the cooperation or lack thereof of trading certain dates. The issue of monitoring didn't surface again until Judge Wettick decided to intervene:

JUDGE: How would you propose [an equally shared custody schedule] be monitored since this is what you have included in [your psychological report]?

DR. SINGER: I think my feeling is a monitoring system has to be built into [the custody schedule].

JUDGE: Since the Court doesn't know what to write in its Order unless you tell us, what type of a monitoring system are we going to have for that situation?

DR. SINGER: It clearly has to be a system where you can get communication in from both sides. I think you have to hear, when a problem comes up, before you make any decisions, you have to hear both sides, and I would think some professional person would have to be retained to be involved. When problems come up . . .

JUDGE: So what would your monitoring system be? The parties would continue to see you?

DR. SINGER: I think that there would be regular appointments and then [sessions as needed] when a crisis comes up.

The dialogue between Singer and the two attorneys resumed. Eventually, the court had heard enough.

JUDGE: I understand both arguments [and] will enter an Order. . . . Everything stays the same until there is a new Order.

DR. SINGER: What is to be my role?

JUDGE: I want you to stay involved.

DR. SINGER: Okay.

The decision was handed down a few weeks later. In a letter to Michael, Leventon told Michael what he might not realize: he won!

ORDER OF COURT

On this 18th day of July, 1988, it is hereby ordered that:

(1) The current custody schedule shall remain in effect until the children begin school.

(2) At the beginning of the school year, the father shall have custody of Nathaniel Nieland and Ariel Nieland as set forth below and the mother shall have custody of the children for the remainder of the time.

Week	Sunday	Monday	Tuesday	Wednesday	Thursday	Friday	Saturday
A	Mother	Father after school to 7:30 P.M.	Mother	Father after school to 7:30 P.M.	Mother	Father after school	Father
B	Father to 5 P.M.	Mother	Father after school to 7:30 P.M.	Mother	Father after school to Fri. school	Mother	Mother
C	Mother	Father after school to 7:30 P.M.	Mother	Father after school to 7:30 P.M.	Mother	Father after school	Father
D	Father to 5 P.M.	Mother	Father after school to 7:30 P.M.	Mother	Father after school to Fri. school	Mother	Mother

(3) When the father has custody of the children immediately after school, upon arrival at their father's house, the

children shall immediately telephone their mother to review their schedule and to inform her of the contents of any notes from school.

(4) Dr. Roland Singer shall continue to monitor the children's progress.

(5) All provisions of the existing custody agreement which are not in conflict with this Order of Court shall remain in effect.

> BY THE COURT:
> R. Stanton Wettick, Jr. [Administrative Judge]

At first, Michael didn't feel much like a winner. Every four weeks Nathaniel and Ariel would spend six nights at Inverness and twenty-two nights at Nancy's residence. Not exactly parity. Furthermore, he steadfastly maintained he and the children shouldn't have been forced to go through this emotional and financial endurance test in the first place.

But, on the other hand, his rights as a father remained intact and he told himself that eventually the schedule would be adjusted on a more equitable basis. After a few sleepless nights he concluded he could live with the court order and get on with his life, although he was dismayed that Roland Singer was still involved in the case.

In the meantime, Michael had a brief telephone conversation with his attorney to find out the status of the child support and personal property issues, which had ground to a halt pending the outcome of the custody hearing. Leventon suggested that with the custody issue settled perhaps Michael should place a call to Nancy and try to "bury the hatchet" on these other issues. Paul also advised his client to stay in the good graces of Roland Singer.

Michael took this advice and in an August 2, 1988 letter apprised his attorney of the outcome. Michael had made the call to Nancy and tried to be conciliatory, but not patronizing. For his effort to bury the hatchet, he said, he was met with a "venomous, vituperative response. "

Michael also mentioned to Leventon that, in the meantime, he had placed a telephone call to Roland Singer regarding the recent court order. During that conversation, Michael learned that Nancy had already called Dr. Singer and Singer said she was extremely upset. Michael responded that he too was upset and disappointed that he did not have even more overnights. According to Michael, the psychologist replied that he had better be sure he could handle what he did get.

In line with that comment, Michael stated to Leventon that at this point he was leaning toward staying away from Singer. "Roland," Michael wrote, "has wimped out on every agreement we made, such as [Nancy and I] allowing each other in our respective homes for the sake of the children's peace of mind, agreeing to stop interrogating the children after visits, and agreeing to let the children bring their toys and clothes back and forth between our houses."

Michael and Nancy were not getting anywhere close to the end. Despite telephone calls, Leventon had been unable to reach Harry Gruener to discuss equitable distribution of the personal property. Michael couldn't understand what Nancy had to gain by further delays. Did she think he was going away?

The news was no better on the child support issue. Because Michael hoped the equally shared custody arrangement Singer recommended in his psychological report would become reality in the near future, he felt child support to Nancy wasn't warranted. She disagreed. Leventon believed the matter would end up in court, probably in late fall. Michael continued to send $1,500 monthly to his ex-spouse.

Despite all of the acrimony permeating the Nieland divorce, Michael, Nathaniel, and Ariel enjoyed the rest of the summer. Michael was pleased he hadn't caved in on the custody issue. Unfortunately, Jennie had chosen not to join in the fun. Apparently, she was too busy driving around in her new car. Just as Michael hadn't given up on seven-year-old Nathaniel and six-year-old Ariel, he didn't plan to give up on Jennie. He was confident that, in time, she would understand the value of a father. As for the little ones, they seemed to be thriving.

Being a stress-free father, seeing the children regularly, was wonderful. Michael couldn't recall the last time he had felt so relaxed. He hoped all the pain and bitterness of his marriage remained forever buried in the past. In fact, when he learned that Nancy's father had passed away in September 1988, he wrote his former spouse a condolence letter.

> I was truly sorry to hear yesterday of your father's death and I continue to feel quite saddened by it. I liked your father very much and I have pleasant memories of a number of visits with him and conversations during those visits. I felt very bad when I last saw him so weakened by Parkinson's disease when previously he had been so vigorous. I was always so impressed by your father's intelligence, wide range of interests and knowledge, and particularly by his even-tempered disposition. Most of all I remember him laughing—he always seemed to pick up on my efforts at humor. . . .
>
> I know this must be a very difficult and overwhelmingly sad time for you and despite all the difficulties between us lately I want you to know that you have my heartfelt sympathy and hopes for happier times ahead for you.
>
> Very sincerely yours,
> Michael

Two days later—on the day before school started—Michael spent his scheduled afternoon with Nathaniel and Ariel and then walked them to Nancy's residence in plenty of time to satisfy the 7:30 P.M. return deadline. He entered in his log what happened as he prepared to walk home:

> Wed., Sept. 7: I said, "so long—see you in the A.M." and started to walk away from the house. Nancy came out of the home followed by Jennie yelling that I was not to come in the morning, that she had custody every other day and I responded that the Court Order let me take the children [to school]. She said absolutely not and Jennie was yelling that Ariel was going with her.

On September 8, the official start of school and the new custody schedule, Nancy refused to permit Michael to provide transportation to Jennie, Nathaniel, and Ariel in violation of the court order. Michael stood on the sidewalk with his heart in his hands while Nancy drove past him with the three children in the car. He placed an urgent call to Roland Singer, their court-appointed monitor, to inform him of the situation. Singer teetered back and forth on the issue, but in the end he declined to intervene. Michael had to deal with a sense of loss one more time, as he related in a letter to his attorney.

> Dr. Singer informed me that since my former spouse felt that she had lost at the Custody Hearing that he felt that she "had to win on something." I told Dr. Singer at that point that I felt he had made a colossal error in judgment and committed a horrendous moral and ethical breach. He threatened me that if I pressed the matter in Court that he would withdraw from the case with obvious prejudice toward me. I replied that I intended to assert my clear right to provide school transportation to my children. . . .

To Michael, it seemed as if Singer's decision was based on the principle "In the best interest of the mom."

Michael's attorney would go before the court to right this wrong. He immediately filed a motion for clarification, which stated:

> ... The Court's July 18, 1988 Order provides: "All provisions of the existing custody agreement which are not in conflict with this Order of Court shall remain in effect."
>
> It is respectfully submitted that there are no provisions of the Court's July 18, 1988 Order which are in conflict with ... [the existing custody agreement provision]: "Father will transport the children to school all mornings, unless prior arrangements are made."
>
> [Starting on Nathaniel's and Ariel's first day of school] Nancy Nieland has refused to permit Michael Nieland to transport his children to school.
>
> [Michael Nieland] respectfully requests that your Honorable Court enter an Order which clarifies its previous July 18, 1988 Order regarding [Michael Nieland's] right to transport his children to school each morning.

Days passed—days that Michael was not able to take his children to school. Days that Michael must have seemed powerless, or perhaps disinterested, in the eyes of his children. Nathaniel and Ariel, in particular, probably didn't understand why he no longer came for them in the morning. It was crucial to Michael that Judge Wettick put an end to the undermining of the court order, especially after what happened next.

Michael had the children for the upcoming weekend, per the court order. His log entry for Sunday, September 11, 1988, doesn't paint a pretty picture:

> Ariel awoke at 4:00 A.M. and had already called her mother to pick her up. I asked Nancy not to come—that I could

handle it—but she came anyway and took Ariel against my will. She told me she would bring her right back. She didn't. Then I called her and she said she'd bring Ariel back at 7:30 A.M. I demanded that she bring her back now. She refused and hung up. I went back to sleep. Nathaniel woke up at 8 A.M. He didn't want to go to Sunday school. I tried to cajole him with a bribe [but] to no avail. I still insisted he go to Sunday school or there would be no baseball in the afternoon (Little League game at 1:00 P.M.). He called his mother, very upset. I explained the situation to her and again demanded that she not come over. She came anyway with Ariel (still in her nightgown) about 8:30 A.M. I asked her to leave. When I stepped away from the door she stepped into the house and started grabbing his baseball equipment. I kept telling her this was intolerable, that she was undermining the children's discipline by giving them an "out," etc. She just didn't seem to care. They left without the baseball uniform. I called Nancy after a while and demanded that the children be returned. She said she would after she "gets them calmed down." At 10:00 A.M. she brought them back (probably because she didn't have the baseball uniform). . . . I took Nathaniel to Sunday school (Ariel stayed behind with my babysitter, Dorothy), got him registered, and delivered him to his teacher, Danny Jacob, the rabbi's son. Nathaniel walked in and sat down. . . . No more than fifteen minutes later I came back for Ariel who was extremely upset and was trying to get out the door. Apparently, she had called her mother to be picked up. Dorothy locked the doors to keep her from leaving again until I got back. I let Ariel leave. [She] ran down the street with a bag of her clothes and with me following. I came to Nancy's door and told her what had happened and asked her to bring Ariel back. During the rest of the morning I had several conversations with Nancy and Ariel to no avail. . . . I picked up . . . Nathaniel . . . at Sunday school. His teacher said he had a good morning. . . . We got home, changed into his uniform and went to his Little League game.

Just another relaxing Sunday with the kids. Singer learned of the day's events from Michael, but did nothing. Michael realized his parental authority was fading with each passing day. His only hope seemed to rest with the court.

Meanwhile, what was taking Judge Wettick so long to rule on the motion for clarification? Didn't he understand what was at stake?

Michael's worry increased after a conversation with his attorney, who informed him that Nancy's lawyer had told Judge Wettick at motions that Singer was totally opposed to Michael taking the children to school. Gruener and Singer had already talked privately preceding the custody hearing—and now this. To Michael's way of thinking, Gruener had had at least two questionable conversations with the psychologist in less than three months. Was this fair? Was it permissible?

As had been the case previously, Leventon gave Gruener and Singer the benefit of the doubt concerning their private conversation about the case. Moreover, Leventon believed logic dictated that the contents of the existing court order, not Singer's opinion, would be the overriding factor in Judge Wettick's decision.

Leventon was in for a surprise. Two weeks after the first day of school, the court responded. Leventon sent a copy to Michael's home:

ORDER OF THE COURT

And now, to wit this 21st day of September, 1988, Plaintiff's [Michael L. Nieland's] Motion for Clarification having come before the Court it is hereby ordered and decreed that this issue will be resolved by Dr. Singer who will determine what is within the children's best interests.

BY THE COURT:
R. Stanton Wettick, Jr. [Administrative Judge]

In his accompanying cover letter, Michael's attorney lamented: "Frankly, I am disappointed and upset that Judge Wettick has adopted such a 'hands off' approach in your case. I think you can expect comparable or similar treatment on any or all issues which may ultimately be before Judge Wettick."

Singer, not Judge Wettick, would determine what is within the children's best interests. This is the same Roland Singer who two months prior Michael had reported saying (in effect): "You'd better be sure you can handle whatever custody time you get." The same Roland Singer who less than two weeks previously Michael had noted as threatening to withdraw from the case with obvious prejudice toward Michael if he pressed the matter in court. The same Roland Singer who didn't perceive Nancy's actions as undermining her ex-husband's relationship with the two younger children even though his teenage daughter, Jennie, wouldn't take his telephone calls any more. Michael realized that not only wasn't Singer withdrawing from the case as he had threatened, but that the custody battle was far from over. Would it ever be over? He wondered if he had the strength to fight on. For the sake of Nathaniel, Ariel, and Jennie, too, he hoped so.

3. The Monitor

Roland Singer had already had multiple conflicts of interest in my family's case as (1) evaluator, (2) therapist, and (3) monitor. Now, the court—in response to my motion for clarification—empowered Roland Singer as judge-surrogate as well. Subsequently, Dr. Singer ran amok, demolishing one provision of the court order after another, and I couldn't stop him. He was too powerful.

—Michael L. Nieland, M.D.
Divorced Father; Dad under Siege

If at all possible, Michael wasn't going to think about his woes for one evening. He had a blind date—with a friend of a friend. He was looking forward to the evening ahead, but there was no schoolboy enthusiasm. They would go to dinner and, perhaps, to a movie or a concert. Maybe there would be a second date? And a third? Even some intimacy? But most likely they wouldn't ride off into the sunset together.

Remarriage was not a high priority. At least, not then. Maybe never. Michael had always thought of himself as the marrying kind, but the madness he had been experiencing had caused him to worry: "Can I trust my own judgment?" He did once—eighteen years previously. The thought of making a second misjudgment made him shudder. Yes, he would have an occasional date. But would he dare to live under the same roof with someone again? He was not sure. Not after all of the emotional and financial consequences he had experienced from a marriage gone bad.

The date went well. The evening ended pleasantly. Unfortunately, so did Michael's pleasant frame of mind. Thoughts of Roland Singer kept him tossing and turning all night long. Why wouldn't the psychologist permit him to take his children to school? Why was Nancy permitted to undermine the court order?

Michael's worries seemed to be well-founded—particularly in regard to Ariel. His daughter's time with her father continued to wither away, according to excerpts from Michael's daily log. And in each of his entries, Nancy is portrayed to be at the problem's core:

Sun., Sept. 11: I asked Nancy not to come [pick up Ariel at 4:00 A.M.]. She came anyway and took Ariel against my will.

Thur., Sept. 15: Met Ariel at 3:40 at the bus stop. She insisted on going to her mother's house first.

Wed., Sept. 21: Nathaniel wanted to play catch and Ariel wanted me to play with her. Ariel got mad about 4:15(?) and [demanded to go] to her mother's house. Called several times to have her returned but to no avail.

> Thur., Sept. 29: I asked Ariel what she wanted packed for
> her school lunch tomorrow and she told me she was going
> to her mother's house at 7:00 and wasn't staying overnight.

In fact, Ariel had yet to sleep over at her dad's house since
the September 8 incident.

The school transportation issue had apparently set a
precedent in the Nieland case: The legally binding custody
schedule could be tampered with in certain instances, provided Singer had no objections.

Morning finally came. Michael went to the neighborhood
newsstand and picked up Sunday's *New York Times*. Before
walking home he stopped at a bakery for some pastries. By
the time he was home he had done his best to shake off the
night's nightmarish thoughts and to give Singer the benefit
of the doubt. After all, Michael knew that Nancy could be
quite alluring. (He had married her, hadn't he?) Surely
though, it would only be a matter of time until Singer understood what was really happening.

Michael had to place some faith in the court-appointed
psychologist. He had no other choice. He had found it impossible to reason with Nancy. She wouldn't respond to his
letters or take his telephone calls. Unilaterally forcing the
children to stay with him wasn't an option, not when their
mother, with Singer's approval, said they didn't have to
abide by what their father or the court said. He couldn't go
right back to court to have Singer removed, either, not on the
heels of the motion for clarification. What would he have
claimed? "My daughter doesn't want to stay with me any
more, but it's not because of me, it's because of my ex-wife
and Roland Singer." The judge might reply, "What are you
talking about? Where's your proof? I think there must be
something wrong with you, Dr. Nieland, if your little girl
runs away from you. Dr. Singer is only trying to help. The

Court will therefore consider a reduction in your custody time. Court adjourned."

Michael realized that unless Singer reassessed Nancy's behavior, it was highly unlikely the court would recognize what Michael swore to be true: that Nancy was doing everything in her power to thwart the court order by undermining his relationship with Ariel. He would do what he must. He planned to call Singer's office the first thing the next day in order to resume the weekly sessions.

At his Wednesday afternoon appointment he told Singer again that Nancy was not obeying the custody order. Ariel, in particular, was not spending anywhere close to her allotted time with her father. He alleged that Nancy's subtle maneuvering (e.g., having babysitters and playmates at her house or serving Ariel dinner during his custody time) in effect kept her away from his home. Michael went on to tell Singer that, if he permitted this to continue, he, the children's father, may be squeezed out of the picture altogether. He pleaded with Singer to do something. The psychologist replied that in his "thirty years' experience" he had "seen everything" and he would "get to the bottom of this."

Then, the subject switched to the main feature, Nancy's charges of the week, concerning Michael's handling of Nathaniel and Ariel. On this occasion there was more than a week's worth of charges. Michael learned that Nancy, on her own, had been meeting regularly with Singer (presumably at $80 a session) since the July custody hearing. In addition to hearing only Nancy's side of the story, Singer also admitted to Michael that he had spoken to attorney Harry Gruener privately in regard to the motion for clarification just one day prior to the attorneys arguing the pivotal motion before Judge Wettick.

Michael had heard enough for one day, but Singer wasn't

quite finished. He related to Michael that in a recent session he had had with Jennie, she told him that her father called her "worthless."

Michael had already heard this from Jennie, but he was infuriated nonetheless. Why was Singer talking to Jennie anyway? She wasn't involved in the custody evaluation. Had he taken on yet another role (and more billable hours) as Jennie's therapist? Of course, Michael denied the "worthless" charge point-blank, but he wondered if Singer believed him.

As for the inflammatory statement, where did this stuff come from? Michael was sure he knew the source. He had tried to talk to Jennie since she hurled the accusation at him in person a few days ago, but she wasn't taking his telephone calls. He feared his lovely, bright, witty daughter had all but slipped away from him.

After leaving Singer's office Michael knew he must somehow get through to Jennie before it was too late. In another two years she would be off to one of the Ivy League schools she had set her sights on. By then it might be impossible ever again to have a normal father-daughter relationship with her.

Just as Michael refused to give up on Nathaniel and Ariel he refused to give up on Jennie. He sat down and wrote her a letter:

September 29, 1988

Dear Jennie,

I have tried over and over again, as you know, to engage you in conversation in the last few weeks and you have refused to speak with me. I truly do not understand why although I do think I understand what has been happening to you in the last year.

Dr. Singer told me that you repeated to him in person

that I had called you "worthless" in our last conversation. You know in your heart that I never used such a word nor did I think it. When you sat down with Ariel and me at the kitchen table on Saturday evening, August 20, you apparently had just returned from Hilton Head where, as I recall, you told me you had gone with two friends. You told me you had a very unhappy time. At that point you started talking about the children, said I "shouldn't get custody" and that I "had never paid attention" to you. I responded that that was preposterous. You immediately got up and stormed out the side door. . . .

Despite what someone else may try to tell you about your childhood you know that I always, and still do, love you, always spent time playing with you, talked with you, and laughed with you. For your sake don't continue to reject the only father you're ever going to have. You'll never replace me and you'll miss me terribly. Before it's too late come to your senses and come home. I miss you very much and you know deep down that you want to do the right thing. Always do the right thing, no matter how hard it is.

Love,
Dad

The letter induced no response. Michael wasn't surprised. Jennie was in the middle of something most adults would find overwhelming—let alone a sixteen-year-old girl. He would just have to keep trying.

In the meantime, another week passed. Another week filled with Jennie's silence . . . with Ariel's refusal to stay at his home . . . with Nancy arranging the school transportation . . . with Singer doing nothing but reiterating Nancy's latest concoctions.

The resumption of sessions with Singer had become almost unbearable for Michael. After his next regularly scheduled interrogation he left the court-appointed evaluator/ monitor/judge-surrogate's office with an incredible amount of pent-up frustration. He picked up his pen and began writing:

October 3, 1988

Dear Roland,

I am not going to keep my appointment with you on October 10 and I hope you will withdraw from this case right away as you indicated you would do in several of our recent conversations.

I am not requesting that you withdraw out of pique. On the contrary, my loss of confidence in you has come about from observing over a period of a year that you simply will not adhere to the set of principles all parties agreed to at the beginning of your involvement and you simply will not follow any principles of logic in solving problems. While you have vehemently stated over and over again that you want to do what's in the best interests of the children, a sentiment in which I heartily concur, I do not believe that you are capable of dealing with the unusual circumstances of this case.

Let me document the issues that I find particularly troublesome:

1. In January you urged [and reiterated in writing] that the children spend increasing amounts of time with me. Nancy tenaciously resisted this for months until the court finally intervened. Now, despite all that has happened and been mandated, Nancy still will not comply with the court's order, particularly in regard to Ariel. . . . I've been telling you over and over again for a year that Nancy refuses to bring Ariel to my house on Sunday mornings. This seems not to bother you at all. Yet over and over again you badger me about bringing the children back at the appointed time in the evenings when I always do so. . . .

2. We agreed last year that to ease tension for the children . . . we would be permitted within reason to enter into each other's houses at transition times. Over and over, Nancy came into my house, but she has refused ever to let me in her house and has endlessly slammed the door in my face . . . in front of the children. If I protest verbally her outrageous behavior she complains to you that I'm being abusive. . . .

You have unilaterally broken the agreement [that I take the children to school] for no reason that makes sense, other than the fact that Nancy doesn't want me to. . . . I think your breaking this bond I had with my children is outrageous. When you claim that my taking the children to school adds to their tension you are not acting in the best interests of the children. Rather, you are hiding behind them because you cannot abide by our agreement for reasons which I do not understand.

3. We agreed in your office that neither parent would interrogate the children after their stays. I have adhered to this, but Nancy has relentlessly grilled the children after every stay and you have demanded of me endless explanations for this or that *ad nauseam*. . . .

4. The issue of controls. We agreed long ago that the parents were going to make decisions for the children and not vice versa. Nancy's refusal to insist to Ariel that she adhere to the ordained schedule is intolerable. Nancy could very easily influence Ariel's behavior, but she refuses to do so. For instance, instead of giving her dinner on the evening of Friday, September 3 [on my time] she should have insisted that Ariel have dinner with me. . . . Instead of storming into my house on Sunday morning, September 11, looking for Nathaniel's baseball uniform she should have backed up my insistence that it was Sunday school in the morning or no baseball in the afternoon. How can I possibly function as a parent if you permit her to undo all my undertakings?

5. I became concerned a long time ago that you would be less than impartial in this case because of your prior working with Harry Gruener. . . . You have had several conversations with him about this case, conversations to which my attorney was not privy. I consider this to be a gross impropriety on your part, an issue to which you seem completely insensitive. . . . Your speaking to Harry Gruener about my taking or not taking the children to school seriously undercut my legal efforts to have Judge Wettick clarify his order. . . .
[Unfinished.]

[unsigned]

Michael didn't send the letter. He feared that Roland Singer, in his multiplying roles, would take offense and declare him an unfit parent. Michael couldn't take the risk that the court would again subserviently follow whatever came out of the psychologist's mouth. Michael would keep his October 10 appointment.

The status quo remained. With nothing or no one to keep her in check Nancy had endless opportunities to continue attacking Michael's parental prerogatives. When it came to Nathaniel's cello lessons, Michael alleged that not only did Nancy refuse to insist he continue his musical training, she also offered him a haven for goofing off. If Michael thought about pressing his son to attend a lesson or to practice, he knew—and Nathaniel knew—that he could bolt to his mother's house where she would in all likelihood greet him with open arms.

The foundation for becoming an accomplished musician which was passed to Michael from his parents would not be passed on to his son or to his daughters. For that Michael blamed Nancy, but he blamed Singer, too, for letting his ex-wife get away with it.

Music wasn't the children's only loss. They weren't getting a religious education, either. Again, Michael couldn't put his foot down. The situation was too fragile. For now, Nathaniel was attending classes at Rodef Shalom Congregation when he was in his father's custody, but Michael saw the handwriting on the wall. Nathaniel, like many children, didn't always want to climb out of bed for Sunday school. How long could Michael continue being the bad guy in Nathaniel's eyes? Without Nancy's assistance the days of Sunday school were numbered. As for Ariel, she never attended Sunday school because she no longer slept over at her father's house. Just as with music, the children were being deprived of their heritage.

To Michael, "the best interests of the children" in the Nieland case seemed to be nothing more than a convenient phrase to hide behind. If Singer truly wanted to act in the best interests of the Nieland children Michael believed he should end the terrible stress and clever manipulation which were taking over the children's lives. Why couldn't Singer with his "thirty years' experience," understand that? If he didn't believe it was happening, then how did he explain Jennie's abrupt departure from her father's life, or Ariel's unwillingness to stay with her father throughout his custody periods, or her adamant refusal to sleep over in the only home she had ever known prior to the divorce? Only a little more than two months prior, Michael wrote to Singer: "the children had a good summer and they seem quite happy. The custody schedule has continued as before without incident. And three months ago Singer himself had testified: "the children enjoy both homes. . . . [Michael] is a good parent. . . ." So, if Michael was a capable, loving father (and he dared Singer or anyone else to prove otherwise) then why did his children, all of a sudden, want so little to do with him? Michael had a one-word explanation: Nancy.

As to what motivated her behavior, he hadn't a clue. He had come to realize he hadn't understood Nancy from practically day one. He knew of nothing he had done in their marriage that ever warranted or justified this kind of post-marriage behavior—including the stealth of her departure from Inverness Avenue.

He wondered if Alex Wanger had had some of these thoughts when Nancy removed him from the lives of Brita and Sarah. Maybe she hates men, Michael speculated, or perhaps she just wants to be in control. Who knows? Nancy wasn't his concern any more—but her actions were. He yearned for the opportunity to function as a father—the primary reason he had sought a divorce.

These were the crucial points Michael wanted to make to Singer, but he couldn't. Michael couldn't afford to antagonize the court-appointed evaluator/monitor/judge-surrogate who very likely would have taken offense at the criticism and recommended to the court no more Daddy for Nathaniel and Ariel.

So, when Singer prescribed his next illogical action—to suspend formally Ariel's overnights inasmuch as "she isn't sleeping over anyway"—Michael gritted his teeth. He was in no position to offer a challenge.

Until December. Michael decided he couldn't bide his time any longer. It had been three months since the motion for clarification and Ariel was spending less time than ever with her father and Jennie remained very distant. (Nathaniel, somehow, displayed what Michael described as "heroic resistance" to his mother's undermining.) The benefit of the doubt Michael had given Singer was now gone. Michael informed his attorney that he was ready for the next step, whatever it might be. Leventon told him their only recourse was to charge Nancy with contempt of the court order. That sounded reasonable to Michael (even if it meant more legal bills). Leventon asked Michael to compile a list of Nancy's actions that would demonstrate her disdain for the court's order. Michael hardly knew where to begin, but the allegations came tumbling out:

1. Repeated telephone calls to Ariel while she is in my custody, followed by:

2. Instigated calls from Ariel to her mother (e.g., telling Ariel to call her before Ariel went to sleep, when she awoke, etc.), followed by:

3. Repeated trips to my house in her car while the children were with me, occasionally to bring Ariel's kitty, in response to phone calls from her. This progressed to:

4. Driving off with Ariel to her house or sitting in her car with Ariel with the doors locked, or walking off with Ariel while whispering in her ear, in conjunction with:

5. Driving over to my house to take the children away if they didn't want to go to school, Sunday school, or a music lesson.

6. Failing to return Ariel promptly if she ran or returned to her house. Keeping her for an entire weekend despite calls and visits from me.

7. Despite admonitions from Dr. Singer, providing Ariel with breakfast, lunch, or dinner when Ariel was supposed to be with me.

8. Despite requests from Dr. Singer that she not do so, making Ariel comfortable and taking her out to eat, go shopping, or go to the movies with Jennie when she was to be with me.

9. Despite entreaties from Dr. Singer that she not keep Ariel entertained, allowed schoolmates to come over or the children of her babysitters. Allowed Ariel to go to a

birthday party from her house when she was to be with me.

10. Indicating to Ariel that it was all right for her to stay at Nancy's house, and that she expected her to, by invariably having a babysitter at her house when Ariel was to be with me.

11. Failing to insist that her babysitters firmly resist Ariel's remaining at her house. (Of course, the babysitters won't jeopardize their jobs by insisting that Ariel come back to my house or go to my house in the first place. They know what Nancy really expects them to do. The babysitters should not let Ariel in when I am there to take care of her.) . . .

12. Indicating to the children that they are not to wear clothes that I bought for them back to her house. Repeated complaints to Dr. Singer that I buy inferior, poor quality, or the wrong clothes, poorly fitting, etc.

13. Within hours, if not minutes, returning clothes the children did wear by leaving them at my side door, including soiled, dirty, unwashed underwear. By this means implying to the children that they are displeasing her or getting "tainted" themselves by wearing my clothes.

14. Always sending clothes with the children as well as "special" pillows, stuffed animals, and pacifiers to remind them of her. Children [ages eight and six] never paid attention to stuffed animals, stopped using pacifiers. (Up to this summer she was still infantilizing them by putting them in diapers and giving them bottles.) . . .

15. Perpetually slamming the door in my face every time I come for the children or return them, loudly throwing the dead bolt while keeping me waiting outside to

show the children how objectionable I am. Rarely letting me step inside, even if raining.

16. Refusing to allow Ariel to bring her cat or any other possessions to my house.

17. Refusing ever to allow Nathaniel to bring his school books or library books to my house.

18. Arranging children's activities on my time without ever consulting me ahead of time. Excluding me from transportation arrangements or deceiving me about transportation arrangements so that children had to go to or from her house.

19. Preventing me from picking up Ariel directly at school on early dismissal days [during my custody period] by telling her that a babysitter would pick her up or arranging for Jennie to pick her up and not telling me while I would wait in the cold or rain for a school bus at her stop near the house.

20. Whenever going out of town always sending children to a babysitter's home instead of giving them the option of staying with me. Telling them to keep it a secret from me.

21. Refusing to let me take the children to doctors' or dentists' appointments. Frequently sends them with a babysitter. . . .

On and on the list went.

Leventon was satisfied that grounds existed to file contempt charges. He asked Michael to prepare a specific list of the alleged violations based on his daily log. Once Michael completed the time-consuming task they decided to give Singer one last chance to identify Nancy's alleged undermining. Leventon sent a letter to Singer; including a summary of Michael's complaints. Copies also went to Michael and to Harry Gruener.

The summary is fourteen single-spaced, typed pages; the opening paragraph states: "Michael L. Nieland, M.D., has diaried the methods and devices by which he believes Nancy S. Nieland, M.D., has undermined, obstructed, and violated both the letter and spirit of Judge Wettick's July 18, 1988 Shared Custody Order of Court." In all, there are 179 infractions that allegedly occurred from July 19, 1988, through December 31, 1988. That breaks down to more than two charges for every day Michael had custody.

Needless to say, Gruener responded to these allegations with his own correspondence to Singer, including Nancy's responses to Michael's list. Nancy rebutted each of Michael's charges in her summary, which totals fifteen single-spaced typed pages. A few comparisons:

Michael claimed that Nancy never took Ariel to Sunday school. Nancy countered that Singer had agreed that Ariel had enough stress already without trying to force the Sunday school issue at that time. As for Nathaniel, Michael contended that Nancy had taken him to Sunday school only twice—once late and the other time picking him up early. On one particular day, Michael actually saw the children playing outside at Nancy's house during Sunday school hours. Nancy replied that Michael did see Nathaniel playing outside because the youngster was waiting for her to get the car out of the garage so they could drive to Rodef Shalom Congregation for class. Nancy also pointed out that Nathaniel disliked Sunday school very much and had never stayed for the entire three hours even while in Michael's custody. Furthermore, Nancy wrote in her summary that she had taken Nathaniel as many times as Michael had.

Regarding Nathaniel's cello lessons, Michael declared that Nancy refused to arrange for or take Nathaniel to a cello lesson despite entreaties from his teacher. On the contrary, according to Nancy, she recalled contacting Nathaniel's cello teacher on at least four occasions during the past few months. She added that Nathaniel disliked cello lessons very much so she told his teacher that it might be easier for Nathaniel if the lessons could sometimes be taken at home. Nancy stated that she even offered to pay the teacher for the travel time, that she also went to the expense of renting a cello for Nathaniel, and that she purchased tapes that were recommended by his teacher. She disputed the notion that she had ever indicated in any way that she disapproved of Nathaniel's cello lessons, or Sunday school for that matter, and said that Nathaniel himself had confirmed this with Dr. Singer.

With respect to Ariel's custody time with her father, Michael pointed out one instance in which Nancy came for Ariel at the ridiculous hour of 4:00 A.M. despite his assurance to Nancy that everything was under control and that he did not want her to come and take Ariel away. Nancy's recollection was that Ariel called her at 4:00 A.M. crying and begging her mom to come get her. Nancy said she told her that she should talk to her father. Michael got on the phone and Nancy told him she would like to come and comfort Ariel for a few minutes. Nancy claimed that Michael did not object. When she arrived at Michael's house, Nancy said that Ariel would not stop crying. She told her former husband that she was going to take Ariel to her house and would return her to his house after she had quieted down. Michael seemed to have no objection to this, according to Nancy. Ariel went to sleep at her mother's house and Nancy returned her to Michael's house at 8:30 A.M.

Michael could not believe what he had read. He marveled at Nancy's skill in taking the elements of truth and, with a twist here and a twist there, stating the exact opposite of what had actually occurred. He dubbed each of Nancy's rebuttals complete fabrications that, most likely, were written around the facts of his summary. (Neither Singer nor the children had ever mentioned that Nancy kept any kind of daily log, so how could she remember the exact times of the events depicted in the summary which had occurred months ago?)

Gruener had also made a jab in his letter to Singer that Michael was no longer paying child support, which was true—Michael had stopped sending Nancy checks. The reason was simple. The court had awarded him equally shared custody—at least that was Leventon's interpretation. And that implied shared expenses to Michael. Therefore, until there was a child support hearing, Michael had suspended all child support payments and, in turn, was not asking for any child support payments from his ex-spouse.

Both sides waited for Singer to respond to the dueling summaries.

But there was no response. Just more appointments with Nancy and Michael. Each passing day seemed to erode further Michael's relationship with Ariel. There was only one viable option left for Michael:

PETITION FOR CONTEMPT

... On January 20, 1989, following frequent written and verbal communication from Petitioner Michael L. Nieland [to Court-appointed Monitor Dr. Roland Singer] that the Respondent, Nancy S. Nieland, has repeatedly violated [the] July 18, 1988 Custody Order, the undersigned, as counsel for Petitioner, forwarded a letter to Dr. Singer with a summary attached thereto detailing the incidents complained of by Petitioner, and requesting Dr. Singer's attention with regard to said dispute. . . .

To date, the undersigned has received no response from Dr. Singer. Respondent [Nancy Nieland] continues to violate the July 18, 1988 Custody Order, in direct conflict with the parties' minor children's best interests. . . .

WHEREFORE, Petitioner requests that this Honorable Court enter an Order scheduling a Hearing on the within Petition for Contempt.

Respectfully submitted,
Paul J. Leventon

The court granted Michael his wish. A showdown was coming:

ORDER OF THE COURT

On this 27th day of February, 1989 it is hereby ORDERED Plaintiff's [Michael L. Nieland] Petition for Contempt is referred to a special master [Carol S. Mills McCarthy, Esquire].

Each party shall deposit ONE THOUSAND DOLLARS with the master within 30 days to cover the master's fees. . . . The master shall conduct a Hearing within 30 days after the fees referred to above are deposited with her, and the master's report shall be submitted to the Court within 14 days after the Hearing. . . .

BY THE COURT:
R. Stanton Wettick, Jr. [Administrative Judge]

Although the outcome of the contempt hearing was far from a sure thing for Michael, this was the first moment in the last six months that he believed his case was truly headed in the right direction. Since the motion for clarification he had watched Singer time and time again fail to challenge Nancy's alleged undermining. In Michael's mind, the contempt hearing was as much a condemnation of the psychologist's behavior as Nancy's.

Depending on which way the court ultimately ruled, Michael hoped that Singer's days as the Nieland family's czar were numbered. With this optimistic frame of mind he trekked to the psychologist's office for his weekly session which had fallen, oddly enough, on the same day the court responded to Michael's petition for contempt.

Michael never considered canceling the appointment even though Singer hadn't even had the courtesy to answer Leventon's January 20 letter. He knew he must still play Singer's tit-for-tat game a while longer although Leventon had suggested it may be time to pressure Singer into withdrawing from the case despite all the power he had accumulated. Michael couldn't have agreed more. Little did he know, however, that this would be his last meeting with Singer. Neither Michael or Singer could have anticipated what was about to happen. Once the dust settled Michael related the details to his attorney in a March 1, 1989 letter: The session started rather uneventfully. Dr. Singer brought up some more complaints from Nancy about some incident relating to Nathaniel's homework in February and Michael said he presented to Singer the "true facts about the matter." Then, Michael recalled, he changed the focus of the discussion by saying, "Roland, it's now eight months since the hearing, six months since the start of school and there's been progressive deterioration of the situation and I don't think it has anything to do with any fault of mine." Michael went on to say, "Just this past weekend Nathaniel went to the movies with me, practiced cello on all three days with his grandfather, went to Sunday school and, as usual, had a good, productive time. I think it's about time to normalize at least Nathaniel's schedule by allowing him to remain overnight with me on those days when I'm supposed to bring him back to Nancy's house at 7:30."

According to Michael, Dr. Singer replied, "Well, I'm not ready to recommend that and you won't tell me what to do."

Michael said he responded by telling Singer that appeasing Nancy, as he had done constantly, would never succeed in resolving this situation. He reminded Singer again that he thought the psychologist had made a "terrible blunder" the previous fall by disrupting his taking the children to school.

At that point, according to Michael, Singer started getting agitated and said sternly, "Michael, I won't have you yelling at me, this session is over," and he started getting up from the sofa.

"Wait a minute," Michael said, "I haven't finished saying what I want to say."

Singer tried to get Michael to leave and, as Michael recalled, the psychologist got very red in the face and his right arm started shaking uncontrollably.

"All right," the psychologist uttered, "What else to you want to say?"

"You claim you have so much experience," Michael replied, "Haven't you ever encountered a willful, vengeful woman before who wants to take the children away from their father?"

"I've also seen willful, vengeful fathers who want to take children away from their mothers."

"Well," Michael responded, "If you can't figure this case out you ought to take a refresher course in psychology because it would be obvious to any of your colleagues. Surely, you have some intuition about what's going on here. You've got to have the balls to stand up to her."

"Michael," exclaimed Dr. Singer, "There are other people in this office. How dare you talk to me in this way."

"Roland, I haven't seen anyone else in this office in a year!"

"Now I see what Nancy is up against," countered Dr. Singer. "You owe me an apology. Don't call me again unless you're going to apologize."

"Roland," Michael said as he prepared to leave, "you owe *me* an apology, you're fired from this case."

To the best of Michael's recollection there were no more words between the two.

In the days that followed the episode, Michael felt exhilarated. At last he had had an opportunity to tell Singer what he really thought of him.

The exhilaration soon wore off while Michael waited day after day for the contempt hearing date to be set. Each passing hour was time forever lost for his children to have the unrequited and *unimpeded* love of their father.

Michael grew more and more frustrated. Why did everything seem so dragged out? It had been more than two years since he and Nancy officially separated, but there was still no final settlement on the custody, property, or child-support issues. To Michael, the Nieland divorce had become an industry profitable only to those running it and responsible for depriving his children of their father's love and attention. Michael, outraged at what the industry had done to his family, asked Paul Leventon about the possibility of a malpractice suit against Roland Singer.

With so much of the Nieland case still unresolved, Leventon advised his client that talk of a malpractice suit was premature. First things first. The statute of limitations for such a suit would allow them to address Singer's alleged culpability at a later date. Michael's number-one priority must be his children. But he vowed that Singer would not get off the hook for the damage he had done.

Leventon suggested that his client confer with another psychologist in order to get a second professional opinion concerning Singer. Michael, though wary of psychologists by this time, made an appointment with Stephen P. Schachner, Ph.D., a respected Pittsburgh psychologist. The appointment certainly went much better than Michael's last encounter with Singer. Michael wrote to Leventon that Dr. Schachner confirmed what Michael already knew—that he and his children were horribly wronged. "Steve feels very strongly that Singer's approach was totally wrong, and that he was in 'way over his head' in this case. Steve also told me again that the failure of a parent to share can be grounds for changing legal custody."

The contempt hearing couldn't come soon enough for Michael. He knew he was going to win. He had to. Just as he prepared to contact Leventon's office again to see if there was any news on a hearing date he received an update in the mail from his attorney: "I suggested that [Attorney Mc-Carthy] schedule [the hearing on your petition for contempt] during the latter part of April [1989]."

As the contempt hearing inched ever closer, Nancy's attorney was apparently hard at work, too—on money issues. He wanted the court to order Michael to resume child support payments.

Michael told his attorney he felt sorry "for this poor woman who earns about a half million dollars a year." In reality, Michael believed that, if anyone was owed child support, it was he, but he would never stoop so low as to demand it because he, too, earned a six-figure annual income. Nonetheless, Michael was well aware that Nancy was a formidable opponent in getting the court to see things her way so he knew that her child support petition must be taken seriously. In actuality, he would have loved to settle all the financial issues once and for all—starting with an equitable property distribution.

Leventon informed Michael what he could have guessed. All financial issues would most likely be delayed until after the contempt hearing. At last, though, there was a date! April 28.

Michael's anticipation of his family's Judgment Day heightened. He truly believed his nightmare was finally coming to an end.

In a follow-up meeting with Dr. Steve Schachner, Michael

learned that Schachner had recently conferred with Singer. (Michael had signed a release earlier giving Schachner permission to discuss his case with Singer.) Schachner told Michael he scheduled the meeting because he was bound by the *Ethical Principles of Psychologists* to inform Singer that he believed Singer had compromised his position in the Nieland case and it was Singer's professional obligation to withdraw from the case immediately. Not surprisingly, Schachner informed Michael that Singer disagreed with the assessment and replied he would not withdraw.

Instead, Singer finally wrote a letter to Michael's attorney. In it, the psychologist critiqued the Nieland case from the beginning to the present, but it is the conclusion that is most astounding.

Dr. Singer had his own version of his last face-to-face contact with Michael. He recalled Michael's suggestion that Nathaniel should have more equitable custody time with his father and also that Michael wanted him to get to the bottom of Ariel's resistance to spending time with her father. However, Singer stated that Michael's behavior did not warrant additional time with Nathaniel based only on what Singer described as "the way things were being handled." As for Ariel, Singer's perception was that the youngster was avoiding visits with her father essentially because of fear and distrust of him which had been built up by Michael's actions, although Singer didn't specify what those actions were.

When it became clear during their session together that there would be no immediate custody time changes, Michael became irritated and, according to Singer's description, loudly began to utter very cruel personal attacks on him. This was especially painful to him, he lamented, because he had worked so hard to get Michael to a position where the psychologist could comfortably support Michael's wish to spend more time with the children.

Singer remembered asking Michael to leave, but Michael refused to go, asserting that he had more to say. Michael declared that if Singer did not comply with his demands he should consider himself fired. Singer said he had never seen Michael so agitated, though he had heard tapes of such behavior that Nancy had played for him when she felt that he did not believe her description of her former husband's behavior. Michael, Singer noted, had also shared an audiotape to show how abusive Nancy could be to him. Though Singer said he had seen Michael angry before, he stated that he never leveled a personal attack toward him as he did on that particular day. Prior to that session, Singer said he considered Michael to be a very charming, friendly, intelligent man. However, on that day Singer reported that he saw the symptomatology of a "severe personality disorder who had been able to cover up his psychopathology." He believed that he had now himself experienced the "battering" from a man whom he had heard about from Nancy, Brita, Sarah, and Jennie.

As for Nancy, Singer considered her actions since the divorce to be warranted and described her as a responsible, caring, and concerned parent.

In his closing comments to Leventon, Singer wrote that he would not advise Michael having any more "visitation time" with Nathaniel than he now had. Visits with Ariel should start up with the short intervals recommended until Ariel could begin to trust her dad again and he could commence to interact more maturely with her than he had previously.

Regarding Michael, Singer strongly advised that he obtain psychotherapy for a "deeply rooted character disorder." The psychologist depicted Michael as a "troubled man" who was "able to mask his disturbance quite successfully" from him for some time. Despite these personality problems, Singer did believe that Michael had many strengths and talents to offer to his children, which was why the psychologist strongly recommended that Michael submit to treatment so he could fully enjoy the delightful children he had helped create.

And, in the last sentence of his letter to Leventon, Singer said that at the present time he did not suggest equally shared custody of Ariel and Nathaniel.

Michael read again and again a copy of the letter Leventon had sent him. Michael found most detestable Singer's claim that he (Michael) had a "severe personality disorder" and/or "a deeply rooted character disorder" which had somehow gone undetected by Singer for the last year and a half. Michael was stunned at the psychologist's irresponsibility and abuse of his position. First of all, Michael didn't believe for one moment he had any such disorder. Second, he couldn't believe any competent mental health professional would arrive at such a conclusion without first conducting psychological testing and making valid clinical observations to support such a claim. All Singer seemed to do was lose his temper with Michael and then vent his anger.

This was more than calling someone a name. It was clear to Michael that Singer had used his authority in a vengeful and cowardly manner following their disagreement in his office.

The rest of the letter also infuriated Michael as Singer took advantage of an opportunity to recycle the same groundless accusations Michael had been faced with since he filed for divorce from Nancy:

- In his acknowledgment that his involvement in the case had totaled to date "one and a half years," Singer seemed to have forgotten he was originally appointed by the court to "conduct psychological evaluations" only. To have assumed or accepted multiple roles (i.e., evaluator, monitor, arbitrator, and judge-surrogate) had clearly created for him conflicts of interest.

- Singer also affirmed, while serving early on as court-appointed evaluator, he "advised that the parents contact me to discuss how things were going with respect to the parenting agreement and to share problems as they come up." In other words, Singer had imposed himself as a therapist in addition to evaluator—another conflict of interest.

- During the period in which Singer was serving only in his court-appointed evaluator capacity, he pointed out that "the parents were willing to participate with me . . . if a conflict arose which they could not settle together, I was to resolve it." He followed this up by saying "both parents stated a desire to continue working with me in an attempt to resolve the custodial impasse." What choice did they have? As court-appointed evaluator he could have declared either of them an unfit parent, if one or the other did not cooperate with him.

- When questions of *bias* arose from "both parents at different times" during Singer's evaluation, he said he had "offered to withdraw from my role as helper and mediator and told them they could request someone else to work with in whom they might have more confidence." But, later, when Michael complained to Singer about Nancy's refusal to let him take the children to school, the court-appointed monitor, according to Michael, responded that he would withdraw from the case with obvious prejudice toward Michael if Michael pressed the matter in court.

- Singer didn't shy away from making other bold assertions: "Mother was the more nurturing, child-focused parent. She was much more competent at parenting than was father. . . . The children are more comfortable and content with mother." Based on what? Singer had no valid data. He had never conducted any psychological testing, there were no home visits, and almost no observations of the children and Michael together without Nancy. Later, he did mention "I had lots of data," but he never went into any detail. Was he referring to the hearsay volunteered by Nancy's ancillary contacts?

- Perhaps Singer's most inflammatory contention concerned the grounds for Ariel's curtailed visits with her father: "I perceived that Ariel was avoiding visits with father because of her fear and distrust which had been built up by his actions." What *actions*? Reported or observed by whom? Once again, he drew a conclusion for which he provided no evidence or support whatsoever (because there was no truth to the accusation). Moreover, Ariel never avoided visits with her father until Nancy thwarted Michael's right to take the children to school. In so doing, Nancy discovered she could bend the custody schedule more to her liking.

- In regard to doing what he was appointed by the court to do—to evaluate—Singer stated: "It was difficult to tell who was telling the truth as both [parents] were very convincing." Wasn't that what he was being paid as a professional to do—separate truths from falsehoods? Wasn't this an admission of failure?

Michael could reread the letter no more. It was too gut-wrenching. He just shook his head in disbelief at what Roland Singer had done: The psychologist had promised repeatedly to Michael that he would withdraw from the case if either party ever made such a request. He had not withdrawn. Instead, Michael found Singer taking one last shot at him.

Apprehensively, Michael contacted Steve Schachner to hear his opinion on Singer's critique. Dr. Schachner responded by saying that Singer didn't seem to know what he was talking about. "It's impossible," Michael recalls him saying, "that you could be any of those things Roland called you."

Schachner's opinion should have cheered Michael up. But it didn't. How could he be happy when two of his children, Jennie and Ariel, had been turned against him? As Michael turned out his bedroom light on the eve of the contempt hearing he asked himself the one question he could not answer: "What demons are driving this woman to do this to me?"

4. Under Oath

Dr. Singer logged 220 hours of interview time, billable for a sum of $17,600, while he watched my family disintegrate. The court order had become meaningless at the hands of Singer and my former spouse. I had all but lost Ariel and Jennie. Would Nathaniel be next?

All along, I had continued to meet with Singer because Judge Wettick had left me with no other choice. I clung to the hope that if I took the "high road," things would ultimately work out fairly. I knew I had always been a good parent and had a loving relationship with Jennie, Nathaniel, and Ariel.

So, why had Jennie become so distant and why did Ariel no longer sleep over at my home or—at times—refuse even to see me? Singer had no jurisdiction over Jennie, but why in the world didn't he investigate the origin of Ariel's behavior? Was Ariel afraid of me, as purported by Nancy, or did my wife induce my six-year-old child's behavior?

Singer didn't delve into anything (except our bank accounts). He hadn't adhered to any recognizable standard of per-

139

formance during the custody evaluation. He had amassed moun-
tains of so-called data, but it was tainted and one-sided because it
hadn't been obtained by adherence to ethical rules that foster ob-
jectivity. Moreover, when Ariel did not adhere to the custody
schedule, Nancy was only too happy to provide more self-serving
corroboration that "proved" Ariel was afraid of me. I asked Judge
Wettick to intervene by way of the motion for clarification. In-
stead of acting like a judge, he empowered Roland Singer, a psy-
chologist, to be (in effect) the judge-surrogate.

My ex-wife had certainly taken full advantage of the inepti-
tude of all involved and—just as had been the case with Brita,
Sarah, and to some extent Jennie—Ariel was disappearing from
my life. I could only hope that the judicial system would see the
error of its ways and act in the best interests of the children by
finding Nancy in contempt of the court order and, thereby, save
Ariel and possibly Nathaniel from what, otherwise, would be-
come a one-parent childhood.

—Michael L. Nieland, M.D.
Contempt of Court Petitioner

Two months after Judge Wettick appointed a special master
to conduct a contempt hearing the moment had finally arrived.

The setting was the downtown Pittsburgh law office of
the master, Carol McCarthy, Esq. The hearing would be conducted in a book-lined, windowless conference room with all
of the participants sitting in close proximity at a rectangular
conference table. Michael and Paul Leventon on one side,
Harry Gruener and Nancy on the other, the master at the
head, and the court reporter tucked away in a corner.

While he waited for Mrs. McCarthy to enter, Michael sur-
veyed the scene. The attorneys were engaged in small talk.
The plaintiff then turned his gaze to Nancy. She didn't return
his glance. It saddened Michael that it had come to this, but
what other choice did he have?

Michael took a deep breath. He realized there was no guarantee he would prevail. However McCarthy ruled, Leventon had informed Michael that Judge Wettick would have the final say, but, generally, a judge would simply rubber-stamp a master's findings—particularly one he or she had personally appointed.

The proceeding began. It was the first of what would be five sessions during April and May 1989. When it was all over the transcript numbered 1,100 pages. The testimony of Michael and then Nancy could not have been more conflicting:

PROCEEDINGS
[condensed]

Michael Louis Nieland, Having Been First Duly Sworn, Was Examined and Testified as Follows:

DIRECT EXAMINATION BY MR. LEVENTON:

LEVENTON: Would you tell the master in your own words why you brought this action?

MICHAEL: I brought this action because I have a Court Order which stipulates that I'm supposed to have my children at certain times of the week and I don't get to have my children during those times and . . . it hurts very much. And I believe it is hurting the children also.

LEVENTON: Prior to the issuance of that Court Order, had you had a different work schedule in place?

MICHAEL: Somewhat, yes.

LEVENTON: Did you have to modify your work schedule . . . to accommodate the provisions contained therein?

MICHAEL: I had to reverse my Saturday mornings so I would always be home when the children were to be with me [and] I adjusted my work schedule a long time ago so I would be home in order to pick the children up in the afternoon [on my custody days].

LEVENTON: Now, when this Order was issued, were you happy with it?

MICHAEL: Well, I would like to have had more time with the children, but I could live with it.

LEVENTON: What is your understanding of the validity and authority of Judge Wettick's Order of the Court?

MICHAEL: I believe it has to be followed exactly as stipulated. . . .

LEVENTON: Do you have an opinion as to whether your ex-wife Nancy tried to comply with the provisions of the Court Order?

MICHAEL: . . . I believe she did everything possible to undermine it—to violate it.

LEVENTON: Why?

MICHAEL: I don't understand why. I never wanted to do anything more than share the children with her. I never wanted to take the children away from her. I just wanted to be their father and to have a reasonable share of the time with them.

LEVENTON: Who prepared the summary [and addendum to the summary] of purported violations?

MICHAEL: I prepared it.

LEVENTON: And from what basis? Do you have a photographic mind?

MICHAEL: No. I have a very careful and accurate [handwritten] chronology from the very beginning of everything that went on with the children every day the entire time they were with me.

LEVENTON: Why did you do that?

MICHAEL: I did it in part to satisfy Dr. Singer's relentless grilling and questions about what I did with the children every day. He would approach me every day . . . asking me what I did with the children in excruciating detail, and therefore, I felt obligated to keep this information at hand.

LEVENTON: Did anything unusual occur during the time, let us say, from the time after Labor Day 1988, until you brought this action when the children were with you?

MICHAEL: Yes. I found I had less and less time with the children than I felt was to occur.

LEVENTON: Specifically . . . ?

MICHAEL: . . . Nancy would continually interfere with my having the children, my taking care of the children, by making phone calls to the children, making trips to my house, taking the children away, coming unexpectedly, grabbing the children.

LEVENTON: Take your time. I'm not directing you to summarize everything. . . .

MICHAEL: Well, for instance, one afternoon I was out front with Nathaniel and a lot of kids on a sunny day in September and I was to take Nathaniel to his cello lesson. He doesn't always like to go to cello lessons. He started resisting and crying and saying he didn't want to go to his cello lesson and he started running away. I went after him and I grabbed his arm and I said, "Hey, we have an appointment." And just at that moment Nancy drove by in her car—this is two houses down from mine—during a time when Nathaniel is to be with me, and Nathaniel saw Nancy and ran to her car. She let him in and drove off with him. . . . This occurred, I believe, on September 9th of 1988.

*　　*　　*

LEVENTON: Michael . . . in your initial [summary] attached to your petition for contempt I think I counted 46 specific examples of . . . Nancy's alleged failure to return Ariel promptly if she [returns to her mother's house]?

MICHAEL: What I'm talking about is I would pick up Ariel all the time at her school bus stop and initially she would come with me directly home as she was supposed to. [But] as the fall term progressed Ariel got more and more in the habit of dropping off her lunchbox or papers she was carrying at her mother's house before coming over to my house. As time went on . . . she stopped at her mother's house, [then] would not come with me. Now, at times Nancy was home; most of the time, a babysitter would be there. . . . Ariel would walk right in and start playing with her kitty or some other attraction in the house and it was very difficult at that point for me to get Ariel to come with me. . . . I would then be in a position, if I wanted to get my daughter, I would have to go in the house, which I felt very uncomfortable doing. I didn't think it was my place to go into Nancy's house to retrieve my child. . . . Dr. Singer had told me that he told Nancy the child is to be returned within 30 minutes. The child is not to be made comfortable . . . to be given dinner. And, over and over again Nancy would violate this. . . . And so, consequently, I had very little leverage left to get my child back.

*　　*　　*

LEVENTON: . . . You say there were certain times that Ariel was taken [by Nancy] to go shopping or the movies during time she was to be with you?

MICHAEL: It happened on a number of occasions. . . .

LEVENTON: . . . Were there any specific incidents when . . . there were other children . . . at Nancy's home [when Ariel was to be with you]?

MICHAEL: There were frequently other children at Nancy's home as playmates for Ariel. . . .

*   *   *

LEVENTON: . . . Did Nancy personally do anything which, in your opinion, had the effect of challenging your equal parenting or your parenting rights with your children?

MICHAEL: Of course. It's very painful and certainly obvious to a child.

LEVENTON: What was that? What were those actions?

MICHAEL: Nancy would close the door in my face . . . loudly secure the dead bolt lock of her door . . . keep me waiting outside her home for the children . . . have babysitters at her house while the children are supposed to be with me . . . exclude me from birthday party transportation arrangements for Ariel during time she was to be in my custody . . . never let me pick up the children and take them to school in the morning. . . .

LEVENTON: And what effect do you believe that this has toward the . . . undermining of your role with the children?

MICHAEL: Well, certainly it undermines the children's feeling that they ought to be with their daddy. . . .

*   *   *

LEVENTON: How important is music to you in your life?

MICHAEL: Music is very important to me. . . .

LEVENTON: Do you feel you have the right as a parent to try to instill in your children the love of music?

MICHAEL: It's my right and my obligation.

LEVENTON: Do you feel with your musical background that it takes a child a while to grow into a musical affinity?

MICHAEL: Absolutely.

LEVENTON: All right. Now Nathaniel takes cello lessons; is that correct?

MICHAEL: That's correct. . . . It's his second season.

LEVENTON: Who arranges the lessons?

MICHAEL: I arrange all lessons.

LEVENTON: During what days or hours are these cello lessons given?

MICHAEL: Always during my time. . . . I have asked Nathaniel's teacher on a number of occasions to make contact with Nancy and try to involve her in his lessons. And [the teacher] has responded, when I have asked her for follow-up, that Nancy will not participate in taking Nathaniel to his cello lesson . . . and, based on what Nathaniel has told me, he has hardly ever practiced his cello at Nancy's house. . . .

LEVENTON: Do you encourage Ariel to be musically inclined?

MICHAEL: Yes. Last summer when Ariel was with me much of the time I took her to her piano teacher's house. . . .

LEVENTON: You have mentioned two separate piano teachers. . . . Did [the first one] become unavailable during the summer of '88?

MICHAEL: Yes.

LEVENTON: Now what happened during that summer so as to cause Ariel not to have her lessons interrupted?

MICHAEL: I took Ariel to [another piano teacher] for her piano lessons and she really enjoyed them and had a good time. . . .

LEVENTON: And what happened . . . ?

MICHAEL: Ariel told me that she no longer had to have two teachers, that she already had a piano teacher, that she didn't have to study with anyone else.

LEVENTON: Did she make that up herself?

MICHAEL: No. She told me that her mother told her she didn't have to have another piano teacher.

*   *   *

LEVENTON: Tell the master . . . with respect to Sunday school, what has occurred.

MICHAEL: . . . On the days when Nancy is supposed to bring Nathaniel to Sunday school he either does not go to Sunday school at all or he arrives late and/or he is picked up early. And, of course, this creates a terrible problem for me [on my custody days] in terms of discipline because he will say to me, "I want to go late," or "I want to be picked up early because that's what my mother does."

LEVENTON: Has Ariel been going to Sunday school?

MICHAEL: Ariel has not been going to Sunday school.

LEVENTON: Is she enrolled in Sunday school?

NIELAND: Ariel is enrolled in Sunday school.

LEVENTON: Who paid for the tuition?

MICHAEL: I have paid the tuitions for both children for Sunday school.

LEVENTON: Was there any particular provision in the interim agreement, to the best of your recollection, concerning Sunday school?

MICHAEL: . . . I was to be allowed to pick them up and take them—or—Nancy would do it.

LEVENTON: Was there anything inconsistent—in your opinion—with Judge Wettick's Court Order that repudiated or changed that provision?

MICHAEL: Absolutely not. Nancy should have taken the children to Sunday school on all the alternate Sundays regularly.

LEVENTON: What effect, if any, do you think attending Sunday school has on young children?

MICHAEL: I think no question that the influence is a positive one. . . . I think it's positive in terms of giving the child some ethical guidelines while he or she grows up.

LEVENTON: Do you think this is particularly important in a situation where there is a break-up of the nuclear family?

MICHAEL: Absolutely. I think children have to learn there is a concept of right and wrong, moral right and wrong.

LEVENTON: Do you find this issue particularly egregious?

MICHAEL: It troubles me very much because I had always gone to Sunday school myself and I always found it to be a rewarding experience. And I wanted my children to have the same opportunity.

*   *   *

LEVENTON: Now, on a few different occasions in your summary or addendum, you made reference to an issue of soiled or clean or types of clothing for the children. . . . I doubt very much if it's important for the master to hear dates and places and times about the clothing issue, but could you tell the master in your own words what you think is occurring and how you feel it impedes the spirit of Judge Wettick's order?

MICHAEL: I have plenty of clothing for my children. . . . Almost invariably [when] I pick up the [children], a bag of clothing is delivered to my door with the children's clothing from Nancy's house in it. . . . It carries the implication that Daddy doesn't provide clothing, that you have to wear clothing that Mommy brings. . . . The children—when they are with me . . . are very happy to wear anything that I suggest . . . particularly my son. . . . He will then wear something back to Nancy's home. And, sometimes, within minutes, if not that evening, the clothing is delivered to my side door. . . .

LEVENTON: Do you have any [opinion] as to [what] it implies?

MICHAEL: It implies to the children that there is something wrong with the clothing.

* * *

LEVENTON: Have you been tortured through this . . . ?

MICHAEL: This has been a horrible experience for me not to have my children with me when they were supposed to be with me, to have them grabbed in the middle of the night, to have them taken away from me and not returned to me when I am supposed to have them. It's an impossible way to parent. It has to make the children terribly uncomfortable and it's absolutely wrong.

LEVENTON: Ariel is going to be seven years old; is that correct?

MICHAEL: That's right.

LEVENTON: Has her personality changed somewhat in the past six, seven months?

MICHAEL: Well, she is becoming more and more disobedient and [less] playful. . . .

* * *

LEVENTON: Ariel is, what, in second grade?

MICHAEL: She is in first grade.

LEVENTON: Were you delivered copies by Nancy of the children's schoolwork this year?

MICHAEL: I have received next to nothing of Ariel's schoolwork this year. Even things she brings home on my days I never get and I don't get most of the school announcements any more. . . .

LEVENTON: Have you contacted Ellis [Ariel's school] and asked for copies of these?

MICHAEL: I have talked to her teacher [who] says she sends home two copies of everything in [Ariel's] book bag and I just never get them.

LEVENTON: Have you requested them?

MICHAEL: Yes, of course.

LEVENTON: What grade is Nathaniel in?

MICHAEL: He is in second grade.

LEVENTON: Do you get copies of his work products?

MICHAEL: Yes.

LEVENTON: Directly from Shady Side Academy [Nathaniel's school]?

MICHAEL: Yes. Nathaniel always has two copies with him and I take one and I put Nancy's name on the other and send it to her house with Nathaniel's book bag so she realizes she is getting copies of Nathaniel's schoolwork. She has never done that for me.

LEVENTON: You do that on days you get him after school?

MICHAEL: That's correct.

LEVENTON: Ariel, I assume, doesn't bring anything home directly?

MICHAEL: She sometimes brings home things directly, but I may not get them. She may not show them to me or let me have her book bag. . . .

* * *

LEVENTON: Concerning Ariel's sleeping habits, under Judge Wettick's order, she was to sleep over at your home . . . six nights out of a 28-day cycle; is that a fair statement?

MICHAEL: Yes. It would be six nights out of the month. Since the start of the school year it's only two or three times at most that she stayed overnight with me—and none since October.

LEVENTON: . . . Did you compute the number of days [from September through December] that you were to have been with your children under Judge Wettick's Order of Court?

MICHAEL: . . . The children were supposed to be with me sixty days, all or in part.

LEVENTON: . . . Do you have an opinion as to how many of those 60 days you had your children . . . ?

* * *

MICHAEL: It's probably 10 out of 60 times.

LEVENTON: In your mind's eye what impact or effect have those types of activities that you have described had with respect to your children and yourself?

MICHAEL: Well, it certainly is psychologically painful to me. I can live with some of these things with great difficulty, but I think they are absolutely horrible from the point of view of the children. I have made the point over and over again that these children should have equal unimpeded access to both parents. They should not have to choose between parents. . . . I think all this kind of strife is a time bomb for these children and I think that this is terribly destructive to their development. . . .

*   *   *

LEVENTON: Jumping back to January 5, that's your first [addendum] notation. Did anything unusual happen?

MICHAEL: . . . When I [was returning] Nathaniel to Nancy's house Nathaniel had a soccer picture [and a class picture] with him he had gotten at school. I said to him, "I would like to have one or the other." He said, "Okay. . . ." When I got to Nancy's house with Nathaniel, Nathaniel said to Nancy, "I want to give my father one of the pictures." And right in front of me and Nathaniel, Nancy said to Nathaniel, "Why? He doesn't deserve either one of them." Right in front of my son . . . !

*   *   *

LEVENTON: Is February 22nd a Wednesday that you were to pick up Ariel at the school bus?

MICHAEL: That's right. I did meet her school bus and she wasn't there. Then Nancy's babysitter and Ariel all arrived at the same time at Nancy's house [as I did]. Nancy said to me in front of Ariel she would bring her to my house, but only for fifteen minutes. Then she would pick her up. At 4:15, indeed, Nancy arrived with Ariel. In front of me Nancy said to Ariel, "I'm coming back for you in fifteen minutes." This was a day she is supposed to be with me until 7:30 in the evening. Ariel came into the house. We went upstairs and started feeding her fish. . . . Within minutes Nancy was back at my side door in her car ringing the bell and encouraging Ariel to leave. So Ariel just, you know, felt that she had to leave. . . .

LEVENTON: During any of these periods, . . . did you ever tell Ariel it was her choice whether or not she chose to be with you?

MICHAEL: No. I told Ariel she had to do what the judge said or what her daddy said, that she was supposed to be with me. On one day she said to me, "I don't care what the judge says."

LEVENTON: Did you ask her where she heard that?

MICHAEL: No. I did not.

LEVENTON: Now, you have told us of five or six instances in 1989 through February where Ariel was at your house during a period of time that Judge Wettick's Order covers and that Nancy came to your house which was the marital residence at one time . . . and wouldn't leave. What dilemma are you faced with in those situations?

MICHAEL: . . . Certainly it violates my custody when the children are with me and Nancy comes into my house and takes the children. . . . I don't do that to her. I have never kept the children from her. I have always dropped them [off at her house] within minutes of being on time. I have never interfered with Nancy's time with the children and I have never spoken to the children disparagingly of their mother. As painful as all these events have become I have never talked to the children and told them how bad their mother makes me feel or anything like that. . . .

*   *   *

LEVENTON: . . . There seems to be a pattern evolving. Is that the way you perceived your custody time with Ariel, Nancy dropping her off and picking her up within fifteen or thirty minutes not withstanding the specific provisions of Judge Wettick's Order?

*   *   *

MICHAEL: Of course. . . .

LEVENTON: Each and every time this happened did you protest to Nancy?

MICHAEL: I vociferously protest to Nancy and she usually turns away from me and doesn't speak to me at all, gets in her car with the child and drives off.

LEVENTON: What are your alternatives?

MICHAEL: Well, I guess one alternative is to come here as I have done today. There are other unreasonable alternatives which I simply wouldn't pursue in terms of physical response to these things. It's a maddening situation. . . .

* * *

MICHAEL: . . . [One] day Nancy said to me, "I had to agree to come back for Ariel in thirty minutes or she wouldn't come."

LEVENTON: She said that in front of Ariel?

MICHAEL: Said that in front of Ariel! Well, Ariel and I went into the backyard. She was picking berries. . . . Then we left my backyard. We walked down Plainfield to the next street which is Bennington Avenue. Then we walked about a block or two up to Maynard and we were having a good time together. . . . Nancy came along in her station wagon and tried to cajole Ariel into getting into her car and leaving. Ariel didn't want to get into Nancy's car. She said, "Well, I'm going back to Daddy's house first." So while Ariel is slowly walking down the street back to my house, . . . Nancy is slowly following her in the car. I'm sort of left behind with my mouth open. . . .

CROSS-EXAMINATION BY MR. GRUENER:

GRUENER: Dr. Nieland, do you have a copy with you of the July 18th Court Order?

MICHAEL: Yes.

GRUENER: Could you take it out, please, and have it in front of you while I'm examining you . . . and, if you have a copy of the Petition for Contempt that your lawyer filed, you could look at the [summary] that you supplied. . . . Okay, Michael, I would like you to take a look at your first complaint, which is repeated telephone calls to Ariel and Nathaniel while they are in your custody. Do you see that?

MICHAEL: Yes.

GRUENER: Could you take a look at the Court Order and tell me whether or not the Court Order prohibits Nancy from calling the children when they are in your custody?

MICHAEL: It doesn't prohibit it, but it doesn't make a provision for it. . . . I think it depends on the definition of custody.

*   *   *

GRUENER: Is Ariel, by the Court Order, prohibited from calling her mother when she is with you?

MICHAEL: It doesn't say anything about that in the Court Order.

GRUENER: Well, as a matter of fact, it does say something about it, doesn't it, Michael? . . . It directs that when the children are in your custody after school and upon arrival at your house they are to immediately telephone their mother, isn't that true?

MICHAEL: That's correct.

GRUENER: Okay, and I presume you have complied with that; is that correct?

MICHAEL: I have attempted to comply with that, yes.

GRUENER: Well Michael, I'll tell you, I have reviewed very carefully all of your very copious statements in your diary and I couldn't find any instance in which you urged either child to call their mother in compliance with this Order upon arrival at your house.

MICHAEL: I don't recall that I specifically mentioned that.

GRUENER: Oh, so if there were instances in which you did not comply with the Order, I take it you didn't write that down; is that correct?

MICHAEL: There were no instances in which I did not comply with this Order to the best of my ability to do so.

GRUENER: Of course. So there are instances in which you could not comply; is that correct?

MICHAEL: Yes.

GRUENER: Okay, would you look at the Court Order and tell me [if] there is a directive to Nancy to deliver anybody anywhere?

MICHAEL: . . . No.

GRUENER: . . . Is there anything in that Order that requires her to return a child?

MICHAEL: No.

GRUENER: . . . I presume, also, Michael that the Order does not provide in any way a duty on my client to return Ariel should she run away from your house; is that correct?

MICHAEL: I believe the Court Order provides that.

GRUENER: I see. Could you show me where?

MICHAEL: It says the father shall have custody between certain times on certain days. You cannot deprive the word "custody" of its meaning. Custody means the child should be with the parent with whom the child is to be.

GRUENER: If Ariel runs away from you while she is in your custody, that's the mother interrupting your custody . . . ?

MICHAEL: If she is not returned to my custody, the mother is interrupting it.

GRUENER: Is there anything in the Court Order that prohibits my client from feeding her children?

MICHAEL: Well, there is. While they are in my custody, they are not to be fed by their mother.

GRUENER: Where is that in the Order?

MICHAEL: The father shall have custody from certain times to certain times. To me, or to any reasonable person with an understanding of the English language, that does not mean that the mother feeds the children at her home.

GRUENER: Michael, I won't take the reasonable understanding of the English language to be insulting; however, I would ask you to stick to my question.

MICHAEL: I am sticking to your question.

GRUENER: Let's move on. . . . Is there a provision in the Court Order which prohibits my client from taking Ariel out to eat or to go to the movies?

MICHAEL: Yes. When she is in my custody, she is to do these things only with me.

GRUENER: If you go to get Ariel on a Saturday morning or a Wednesday afternoon and Ariel refuses to go with you, is it your testimony that that's a violation of the order, then, if Ariel leaves the residence? Is that your testimony, Michael?

MICHAEL: Yes.

GRUENER: Once again, that was something that was taken up with Dr. Singer during the monitoring process; is that correct?

MICHAEL: I complained of this to Dr. Singer and asked him to ensure compliance with the Court Order.

GRUENER: Let's move on. ... Is it your position that my client is in violation of this Order of Court if she has a housekeeper present any time that you're to have custody of the children? Is that your testimony, Michael?

MICHAEL: No. She is allowed to have housekeepers, but they are not to be used to keep my children from me.

GRUENER: Once again, is there anything in the Court Order that prohibits Nancy from retaining babysitters or house-keepers?

MICHAEL: I don't think the Court could possibly have antic-ipated all the ways by which Nancy has attempted to vio-late it.

GRUENER: That's not my question.

MASTER: Dr. Nieland, would you please answer the ques-tion?

MICHAEL: Not specifically.

GRUENER: Does the Court Order in any way require babysitters to deliver children to you?

MICHAEL: Yes.

GRUENER: I see. Is that again what you get from the word custody?

MICHAEL: It certainly is. The mother cannot use replace-ments for herself to avoid obeying the terms of the Court Order.

GRUENER: Okay. Grab your diary, Michael. Do you have your diary handy?

MICHAEL: Yes.

GRUENER: Would you turn to Saturday, July 9, 1988, . . . July 21st, . . . July 27th, . . . August 2nd, . . . August 18th, . . . August 24th, . . . September 1st, . . . [all notations of the babysitters making some effort to get the children to cooperate]. Do you recall [these instances]?

MICHAEL: Yes.

GRUENER: Let's go to September 7th. . . . On that particular day you went at 4:00 for the children, it says, and when you heard someone say, "Come in," you walked in. Incidentally, under the interim Order, you're prohibited from entering that residence, aren't you, under the interim agreement, Michael?

MICHAEL: Yes.

GRUENER: "[The babysitter] asked you if it was okay if Ariel had chicken soup and came later. I said okay." Were you angry that the child was being fed?

MICHAEL: Yes; probably.

GRUENER: Okay. But you said okay?

MICHAEL: Yes. . . . I did the reasonable thing.

GRUENER: I know. I understand. That is reasonable, Michael. . . . If the child wants something to eat when she comes home, she should have it. And you did the reasonable thing, didn't you. Didn't you? Michael?

MICHAEL: Yes.

* * *

GRUENER: We have covered from July to November, Michael . . . so [these babysitters] hired to keep you from your children not only deliver the child but [in several instances they] help you and suggest that you persist; isn't that what you wrote?

MICHAEL: Yes.

GRUENER: December 2nd, Michael . . . was a day when you returned from a trip and had a present for your daughter. Do you recall that?

MICHAEL: Yes.

GRUENER: You told her she could have the present only if she came to your house. Do you remember that?

MICHAEL: Yes.

GRUENER: You also told her that if she came she could come right back. Do you remember writing that?

MICHAEL: Yes.

GRUENER: That was in accordance with an agreement that you all [Nancy, Dr. Singer, and Michael] reached for short periods; isn't that correct?

MICHAEL: No. It's not correct.

GRUENER: So, if Dr. Singer says it's correct or your ex-wife says it's correct, they are both liars; is that correct?

MICHAEL: Yes.

*   *   *

GRUENER: Okay. . . . You testified [that] when you would attempt to enter [Nancy's] residence the door was slammed in your face. Do you recall testifying to that?

MICHAEL: Yes. On many occasions.

GRUENER: . . . Do you recall the provision in the interim agreement that father is not to enter the property of mother at any time for any reason unless with mother's consent or by Court Order. Do you recall that?

MICHAEL: Yes. . . . But I can't imagine that the interim Order would provide for such churlish, uncivilized behavior as keeping someone waiting outside the door when it is raining or snowing.

GRUENER: Well, you agreed to that churlish behavior . . . ?

MICHAEL: Under duress, yes. . . .

GRUENER: Let's go on. . . . Whenever Nancy goes out of town the children should be with you. . . . Now, that's not in our Order of Court, is it Michael?

MICHAEL: No.

GRUENER: So, Nancy is not in contempt if she does not deliver the children to you when she is out of town, is she?

MICHAEL: No.

GRUENER: . . . Any provision in the Order of Court that my client is to take any child to any lesson?

MICHAEL: No.

GRUENER: So, if Nancy doesn't share your enthusiasm for music and make Nathaniel go to the cello lesson, she is in contempt of the Custody Order; is that your position?

MICHAEL: No, that is not my position. My position is that she should be sharing responsibilities for taking the children to their appointments, lessons, school, Sunday school on time.

GRUENER: And, if she isn't, she is in violation of the Court Order?

MICHAEL: She is certainly in violation of the spirit of it.

GRUENER: Okay. Now, talking about the spirit of it, Nathaniel has a cello at Nancy's house, doesn't he?

MICHAEL: Yes.

GRUENER: And Nancy rented that, didn't she?

MICHAEL: I assume that she did.

GRUENER: So, to undermine your efforts at Nathaniel playing the cello she went out and rented a cello; is that right?

MICHAEL: Well, that doesn't make sense. Of course not.

GRUENER: . . . There is nothing in the Court Order with regard to taking children to Sunday school, is there?

MICHAEL: Yes, because it's in the interim agreement and the Court Order says that all provisions of the existing interim agreement hold.

*   *   *

GRUENER: . . . Except for two occasions, every time that Nancy had custody of Nathaniel, which would be every other Sunday, according to you, he would be marked absent . . . ; is that correct?

MICHAEL: Yes.

GRUENER: . . . Does the record substantiate that?

MICHAEL: I don't specifically recall looking at his attendance record. I have relied on what Nathaniel has told me.

GRUENER: Let's go on to the failure to deliver notes and notices from school. . . . Is there a requirement in the Court Order that she deliver notes and notices from school to you, Michael?

MICHAEL: They are not specifically mentioned.

GRUENER: Now, you told us, Michael, on direct examination that you're a loving and caring parent; is that right?

MICHAEL: Yes.

*   *   *

GRUENER: Now, from examining your compendium, Michael, it appears that Nathaniel visits with you much more regularly than Ariel; is that correct?

MICHAEL: That's correct.

GRUENER: Is that, in your view, because Nancy is not suc-·cessful in keeping him away from you?

MICHAEL: Yes. I think that is exactly correct. I think a six-year-old girl is going to be more responsive to Mommy saying, "I don't want you to be at Daddy's house," or "Daddy may make you go to a piano lesson," or "Daddy won't give you everything you want. You better stay here with me. . . ."

GRUENER: I want to know if you have personal knowledge, since you haven't testified to it, that Ariel has been told these things that you just rattled off?

* * *

MICHAEL: I have no knowledge of specific things that Nancy has said to Ariel except, "Call me on the telephone."

GRUENER: Is Ariel afraid of you, Michael?

MICHAEL: Absolutely not.

GRUENER: Let's back up. . . . Once you pick up Ariel at the bus stop, you have custody of her?

MICHAEL: That's correct.

GRUENER: And if Ariel wants to go home first, that is up to you, isn't it? Nancy is not standing there, is she?

MICHAEL: I do not force Ariel to—

GRUENER: But you expect Nancy to force Ariel?

MICHAEL: No. I never said that. I expect Nancy or the babysitter to explain to Ariel that she is supposed to be

with her father and not let her into Nancy's house. What is
the difference between that and Ariel going into any neighborhood house and my not getting my child back?

GRUENER: . . . You have drawn the line at physical force and
would draw that same line for others; isn't that right?

MICHAEL: Correct.

GRUENER: . . . What did you regard Dr. Singer's role to be [as
monitor]?

MICHAEL: To assess the children's progress.

GRUENER: In a letter to [Dr. Singer] . . . , written by your
lawyer with a carbon copy to you . . . , it says, "In Judge
Wettick's Order of July 18, 1988, and again on September 1,
1988, you were to monitor, resolve, and determine what is
in the children's best interest." Do you agree with your
lawyer's description of what Dr. Singer was to do?

MICHAEL: . . . This does not agree with what the Court
Order was . . .

GRUENER: So, you don't agree . . . ?

MICHAEL: No. . . .

GRUENER: What did you do when you got a copy of this
letter?

MICHAEL: Well, I didn't do anything. . . . Dr. Singer, according to the Court Order, which was mandatory, was to
monitor the children's progress based upon the Court
Order being complied with.

GRUENER: And, in monitoring that progress, certain refine-
ments were made, . . . Dr. Singer's entreaties as you call
them . . . . Is that right?

MICHAEL: That's correct.

GRUENER: Have you . . . violated this Court Order by attempting to fire the Court-appointed expert?

MICHAEL: No.

GRUENER: Well, as your lawyer pointed out, . . . the Order provided that Dr. Singer was to monitor this matter; is that right?

MICHAEL: Yes.

GRUENER: And you haven't seen Dr. Singer since February; have you?

MICHAEL: That's correct.

GRUENER: And you fired him; didn't you?

MICHAEL: Yes.

*   *   *

GRUENER: I have nothing further.

REDIRECT EXAMINATION BY MR. LEVENTON:

LEVENTON: Okay. Mr. Gruener points out or assisted you in pointing out and agreeing that the Court Order does not: . . . specifically deal with cooperation by babysitters; . . . prohibit Nancy from calling the children; . . . prohibit Ariel from calling Nancy; . . . [require] Ariel's bringing her kitty to your house; . . . [forbid] Nancy sending clothes and having them cleaned right away and, you know, these sundry little things?

MICHAEL: It does not specifically mention those.

LEVENTON: Okay. With respect to those types of issues do you have an opinion, first of all, as to what the intent of the Court Order is with respect to those types of matters?

*   *   *

MICHAEL: [A]ll of these additional items and obstacles put in the way and behavior and subterfuges have been a very thoughtful attempt on the part of Nancy to undermine the spirit of this Court Order. No judge could possibly have anticipated all the insidious, ugly things that have been done to undermine, to rip the heart out of an agreement or an Order whereby parents are to share parenting of two children.

*   *   *

LEVENTON: . . . Can you tell the master why it . . . took this long to get this action before the Court through a master?

MICHAEL: I had very few difficulties with the children during last summer after the Hearing. . . . Everything was going beautifully. All of a sudden, at the start of the school year, when I expected to take my children to school, Nancy told me absolutely I was not to. . . . I complained about this to my attorney and Dr. Singer. Dr. Singer said, "Well, I don't think you should take the children to school," and the next morning he said to me on the phone, "I understand your position. There is nothing in the Court Order that prevents you from taking the children to school." Then, he called me back again and he said he had changed his mind again, that "Nancy felt she had lost at the Hearing" and he felt that now "she ought to win at something. . . ."

*   *   *

LEVENTON: Why did it take so long?

MICHAEL: Dr. Singer kept telling me to wait and be patient.

LEVENTON: There was a suggestion that . . . you have no relationship with Jennie now. . . . Very briefly, since she is not the subject of this proceeding, how can you . . . describe your relationship with Jennie prior to your separation?

MICHAEL: I always had a warm, loving, adoring relationship with my daughter whom I am crazy about and whose absence from my life just pains me no end.

LEVENTON: When you came back home from a medical meeting and found [Nancy and the children had moved out] did you also find a letter or a document?

MICHAEL: I found a note from Jennie.

LEVENTON: And I show this to you. . . . I will ask you to read this into the record.

MICHAEL: "Daddy. Don't be mad at me, please. I had no involvement with the move—it's only between you and Mom. Custody will be worked out and I'm planning on spending time with both of you. I love you! Jennie."

*   *   *

LEVENTON: What happened between separation and the present, in your opinion . . . , to explain what has now been described as an estrangement or no relationship with Jennie?

MICHAEL: I think Nancy has done everything possible to influence Jennie adversely against me . . . and this is exactly what I went through with Nancy and her first husband and the older girls. . . I see the same thing happening with Ariel. . . .

*   *   *

LEVENTON: Has Ariel ever indicated that she was afraid of you?

MICHAEL: Ariel has never been afraid of me. Quite the contrary. . . .

*   *   *

LEVENTON: Michael, there was testimony in cross-examination of approximately fifteen instances when the babysitters . . . cooperated with you in having time with either or both children . . . The dates are of record, of course, and they [occurred in 1988] . . . Now, how many times have you even had the minimal cooperation alluded to in 1989?

MICHAEL: I don't think even once. . . . I would just like to say there were hundreds of occasions of noncompliance and I think [the instances of cooperation] attest to the accuracy of my notes.

LEVENTON: What was Dr. Singer's ultimate goal as communicated to you for the children?

MICHAEL: . . . To have an equal, shared Custody Order arrangement with the children. . . .

LEVENTON: When you would go in and complain that you were getting less and less time with your children?

MICHAEL: . . . He would refuse to give me an answer . . . .

LEVENTON: I have nothing else.

RECROSS-EXAMINATION BY MR. GRUENER:

GRUENER: So, now, Michael, your testimony today is, of course, that your estrangement from Brita . . . and Sarah . . . and Jennie . . . is Nancy's fault?

MICHAEL: Absolutely. . . .

GRUENER: So, if Brita and Sarah and Jennie come here and testify to the contrary, they are lying; is that right?

MICHAEL: I don't know that it is lying. I think it is a gross misunderstanding on their part. I feel sorry for Brita and Sarah because [they] not only are estranged from me, [they] are estranged from their natural father. Nancy has planned to deprive [them] of both parties. . . .

GRUENER: In addition, you testified . . . that Dr. Singer could find no reason why Ariel would not want to go with you; isn't that right?

MICHAEL: That's correct.

GRUENER: . . . I'm going to ask you whether or not this [quote from Roland Singer's report] was ever expressed to you by Dr. Singer . . . "I perceive that Ariel was avoiding visits with father because of her fear and distrust which had been built up by his actions. . . ."

MICHAEL: No. He never told me that Ariel was afraid of me or distrusted me.

GRUENER: So, if he thought that, he didn't tell you; is that it?

MICHAEL: That's correct.

GRUENER: And what reason would he have to keep that from you, doctor?

MICHAEL: Because I don't think he knew the reason. I don't think professionally he was capable of evaluating it.

GRUENER: Okay. Well, so is what you're telling us now is Dr. Singer is not qualified?

MICHAEL: I think he is professionally incompetent.

GRUENER: So, Judge Wettick in this case appointed in your judgment a professionally incompetent individual? . . .

MICHAEL: With hindsight, yes. [Judge Kaplan actually appointed Roland Singer.]

GRUENER: I have nothing further.

Nancy [Rose] Selove Nieland, Having Been First Duly Sworn, Was Examined and Testified as Follows:

DIRECT EXAMINATION BY MR. GRUENER:

GRUENER: . . . Would you state your full name for the record, please?

NANCY: Nancy Selove Nieland.

GRUENER: . . . Describe Michael Nieland's relationship with Nathaniel and Ariel prior to separation.

NANCY: There virtually was no relationship. . . . He had almost nothing to do with them unless they were in his way or they were annoying him while he was playing the violin or listening to records—which he spent most of his time doing when he was at home.

GRUENER: Now, Michael has also described in his examination his relationship with the other children, Jennie, Brita, and Sarah. Could you briefly describe for the master what that relationship was and is?

NANCY: . . . No matter what they did in school, whether it was mediocre or good or not good, it never satisfied him. . . .

GRUENER: What is the current relationship that he has with Brita and Sarah?

NANCY: They want to have nothing to do with him. . . . They don't want to acknowledge him as a father.

GRUENER: What is his current relationship with Jennie?

NANCY: Jennie wants nothing to do with Michael.

GRUENER: Now, is that your fault?

NANCY: This has nothing to do with me. . . . I have never in any way tried to influence Jennie not to have something to do with Michael.... I think it's very important to have a balanced parental relationship, if at all possible.... She has been verbally and physically abused by Michael over and over—humiliated and embarrassed by him over and over again. I cannot remember any kind of pleasant relationship or pleasant time she spent with him.

* * *

GRUENER: After your separation—and I want you to go back to Ariel and Nathaniel now—did you and Michael have an interim agreement with regard to the times of partial custody?

NANCY: Yes. We did.

GRUENER: Could you tell me, Nancy, how the children tolerated that arrangement? What happened?

NANCY: It was very difficult. There was no relationship with Michael to begin with. He suddenly went from completely ignoring these children to being very pro—oppressive and wanting half-time with them. And it was very difficult to talk them into going most of the time when they were supposed to go.

GRUENER: All right. Now, what did you do to facilitate the temporary arrangement?

NANCY: I bribed them on many occasions. I would say, "Look, you go with Daddy now and when you get back we will do something . . . ." I enlisted the help of my daughter Jennie and . . . the help of my housekeepers because I thought maybe, if I wasn't the one from whom they were separating at the time they were supposed to go to Michael's house, it might be easier for them.... We did everything humanly possible to persuade them and cajole them to go.

GRUENER: . . . There came a time when there was an Order of Court entered. This is the subject of this Proceeding; is that right?

Nancy: Yes. . . . This is an Order of the Court which expanded the amount of time which Michael was to spend with the children.

GRUENER: And—what happened under that Court Order with regard to the children?

NANCY: It rapidly became much, much more difficult to get both of the children to go. . . . They both ran away from Michael over and over again. They expressed great fear and distrust of Michael.

* * *

NANCY: Ariel would cry and say, "I'm afraid to go," or she would say, "Daddy is always mad at me." Nathaniel would say he didn't want to go; there was nothing to do. . . . They detested having to go there.

GRUENER: What did you do to facilitate their going?

NANCY: Again, I enlisted my daughter Jennie and the housekeepers to help. . . . I let Ariel take her kitten over a few times. I always sent their pillows and blankets and their favorite stuffed animals because they have slept with these things since they were babies so I thought that might make them feel a little more comfortable.

GRUENER: Did you deliver the children on occasion?

NANCY: Yes. I did. On many occasions.

GRUENER: . . . Did you bring to Dr. Singer's attention the problems that you have described here that were going on?

NANCY: Yes. I did.

GRUENER: And did you and Dr. Singer and Michael reach any agreements with regard to the Order?

NANCY: Yes. There was . . . a list of modifications [that included], sometime in late January or in February, daylight periods with Ariel curtailed to twenty minutes, but, sometime long before that, sometime in November probably, it was agreed that Ariel's visitation periods would be much more brief than the time from after school until 7:30 because she wasn't able to cope with that, nor was Michael, at all.

GRUENER: Why was that done?

NANCY: Because the schedule simply was not working as it was outlined in the Order. So, it was agreed that Ariel would spend short, pleasant visits instead of these very frightening, forced longer visits that Michael was attempting to institute.

*   *   *

GRUENER: I want to direct your attention to some of the specific dates that were referred to by Michael Nieland, okay? . . .

NANCY: Yes.

GRUENER: Michael Nieland testified . . . [Mr. Gruener reads into the record Michael's testimony regarding Nathaniel's refusal to go to his cello lesson]. Could you describe what occurred on September 9, 1988?

NANCY: Nathaniel had gone to Michael's house after school. He called me to ask me to bring over some baseball equipment. . . . Michael was in the background prompting him, saying, "If you want your bases, be sure to tell her . . . ," and so on. So, Michael was well aware of the phone call. He knew I was going to bring over the supplies. . . . So, I was taking those things to Michael's house and, as I was driving over, Nathaniel was running down the street from Michael's house toward my house, crying, and

Michael was chasing him. Michael was hitting him and screaming at him about a cello lesson. Nathaniel was crying and he fell down on the sidewalk and Michael took his arm and hit it twice and tried to yank him up, still yelling about the cello lesson. Nathaniel was begging me to take him back again. Apparently, there was an argument because Nathaniel didn't want to go to the cello lesson and Michael was trying to force him to go. . . . Nathaniel was so upset I told Michael if he'd let me take Nathaniel to my house I thought I could get him calmed down. . . . Michael shouted at me over and over again, and at Nathaniel, and there were neighbors passing. It was an incredible scene.

GRUENER: When Michael shouts, what are we talking about here . . . ?

NANCY: That I am defying the Court Order, that I have no right to be here, that I am undermining his right, that I'm spoiling the children, that I'm trying to interfere with his custody rights, and—

GRUENER: This is out on the street?

NANCY: This is in the street, in an extremely loud voice so he can be heard at least a block away. Several of my neighbors have commented to me on some of the scenes that he created.

GRUENER: Did you take Nathaniel and quiet him down?

NANCY: Yes. I did. This was with Michael's permission. I told him I thought I could do it. He finally did agree. I was trying to end the scene.

GRUENER: Did you return Nathaniel to Michael's house?

NANCY: Yes. I did.

GRUENER: . . . Did you have difficulty with the overnights from the time of separation?

NANCY: A great deal of difficulty with the overnights. Those were particularly painful for Ariel and also for Nathaniel for a long time.

GRUENER: But Nathaniel adapted better than Ariel; is that right?

NANCY: I was able to do a better job with Nathaniel in convincing him that whether he liked it or not he had to do it. I wasn't as effective with Ariel.

GRUENER: You have heard Michael testify that he doesn't force the children. Do you force the children?

NANCY: No. I don't bind and gag and tie them ever. It's not possible to do that. I do everything in my power to get them to go, but I don't physically force them to go.

GRUENER: Did you prohibit Ariel from taking the cat [to Michael's house] or did you refuse to bring the cat over, if that was requested?

NANCY: Never.

GRUENER: Were there any occasions where you initiated a telephone call to Ariel when she was in Michael's custody?

NANCY: There were a few occasions when Ariel called me that I wasn't home and I would return her call a few minutes later.

GRUENER: I want to know if you began the chain?

NANCY: No.

GRUENER: . . . Did the Court Order require you to take anybody to Sunday school?

NANCY: No.

GRUENER: All right. And there is also a reference in Dr. Singer's report to the interim agreement which only applied to Nathaniel. Can you tell the master what that chronology was that went from interim order typed up, to what Dr. Singer has, to the Court Order?

NANCY: The interim Order was typed up around September, October 1987 and Michael insisted that part of the Order include that the children go to Sunday school. I agreed to it at the time and tried as hard as I could to do it. Ariel absolutely was very upset by it and refused to go and Dr. Singer agreed that she was under so much stress at that time that it was not in her best interest at all to force the Sunday school issue, that that should be dropped completely by Ariel.

GRUENER: Was that agreed to by you, Michael, and Dr. Singer?

NANCY: Yes.

GRUENER: Michael has alleged that you took Nathaniel to Sunday school only once late and another time picking him up early. . . . Does the Sunday school, Rodef Shalom, keep attendance records of children?

NANCY: Yes. It does.

GRUENER: I'm going to show you what has been marked for identification as Defendant's Exhibits E and F. . . . What are they?

NANCY: These are the Sunday school comments and attendance records for the semester last spring and this fall. . . . January to June of 1988 and September through December of 1988.

GRUENER: . . . Take a look at . . . the period of time the Court Order was entered [September through December] . . . how many absences is Nathaniel marked for?

NANCY: Four. . . . Two of those absences were probably on days when I had Nathaniel and two of the absences were on Michael's day.

GRUENER: ... Are there any comments of him either being late or leaving early?

NANCY: No.

GRUENER: Are the comments generally favorable?

NANCY: Yes.

GRUENER: So, if Michael has testified, as he has, that you have taken Nathaniel only twice to Sunday school, I presume, since the Order was entered, is that right or wrong?

NANCY: Absolutely wrong.

GRUENER: Did you regard it as your responsibility to return Ariel to Michael's house, if she ran away?

NANCY: Not a legal responsibility, although I did return her many times.

GRUENER: Have [your housekeepers] on occasion had occasion to either deliver or return Ariel to Michael's house, to the best of your knowledge?

NANCY: Many times.

GRUENER: Is that pursuant to any instructions that you give them?

NANCY: Yes. I have instructed them to do everything within their power, everything possible to get the children to go to Michael's house and return them to Michael's house if they run away.

GRUENER: Now, have there been occasions where you have been present when Michael has come to the residence for his partial custody period and you have been unable to get Ariel to go?

NANCY: Yes, there have been.

GRUENER: Tell the master what happened and why you're unable to; what goes on?

NANCY: Ariel is frightened to go. She simply refuses. What-ever the bribe or the threat or the—however hard we try to get her to go, she simply won't do it. She is afraid to go.

*   *   *

GRUENER: . . . Do you know [of what] Ariel is afraid?

NANCY: . . . That when she is there, she is locked in. She is not permitted to call. There is nothing to do, that Michael's parents, who live in the house, either won't talk to her and won't look at her for weeks at a time or else will taunt her, just following her around teasing her, taunting her. She cries frequently on days she is supposed to go there. She begs me to stay at home. She doesn't trust Michael when he tells her, as he has many times, she will be able to leave after twenty minutes or thirty minutes, if she comes over. He will tell her that and not let her do it, or promise her money and promise a gift and then not give it to her or promise they are going to do something. She doesn't trust him because he has either lied or broken promises. She doesn't trust him because he has locked her in and refused to let her out. He shouts at her, telling her over and over again how bad she is. He has told me in front of her many times that he is going to call the police, she's defying a Court Order—does she know what that means? She is being a very bad little girl. He told her in late April that she has to go see a psychoanalyst. . . . She isn't accustomed to being smacked and shouted at and threatened and to have this language used. She has been treated very gently all the years by me and by the housekeepers and by her sisters and this is just very frightening, unsettling behavior for her. . . . She is just a little six-year-old girl. . . .

GRUENER: Do you have any discipline problems with Ariel?

NANCY: No. I don't. . . .

GRUENER: Michael complains that despite admonitions from Dr. Singer, you're in contempt of the Order by providing Ariel with breakfast, lunch, or dinner when Ariel is supposed to be with him. Could you respond to that allegation, please?

NANCY: I have spoken with Dr. Singer about this several times and Dr. Singer agrees that when the children don't go, or if they come back from Michael's house, they shouldn't be immediately fed and that I should tell them, if it's around dinnertime, they are to have dinner with their father. This is what I do. Dr. Singer also agrees, however, it would be unreasonable to expect the children to go for an entire weekend without having breakfast, lunch, or dinner. . . .

GRUENER: And so, on those occasions that you're aware of, when Ariel has had something to eat, that has not stopped her from ultimately going, if she was going to go?

NANCY: No.

GRUENER: You're alleged, Nancy, to have violated this order by refusing to allow Nathaniel to bring his school books to Michael's house or . . . refusing to allow him to bring over a special notebook for his reports. . . . Could you comment on whether or not you're aware of any requirement of Shady Side Academy that book reports be done in some special notebook?

NANCY: There is a book report notebook they can do it in, or they can be done on any paper . . . and then just attach it to the [three-ring composition notebook].

GRUENER: Now, is he prohibited from bringing his notebook to Michael's house?

NANCY: No.

GRUENER: . . . Now, Michael has continued to refer to the [housekeepers] as babysitters. Do they do more than babysit?

NANCY: Much more.

GRUENER: . . . What would you say their percentage of babysitting is versus the other duties that you have described?

NANCY: It's hard to say. I would say probably 66 percent housework; 33 percent babysitting, something like that.

GRUENER: Have you ever instructed any housekeeper to keep the children away from Michael?

NANCY: Absolutely not.

GRUENER: . . . Michael complained that you have arranged children's activities on his time without consulting him and excluded him from transportation arrangements with regard to the children. Specifically, he alluded to the date of December 16, 1988 [in regard to a birthday party for Ariel] . . . ?

NANCY: . . . Let me just find that in my notes here. . . . Michael did not offer to take her to the party. . . I let her go to the party for a short time. . . . He did say to try to bring her to his house before the party, if possible.

GRUENER: Did you try to do that?

NANCY: Yes. I did.

GRUENER: Where he says . . . you prevented him from picking Ariel up at school on early dismissal . . . ?

NANCY: . . . I was astounded to find this as one of his complaints. . . .

GRUENER: So, in . . . these instances, then, he was not prevented from picking Ariel up at school; is that right?

NANCY: Not at all.

GRUENER: Was there ever an instance in which you learned during the day that due to illness or other problems, that a child was not going to be on the [school] bus and you didn't try to communicate with Michael either by answering machine or by housekeeper?

NANCY: Never. There was never a single instance.

GRUENER: . . . I'm going to ask you, generally, have you at any time canceled any arrangements that Michael has made with the children with any third party?

NANCY: Absolutely not. . . .

GRUENER: Okay. . . . Michael complains that whenever you're out of town the children are not with him. To your knowledge, is there any outstanding Order that requires that you deliver the children to him when you go out of town?

NANCY: No. I discussed this with Dr. Singer because Michael has made quite an issue of this and Dr. Singer said it's up to me to make the arrangements I want to.

GRUENER: . . . Now, Nancy, he alleges that you're in contempt of this Order because you refused to arrange to take Nathaniel to a cello lesson. First of all, do you know anything in the Order that requires you to take him to cello lessons?

NANCY: No.

GRUENER: All right. What have you done with regard to Nathaniel's cello lessons?

NANCY: . . . I did everything I could to try to facilitate the lessons. Nathaniel—I have to use the word—despised having cello lessons and practicing and complained about it bitterly. I did not support Nathaniel in this at all. I rented a cello. . . . I bought books and tapes that his teacher recommended I have. . . . I went to [the teacher's] house and . . . spoke to her on the telephone about his lessons. . . . Michael has excluded me completely from anything having to do with Nathaniel's lessons. I do have Nathaniel practice occasionally at my house, but I don't know what his assignments are and I don't have the most recent music probably that he is using.

GRUENER: Okay. Let's move on . . . [to] the allegation . . . that you're in contempt of this Court Order because you disrupt the relationship between Ariel and the piano teacher that Michael has selected. Can you tell us briefly what your position has been with regard to Ariel and her music lessons?

NANCY: . . . Michael was well-aware that Ariel was studying [piano with a very fine primary piano teacher] for six or eight months before Michael had her start taking piano lessons. The woman he selected, it's true, is a concert-quality pianist. . . . But Ariel was already well-established with a teacher of whom she was very fond. . . . I did not feel it was necessary for her to have two piano teachers at one time, but neither did I try to interrupt them. Michael made it exceedingly unpleasant by insisting that she go whether she wanted to or not. He caused a scene [on Thursday, September 29, 1988—an occurrence Michael also testified about] where he pulled her out of the car and kept hitting her while she was in the car, pulled her out of the car while she was crying, spanked her in the middle of the street and tried to drag her. And I believe that was the last time she had a piano lesson. . . . It had nothing to do with my trying to interfere with the lessons.*

GRUENER: Okay. . . . Michael alleges that you violate this Court Order by somehow indicating to the children that they are not to wear the clothes that he buys. . . ?

---

*Michael's testimony explains that at the time Ariel was spanked she was throwing a temper tantrum outside her piano teacher's house while Nathaniel was running down the street, furious because his father would not go immediately to get him a skateboard. Michael stated "I smacked her on her rear . . . not to get her out of the car, but to get her back in so we could go get Nathaniel."

NANCY: Occasionally the children have worn clothes, Nathaniel has worn clothes, to my house that belong to Michael. Many times Nathaniel has worn clothes from my house to Michael's house and [when Ariel participated in overnights] she did also. . . . Michael has repeatedly and continues to keep many of those items. . . . I have never indicated to the children that there was any reason not to wear [clothes Michael has purchased]. The children, [after] they come back to my house and after they are bathed and ready for bed, then I put the clothing in the bag and hope that he would do the same thing and return my clothing promptly so it doesn't get mixed up. And he doesn't have any excuse for not returning it.

*   *   *

GRUENER: . . . [Michael] complained that we are in contempt of the Court Order for the failure to deliver notes and notices from the school. . . . Now, Michael is the one who's meeting these children at the bus stop?

NANCY: Every other day of their lives. Yes.

GRUENER: And, so, the first person to see these notices, then, on those dates would be Michael?

NANCY: That's right.

GRUENER: And you have not received on a timely basis any notices of any school activities; is that right?

NANCY: That's correct.

GRUENER: What is this business about you whispering in [Ariel's] ear?

NANCY: I don't know what that's about. . . .

GRUENER: Have you ever been present when this six-year-old girl continued to slam the door in Michael's face . . . or said to him, "Go away, Stupid"?

NANCY: No. She stays as far away from him as she can because she is afraid he is going to grab her.

GRUENER: Has he threatened you with the police in front of Ariel?

NANCY: Several times.

GRUENER: Has he threatened Ariel with the police?

NANCY: Yes. He has told her that she is going to be in trouble with the police. And it gets more and more difficult to have her go because of these scenes when I drop her off and pick her up, this terrible shouting, arguing, and threatening. So, it's almost impossible to have her go sometimes because she is afraid of this.

GRUENER: Nancy, let me ask you something? Why do you deliver her at all?

NANCY: Because, otherwise, she wouldn't go at all. It would be impossible because Michael cannot get her to go with him. It's only if we take her over that she will go. . . .

GRUENER: By delivering Ariel, is it your intention to violate this Court Order?

NANCY: No. I am working as hard as I can to comply with the Court Order. . . .

GRUENER: Let me ask you a question about Brita's natural father who, Michael testified, was alienated from Brita by you. Was Brita's natural father at the wedding?

NANCY: He was at the wedding and his daughter and son were members of the wedding party.

GRUENER: Did he also give Brita a gift?

NANCY: Yes. He gave her a check for $5,000.

GRUENER: And he and Brita have a relationship, do they?

NANCY: Yes. They have a very friendly, close relationship and have, except for the years when Michael prohibited her and Sarah from seeing [Dr. Wanger].

*   *   *

GRUENER: Nancy, based upon the period of time now that you have been working under the Court Order and based upon your experiences under the Order with the children and your conversations with the children, why don't the children go with Michael Nieland?

NANCY: There are several reasons. One, Nathaniel and Ariel are both afraid of Michael. He shouts at them, he shouts at me, he shouts at the housekeepers in front of them. . . . On many occasions he has hit or chased both of them. . . . He has on several occasions locked Ariel in. . . . He has not kept promises he has made to both children, but particularly to Ariel. . . .

GRUENER: Have either one of them expressed any fear of his parents?

NANCY: Yes.

GRUENER: Where did [Michael's parents] live before they moved to Pittsburgh?

NANCY: They lived in Boston. . . . I took the children to Boston to visit them on a few occasions. . . . They moved to Pittsburgh near Labor Day of 1988. . . .

GRUENER: Now, Nancy, . . . could you tell us, aside from what you have already told us, those things that you believe you have done to aid—both before and after the Court Order was entered—his partial custody rights?

NANCY: Well, for one thing, when I moved, first I rented a house that was just a few blocks from Michael's house, then I purchased a house that was only a block away. I could have gone anywhere, but I felt it would make it easier for the children to be near . . . I did this for the children, also, because they had friends there, but I felt that would facilitate custody and visitation and so on.

GRUENER: Nancy, Michael testified in direct examination that Ariel and Nathaniel want very much to be with him. Have you seen evidence of that?

NANCY: Quite the opposite. . . . It's just more and more difficult and ugly to get them to go there. It is not my responsibility; yet I tried repeatedly, constantly and valiantly, had the housekeepers try as well to have the children go when it was Michael's time to have the children.

GRUENER: Your witness.

CROSS-EXAMINATION BY MR. LEVENTON:

LEVENTON: Nancy, . . . I have reviewed Dr. Singer's March 1988 psychological report and . . . isn't it true that you told Dr. Singer that you had more confidence in your housekeepers' handling of the children than entrusting them to their father?

NANCY: That was said in a reply to Michael's request that when I was out of town the children would be left with Michael instead of with a housekeeper. . . . I told Dr. Singer that the children and I both felt more comfortable in having a housekeeper take care of them, if I was no longer in town.

LEVENTON: That's what you told Dr. Singer?

NANCY: Right.

LEVENTON: Talking about Jennie, in March of 1988, Dr. Singer writes, "Recently she has started to spend more time at father's home." . . . Was that true?

*   *   *

NANCY: . . . [R]ight before this letter was written, yes, it was true. . . .

LEVENTON: Now, [in the report] Dr. Singer says apparently some very positive things about both you and Michael. He says you're both "very charming, pleasant, very intelligent and extremely articulate people. . . . [and] they each have much to contribute to the growth and development of their children." Do you see that [in your copy of the report]?

NANCY: Yes.

LEVENTON: Do you agree with that statement?

*   *   *

NANCY: It was Dr. Singer's perception that was the case.

LEVENTON: Let me ask it a different way. Do you think that Michael has much to contribute to the growth and development of Ariel and Nathaniel?

NANCY: Yes. I do.

LEVENTON: In what capacity. . . ?

NANCY: I believe that children, in general, are better to have a relationship with both parents no matter what the disparity in ability to parent or how the children feel about spending time with each parent. I believe that it's better for the children to feel that both parents care about them rather than being abandoned by one parent. . . .

LEVENTON: What about when it comes to the issue of discipline of children and authority figures? . . . For instance, do you think it would be best for Nathaniel to perceive both you and Michael as equal authority figures?

NANCY: I haven't thought about that question specifically.

LEVENTON: Would you?

NANCY: Yes, I think it would be, in general.

LEVENTON: No, I'm asking specifics with respect to Nathaniel?

NANCY: Okay. But I'm saying generally, with regard to Nathaniel, I think it would be, under ideal circumstances, better if he could regard each of us as equal authority figures.

LEVENTON: Same with Ariel?

NANCY: Yes.

LEVENTON: Do you think, if one parent undermines the authority of the other, that he or she may be doing a disservice to the child and to the other parent?

NANCY: If it truly is an attempt to undermine the authority, yes.

LEVENTON: . . . Concerning the interim custody agreement, . . . do you have a present recollection of the discussion with Dr. Singer as to how potentially destructive it would be to let the children make choices and the children manipulate one or the other parent to their own advantage?

NANCY: The terms "mutually destructive" or "manipulative" were not used. . . .

LEVENTON: Now, are you telling us that you don't think that Dr. Singer specifically used the word "manipulative" with respect to the children?

NANCY: No. He used the word "manipulative" with respect to the children. . . . But he did not imply that somehow I was manipulative. . . .

LEVENTON: I wasn't talking about you being manipulative; I'm talking about him stating that the children could be controlling and manipulative.

NANCY: He felt that children this age were not capable of making final decisions about how the time would be divided.

LEVENTON: And you agreed with that?

NANCY: Yes.

LEVENTON: Okay. . . . Dr. Singer writes Ariel and Nathaniel . . . "can be exceedingly controlling and manipulative in their behavior." . . . Did you discuss with Dr. Singer what he meant . . . ?

NANCY: Yes. . . . He meant that when they didn't want to do something they try to find—if they felt frightened and anxious and upset, that it would be more difficult to have them comply with this. . . .

LEVENTON: Are you telling me that . . . prior to the issuance of that report in early March 1988 that you had communicated to Dr. Singer or the children had communicated to Dr. Singer that they were afraid of their father and didn't want to spend time with him?

NANCY: I don't know whether those exact words were used. . . .

* * *

LEVENTON: . . . Do you think that [it] is appropriate to bribe the children to go to Michael's?

NANCY: Yes, I think in some circumstances it is because I think that the unpleasantness only escalates each time Ariel doesn't go and, I think in desperation, if bribing will enhance the chances of getting her to go over there, even for a brief time to try and build up to more time, then it's worth that. . . .

LEVENTON: . . . Dr. Singer recommended . . . that an equally shared custody arrangement be attempted; is that correct? . . .

NANCY: Yes. That was Dr. Singer's recommendation.

LEVENTON: [Dr. Singer states in the report] "if the shared custody recommendation is followed," what's the next phrase?

NANCY: "That the arrangements are . . . not a decision to be made by the children, though the expression of feelings is to be encouraged."

LEVENTON: Do you agree with that statement?

NANCY: Yes.

LEVENTON: Now, this was written in March. . . . Then there was a Court Hearing July 7th . . . at which point in time Dr. Singer testified. . . . [D]o you remember what Dr. Singer said and what he recommended to the Court with respect to Ariel?

NANCY: Yes. . . . He recommended an arrangement whereby the children would spend equal time at each house.

LEVENTON: Eleven days later Judge Wettick did issue an Order, did he not?

NANCY: Yes.

LEVENTON: . . . What is your interpretation of a Court Order?

NANCY: . . . It's a document which must be complied with. . . .

LEVENTON: What was your reaction when you received it?

NANCY: I'm not going to say that I liked the Court Order, but I had every intention of complying with it completely. It wasn't up to me to decide whether I liked it or approved of it or not.

LEVENTON: But I'm asking what your reaction was?

NANCY: I felt it was a Court Order that was not—that was going to be very difficult with which to comply, but I intended to do it.

LEVENTON: But there was no question in your mind that it wasn't up to the kids when they wanted to go and when they didn't want to go; . . . is that correct?

NANCY: Right. . . .

LEVENTON: The Order was to be implemented when school started, so we will say roughly after Labor Day; is that correct?

NANCY: Right.

LEVENTON: In September, . . . there were 46 examples starting September 11th—I guess that is within a week or so of when the Order was issued—as to alleged noncompliance. . . . Let's state facts. Starting from the issuance of the Court Order, . . . how many days or weeks would you say the Order was strictly fulfilled?

NANCY: I have not computed this. I don't know.

LEVENTON: Well, let's do the opposite then. How many days or weeks do you think it was not fulfilled?

NANCY: . . . I don't know. I know there have been many problems, but not because I have tried to not comply with the Court Order. . . .

LEVENTON: You have testified that you sometimes felt it was necessary to bribe them . . . cajole them, . . . you promised them things if they would go?

NANCY: Yes.

LEVENTON: Did you ever tell them that they had to go?

NANCY: Well, I told them every time they had to go, that this was not something they had a choice about. But, on the other hand, neither was it possible for me to tie them up and drag them there, nor was it possible for Michael who had first shot at them because he met them at the school bus to get them to go.

LEVENTON: . . . You did everything in your power to get your housekeepers/babysitters to assist the implementation of the Order of Court?

NANCY: Yes. I did.

LEVENTON: . . . Under what basis did you feel [per the Court Order] during Michael's custody time with Ariel and Nathaniel that it was appropriate for you, when you weren't home but there was someone caring for your home, to authorize or permit them to let Ariel or Nathaniel come into your home . . . ?

NANCY: . . . They were not there to interfere with Michael's time with the children; they were to do the work I had assigned them. . . .

LEVENTON: . . . We can assume they are doing housework, right?

NANCY: Yes.

LEVENTON: Have you discussed with them specifically what they are to do when Ariel comes to the door with Michael?

NANCY: Yes. . . . I have told them to do everything within their power to have Ariel go as promptly as possible to Michael's house, short of using physical force.

LEVENTON: Okay. Have you told them to provide treats for Ariel, food treats, if she says she is hungry?

NANCY: I have not. . . . On occasion she has come in and has wanted to have something to eat before she goes to Michael's house. . . .

LEVENTON: [Are your housekeeper/babysitters' children] ever [at your house], to the best of your knowledge, on days Michael is to have custody of Ariel and Nathaniel?

NANCY: Yes.

LEVENTON: Now, do you think that impedes Michael's custody rights and opportunities with Ariel and Nathaniel when Ariel knows that [two little girls, an eight-year-old and a ten-year-old] are there to play with in your home?

NANCY: No. I don't think so at all. . . . Michael has been told that the [housekeepers' children] and Ariel do not play together. . . . They are not used as an inducement to get Ariel not to go.

LEVENTON: . . . Okay. You testified that Ariel told you she is afraid of her father?

NANCY: Yes.

LEVENTON: She told you that she is afraid of him because he has shouted at her, correct?

NANCY: Yes. That he is mad at her all the time and that he will yell at her.

LEVENTON: And you also said she is afraid of him because she thinks she is either being accused of or actually is being bad?

NANCY: Yes. That he tells her—he has told her this in front of me also—that she is very naughty and bad many times.

LEVENTON: Do you have any present knowledge of whether, in fact, she was naughty when he told her she was naughty?

NANCY: Certainly, she wasn't naughty when he told her that at my house.

LEVENTON: When? When is the last time at your home that Michael told Ariel that she was being naughty?

NANCY: If you'll give me a few minutes, I can come up with the date probably. . . . He told her that on February 28th, that she was being naughty and the judge said she must come or she would be in trouble.

LEVENTON: Again, this has to directly do with her reluctance to go with her father?

NANCY: Yes. He shouted at her on Monday, April 3rd, told her to come with him immediately. "The choice is not yours." Talked to her a long time in a loud, angry voice, including the statement that she is being very naughty. . . . She told me on Sunday, April 23rd that he was always mad at her. . . . Those are the most recent times, but . . . it doesn't include all the times.

LEVENTON: Excuse me! These times had to do with [Ariel refusing to follow the custody schedule]; is that correct?

NANCY: They were times when he was at my house trying to talk Ariel into going to his house, yes.

LEVENTON: . . . Earlier, the very beginning of your cross-examination, . . . you agreed that the choice is not hers; is that correct?

NANCY: Right.

LEVENTON: . . . So, we now agree the choice . . . certainly isn't Ariel's. It was a Court Order to be obeyed, correct?

NANCY: Yes.

LEVENTON: Now, do you think that Michael, in order to . . . implement some sort of discipline, had every right in the world as a loving parent to get angry?

NANCY: I think he certainly didn't come across as a loving parent. . . .

LEVENTON: That might have been true, but his motive was as a loving parent: to have time that the Court ordered with his daughter; is that not true?

NANCY: I have no way of knowing why Michael did what he did.

LEVENTON: Why do you think he is doing this? Why do you think he initiated this proceeding, Nancy?

NANCY: Mr. Leventon, I would like to know that myself. . . .

LEVENTON: . . . Do you want Michael to have a healthy and loving relationship with Ariel and Nathaniel?

NANCY: I think that would be ideal, if Michael were capable of ever having such a relationship.

LEVENTON: Do you think it's appropriate for a parent to yell at a child?

NANCY: I think there are better ways of dealing with situations.

LEVENTON: . . . Do you think that promising Ariel a reward to spend time, as you categorize it, to spend time with her father is not exceedingly manipulative behavior for a six- or seven-year-old girl?

NANCY: Quite the contrary, I think that there is no way to overcome this block and I have tried as hard as I can to comply with the Court Order. . . .

LEVENTON: There is no reference to a block in Dr. Singer's report of March 1988, is there?

NANCY: The children were then spending far less time with the agreement that was in effect at that time than they are to spend with the Court Order that's in effect now.

LEVENTON: What about Dr. Singer's testimony in July of 1988 in front of Judge Wettick. . . ?

NANCY: I don't remember specifically what he said.

LEVENTON: "I think that what would be consistent with their best interest would be to have more time with the father—to work toward half time with the father." Do you remember him testifying as to that?

NANCY: Yes.

＊　　＊　　＊

LEVENTON: Nancy, you talked about the relationship between Michael and Sarah and Brita?

NANCY: Yes.

LEVENTON: . . . You testified as to the renewed relationship between Dr. Wanger and Brita; is that correct?

NANCY: I didn't call it a renewed relationship. I said it was always that. Except for the time when Michael deliberately obstructed the relationship—they had a good relationship and they still do.

LEVENTON: Nancy, I show you an opinion or a document . . . and ask if you can identify it?

NANCY: It's the, I think, Adoption Order [by Michael] for Brita and Sarah.

LEVENTON: And was there also an involuntary termination of parental rights associated with that?

NANCY: I don't think it was involuntary. I think that Dr. Wanger agreed to the adoption.

LEVENTON: Is that your present recollection?

NANCY: I haven't seen this for at least 15 years, so I cannot tell you accurately what my recollection is. . . . As a matter of fact, I don't think I have ever seen this thing. . . . I have never seen this.

LEVENTON: Well, let me direct your attention to a few provisions contained therein.

GRUENER: Why don't we first get on the record what this is. . . .

LEVENTON: . . . This is the Opinion issued by the Court . . . concerning the adoption of Brita and Sarah by Dr. Michael Nieland. . . . Nancy, would you like to take a few minutes and refresh your recollection or at least read this document? . . .

NANCY: [Nancy is instructed to read the following excerpt]: "[Dr. Wanger] testified that he is now, and always has been, ready, willing, and able to support his children and discharge his parental obligations to them. He testified that he had been thwarted in his attempt to perform his parental duties. He testified that he has been attempting to see his daughters on numerous occasions since the year 1971 and has yet to be permitted to see and visit them. . . . Dr. Wanger testified in part: "I am contesting this adoption because I love my daughters and need to be a parent to my daughters and I have been thwarted at every turn in efforts to be that."

NANCY: I'll tell you that I have never seen this. . . .

GRUENER: I object [to this document being admitted as evidence] on the basis of relevance. . . .

LEVENTON: To respond, number one, I think it's extremely relevant to show a pattern that Nancy Nieland is trying to, once again, . . . cause an estrangement between her husband and a daughter. Secondly, and also for purposes of relevance, in Nancy's direct examination [she testified Brita and Sarah] have had a friendly, close relationship with [their natural father] except for the years Michael prohibited Brita and Sarah from seeing him. I think this document which is a judicial record goes genuinely to the heart of this proceeding and to the credibility of the parties.

MASTER: All right. . . . I would agree with Mr. Gruener it is somewhat irrelevant in terms of this action and therefore I'm not going to admit this document. . . . She has read the parts that you wanted her to read, and therefore, I simply will not admit the document to read the whole thing.

*   *   *

LEVENTON: Have you ever seen Michael get frustrated with the children?

NANCY: Yes, on many occasions.

LEVENTON: Do you think . . . that is a normal reaction?

NANCY: I think it far exceeds a normal reaction.

LEVENTON: You think your way is the preferred way?

NANCY: No. I think that it's much less frightening for the children. I'm not sure that a panel of child experts will agree there is one preferred way, but I think, in general, they agree it's better not to scream, strike, and threaten.

LEVENTON: But it's better to bribe, cajole, and coddle?

NANCY: I don't do that ordinarily. Because I was so desperate to somehow make this Court Order work to try to help Michael out, I have bribed on occasion. . . . I have done everything.

LEVENTON: You told us that one of the reasons you believe that Ariel fears her father is because he "smacked" her. . . ?

NANCY: Well, that's one of the reasons.

LEVENTON: You ever see him smack her?

NANCY: No. But she told me about it [the piano lesson episode]. Dr. Singer told me about it. . . .

LEVENTON: Dr. Singer wasn't present; is that right?

NANCY: No. Michael told Dr. Singer about it.

LEVENTON: Okay, and Michael told Dr. Singer that that was to discipline Ariel, was it not?

NANCY: It was because she wouldn't get out of the car and go in and take a piano lesson at her piano teacher's house.

LEVENTON: Disciplined, and it was on one occasion.

NANCY: That episode was one occasion.

LEVENTON: How many other times do you have personal knowledge ever of Michael striking Ariel?

NANCY: One.

LEVENTON: One other occasion, tell us about it?

NANCY: . . . She was trying to get out of the house and he was trying to prevent her from getting out of the house. And there was another time when she and Nathaniel were arguing about something and he was trying to separate them.

LEVENTON: As a parent?

NANCY: He was acting as a parent.

LEVENTON: When you and Michael lived together as husband and wife for approximately 15 years, did Michael ever raise his voice in the house?

NANCY: Many times.

LEVENTON: Was Ariel present when he raised his voice?

NANCY: Yes . . . and it frightened her then, also.

LEVENTON: Did she tell you it frightened her then?

NANCY: Yes. . . . That she didn't like it when he shouted or when he screamed.

LEVENTON: Are you considering, "that she didn't like it" and "frightened her" as the same thing?

NANCY: I think that's what she meant.

*   *   *

LEVENTON: . . . Do you recognize the fact that there is a Court Order in full force and effect . . . ?

NANCY: Of course I do. I was happy to have it.

LEVENTON: Now, that's an interesting point. You were happy to have it?

NANCY: I was happy to have a Court Order.

LEVENTON: You were?

NANCY: Yes.

LEVENTON: Weren't you really, really angry at Judge Wettick's Court Order when he issued it . . . ?

NANCY: I doubt that there are ever any parents who are 100 percent . . . I don't think I was any more upset than any other parent would be. I wasn't very upset.

LEVENTON: Isn't it true that starting in September of 1988 you did everything in your power to undermine Michael's custody arrangements with the children?

NANCY: Absolutely not.

LEVENTON: I have nothing else of this witness.

MASTER: Any redirect, Mr. Gruener?

GRUENER: I don't have any questions on redirect. . . .

MASTER: . . . Mr. Gruener, it's your turn to call your next witness.

5. The Witnesses

After hearing Nancy testify, I didn't know whether to be confident or worried. Could anyone take seriously the nonstop accusations that I physically and verbally abused the children? Or the accusations against my elderly parents, who adored their grandchildren? I hoped not.

If her abuse charges were true, why would Nancy send the children back for more? Why didn't she file a complaint with the proper authorities? Why didn't she initiate court proceedings to protect Ariel and Nathaniel from this evil man who had already "verbally and physically abused" Jennie "over and over again"? Why, after describing endless chasing, threatening, taunting, hitting, and screaming on my part, would she testify to doing "everything humanly possible to persuade [Nathaniel and Ariel] and cajole them to go" with me?

Even though I found Nancy's answers to be filled with contradictions I worried that her explanations might sound convincing to the master. I could only hope the master wasn't taken in by her per-

formance. I worried, too, that my former spouse's attorney might somehow find a way to corroborate his client's story in the testimony yet to come from the housekeepers, Roland Singer, and even the children themselves.

Despite all these concerns I tried to remain upbeat because I knew I had an important ally: the truth. The truth was that Nancy had done everything possible to undermine and thwart the court-ordered custody schedule.

—Michael L. Nieland, M.D.
Defamed Parent

While waiting for the resumption of the contempt hearing Michael continued to brood over Nancy's testimony. It was painful to hear and even more painful to think that it might be believed. Naturally, he contemplated how much impact her recollections would have on Ms. McCarthy.

Michael worried further that his attorney might have found some of what Nancy said to be plausible. Before the hearing resumed in a few days, Michael reassured Paul Leventon that the accusations were unfounded.

Even though Michael found there were barely enough hours in the day for dealing with the contempt hearing and running his household after completing his work at his medical offices, he still made the time to search for just the right birthday card for Jennie's seventeenth birthday on May 13. At last he found a fitting one. It read: "Happy Birthday! And thanks for being born during my lifetime!" Love, Dad. Miss you!

Michael enclosed the following note in the card:

May 11, 1989

Dear Jennie,

Hope my birthday card made you laugh. I looked a long time for just the right message. . . . I've had a present for you which I've been waiting to give you for a long time and I sure hope you'll pay me a visit soon so that I can give it to you.

Jennie, I miss you terribly and cannot fathom your remaining so remote from me. We used to have so many laughs together. . . .

I'm not mad at you. At long last, come home!

Love,
Dad

Jennie didn't respond.
The contempt hearing resumed on May 16:

PROCEEDINGS

[condensed]

Karen Warych, Having Been First Duly Sworn, Was Examined and Testified as Follows:

DIRECT EXAMINATION BY MR. GRUENER:

GRUENER: . . . Where are you employed?

WARYCH: I work for Dr. Nancy Nieland. . . . My hours are generally from 2:00 or 2:30 until 9:30 during the week . . . although that varies depending upon [the other house-keeper/babysitters'] schedules.

GRUENER: . . . Are you frequently at the residence if Michael Nieland comes to pick up Ariel?

WARYCH: Yes.

GRUENER: Have there been occasions when Ariel has refused to go?

WARYCH: Yes.

GRUENER: And could you describe to me, then, what happens . . . ?

WARYCH: Michael will try to get her to go. I, also, have tried to get her to go. Sometimes she gets angry because Michael has gotten angry or yelled at her and then she'll—

GRUENER: Explain to me what you mean by Michael getting angry and yelling at her . . . ?

WARYCH: He has told her that it's the law, that she must go, that she'll be in Contempt of Court if she doesn't go. . . .

GRUENER: Describe for the master, if you will, the tone of voice we're talking about here. Is it a normal tone of voice—or not?

WARYCH: It may start out normal, but it does get louder and angry sometimes.

GRUENER: Okay. What have you done to attempt to get Ariel to go?

WARYCH: I've done lots of things. I've tried to get her to go. I've talked to her, telling her she's supposed to go and I have, at times, taken her over myself. One time I gave her my watch [because] she said she would only go over for a few minutes. . . . I could not get her to go the next time. She just ran up to her room and wouldn't come out. She shut the door. She was mad at me because I was trying to get her to go.

GRUENER: In your conversations with Ariel over the course of last year has she ever expressed to you why she won't go?

WARYCH: Sometimes she does. . . . She'll say—her grandmother ignores or apparently teases her. . . . It's boring over there. . . . Michael won't let her come back home, if she wants to come home. . . . She did tell me one time that he . . . locked the doors on her and that's why she doesn't want to go. That she has tried to get out and couldn't get out.

GRUENER: Have you personally been blamed by Michael Nieland for the children not going?

WARYCH: Yes . . . at different times. One time I know he told me that I was there specifically to keep Ariel from going, which is not true. I've had those same hours for many years now. . . . I do have other work to do. Not always; I mean, there are times that I'm not busy and I do sit down. I'm not required to work the whole six to eight hours I'm there. . . .

GRUENER: You talked about other duties. What other duties do you have in the residence?

WARYCH: [I] clean, cook, run errands, go to the grocery store, do laundry. . . . Anything to keep the house running smoothly.

GRUENER: What are you instructed by Nancy to do when it comes to that particular problem of Michael coming into the house to pick up Ariel?

WARYCH: To encourage Ariel to go, . . . to take her over if she doesn't go. If she agrees to go a little later, you know, to take her over a little bit later on. . . .

GRUENER: Have you ever, in all the days that you have been there, heard Nancy discourage the child about going?

WARYCH: No.

GRUENER: Are your children [seventeen-year-old son and eight-year-old daughter] present when you're at the residence?

WARYCH: Sometimes my daughter is with me, but not always. . . . In fact, on days when Michael was to have the children I generally try my best to not bring her. . . . Sometimes I have to because of my own situation at home.

GRUENER: Is that in response to an objection by Michael?

WARYCH: . . . That's of my own—because I felt that maybe if my daughter was there that [Ariel] would rather stay and play there and I didn't want to be put into that situation.

GRUENER: No further questions.

CROSS-EXAMINATION BY MR. LEVENTON:

LEVENTON: You said that occasionally Michael would come in and try to get Ariel to go with him . . . and you indicated that the tone of his voice would generally start out normally?

WARYCH: Yes.

LEVENTON: . . . And you said he would become, in your opinion, angry?

WARYCH: Yes.

LEVENTON: Was this a sense of frustration that you saw in him?

WARYCH: I don't know.

LEVENTON: Was he trying to reason with Ariel . . . that she was to be with him?

WARYCH: Yes.

LEVENTON: Would you participate in these discussions?

WARYCH: Yes.

LEVENTON: And, if she said she didn't want to go, what would you then do?

WARYCH: I would still keep trying. I would still keep saying, "But you have to go. . . ." I'm not going to pick the child up and bodily put her out of that house. That, I don't feel is my job.

LEVENTON: Did you ever see Michael come in and bodily pick up Ariel and take her with him [or] strike Ariel?

WARYCH: No.

LEVENTON: You told us that . . . the focus of her dislike for being back over on Inverness Avenue is the grandmother now?

WARYCH: That's not the only focus.

LEVENTON: The primary thing that she's complained of?

WARYCH: To me, it's her grandmother mostly, I'd have to say. . . . Ariel said to me, "She doesn't like anything I do. She doesn't even like the way I walk across the . . . room" [and] "She made fun of me."

LEVENTON: You also told us that she felt that it was boring there some of the time . . . ?

WARYCH: Some of the time, yes. . . . She has said to me, "there's nothing to do."

LEVENTON: Is there always something for her to do at Nancy's house?

WARYCH: Something to do—she's got lots of things to do. . . .

LEVENTON: Do you do them with her? . . .

WARYCH: I've always played with her when she wanted it.

LEVENTON: So, you were there as a playmate as well as a housekeeper and a babysitter; is that correct?

WARYCH: Playmate, yes. I could say I was a playmate. But not—I mean, I would sit and color with her—things like that.

LEVENTON: There was testimony from Michael that he, I think the term was "blamed you," for Ariel not going with him . . . and you remember that specifically?

WARYCH: Pretty specifically. . . . I said, "I'm here when I'm supposed to be here," is what I remember saying. And he said, "Well, you can't possibly have that much laundry or work to do. I've seen you sitting here."

LEVENTON: And, that's true; isn't it?

WARYCH: Yes. That's true. I have sat down.

LEVENTON: And you didn't deny to Michael that one of your functions [as playmate/housekeeper/babysitter] was to be there on days that Ariel came after school?

WARYCH: I am there the days I'm supposed to be there . . . whether Ariel is there or not.

LEVENTON: Did Ariel ever tell you that she fears her father?

WARYCH: Yes. . . . When he's angry or if he raises his voice with her, then I think she is afraid because she will—there are times that she would refuse to come down to the door. Now, these are days when she'd maybe come home and Michael would come back over to get her. You know, get her to come back over to his house. . . .

LEVENTON: So, she was afraid of his loud voice.

WARYCH: Yes.

LEVENTON: She ever express any fear of her father, though, other than him yelling at her?

WARYCH: You mean like that he would hit her or something like that?

LEVENTON: Yes.

WARYCH: No.

LEVENTON: I have nothing else.

MASTER: You may be excused.

Virginia Ingoldsby, Having Been First Duly Sworn, Was Examined and Testified as Follows:

DIRECT EXAMINATION BY MR. GRUENER:

GRUENER: By whom are you employed?

INGOLDSBY: Nancy [Nieland].

GRUENER: And how long have you been employed?

INGOLDSBY: Nine years.

GRUENER: So you were employed, then, prior to the time that the parties separated?

INGOLDSBY: Yes.

* * *

GRUENER: What are your duties?

INGOLDSBY: Take care of the children, do the housekeeping.

GRUENER: Do you run errands?

INGOLDSBY: Occasionally.

GRUENER: Do you get groceries?

INGOLDSBY: Yes.

GRUENER: Have you had any confrontations with Michael?

INGOLDSBY: . . . The only time, the one argument that we really had . . . he had come over earlier to get Ariel and Ariel said, "[Come back] later" and I said I'd try to bring her over. Well, she didn't [go over] and then Michael came back and Ariel still wouldn't go so he was angry with me.

GRUENER: Have you ever done anything that you know of to keep him away from his children?

INGOLDSBY: No.

GRUENER: Have you observed Nancy encourage Ariel to go?

INGOLDSBY: Yes.

GRUENER: Have you had occasions, knowing Ariel all her life, to have talked to her about why she resists going with Michael?

INGOLDSBY: Yes . . . the main one that she has given to me was . . . the grandparents. . . .

GRUENER: Has she given you any other reasons?

INGOLDSBY: Just that she wants to be home, she's bored.

GRUENER: Has she ever indicated to you any problems with trust of Michael?

LEVENTON: Objection. Leading.

MASTER: Overruled.

GRUENER: Has she ever complained to you that he breaks promises?

INGOLDSBY: Yes.

GRUENER: What was that occasion? Do you remember a specific instance, or instances, or was it a general context?

INGOLDSBY: It's just a general—well, he had promised her to go to Chuck E. Cheese and for some reason they could not go. She was upset about that. They didn't go that day.

GRUENER: Have you in any way encouraged Emily [Mrs. Ingoldsby's nine-year-old daughter], on the [days] that she is there, to get to playing with Ariel or doing something to interfere with Michael?

INGOLDSBY: No. When Emily comes, I tell her—if it's a Michael day, I tell her that. She knows that there's a good chance that [Ariel] won't be there. Regardless, if it's a Michael day or a Nancy day, Emily goes home at 4:30 P.M., period.

GRUENER: Your witness, Paul.

CROSS-EXAMINATION BY MR. LEVENTON:

LEVENTON: Were you aware of when Judge Wettick issued his Order in July of '88?

INGOLDSBY: Yes.

LEVENTON: Did Nancy tell you whether she was pleased with that Order?

INGOLDSBY: She wasn't happy about it.

LEVENTON: Was she very unhappy?

INGOLDSBY: Yes.

LEVENTON: During your eight or nine years with the Nielands when Nathaniel and Ariel were born, and prior to separation, . . . did either of the children ever express any fear of their father to you?

INGOLDSBY: No.

* * *

LEVENTON: . . . Effectively, two out of every three days you were at [Nancy's home] after school, Emily was with you?

INGOLDSBY: How do you figure that? She's there once a week.

LEVENTON: Right. And you're there three [schooldays] every two weeks?

INGOLDSBY: I don't get the point of this.

LEVENTON: . . . Now, this confrontation with Michael, [Ariel] was there; is that right?

INGOLDSBY: And Emily.

LEVENTON: And Emily! Well, this was on a Saturday. Emily was there on a Saturday this week, too?

INGOLDSBY: Right.

LEVENTON: Was she there Saturdays also?

INGOLDSBY: No. Rarely.

LEVENTON: But—she was there this time?

INGOLDSBY: Yes.

LEVENTON: And—this was a day that Ariel said she would come later; is that right?

INGOLDSBY: [T]he first time that Michael came Emily was not there. They were to be taking skating lessons. Emily was dropped off after her skating lesson which Ariel did not go to. . . .

LEVENTON: Are you telling me that sometimes Emily and Ariel would take skating lessons together?

INGOLDSBY: On Nancy's weekend. On Michael's weekend, my husband took Emily.

LEVENTON: So that was a weekend that was Michael's weekend?

INGOLDSBY: Right. My husband had taken Emily [to] her skating lesson. She was dropped off and we were leaving.

LEVENTON: And Ariel knew that on Michael's weekend she couldn't take her skating lesson *with Emily*; isn't that true?

INGOLDSBY: Right.

LEVENTON: And you don't think that undermined her decision to spend time with her father?

INGOLDSBY: No, because there were weeks that I would take [all the children] skating and Ariel would not go.

LEVENTON: So?

INGOLDSBY: So just because Emily, Nathaniel, and [his friend] are skating, if Ariel wanted to skate, it was . . . fine.

LEVENTON: It was what Ariel wanted to do?

INGOLDSBY: No.

LEVENTON: Isn't that what you said?

INGOLDSBY: No, that's what you are trying to say.

LEVENTON: That's what it sounds like to me!

INGOLDSBY: Well, I'm sorry.

LEVENTON: Okay. So Ariel has known Emily, your daughter, who is nine, . . . her whole life?

INGOLDSBY: Right.

LEVENTON: Are Emily and Ariel friends?

INGOLDSBY: . . . This is a very gray area. They are friends, they play well together, but does Ariel come down to my house on an off day? No.

LEVENTON: Do you take Ariel to your home for overnights?

INGOLDSBY: Yes.

LEVENTON: How often?

INGOLDSBY: When needed. And I have always done that. My hours and patterns have not changed.

LEVENTON: Were you ever present when Michael came to pick up Ariel on the weekend when Nancy was present?

INGOLDSBY: Yes.

LEVENTON: To the best of your recollection, what did Nancy do in those instances?

INGOLDSBY: The same thing [as I do]. . . . She tries to tell Ariel to go.

LEVENTON: And if Ariel would say, "I don't want to go?"

INGOLDSBY: And then [Nancy] would say, "Well, why don't you go for a little while and then see how things go."

LEVENTON: Thank you. I have nothing else.

REDIRECT EXAMINATION BY MR. GRUENER:

GRUENER: When Ariel resists going and her father is standing there, he doesn't do any more than you do, does he?

INGOLDSBY: No.

GRUENER: Neither of you has decided to take the kid kicking and screaming into a car; have you? Neither you nor Michael?

INGOLDSBY: I will not do that.

GRUENER: And Michael hasn't done it, has he?

INGOLDSBY: No.

GRUENER: I have nothing further.

Ariel & Nathaniel Nieland, Having Been First Duly Sworn, Were Examined and Testified as Follows:

EXAMINATION BY THE MASTER:

MASTER: . . . I am Mrs. McCarthy and I hope you don't mind that we took you out of school today. Is that okay?

NATHANIEL: Yes.

MASTER: What grade are you in, Nathaniel?

NATHANIEL: Second.

MASTER: What grade are you in, Ariel?

ARIEL: First.

MASTER: What are you going to do this summer, Ariel?

ARIEL: I don't know.

MASTER: Are you going to go to camp at all?

ARIEL: No. I hate camp.

MASTER: You both went to Shady Side camp last summer?

NATHANIEL: Yes.

ARIEL: Yes.

MASTER: But you didn't like it, Ariel?

ARIEL: No.

MASTER: How come?

ARIEL: They make you do everything.

NATHANIEL: They don't make me do everything.

MASTER: . . . So you don't know whether you are going to camp at all this summer?

ARIEL: No, but I might be going to Chatham Music Camp.

MASTER: I know somebody that went to Chatham Music Camp last summer . . . and he really liked it a lot. . . . His dad is a real accomplished pianist and he likes to play. . . . Do you like to play the piano, Ariel?

ARIEL: Yes.

MASTER: Do you have one teacher or do you have several teachers?

ARIEL: I used to have one of my dad's friends, but I didn't want to take piano with her any more.

MASTER: Do you practice when you are home?

ARIEL: Yes. Sometimes.

MASTER: Do you practice when you go to your dad's?

ARIEL: Yeah.

MASTER: Do you take piano lessons, too, Nathaniel?

NATHANIEL: I take cello and I absolutely hate it.

MASTER: How come?

NATHANIEL: Because see, it's so hard. . . .

MASTER: Do you practice your cello lesson even though you hate it?

NATHANIEL: I only practice it before Sunday school so I can miss it.

MASTER: . . . Is there another instrument that you would want to take besides cello?

NATHANIEL: Yes.

MASTER: What would that be?

NATHANIEL: The tuba or, maybe, the drums or guitar.

MASTER: Do you like being able to play a musical instrument?

NATHANIEL: Sort of. I don't like my cello lessons because they're always getting in my way when I'm playing something. I don't like them and I am bored half to death.

MASTER: . . . Do you like your cello lessons once you get there?

NATHANIEL: No.

MASTER: What about you, Ariel? Do you like taking piano lessons?

ARIEL: Yes.

NATHANIEL: She plays at my mom's and my dad's.

MASTER: But mostly at your mom's.

NATHANIEL: Because she barely goes over to my dad's.

MASTER: You barely go over to your dad's? How come?

ARIEL: I don't know.

NATHANIEL: I'm going over there every day I'm supposed to.

MASTER: Do you like going over there every day when you are supposed to?

NATHANIEL: I don't care where I go.

MASTER: Does it get confusing to know which day you are supposed to be at whose house?

NATHANIEL: No. This weekend I am with my dad and the next weekend I am with my mom. . . . Yesterday I was with my dad. Today I go with my mom and I sleep over and I go to my dad's. He brings me back and I sleep over again and . . . then I sleep over at my dad's Friday, Saturday, and Sunday.

*   *   *

MASTER: So, what is it like at your dad's? . . . Do you have all the same kinds of toys?

NATHANIEL: Not the same kind of toys. . . .

MASTER: Ariel, is your room different at your dad's than at your mom's?

ARIEL: Yes.

NATHANIEL: It's the same.

ARIEL: It's smaller.

MASTER: Do you have all the same sorts of things at your dad's that you do at your mom's?

ARIEL: No.

NATHANIEL: I have more gerbils than anyone in the family. I had four and two of them died, the baby and the mother.

*   *   *

MASTER: Where are the gerbils? At your mom's or your dad's?

NATHANIEL: My mom's.

ARIEL: I have a gerbil at my dad's.

MASTER: How often do you go see your gerbil at your dad's; do you know?

ARIEL: No.

NATHANIEL: Me and my dad are always working on it. We're trying to clean the cage and everything. It's like squiggling around.

MASTER: Ariel, what days do you go to your dad's? Do you have your schedule memorized like Nathaniel does?

ARIEL: No.

MASTER: Do you just go when you go?

ARIEL: Hardly ever.

NATHANIEL: She doesn't go when I go.

MASTER: Why do you hardly ever go?

ARIEL: Because.

MASTER: Why?

ARIEL: I don't know.

NATHANIEL: Me and dad are always inviting her to go to Chuck E. Cheese and she doesn't want to go.

ARIEL: Sometimes I go.

MASTER: Do you not go to your dad's at all or do you just not stay overnight at your dad's?

ARIEL: Me . . . I go to my dad's sometimes, but I don't stay overnight. . . . Before I slept over when I was supposed to. Not any more.

MASTER: Do you remember the last time you stayed overnight at your dad's, Ariel?

ARIEL: No.

NATHANIEL: Neither do I.

MASTER: Do you mind that she doesn't sleep over, Nathaniel? Does it bother you to be over there without Ariel?

ARIEL: Of course not.

NATHANIEL: Sometimes I even like her not being there.

MASTER: So, it's sort of like you get to have some time away from your sister going to your dad's?

ARIEL: I am glad to have some time away from him, too.

MASTER: I had a brother when I was your age, Ariel, so I understand what you are going through. . . . Does it scare you if you have to stay overnight at your dad's? Is that why you quit staying overnight at your dad's?

ARIEL: I guess so.

MASTER: You don't like sleeping in a different bed?

ARIEL: Yeah.

MASTER: Do you get mad at Nathaniel ever—if you go to your dad's?

*   *   *

ARIEL: Yeah.

MASTER: Do you get mad at your mother, too?

ARIEL: Yeah.

MASTER: Do you get mad at your father?

ARIEL: (laugh) I get mad at everybody.

MASTER: What about you, Nathaniel?

NATHANIEL: What about me?

MASTER: Do you ever get mad at Ariel?

NATHANIEL: You should see me! . . .

*   *   *

MASTER: Do you ever get mad at your mom?

ARIEL: Say yes, Nathaniel. Admit it.

NATHANIEL: Yes. . . . Sometimes. Very little.

MASTER: How about your dad? Do you ever get mad at your dad?

NATHANIEL: Very little.

MASTER: So your prime source of trouble in your life is your sister; is that it?

NATHANIEL: Yes. She causes trouble every time in my room. . . . I know Ariel had a fight with Mom this morning. You have to admit it.

ARIEL: Yes.

MASTER: What did you have a fight with Mom about this morning?

NATHANIEL: Her hair. Brushing it. . . . She started crying, "Mom, Mom. If you don't brush this hair I am not going to go to school today." She was crying over a little thing like that.

MASTER: Do you like your grandmother and grandfather [Michael's parents], Nathaniel? Do you get along with them? Do you ever get mad at them?

NATHANIEL: Yes. My grandmom makes me eat dinner at the table and I don't even feel like it.

ARIEL: I hardly even eat dinner.

MASTER: Is she strict? Is that what you mean?

NATHANIEL: Sort of. Most of the time.

MASTER: What about you, Ariel? Do you ever get mad at your grandma and your grandpa?

ARIEL: I don't think so.

NATHANIEL: Because she is barely over there. That's right, you never even got in a fight with them because you are never over there.

ARIEL: But last year when I was in kindergarten I always went over there.

MASTER: You always went where?

ARIEL: Dad's house.

MASTER: Do you know why you changed between kindergarten and first grade that made you stop going over to your dad's?

ARIEL: I don't know. Well . . .

MASTER: Ariel, do you get mad at your mom if she makes you go over to your dad's house if you don't want to go?

ARIEL: I guess so.

MASTER: . . . Now, does your mom say it's okay if you don't go to your dad's?

ARIEL: Yeah.

MASTER: Have you ever told anybody why you don't want to go, Ariel?

ARIEL: Yeah.

MASTER: Who have you told why you don't want to go?

ARIEL: Dr. Singer, my mom, my sister Jennie.

*   *   *

MASTER: Have you ever told your dad why you don't go there?

ARIEL: No, I guess not.

MASTER: Why haven't you told him? It seems that he would be the most important person to tell.

ARIEL: He would probably get mad at me.

NATHANIEL: Everytime when I play soccer over at somebody's house I am almost breaking a window because I kick it so hard.

ARIEL: I almost raised my right hand.

MASTER: What is your question, Ariel?

ARIEL: I have to tell you something. When my dad—sometimes he tells somebody something mean and then I tell him he said that sometimes and then he says, "I never said that." It's just like one time my sister came over my dad's house when I was there. He said that she was . . . worthless. When my sister told him he said that he said, "I never said that. No, I would never say that. . . ."

MASTER: . . . Well, let me ask one more question. . . . I am going to ask you both the same question. . . : If you had three wishes, what would you wish for? Nathaniel?

NATHANIEL: About a hundred million dollars, twenty credit cards, and a new house and five Nintendos.

MASTER: Where would you want your new house to be?

NATHANIEL: I don't want it to be in Brazil!

MASTER: What adults would you want to live there? Would you want to live there all by yourself?

NATHANIEL: My dad, my mom—not Ariel.

MASTER: Ariel is not an adult.

NATHANIEL: She's still not my friend.

MASTER: You want your dad and your mom; is that what you said?

NATHANIEL: Yeah.

MASTER: Are there any other adults that you want to live there?

NATHANIEL: I don't care if my mom and dad fight. I mean, it's their problem. I don't get into anything. I am just playing Nintendo.

MASTER: It doesn't bother you when your mom and dad fight?

NATHANIEL: No.

MASTER: Ariel, you have had lots of time to think. If you had three wishes, what would they be? And—Nathaniel has already taken all the money in the world.

ARIEL: I don't want any money.

MASTER: Ariel, what else would you want?

ARIEL: You didn't take all the pets; so I get all of them. . . . All the animals in the world, actually.

MASTER: That's one. What is two?

*   *   *

ARIEL: For my mom and dad to stop fighting.

MASTER: That is number two and what is number three?

ARIEL: If I wouldn't have to go to school any more. I like school, but my mom wants to wake me up so early.

NATHANIEL: Can I have a fourth wish?

MASTER: Fine, Nathaniel. You can have a fourth wish.

NATHANIEL: Tell her to go up to heaven.

MASTER: Eventually, I am sure she will be there.

ARIEL: But you will be there before me, but don't worry.

MASTER: Do you want a fourth wish, Ariel?

NATHANIEL: I want a fifth wish, too.

MASTER: Enough. I only have so many wishes to give.

ARIEL: No.

MASTER: You don't want a fourth wish?

ARIEL: No.

MASTER: Well, you have answered all my questions.

DIRECT EXAMINATION BY MR. LEVENTON:

LEVENTON: There are babysitters at your mom's house; right?

ARIEL: Yes.

LEVENTON: They're always there; right?

ARIEL: Yes.

LEVENTON: Their daughters are there sometimes; right?

ARIEL: Yes.

LEVENTON: You play with them sometimes; right?

ARIEL: Yes.

LEVENTON: . . . Your grandparents . . . are not as much fun to play with; is that right?

ARIEL: Yes.

LEVENTON: Do you think when you spend time with your dad that it hurts your mom's feelings?

ARIEL: No—maybe.

LEVENTON: Do you love your dad?

ARIEL: Sometimes.

LEVENTON: Do you know what love means? . . . Well, let me ask you this: Do you love Nathaniel?

ARIEL: No, no way!

NATHANIEL: I don't love her!

*   *   *

LEVENTON: Do you love your mom?

ARIEL: Sometimes.

LEVENTON: Do you love your dad?

ARIEL: Sometimes. Same thing.

LEVENTON: When you are with your mom, do you miss your dad?

ARIEL: Not really.

LEVENTON: When you are with your dad, do you miss your mom?

ARIEL: Not really.

LEVENTON: Do you pretty much decide when you are going to your dad's and how long you are going to stay?

ARIEL: No, because my mom says, "Do you want to stay for—" she says, "Okay, you can stay for twenty minutes." I usually say, "Okay." And then she says, "Do you want to stay for ten minutes?" I might want to stay longer times.

LEVENTON: When you are there [at your father's], are you worried about how long you are there?

ARIEL: Yeah—no.

LEVENTON: Thanks, Ariel. Thank you for talking to me.

CROSS-EXAMINATION BY MR. GRUENER:

GRUENER: Just a couple of questions, Ariel. . . . You said that your dad was mean because he screams at you. Does he do that often?

ARIEL: Pretty much.

GRUENER: Does that frighten you?

ARIEL: Yeah, I guess so.

GRUENER: Does [it] bother you when your dad says things and said that he didn't say them?

ARIEL: Yeah. I guess.

GRUENER: When you go over to your dad's house, sometimes you meet [him] at the bus stop; is that right?

ARIEL: Yeah.

GRUENER: Do you sometimes go straight to his house or do you go home first?

ARIEL: Well, sometimes I go home and then sometimes I say, "Let me drop my stuff off" and I go stay at my house and I will ask him to stay with me.

GRUENER: Ariel, when you don't want to go to your dad's does anyone try to make you go?

ARIEL: Yeah.

GRUENER: Who?

ARIEL: Sometimes it's my babysitters, but it's mostly not. Sometimes it's my mom because she says, "Why don't you go?" or whatever.

GRUENER: . . . What do you do then?

ARIEL: I guess I try to ignore them. . . .

GRUENER: . . . You want to keep seeing your dad, don't you?

ARIEL: I guess so.

GRUENER: You guess so?

ARIEL: But nobody makes me stay home, either. I don't stay at my mom's house, either.

GRUENER: So, it's making you stay [at your dad's house] that bothers you the most; is that it?

ARIEL: Yeah.

GRUENER: Has your dad ever hit you, Ariel?

ARIEL: Yeah.

GRUENER: Has your mom ever hit you?

ARIEL: No.

GRUENER: Do your babysitters hit you?

ARIEL: No.

GRUENER: Nathaniel, it's your turn. . . . Has your dad ever hit you?

NATHANIEL: Sometimes. One time my mom hit me.

ARIEL: By accident?

NATHANIEL: No.

*   *   *

MASTER: I have a question for you Nathaniel. . . . Do you know why Ariel doesn't want to go over to your dad's? Do you have any ideas?

NATHANIEL: Yeah.

MASTER: What is your idea?

NATHANIEL: He always makes us eat down at the dinner table when we don't want to.

ARIEL: Nathaniel!

MASTER: All right, kids.

Roland Singer, Ph.D. , Having Been First Duly Sworn, Was Examined and Testified as Follows:

DIRECT EXAMINATION BY MR. LEVENTON:

LEVENTON: Dr. Singer [a clinical psychologist], . . . what does "clinical" mean in terms of a clinical psychologist?

SINGER: Offering services with troubles, problems, things of that nature.

LEVENTON: Is there a distinction between a psychologist and a clinical psychologist?

SINGER: Well, psychologist I would consider to be a generic term in clinical, industrial and, especially, academic psychology.

LEVENTON: Are there any specific educational courses or degrees that you have that qualify you to call yourself a clinical psychologist?

SINGER: Well, most of the training that I have had in graduate school has been in clinical service, clinical work.

LEVENTON: When did you go to graduate school?

SINGER: I got my Ph.D. in 1957.

LEVENTON: Have you had any educational or academic background since 1957?

SINGER: No. Just training courses while I have been working and things like that.

LEVENTON: Is it true that on September 23, 1987, you were appointed by the Court in the Nieland case?

SINGER: Yes.

LEVENTON: Do you specifically recall what your Order on that date directed you to do?

SINGER: To do an evaluation with respect to a custody problem.

LEVENTON: Is it also true that it was not until March of 1988 that you issued a written recommendation?

SINGER: Right.

LEVENTON: Do you recall a Custody Hearing before Judge Wettick in July of 1988 dealing with this case?

SINGER: Yes.

LEVENTON: And, in fact, you were the only witness who testified; is that correct?

SINGER: Yes.

LEVENTON: At that Hearing, I believe you testified that you had spent, since your Court appointment in October, roughly 155 billable hours [as of that time] on the Nieland case. Is that your recollection?

SINGER: That would be about right, yes.

LEVENTON: In fact, I believe you said, and correct me if this statement isn't correct, that you think you had spent as much time and effort on this case from September until the trial in July as you ever had in your 30 years?

SINGER: That's correct.

LEVENTON: I assume you're also familiar with the fact that eleven days [after the Hearing] Judge Wettick issued a Court Order in this case?

SINGER: Yes.

LEVENTON: Did you feel [the] one-sentence provision that says, "Dr. Roland Singer shall continue to monitor the children's progress" was the most important provision in this [Court Order]?

SINGER: No, not at all. All of the things were important.

LEVENTON: Would you tell the master what your understanding of a Court Order is generically?

SINGER: It stipulates what people are to follow, and you're to follow that.

LEVENTON: It's the law; is that correct?

SINGER: Yes.

LEVENTON: And—you believe in that?

SINGER: Yes, I do.

LEVENTON: Were you familiar with the provisions in the existing custody agreement between the parties?

SINGER: Yes.

LEVENTON: Do you have a specific recollection that there was a specific provision in the existing custody agreement that Michael Nieland was taking his children Ariel and Nathaniel to school every morning?

SINGER: Yes.

LEVENTON: In other words . . . that was part of Judge Wettick's continuing Court Order?

SINGER: Yes. But when problems came up I was to attempt to immediately monitor and that had been my position all along, discussed by the judge.

LEVENTON: . . . Would you define for the master the word "monitor"?

SINGER: I guess monitoring is checking and observing and trying to help people work out a solution.

LEVENTON: Okay. Fine. Now, after Judge Wettick issued his Order . . . do you have a present recollection of whether or not Dr. Nancy Nieland was happy or pleased or angry with that order?

SINGER: I think she was upset with the Order.

LEVENTON: Did you continue to monitor the progress of the children?

SINGER: . . . Correct. Yes. Also my understanding was that I was to resolve problems when they came up.

LEVENTON: You mean you were going to be the Superjudge?

* * *

SINGER: I was not trying to be Superjudge.

LEVENTON: Now, since the issuance of this Order, you have remained involved with monitoring the progress of the children; is that correct?

SINGER: Yes. That's correct.

LEVENTON: So, it's your testimony that you have a direction from Judge Wettick to monitor the progress of the children. . . . Out of your 220 [total billable] hours, you have seen the children—not necessarily by themselves even—for a total of thirteen and a half hours?

SINGER: True.

LEVENTON: You may want to look at your bills. . . . So, is it a fair summation of your time that you have spent approximately one to two hours alone with Ariel and approximately two or three hours alone with Nathaniel?

SINGER: Alone?

LEVENTON: Out of your 220 billable hours?

SINGER: Alone, yes.

LEVENTON: During those periods of time alone with the children, did you perform any psychological tests on either of the children?

SINGER: No, I did not. I just observed them. I talked with them. Talked and observed. Interviewed and observed their play.

LEVENTON: Okay. And during the balance of the in-excess of 200 hours with Nancy Nieland and Michael Nieland, did you perform any psychological tests such as Minnesota Multi-Personality or anything else?

SINGER: No, I did not. I—just observations.

LEVENTON: I go back to [the Court's] original Order which was to conduct psychological evaluations; is that correct?

SINGER: Yes. But I make that determination of—psychological evaluation is very broad and, in my general evaluations, I do not include tests. And I have done close to 100 of them.

LEVENTON: In your 30 years of practice you have indicated that you have never worked so hard in a case or spent as much time?

SINGER: Both.

LEVENTON: Okay. So, wouldn't it be fair to suggest that if you were going to spend so much time, . . . that you would have also done tests, particularly on the two children . . . when, in fact, your instructions from the Court were to conduct psychological evaluations and subsequently to monitor the children's progress; correct?

SINGER: Yes.

LEVENTON: Okay. You still chose not to?

SINGER: Because I saw myself eventually trying to help the parents.

LEVENTON: Wait. What did Judge Wettick instruct you to do [in the Court Order]?

SINGER: To monitor the children.

LEVENTON: To monitor the children's progress. Are you instructed to monitor the parents' progress? Yes or no? . . . Do you want to look at it again?

SINGER: Yes. [He reviews the Court Order.] It says to monitor the children's progress.

LEVENTON: Now, how were you monitoring the children's progress by never meeting with the children or by never testing the children?

SINGER: Because I worked with the parents to get the information.

LEVENTON: And you, based on your reports, received from [the parents] conflicting data?

SINGER: Yes I did.

LEVENTON: So we were getting—what we call legally— hearsay information from the parents who had very deep hostility toward each other?

SINGER: Yes. . . . I did it through the parents because I think both these parents love these children and want to do what's right for them.

LEVENTON: But, obviously, what one thinks is right for the children is in conflict with what the other thinks.

SINGER: I attempted to help work that through with them. That's what I attempted to focus on in attempting to mediate and monitor this.

LEVENTON: Wait a second. What do you mean, "mediate and monitor"? What does mediate mean? Now you're becoming a Superjudge again.

*   *   *

LEVENTON: Specifically, in Judge Wettick's Court Order, it does specifically say, "All provisions of the existing custody agreement which are not in conflict with this Order of Court shall remain in effect." "Shall" is mandatory; correct?

SINGER: Yes.

LEVENTON: Now, when faced with that, what did you think was your responsibility to do if you have a Court Order and a provision of an existing agreement that says Michael is to take the kids to school, but you're faced with a conflict between the parties?

SINGER: My understanding was that I was to attempt to help them resolve it.

LEVENTON: Obviously, they were unable to resolve it.

SINGER: When they were unable to resolve it, I was to make the decision.

LEVENTON: You mean you were to superimpose your decision on that issue over what Judge Wettick said in his Order?

SINGER: That was my understanding.

LEVENTON: So you felt this Order wasn't worth the paper it was written on, I imagine.

SINGER: I interpreted monitoring very broadly.

LEVENTON: Okay. . . . I have nothing else for this witness.

DIRECT EXAMINATION BY MR. GRUENER:

GRUENER: You have been appointed by the courts of Allegheny County to evaluate custody matters now for how many years?

SINGER: Ten.

GRUENER: And in that ten-year period, has any judge of our Family Division ever issued as part of its Order appointing you an Order that you do psychological testing?

SINGER: No.

GRUENER: So, that's a decision that psychologists make; is that correct?

SINGER: Yes.

GRUENER: Was there ever a time that either parent asked to bring the children in to see you that you declined?

SINGER: No.

GRUENER: Dr. Singer, on direct examination you were asked about a second Court Order that was entered . . . in which

Judge Wettick ordered you to deal with an issue concerning school transportation. . . . Did you deal with it?

SINGER: I tried.

GRUENER: And you made a recommendation with regard to that pursuant to Judge Wettick's Order; did you not?

SINGER: Yes.

GRUENER: And that recommendation that you made was not what Dr. Michael Nieland wanted; was it?

SINGER: No.

GRUENER: Now, I want you to take a look at your notes of February 8, 1989. . . . Did Ariel on that date . . . make any specific statements to you with regard to why she had not been visiting her father?

SINGER: Yes. She did.

GRUENER: Could you tell the master please?

SINGER: She had a number of complaints. I will try to give them to you in sequence of what I have in my notes. . . . She complained about her grandparents, that they're mean. . . . She wants them to play with her more and just not sit. . . . She talked of wanting to talk to her mother and she wasn't allowed to make a call. . . . She told me about her father, that she can't trust him because she shows him [school] papers and he won't just look at them, he keeps them. . . . She told me that she is scared of her father. I asked her to tell me specifically why and she gave me two reasons: that he yells at her and he hits her. From questioning her about it, the yelling is often and the hitting—all I could get is there was one occasion, but he might hit her again is what she told me. . . . She complained about Nathaniel, talked about him punching and kicking her and, "He bugs me." She really did share more information than she had shared with me in the past.

GRUENER: Had you tried earlier . . . to discuss these matters with her?

SINGER: Yes. . . . At times she would share a little information and at times indicated that she didn't want to talk . . . I think there are just a few more things [from the February 8 session]. . . . I asked her to tell me things about her parents that she likes [and] things she doesn't like. The only thing that she could tell me that she doesn't like about her mother is that she didn't get her a dog. . . . She complained about her daddy that when she wants to leave she has difficulty leaving and that he, at times, won't let her call. . . .

GRUENER: Dr. Singer, when you were at trial in this case . . . Judge Wettick asked you, "Do you see her [Nancy] undermining the schedule?" Answer: "I think there may be some subtle bits of this, but I truly feel that she is attempting to work it out." Question by Judge Wettick: "You are saying it is not intentional?" Your answer: "No, I don't think. I think father feels it is, but from what I think I have seen I think she truly would like to have it work and have things be settled." . . . Now, subsequent to the Court Order, since . . . July of 1988, do you still have that opinion with regard to Nancy?

SINGER: Yes.

GRUENER: I have no further questions of this witness.

REDIRECT EXAMINATION BY MR. LEVENTON:

LEVENTON: . . . Do you remember having a discussion with Michael Nieland after the issuance of that Order when you told him something to the effect, "Well, I will have to let Nancy win one now or else she will have no confidence?"

SINGER: No. I did not say that. . . . I may have indicated there might have to be some trade-offs, particularly since I am attempting to try to improve his parenting skills.

LEVENTON: . . . I would like you to refer to your notes that apparently you have with you from the fall of 1988 [and I would like you to testify] when Michael agreed to the suspension of overnights for Ariel?

SINGER: I don't know whether I can find them specifically, but he did agree or it wouldn't have occurred. . . . I wouldn't have done this without his approval. . . .

LEVENTON: You don't have any specific recollection of when that agreement was made?

SINGER: No. I do not.

LEVENTON: You don't feel that that is significant?

SINGER: I think it is significant, but I can just share information with you [sic].

LEVENTON: Do you feel that it is in the children's best interest to let them decide the time that they are going to spend with either parent?

SINGER: No. But when there is a great deal of discomfort being manifested then I do think that [their feelings] have to be considered.

LEVENTON: Did you discuss this with Ariel?

SINGER: I would hear from the parents. Ariel had indicated to me that she didn't want to spend overnights with her father.

LEVENTON: . . . Other than on February 8, 1989, which is six months after that Order, [when] did Ariel indicate that to you? . . . I would like for you to show me in your notes. You have very copious notes for one incident in February.

SINGER: I have a lot of notes. . . . In October of 1987 Ariel told me that she wanted to live at her mom's and just visit her daddy and she didn't want to sleep there. . . .

LEVENTON: Can you date [this]?

SINGER: On October 6, 1987, when I saw her with her mother. . . .

LEVENTON: In July of 1988, a full eight months or so after that, you testified and made a recommendation to Judge Wettick that . . . involved overnights for Ariel; is that correct?

SINGER: Yes.

LEVENTON: Were there any specific incidents where you interviewed or tested Ariel between October 6, 1987, and your testimony in July 1988 that Ariel indicated [without her mother present] that she didn't want to sleep at her father's?

SINGER: I am looking for that now. On June 9, 1988, I saw Michael with both of the children. They were talking about enjoying playing at both places. Ariel indicated there that she didn't want to sleep over.

LEVENTON: May I see where you are referring to where Ariel indicated that, Dr. Singer?

SINGER: I asked her what was interfering with her going with her father and she denied that she was afraid of anything.

LEVENTON: You just specifically, under oath, said that Ariel told you something about not wanting to sleep at her father's. I would like to see that.

SINGER: I will try to find it.

LEVENTON: You just read from it!

SINGER: I am trying to find it in my notes.

LEVENTON: For the record, Dr. Singer just flipped over to the second page when he purportedly had read something from the first page! . . . Were you just making that up?

SINGER: No. I wasn't making it up.

LEVENTON: Are you flying by the seat of your pants right now in the Nieland case involving these children?

SINGER: No, I am not.

LEVENTON: Are you in over your head with these people?

SINGER: I don't think I am.

LEVENTON: The only reference that you have just been able to say is that both children denied being afraid of anything. Isn't that what you testified?

SINGER: That the children's father had the children for the weekend and there were no protests about anything.

LEVENTON: . . . Do you remember testifying . . . less than five minutes ago—that Ariel allegedly indicated to you that she was afraid to sleep at her father's?

SINGER: I also heard it from Jennie.

LEVENTON: I am asking you what you heard from this child whose progress you were to monitor.

SINGER: Then, I guess I picked it up from the parents.

LEVENTON: I guess you did pick it up from the parents, didn't you?

SINGER: I guess. Yes.

LEVENTON: Who brought Ariel in [for the February 8, 1989 session where she purportedly indicated being "scared of her father"]?

SINGER: Her mother brought her in.

LEVENTON: . . . Did you ask Ariel [whether or not her mother had told her what to say]?

SINGER: I don't think I did then, but I am sure that I have done it in past context with her. I don't think her mother does that.

LEVENTON: I am not asking you if you think her mother did it. I am asking you if you asked Ariel if her mother told her what to say?

SINGER: There are so many things that occurred I am not sure if I asked Ariel. . . .

LEVENTON: Do you think [the Nielands] are functioning more adequately today than they did when they first came in to see you in September 1987?

SINGER: I think that the problems are clearer. At least to me they're clearer.

LEVENTON: You finally focused in on the problem after a year and a half now?

SINGER: I think it's taken me this long to see them because I experienced [the gross pathology in this man in February].

LEVENTON: You are making a diagnosis of a gross pathology?

SINGER: It took me a year and a half to be able to see it, Mr. Leventon. . . . The only time that I ever saw it was on that 27th of February session.

LEVENTON: . . . Because he lost his cool after 200 hours?

SINGER: I think it's one thing losing control and the other thing is really behaving as he behaved.

LEVENTON: Why? Did he punch your lights out?

SINGER: No. He didn't.

LEVENTON: Well—did he scream at you?

SINGER: I had never been attacked like that . . . [especially in light of] how I worked with him and what I attempted to obtain for him in a year and a half.

LEVENTON: Well, so far we have a Court Order from July '88 that is not being complied with and you now say Ariel should play with her father for twenty minutes and you think that you have worked with them . . . ?

SINGER: . . . But I had assumed that, if [Michael] had any complaints about [the agreement], he would have called. He never hesitated to call me before.

LEVENTON: [What if the agreement] was a figment of Nancy's imagination?

SINGER: I had no reason to question that, I knew her for a year and a half, too, Mr. Leventon.

LEVENTON: I have nothing else of this witness.

EXAMINATION BY THE MASTER:

MASTER: . . . I am not asking you to go through your notes— but can you, in your mind, recall how it came about that the overnights with Ariel were suspended?

SINGER: Because she was so uncomfortable, appeared to be so uncomfortable with them, that I was attempting to at least have her not lose the good times that she was having with her dad during the day. . . .

MASTER: Now, how is it that you saw this in her? Is it from things that [the] mother said, [the] father said, the child said?

SINGER: Primarily, things the child said [that] I would hear from the parents.

MASTER: Did you hear this from the mother [and] the father?

SINGER: No. Father tended to indicate that everything was fine, that there were no problems at all and, then, I would hear from Nancy—there would be an indication that there were problems.

MASTER: . . . Would you ask Michael, specifically, did the problem that Nancy described to you actually—

SINGER: He would say they were all fabrications. . . . Again, I would let it ride. Then, hoping that things would be able to either be worked out later or that things would improve because we would move on to another incident I wouldn't hear about it again, but there would be another incident with them.

MASTER: Whose idea was it to suspend the overnight visits?

SINGER: I think—as I was hearing the problems that were coming up—I think that I suggested it, although it very well might have been brought up—the initiator may have been Nancy.

MASTER: . . . Did you approach the problem with Michael to suspend the overnights? That it would be a good idea to suspend the overnight visits . . . ?

SINGER: Yes. I did.

MASTER: What was his response?

SINGER: He was never happy backtracking . . . but my impression was that if I was the expert he would have to go along. . . .

MASTER: So, he accepted it?

SINGER: He accepted it. Reluctantly. He was never happy to give up something that he had gained.

MASTER: . . . The agreement to limit Ariel's visits to twenty minutes [in February 1989]—when did you first learn of that specific agreement?

SINGER: When I met with Nancy on that session [February 8, 1989].

MASTER: So, the first time you heard about it was in February, but you never discussed it with Michael? . . .

SINGER: I assumed . . . if he had any [objection] he [would have called] me. . . . He never hesitated to do that in the past.

MASTER: Those are all my questions. . . .

Stella Nieland, Having Been First Duly Sworn, Was Examined and Testified as Follows:

DIRECT EXAMINATION BY MR. LEVENTON:

LEVENTON: Mrs. Nieland, did you know Ariel and Nathaniel very well or did you spend very much time with Ariel and Nathaniel before moving to Pittsburgh?

STELLA: No. We had numerous visits and they were, on the whole, short but intense visits. I spent a lot of time with them when I was with them.

LEVENTON: What precipitated your move to Pittsburgh?

STELLA: Well, we sold our house in Boston and we thought we would come down here for a short time until we made up our minds just exactly what we wanted to do.

LEVENTON: Now, when you moved [into Michael's home] did you . . . reacquaint yourself with Ariel and Nathaniel or was that unnecessary?

STELLA: Unnecessary.

LEVENTON: Would you briefly describe your relationship with Nathaniel as you perceive it?

STELLA: Our relationship, I would say, was just a relationship between a grandparent and a grandson—funny and intimate and good-natured and affectionate.

LEVENTON: Now, with respect to your relationship as you perceive it with Ariel . . . ?

STELLA: Ariel was very affectionate and very loving and we played lots of games. . . . We played hairdresser and we did puzzles. . . .

LEVENTON: Is this during the past eight months?

STELLA: Yes, and in the beginning.

LEVENTON: Did something change or did you notice a change?

STELLA: Oh, yes, I noticed a change.

LEVENTON: Can you tell the master how or what changes you saw occur?

STELLA: Well [about two months or so after we arrived here], she stopped being friendly. . . .

LEVENTON: Did you ever inquire as to what, if anything, you did to displease her?

STELLA: I would say, "Ariel, why don't you talk to me?" And she would give me a flippant answer, "Because I don't want to" and she said at one time, "My mother says I don't have to talk to you. . . ." Sometimes, . . . she would walk in on her infrequent visits and I would say, "Hi, Ariel," and she would walk right by me as if I wasn't there. It happened many times.

LEVENTON: Did you find that to be disrespectful?

STELLA: It hurt me.

LEVENTON: Did you scold her about it?

STELLA: Oh, no.

LEVENTON: Did you ever discipline Ariel?

STELLA: No. What do you mean by discipline?

LEVENTON: Did you ever smack her fanny?

STELLA: Oh, good heavens, no.

LEVENTON: Do you have anything in your life more precious to you than your grandchildren?

STELLA: They are the only things that we have.

LEVENTON: To the best of your knowledge, have you ever been intentionally mean to her?

STELLA: Never.

LEVENTON: Did you ever hear Michael yell at Ariel?

STELLA: Never. He never yells. He may talk loudly sometimes, but he doesn't yell.

LEVENTON: Did you ever see Michael strike Ariel?

STELLA: Never.

LEVENTON: I have nothing else of this witness. Thank you, Mrs. Nieland.

CROSS-EXAMINATION BY MR. GRUENER:

GRUENER: Mrs. Nieland, isn't it a fact that you have never visited Pittsburgh after Ariel was born until now? This is your first visit here?

*   *   *

STELLA: I visited.

GRUENER: I presume, Mrs. Nieland, that it would surprise you if Ariel told Dr. Singer that you were mean, wouldn't it? Would that surprise you?

STELLA: Yes, indeed.

GRUENER: Would it surprise you if she told Dr. Singer that you ignore her?

STELLA: That would surprise me, certainly.

GRUENER: Would it surprise you if she told other people that you were mean and ignored her?

STELLA: It would surprise me from the point of view that I was never mean nor did I ever ignore her.

GRUENER: Would it surprise you if she told people that you spanked her?

STELLA: That would really shock me.

GRUENER: Because you never have, have you, Mrs. Nieland?

STELLA: Of course not.

GRUENER: Mrs. Nieland, Michael is your only child, isn't that right?

STELLA: Yes.

GRUENER: You wanted to come today and help him out, didn't you?

STELLA: Indeed.

GRUENER: No further questions.

Mischa Nieland, Having Been First Duly Sworn, Was Examined and Testified as Follows:

DIRECT EXAMINATION BY MR. LEVENTON:

LEVENTON: I would like to ask you very briefly to describe, if you can, your relationship with Nathaniel and your relationship with Ariel since you have been in Pittsburgh.

MISCHA: I think I have had a very good relationship. With Nathaniel, there has been no problem. I play football and soccer with him. . . . Ariel also, no problem. For instance, the other day I picked her up at the bus and we were very friendly. . . . I said your gerbil has been asking for you—Pinky—and we talked about that. It was very friendly. In one block, she came to the corner . . . and she just ran [to Nancy's] home. . . . I can't understand why she has suddenly changed.

LEVENTON: . . . Your relationship with Ariel, have you ever teased her?

MISCHA: No, there is no game like that.

LEVENTON: Do you try to be kind to her?

MISCHA: I have always been kind to her. I have handled students. I have been teaching for 58 years now and I have had students of all ages—

LEVENTON: What did you teach?

MISCHA: I teach cello.

LEVENTON: [Are] you gentle with Ariel?

MISCHA: . . . I have always been very sweet and very gentle to Ariel. . . .

LEVENTON: Have you ever seen Michael scream and holler at Ariel?

MISCHA: No. As my wife said, he has a loud voice.

LEVENTON: Did you see Michael get frustrated with the kids?

MISCHA: No.

LEVENTON: Did you ever see him get frustrated himself when the children say, "If I don't get my way, I am going home to Mommy's"?

MISCHA: Oh, that's always been the case. "I am going home."

LEVENTON: How does Michael react to that?

MISCHA: Well, he has given in to them all the time. . . . They are so used to being bribed. Everything they want . . . they get. . . . Rather than frustrate them, he gives in to them. . . . They never have any discipline. . . .

LEVENTON: Do you think [Nancy is] undermining his attempt to discipline?

MISCHA: Absolutely. [There is] no discipline whatsoever.

LEVENTON: Do you think, in your opinion, that, long-term, these children are going to be better off for it?

MISCHA: Certainly not.

LEVENTON: I have nothing else of this witness.

CROSS-EXAMINATION BY MR. GRUENER:

GRUENER: Do you have any notion, Mr. Nieland, as to why Dr. Singer would include in his report the statement that "the arrival of father's parents to his home did not help father's position."

MISCHA: Total lies.

GRUENER: You can also shed no light on why Ariel may have told Dr. Singer, housekeepers, or others, that you are mean?

MISCHA: I am mean?

GRUENER: Yes.

MISCHA: Well, I am sorry to say that that's absolutely false.

GRUENER: Mr. Nieland, this is also your only son; right?

MISCHA: Yes.

GRUENER: You would like to do what you can to help him out in this Hearing, wouldn't you?

MISCHA: Naturally.

GRUENER: That's all. Nothing further.

Stephen Schachner, Ph.D., Having Been First Duly Sworn, Was Examined and Testified as Follows:

DIRECT EXAMINATION BY MR. LEVENTON:

LEVENTON: Dr. Schachner—

GRUENER: [Objection] . . . It would be inappropriate for this witness to testify. This witness has never met until today Mrs. Nancy Nieland, has never seen the children, has never interviewed the children and is testifying on behalf of someone who is now his patient. For that reason I would think that the objection properly goes to the relevance of what this witness has to offer in that limited context of what we're here to try.

MASTER: Well, I'm going to overrule this objection. . . . There has been a great deal of discussion here by Dr. Singer of the various things that he has done and the whole question of monitoring. I believe that it's relevant. I think I am capable of recognizing that he has not met Mrs. Nieland or the children. You may proceed.

LEVENTON: Dr. Schachner, did you discuss Dr. Singer's involvement with the Nielands during your April 18, 1989 visit with him?

SCHACHNER: I made it my responsibility to ask Dr. Singer to give me first the treatment summary and his impressions on the case and he did so.

LEVENTON: Dr. Schachner, is there a standard in your profession for doing [an] evaluation?

SCHACHNER: . . . I believe that there is academically a standard that has been defined through various textbooks.

LEVENTON: Could you briefly explain that, please.

SCHACHNER: There will be two or three visits [by the evaluator] of each [parent and child]—psychological testing or interviewing and, if it's the children, there will be play therapy as well as direct conversations because many children cannot be asked direct questions. . . . School records are reviewed, a home evaluator's report—if one is available—is reviewed, a physician's report [reviewed] and meeting of ancillary personnel. . . . A written report usually occurs no more than three weeks from the completion of the last visit, which is usually not more than two months [from the start]. . . . The encouragement is for the psychologist not to define what is the judge's responsibility—which would be the exact visitation schedule—or to make a specific recommendation. . . . Concerns that the psychologists are supposed to attend to include: attachment and dependency between child and parent figure, evaluation of educational issues, ability of the parent to share the child with the other parent, socioeconomic factors that might impose upon quality of life. . . . It is considered a violation of the ethical standard of psychologists and also common clinical sense dictates that the psychologist cannot evaluate a family and attempt on a regular basis to bring these recommendations to fruition through any type of ongoing consultation. This is a duality of role and it is strictly denied the psychologist.

LEVENTON: When you spoke with Dr. Singer, . . . did he ever mention Ariel's purported or alleged fear of her father?

SCHACHNER: I would like to look at my notes to answer that, if I may have a minute. Dr. Singer did not discuss that with me of his own accord. . . .

LEVENTON: He didn't bring it up on his own?

SCHACHNER: No. . . . He basically felt that the children were healthy children.

LEVENTON: In your opinion, was there any way to determine whether one parent, Nancy, has undermined and intentionally deprived Michael of his custody time with the children?

SCHACHNER: . . . Suffice it to say that if you have these concerns about whether a child is afraid of a parent or being any way verbally or physically abused by a parent, then you as a psychologist are responsible for developing evidence, not just from the parents, and to recommend treatment, if you see a problem.

LEVENTON: Do you think Dr. Singer's procedures and approach are . . . inappropriate?

SCHACHNER: I would not choose to second guess Dr. Singer. I would state that in the current situation that I am reviewing it is clear that his approach has not led him to the success that he would like it to have had.

*   *   *

LEVENTON: . . . With respect to Dr. Singer's monitoring . . . ?

SCHACHNER: . . . When you are an evaluator, and you are also ongoingly involved in attempting to improve or change behavior, you are then working as a therapist or facilitator. You are attempting to develop a sense of trust and confidence with the individuals that you are working with—while they are continuing to hold in their own mind the fact that you have some judgment that you can pass down about them—and that makes the conflict of interest very real therapeutically, even if everybody is saying at the moment we are all getting along and we all like you. So, the psychologist is prohibited from this role, according to the ethics and the interpretation of those ethics by these various organizations that propose them. . . . You really want to avoid this and, unfortunately, many judges and attorneys have not come to this understanding of the clinical process. So, it is not unusual to find a psychologist in the position that Dr. Singer was in. . . .

LEVENTON: Is it appropriate or psychologically healthy for a child to choose whether to be with a parent whether it be custodial or noncustodial?

* * *

SCHACHNER: I think your question is getting to the heart of the difficulty. . . . It is not good for children at a young age to be in charge of when they are going to be placed with an individual who may or may not cause them to be fearful. . . . In plain talk, you are not supposed to say to a child, "Would you like to go to school today?" You are supposed to ask, "Would you like to play with this friend or that friend?" There are certain boundaries that we have in raising children that are generally attested to. . . . I am not prepared to talk about the children in this case—we all know that. . . . Dr. Singer's approach is to try to help parents share and it has not succeeded. . . . At this point in time people are casting a lot of stones. . . . Our [psychologist's] reply in dealing with that would be . . . : If there were evidence of specific—and real concern about—fearfulness in the child, why would there not have been immediately a recommendation or supervised visitation with a neutral party present? Why would there not be consultation time in this case with the father or the mother and the child so that the therapist could see firsthand how they played and interacted and if that play was a false sense of play? . . . These things didn't happen. . . .

LEVENTON: Recommendation as to what should be done presently?

SCHACHNER: . . . I feel that we have to be very concerned about the child and we have to be very curious in learning whether the child, in fact, has suffered some damage and has fears that are above and beyond traditional or typical that might occur in any child growing up. . . . One cannot assess any fear in children through verbalization of comments through adults. That is not how we do it. . . . I don't know what the scenario is here, but there is a strong need to spend time with the child by [a] therapist . . . not only to diagnose, but to offer commentary that is meaningful. . . .

LEVENTON: Thank you, Dr. Schachner. I have no further questions.

CROSS-EXAMINATION BY MR. GRUENER:

GRUENER: Although it's probably abundantly clear on the record from the many times that you referred to it, let me go through this for my own purposes. You have not ever met my client. . . . You have never met the children in this context?

SCHACHNER: That's correct.

GRUENER: You have, therefore, never conducted any interviews, evaluations, or tests of my clients or of anyone in this case except Michael Nieland?

SCHACHNER: Well, I have had a meeting with Dr. Singer, but in terms of evaluation, yes, you're correct.

GRUENER: You have not talked to Brita, . . . Sarah, . . . or Jennie? . . .

SCHACHNER: No. I haven't.

GRUENER: You have also alluded to a [standard in your profession for doing an evaluation]. . . . You have not—nor do you in any way purport to have done—any of these things in this case, right?

SCHACHNER: The only thing that I have accomplished would be the developmental and background history taking of Dr. Michael Nieland and the consultation with Dr. Singer.

GRUENER: Now, is there any problem in your mind—based upon that limited background in this case—in making recommendations . . . ?

SCHACHNER: I don't want to disappoint you in my answer, but I have absolutely no reluctance—in the type of recommendations made. . . .

GRUENER: So these are the kinds of recommendations that you would make in any case . . . ?

SCHACHNER: Well, I think I totally agree with you. . . .

GRUENER: . . . I presume that from your view of what is proper or improper, these types of Court appointments—to continue to monitor a situation—should probably be turned down by people that share your view of what your role is; is that correct or incorrect?

SCHACHNER: I think the essence of what you are saying is correct. Calling it "my view" would not be correct. . . .

GRUENER: But—you testified on direct examination that it is not unusual to find [these Court appointments] . . . ?

SCHACHNER: Unfortunately, that's true. . . .

*   *   *

GRUENER: Of all the things that you took seriously in meeting with Dr. Singer . . . have you taken seriously his recommendation to Michael that he obtain psychotherapy for a deeply rooted character disorder?

SCHACHNER: . . . It would be very difficult for me to make a fair assessment of Dr. Singer's concern about Dr. Michael Nieland—and vice versa. . . .

GRUENER: . . . Based upon your standards of evaluation, you are not prepared here today to offer an opinion as to whether Ariel is afraid of her father or not, are you?

SCHACHNER: Absolutely. You are correct.

GRUENER: You are also not here to render an opinion—nor are you able to—with regard to my client's culpability or willfulness in violating any Court Order; are you?

SCHACHNER: Not in reference to your specific client. No.

GRUENER: Well, that's why we're here. . . . I don't have any other questions.

EXAMINATION BY THE MASTER:

MASTER: One of the concerns here . . . is that the Court Order directed Dr. Singer to do that which has been difficult, and—now that Dr. Michael Nieland has taken Dr. Singer up on his offer not to work with him any more— there is a problem that this could be a continuing pattern of behavior. . . . In other words, whenever we get to a crossroads in any form of therapy . . . if Dr. Michael Nieland flares up, becomes angry, he can just walk out of it and he has to start all over again which [causes another] delay [and can be] expensive. How do you deal with that kind of situation?

SCHACHNER: Well, that is . . . an easy question to resolve from the Court's point of view. . . . It has been recognized that ordering psychotherapy is not consistent with judicial perspective throughout the country or clinical perspective about how to help people, but it happens. . . . But, if you separate the mental health specialist from treatment, . . . the Court-appointed specialist is able to . . . monitor the frequency of broken therapeutic relationships, so that if Dr. Singer . . . had referred [the Nieland] family onward, if he took his position as the Monitor by the Court and said to the family, "Okay, I'm not going to monitor, but I am going to be the one to help facilitate—so here are some people that I recommend you see, make your choice and I would like you to give me permission to talk with them in three months—and then again in six months." If the family were to agree with this, Dr. Singer would be able to offer quite a congenial opinion after three, six months, a year, two years, as to the likelihood of either of the adults to respond [or not respond] to the chosen treatment.

MASTER: So, what you are saying is, if a Court-appointed specialist is asked to be in the role of Evaluator, there has to be someone else that does the treatment and the role becomes coordinator of the treatment process?

SCHACHNER: Or at least a monitor of it—in the true sense of the word, of regulating and watching.

MASTER: I have nothing else.

6. The Verdicts

At the conclusion of the contempt hearing, I believed Paul Leventon had ably demonstrated for all to see what I already knew: Nancy had intentionally undermined and thwarted the court order.

She had defended herself by claiming that Ariel would not adhere to the custody schedule because she was afraid of her father, but neither the babysitters nor the children, nor Roland Singer substantiated Nancy's accusation.

The only charge that my ex-wife's witnesses supported was that I yelled. I'm sure there were times I did raise my voice; maybe, to them, it sounded like yelling. So what? What wounded father wouldn't vociferously object to having his child turned against him?

Even though I was sure Nancy's true intentions and Singer's questionable competence had been revealed during the proceedings I realized my conclusion meant nothing. For all intents and purposes, my family life hinged on the master's decision. When the fifth and final session ended I honestly can't recall how I

thought the master would rule. Paul Leventon had no more cer-
tainty than I. I would just have to wait patiently for the wheels
of justice to grind to a conclusion.

If I were to win, I didn't know what to expect next. I hadn't
asked for any sanctions against Nancy. I wasn't out to punish my
ex-wife or take the children away from her. I suppose my petition
for contempt boiled down to a moral issue more than anything
else. I wanted Nancy to understand that she couldn't get away
with this kind of behavior and I wanted to make sure Jennie,
Nathaniel, and Ariel understood that I loved them very much and
I wouldn't let anyone separate them from me.

I didn't want to contemplate what kind of message would be
sent to Nancy and the children if the verdict turned out to be "not
guilty."

—*Michael L. Nieland, M.D.*
Parent in Limbo

Two years had passed since Michael had returned home from his medical meeting to find Nancy, the children, and most of the family belongings gone. During those two years, with legal bills soaring into five figures, absolutely nothing had been resolved. Michael hoped his luck would finally change when the master issued her decision on his petition for contempt. He was going to have to hold on a while longer, though. Master McCarthy was expected to take several weeks before making her recommendation to the court.

Michael wouldn't have to find something to occupy his time, though. Nancy had taken care of that for him. He was going back to court once more. This time he would be the defendant and Nancy the plaintiff. She wanted child support, and a great deal of it, too.

Michael could not fathom how someone whose annual income was in the hundreds of thousands of dollars could make a credible argument for child support. If anything, Michael contended he should be the one making the demand. But, with an income of well over $100,000 annually he knew—if only all the legal wrangling and the bills it generated would cease—that he had the means to provide for the children when they were with him. In fact, he was already doing so by maintaining the original family home and buying the children clothes, toys, school supplies, and whatever else they might need.

Evidently, Nancy found it a little more difficult to make ends meet on a six-figure salary. Her budget information filed with the court on June 3, 1989, itemized her own average monthly living expense along with the monthly expenses for the reasonable and necessary support and maintenance of Jennie, Nathaniel, and Ariel that Nancy maintained she incurred. The numbers reminded Michael why he wanted a divorce:

MONTHLY EXPENSES FOR NANCY NIELAND AND THREE CHILDREN

	Mother	3 Children
Food, Household Products, Sundries:	$ 350	$ 1,050
Mortgage Payment or Rent:	$ 787.60	$ 2,362.78
Clothing:	$ 1,500	$ 1,400
Car Payments:*		$ 489.81
Car Expense (Fuel, Repairs, Insurance):		$ 215
Loan Payments, Charge Accounts:	$ 4,000	
All Medical and Dental Expense:	$ 100	$ 90
Insurance (Home):	$ 131.66	
Utilities (Gas, Light, Water, Sewer):	$ 107.50	$ 322.50
Educational (Private School):		$ 595.80 Average
Taxes (City & School District):	$ 220.46	$ 661.41 Average
Household Help:	$ 1,500	
Child Care:		$ 2,500
Barber, Beauty Shop:	$ 80	$ 80

*No car expenses are listed in Nancy's column because her car was owned by her professional corporation and therefore could not be claimed as a personal expense.

	Mother	3 Children
Entertainment:	$ 500	$ 500
Papers, Books, Magazines:	$ 25	$ 30
Other Child Support (Brita & Sarah):*	$ 1,850	
Gifts:		$ 600
Charitable Contributions:	$ 440	
Vacations:	$ 200	$ 500
Legal Fees:		$ 1,500
Gardening:	$ 500	
Cable:		$ 41
Music Lessons:		$ 75
Dry Cleaning:	$ 50	$ 50
Summer Camp (Ariel & Nathaniel):		$ 100
SAT Prep Class (Jennie):		$ 45
Upkeep of House—Maintenance:	$ 25	$ 75
Swimming Lessons:		$ 25
TOTAL EXPENSES PER MONTH:	$12,367.22	$13,308.30

Michael couldn't decide which entry he found the most incredible. Could it be the $500 monthly entertainment bill for the children or, perhaps, the $600 spent monthly on gifts for them or, possibly, their $1,400 clothing allowance?

While Nancy's budget rekindled some very unpleasant memories for him, another piece of information she submitted may be even more telling as to why they divorced—the schedule of the housekeepers/babysitters, which was essentially unchanged from when they were married: more than eighty hours a week were regularly scheduled, and there were an additional nineteen "overtime hours sometimes requested by Nancy."

Michael doubted he would ever understand why Nancy didn't seem to want any time alone with Jennie, Nathaniel,

*Although Brita and Sarah were twenty-six and twenty-five, respectively, at the time of these proceedings (and therefore too old to be considered needy of child support), this presumably refers to the money Nancy gave to the older girls to "help" with their living expenses.

and Ariel. Since the divorce Michael derived his greatest pleasure when he was with the children without an entourage of household help. Looking at the housekeeper/child care schedule, he wondered how he had put up with the unending succession of child care providers as long as he did.

He also pondered, on the eve of the child support hearing, how much longer he could endure the pace of the judicial system. Nearly two months had passed since the contempt proceedings concluded, but there was still no white smoke emanating from the master's chambers and, all the while, his custody time with Ariel had remained as chancy as ever.

While waiting for the ruling and preparing for the child support hearing, Michael hadn't forgotten about Roland Singer. He had been hard at work on a complaint to the local branch of the American Psychological Association concerning the evaluator's involvement in the case. Following Stephen Schachner's testimony at the contempt hearing, Michael's attorney concurred that Singer's performance warranted the filing of a complaint. He advised his client, also, that it might be more appropriate for a formal complaint to come directly from a parent rather than from legal counsel. In other words, Michael was on his own.

The more research he did on the complaint the more violations he believed Singer had committed. He also puzzled over the fact that, despite the decades of cumulative Family Division experience among the judges and attorneys involved in his case, no one seemed to understand from the outset that it was ethically forbidden for Singer to have participated in the case in the manner that he had. Michael hoped his complaint would change that.

On July 21, 1989, the preparation of his complaint came to a temporary halt. The Nieland child support hearing appeared on the docket of the Allegheny County Family Division. The cast of characters had been shuffled. Harry Greuner's associate, Kenneth Horoho Jr., was representing Nancy and the court had appointed Jeanne J. Bingman, Esq., a wife and mother in her mid-thirties, as hearing officer for the case. Paul continued to represent Michael.

The proceedings took place in the City-County Building in downtown Pittsburgh. As Michael entered the courtroom, he still had no idea why he was there. He already paid his share of the tuitions for the children's private schools, and he always supported the children when they were with him and he always planned to do so.

To him, it seemed like pure vindictiveness on the part of Nancy to ask for child support when the children were supposed to be in his custody, according to the court order, nearly half the time. To add to the absurdity of the claim, Michael had learned during the depositions taken days earlier that Nancy apparently intended to prove he should be working harder and making more money than he did—even though he already earned well over $100,000 annually. Perhaps Nancy didn't want the hearing officer to be concerned that Michael might have difficulty making monthly child support payments to defray her $13,308.30 monthly expenses (or $159,699.60 annually) incurred for the reasonable and necessary support and maintenance of Jennie, Nathaniel, and Ariel.

Once again, his future lay in the hands of the legal system:

PROCEEDINGS
[condensed]

OFFICER: We are here today [July 21, 1989] on the claim for child support [retroactive to September 15, 1987]. . . . How would you like to proceed . . . ?

LEVENTON: . . . I think it would be appropriate to crystallize the issues for you because it is a fairly complicated financial situation. . . . Both parties are dermatologists. . . . There is a corporation called the Pittsburgh Skin & Cancer Clinic. . . . Nancy Nieland, Michael Nieland, and Dr. Alan Silverman are one-third shareholders in that corporation. . . . There is a second corporation called the Pittsburgh Skin Pathology Lab, Inc. which . . . is owned 50 percent by Michael Nieland and 50 percent by Alan Silverman. . . . I think it will be agreed, Nieland & Francis [Nancy's other practice] is the primary source of income for Nancy [in addition to the Pittsburgh Skin & Cancer Clinic]. . . .

HOROHO: Paul Leventon is reading from one of our exhibits and we might as well give it to the Hearing Officer. . . .

OFFICER: Do you each want to give an opening statement? . . .

HOROHO: . . . We are here today for child support for three children. Essentially the issue is, as I understand it, twofold:

One is what are the respective incomes and/or earning potential capacities of the respective parties? It would be [Nancy Nieland's] position in this case that Dr. Michael Nieland . . . is not working up to his earning capacity, that his earning capacity should be at least equal to, if not greater than, his wife, Nancy Nieland. . . .

And—the second issue would be the reasonable and necessary expenses for the children. . . .

OFFICER: Mr. Leventon:

LEVENTON: The suggestion that Michael Nieland is not working to his earning capacity . . . is a total red herring. His mode of practicing medicine is different from Nancy Nieland's. . . . The second point, which I think this case really will hit upon . . . Your Honor, are the purported expenditures which, as defined by the Supreme Court, must be reasonable and necessary. And it is [Michael's] position that the expenditures listed here for these three children, currently ages seven, eight, and seventeen, are so outrageous they are obscene. To suggest that the moneys that are listed on the budgets for these three children are reasonable and necessary is really very counterproductive and destructive for their growth. Michael will not participate in adding fuel to the fire. . . .

OFFICER: Thank you. Mr. Horoho, would you like to begin?

HOROHO: Yes, Your Honor. I would like to begin by calling Nancy Nieland. And, as is the usual practice in our courts, I would like to proceed with summarizing as much of the testimony as I can.

OFFICER: That would be fine.

HOROHO: . . . On July 18th, 1988, Judge Wettick issued an Order of Court regarding custody. Essentially, the custody situation is that the children primarily reside with the mother. . . .

LEVENTON: . . . The Order of Court does not provide primary custody with Nancy. The document speaks for itself.

HOROHO: Can I please proceed with asking Nancy what is the custody arrangement?

OFFICER: Why don't you try to sum up as much as you can. . . .

Nancy [Rose] Selove Nieland, Having Been First Duly Sworn, Was Examined and Testified as Follows:

DIRECT EXAMINATION BY MR. HOROHO:

HOROHO: . . . Based upon what you personally know and have observed, . . . how often do the children see the father and how oft 'n do you see them?

NANCY: Jennie sees her father practically never and does not live with him at all. Nathaniel spends the hours [outlined in the Custody Order]. Ariel spends probably about four hours a month with Michael at Michael's house.

HOROHO: Your Honor, . . . the child support paid by the defendant has been $1,500 [monthly] for eight and a half months . . . during the twenty-five months of separation. . . . Nancy, can you explain . . . the total hours that you work for [the two clinical practices] . . . per week?

NANCY: About thirty-four and a half hours and, in addition, I may work one or two hours at home late at night with paperwork I bring home with me.

HOROHO: Was the original arrangement when that corporation [Pittsburgh Skin & Cancer Clinic] was formed that both Drs. Silverman and Michael Nieland would work approximately the same amount of hours and accept approximately the same number of patients?

NANCY: Work exactly the same number of hours and have the same compensation and see the same number of patients. . . .

Despite their twenty-year history together (and not together), Michael still couldn't get used to Nancy making statements that sound so sincere but—he contends—are boldface lies. He adamantly denies that the working arrangement Nancy just alluded to ever existed—signed or verbal. The doctors had never had a set schedule. For instance, in the early years at the clinic Michael was also Chief of Dermatology at the VA Medical Center and had responsibilities there. In addition, each physician's compensation from the clinic had nearly always been adjusted from year to year. And, furthermore, an employment contract signed by the three physicians in 1978 makes the only reference to office hours: "Employee [i.e., Michael Louis Nieland; Alan Ronald Silverman; Nancy Rose Nieland] agrees to devote such time as shall be mutually agreeable to the Employer [Pittsburgh Skin & Cancer Clinic, P.C.]."

> HOROHO: . . . Did that arrangement continue for Michael Nieland?

> NANCY: No. It did not. He drastically reduced his hours for scheduling patients and reduced drastically the number of patients he permitted to be scheduled per hour during the time he was in the office.

> HOROHO: Are you familiar [with when] he began reducing those hours?

> NANCY: It was around the time of separation.

> HOROHO: Were there any limitations that you placed on your hours of work? . . .

> NANCY: No. There were never any limitations. . . . I worked until the last week of two pregnancies. One time, during an argument, Michael broke my arm. I went into emergency at 4 A.M. and was—

> LEVENTON: Objection. She testified Michael broke her arm. It's inflammatory and not supported by any medical records or any evidence at trial.

> OFFICER: Sustained as to that portion. Just explain your work schedule.

> NANCY: I have never cut back on my schedule since 1978.

Michael didn't question the veracity of Nancy's testimony concerning her work schedule. However, he noted their different priorities. Nancy gave birth to two more children after 1978. He suggested to her frequently in the following years that their significant incomes gave them the opportunity to reduce their workloads and place a greater emphasis on family life. In fact, near the end of the marriage, he presented to her, through the attorneys, a proposal for avoiding a divorce which included revising the parties' work schedules so that each of them would have sufficient time and energy for their children and for each other.

Nancy never directly, or through her attorney, responded to the proposal except to say to Michael: "That ridiculous letter! My reaction to that letter was that you had a total and complete lapse of psychiatric proportions."

Paul Leventon objected to her statement for different reasons:

LEVENTON: Your Honor, ... until or unless Mr. Horoho could demonstrate what the average or standard fees are earned in this field I think that the offer of proof falls far short to demonstrate that, if Dr. Nancy Nieland makes $600,000 a year, $500,000 a year, [that] every other physician who is a dermatologist should have an earning capacity of that. . . . I am not here to criticize the way Nancy Nieland practices medicine and I think it isn't the province of someone . . . to be here to criticize the way Dr. Michael Nieland practices medicine. The proof of the pudding is in the constant flow of income. . . .

OFFICER: I am going to reserve my ruling on this. There is no jury.

* * *

HOROHO: Referring quickly to the [family] budget sheet, the budget sheet was based on the standard of living for the parties that was established during the marriage for the children. For example, the vacations. Prior to the separation the parents took the children to Disney World, New York City, Boston, Washington, D.C., Miami Beach, and

Georgia. . . . And just briefly explain for the Hearing Officer the child care expense which we list on the budget sheet as household help at $1,500 [and] $2,500 under child care.

NANCY: Yes. The same child care providers have been employed for many years. . . . Their hours have remained the same all of these years. . . . before separation and after separation. . . .

*   *   *

HOROHO: Is there anything else that you would like to present at this time regarding the information that we have supplied regarding your net income and the children's expenses . . . ?

NANCY: . . . When I left the marital residence, . . . I left without getting any pay-out for the marital house, was responsible for renting another house, replacing furniture that was left behind and clothing and toys for the children. . . .

It sounded like Nancy wanted the hearing officer to feel sorry for her. Michael hopes Mrs. Bingman realized that: (1) Nancy chose to leave the marital home with no prior notice to Michael; (2) there had been no equitable distribution of Nancy's retirement fund, which was marital property with a value that more than matched the equity in the marital home; (3) an independent appraisal had verified that she took the vast majority of personal property; and (4) none of the children's clothes and belongings had remained in the family home.

CROSS-EXAMINATION BY MR. LEVENTON:

LEVENTON: Did Michael know when you were moving out?

NANCY: We had discussed for several months that we would separate. I asked him several times to leave and he refused to do it. We each knew I was going to move out, but we hadn't discussed a specific date.

For once, Michael and Nancy were in complete agreement. Both had agreed that she would move out after she found a new home; no deadline was imposed in order that the departure be as orderly as possible for the sake of the children and for each other.

Because the residency question had been settled Michael was under the assumption that the children's living arrangements would be the next issue to resolve. However, in Michael's estimation Nancy's secret departure with the children in tow preempted that discussion.

LEVENTON: Was he out of town when you moved out?

NANCY: Yes.

LEVENTON: Did you unilaterally take that which you chose to take out of the house?

NANCY: I took less than one-half of the appraised marital belongings which were appraised six months before I moved out.

LEVENTON: You are telling this Court, even based on Mr. Simon's appraisal, you are saying that you think you took less than 50 percent of the value of the personal property?

NANCY: Yes. I did.

In light of the appraisals, it was preposterous to Michael that Nancy—under oath—stated that she took less than 50 percent of the value of the personal property.

LEVENTON: The property issues have not been resolved in this case; is that correct?

NANCY: That's right.

LEVENTON: Nancy, on your budget, you show $2,500 a month in child care and an additional $1,500 a month in household help; is that correct?

NANCY: Yes. . . .

LEVENTON: You testified, I believe, that you work approximately thirty-four and a half hours a week?

NANCY: . . . Yes.

LEVENTON: Three children ages seven, eight, and seventeen . . . all healthy?

NANCY: Yes.

LEVENTON: What time do the children leave for school?

NANCY: They leave for school around 8:00 or 8:15 in the morning.

LEVENTON: What time do the children get out of school?

NANCY: Ariel gets home a little bit before 4:00 . . . around 3:00 on Friday; Nathaniel . . . between 3:30 and 4:00; Jennie . . . around 3:30 . . .

LEVENTON: If you average a seven-hour work day [based on your thirty-four and a half hour work week]—

HOROHO: Your Honor, I object to this line of questioning unless Mr. Leventon can establish that this was not the same arrangement that Michael and Nancy had prior to the separation. This is not a changed—she didn't just start experiencing $4,000 worth of child care and household expenses in June of 1987. They were always at or about that amount. The schedules of her and Michael were always about the same. . . .

LEVENTON: What Mr. Horoho said is precisely true. What Michael's schedule was then is precisely what his schedule is now! [Your Honor,] the children are presently in school. You don't have the same child care expenses when you have infants and preschoolers as when you have them in school all day. I will establish through this witness . . . that we are talking a maximum need for child care expense at the most, the most, twenty hours a week. That's giving her the benefit of every single doubt. . . .

HOROHO: Objection. Let's go. This is summary. Cross-examine the witness. Do you have any other questions regarding this issue? Let's move on.

OFFICER: Okay, Mr. Horoho. Please! [Mr. Leventon], I think you made your point.

* * *

LEVENTON: [Based on your budget information sheet] if you combine these two figures [$2,500 per month for child care and $1,500 per month at $9.50 per hour] for household help—which you have testified is reasonably accurate—you are telling the Court that you have someone in your house approximately 98 hours a week?

HOROHO: Objection, she can't—

LEVENTON: Yes she can.

HOROHO: If he wants a breakdown on—

OFFICER: [Mr. Leventon], I think your point is really made!

LEVENTON: Fine. As long as the point is made.

OFFICER: All right. We can move on to another subject.

* * *

LEVENTON: I notice on your budget information sheet you have listed, . . . under the column for children, a car payment of $489.81 per month. . . . Did you buy Jennie a car?

NANCY: Yes.

LEVENTON: Did you discuss the purpose of the car with her father, Michael? Yes or no?

NANCY: No. I did not. It's not possible to discuss anything in a reasonable way with Michael without some incredible argument from him concerning anything. So, it's not possible to discuss this with Michael.

LEVENTON: You also have a car expense of $215 a month for Jennie's car?

NANCY: Yes.

LEVENTON: You were asked to provide documentary evidence to support those expenses. Have you done so?

NANCY: Well, I don't have documents to support the gas and oil expenses because it's all paid in cash. . . .

*   *   *

LEVENTON: You list $500 per month in entertainment for the children, but I notice that there are . . . very few receipts. . . .

NANCY: Because a portion of it is paid in cash. . . . I did not think to keep receipts. Things like the circus, Ice Capades, . . . Pittsburgh Penguin [hockey tickets], . . . Pirate [baseball tickets]. . . .

LEVENTON: You have provided receipts, totally, $95 for the year for entertainment; is that true?

NANCY: I'm telling you I paid cash for a lot of these things and I don't save receipts for the zoo and Sea World and bike rentals and so on.

HOROHO: I want to let the record state . . . we have bent over backwards to get as many of the expenses as we have. . . . We didn't make copies of every—

LEVENTON: I understand that. I am not arguing.

HOROHO: I want to say for the record that questions such as: "This is all you provided as far as travel and entertainment," are unfair.

OFFICER: You have pointed that out.... [Mr. Leventon] do you have anything further on the budget?

LEVENTON: [I have] nothing further on the budget.... On the financial ... I have a bunch [of questions].... Nancy, I show you ... and ask you if you can identify this as the fiscal corporate tax return for Nieland & Francis corporation for the fiscal year ending September 30th, 1987?

NANCY: It's labeled as such.

LEVENTON: Was Dr. Francis. . . .

NANCY: Yes.

LEVENTON: Was he in the office approximately the same [as you]?

NANCY: Yes, about.

LEVENTON: Dr. Francis earned from your corporation $100,322 and you earned $361,976; is that true?

HOROHO: We will stipulate, Your Honor, to it. . . .

LEVENTON: How many patients do you schedule per fifteen-minute units at Nieland-Francis?

NANCY: Usually three.

LEVENTON: How many patients do you schedule per fifteen minutes at the clinic which is downtown where Michael [and Alan Silverman are] involved?

NANCY: Usually three. . . .

LEVENTON: You feel competent to accept, as a medical practitioner, a patient in a maximum period of time of five minutes?

NANCY: This is not an unusual schedule for a dermatologist where visits are brief and volume is high. It's not as though you were doing a complete physical examination. It's usually focusing in on one problem at a time. And, yes, I feel very confident to do this.

LEVENTON: Can you see how a dermatologist who has a different bent than you would be uncomfortable in scheduling three patients per every fifteen-minute unit?

NANCY: I can't answer that, Mr. Leventon.

LEVENTON: Isn't it true that [your partner, Dr. Francis] sees substantially fewer patients than you per hour?

NANCY: He . . . sees fewer per hour.

LEVENTON: And that's his choice. That's the way he chooses to practice medicine. Correct?

NANCY: Yes.

LEVENTON: I have nothing else.

REDIRECT EXAMINATION BY MR. HOROHO:

HOROHO: The standard of living that was indicated by your budget is not any different from the standard of living that Michael Nieland and Nancy Nieland established for their children prior to the separation, is that true?

NANCY: True.

HOROHO: So, things haven't changed. You haven't gone out and increased the standard of living for the children?

NANCY: No. That's right.

HOROHO: Let's just talk very quickly about the child care. . . . Was the usual monthly expense prior to separation . . . about the same amount [as on your budget sheet]?

NANCY: It was probably at or about the same amount.

HOROHO: [Michael] never objected to that, did he?

NANCY: No. Not at all.

Once again, Michael was in awe at how Nancy testified with a straight face. His recollection on the child care issue is far different. He consistently, unflaggingly objected to the babysitters.

As the first phase of the child support hearing concluded, Michael felt reasonably certain Nancy had not proven he was not working up to his earning capacity or that her expenses for the children were reasonable and necessary. But, he also realized he was not the hearing officer and her ruling would impact whether he could afford to support his children in his own home. If she believed him responsible for half of Nancy's "reasonable and necessary" child support expenses retroactive to September 1987, his payments would be around one million dollars by the time Ariel and Nathaniel graduated from high school.

Michael tried not to dwell on such ominous projections. Besides, he knew his opportunity to testify was yet to come.

Meanwhile, it was back to the real world. No Ariel. No Jennie. No contempt verdict from the master. Michael bided his time by preparing his complaint against Roland Singer.

Finally, on July 31, approximately two months after the contempt hearing ended, Carol McCarthy rendered her decision in the form of a twenty-page report. A copy was sent by messenger to Michael at his downtown office. He read:

THE MASTER'S REPORT
[condensed]

DISCUSSION OF EVIDENCE AND FINDINGS OF FACT

... After hearing testimony over five days that spanned one month and produced 1,100 pages of testimony, to simply [state] one of the parties' positions is correct ... would be a disservice to the parties. [This] section will review the evidence and the conclusions drawn therefrom.

... Father's ... central complaint involves what he sees as the overall course of conduct on mother's part to thwart the Order of Judge Wettick. His basic complaint is the failure of Ariel to spend time with him under the Order.

... The evidence that was presented showed that father, either directly or by his conduct, agreed to the temporary suspension of overnight visits for Ariel. Mother and Dr. Singer both credibly testified that father agreed to this modification. ... Father did not vehemently dispute this. ... The master can surmise from the overall evidence and demeanor of the father that it was not his intention that this *temporary* arrangement would be permanent let alone even go on this long. However, his acquiescence prevents this from being a basis for a finding of contempt.

Michael contends he did object, but he couldn't "vehemently dispute" the suspension of Ariel's overnights for fear of annoying Singer who could—in his role as the court's monitor, take offense and recommend further reductions in Michael's time with Ariel.

The next question is whether the father agreed to the twenty-minute limitation of his time with Ariel. Although both Dr. Singer and mother testified that father agreed to a twenty-minute limit to visit time, that position cannot be logically supported by the overall evidence. . . . Dr. Singer did hear an objection [from father]—long, loud, abusive, and unprofessionally so—but a clear objection nonetheless. . . .

The master must be referring to Michael's last session with Singer, but Michael maintains he behaved in a totally civilized manner. Moreover, his account of their disagreement had nothing to do with any twenty-minute limit: How could he argue about something he insists he never knew existed? Singer himself, in a letter to Leventon, never even mentioned the alleged twenty-minute limit when describing his final meeting with Michael.

Of greater significance than whether there was an agreement or not is the problem at the heart of this action. Father does not have significant quality time with his daughter as ordered by Judge Wettick. . . .

The master believes that father does genuinely wish to have, develop, and expand upon his relationship with Ariel. More importantly, Ariel needs, is entitled to, and should have this kind of relationship with father.

However, father's conduct contributes to Ariel's refusal to spend time with him. . . . A simple example. . . . Father glosses over the fact that it is he who picks up Ariel at the bus stop and he who is in control at that time under the Court Order. Father's conduct of walking her to her mother's house has established the pattern that the child can manipulate the situation to her wishes. . . . Father has not exercised his parental authority.

. . . The evidence does not support that [mother's] conduct alone is the cause of his lack of ability to control Ariel's behavior. . . . Father must recognize that while he is correct that Ariel must come with him because it is a Court Order, that yelling at her is not an effective method of ob-

taining the desired behavior. Locking her in the house does
not make her want to stay. Telling her that he will do something, then not doing it, does not create a strong sense of
trust ... regardless of how inconsequential the promised
thing or conduct was. .... Although father denies [these be-
haviors] as true, the master finds it credible that he did engage in this conduct.

Michael couldn't quite follow Ms. McCarthy's logic. On
the one hand, she said "it is he who picks up Ariel at the bus
stop and he who is in control at that time under the Court
Order." On the other hand, she said he shouldn't raise his
voice and he shouldn't prevent his daughter, who is only six
years old, from walking out of his house and down the street
alone. What did the master expect him to do in a situation in
which Ariel had been told over and over again that she
needn't stay with her father and that she could demand to go
to her mother's house where there were babysitters (and
sometimes their children, too) waiting to play with her?

Mother cannot escape responsibility. .... If being found to
be not in Contempt justifies a continuation of the current
situation, then mother is not the woman the master perceived. The master's perception of mother is that she does
have the best interest of the children at heart. Although she
is currently frustrated with father's behavior toward her
and the children, she would like to see them have the kind
of relationship with father he is so forcefully demanding.

Michael couldn't get over how it seems everyone con-
nected with the case wanted to attribute virtuous motives to
the mother.

The master believes that mother has tried to comply with
the July 18, 1988 Order of Court. .... However, ... it is clear

that mother intervened in the father's relationship with the children. Although this could have been well intended, . . . her actions contributed to the noncompliance with the Court Order. [An] example can be seen in [audiotapes] mother presented to show that she did attempt to obtain Ariel's compliance with the Court Order. In one tape mother is attempting to coach Ariel who is hysterically stating her refusal to go to father's during a Court-ordered time period. However, as the parent of a young child, the master is able to identify the background noise to be children's television programming. It is well within the master's experience to know the difficulty in changing a child's direction if the child is engaged in conduct he or she is enjoying. It is possible that Ariel simply did not wish to stop watching television. . . . Further, the child's tone was one of frenzy, not fear. Certainly other approaches, such as attempting to direct the child to father's when the television was not a distraction, come readily to mind.

It is because in many situations mother described that other approaches to the situation are readily apparent that the master must conclude that mother contributed to the noncompliance with the Court Order.

. . . The master gives little weight to the testimony of [Dr. Singer]. . . .

Dr. Singer's testimony was that Ariel told him she was frightened [of her father]. However, . . . he did not go into detail how this fear was harmful or whether it was based on anything of significance. The child gave very superficial reasons for her stated fear. . . . If Dr. Singer had thought this fear was cause for concern, the master believes he would have pursued Ariel's statements further . . . [as to] whether [it] is real or simply a tactic to avoid doing something she does not wish to do for childish reasons. . . .

In summary, the question of father's right to and the amount of time he is to have with his children was determined in the July 18, 1988 Order of Court. This Order has not been modified nor has either party sought to modify it. Therefore, it must be followed. . . .

LEGAL CONCLUSIONS AND RECOMMENDATIONS

. . . It is the master's finding that the mother is in Contempt of the July 18, 1988 Order. . . .

The master does not find that mother met her burden of persuasion on the issue of impossibility of complying with the Court Order. Although mother did make many efforts to encourage Ariel to be with her father, the fact is that her efforts cannot be viewed as those which are likely to breed success. . . . Mother interfered by going to get Ariel regardless of how upset the child sounded in her telephone call. The mother interfered when she did not advise the child and the housekeepers that, if the child did not go to or stay with her father at the designated times, she would not be allowed to do anything else in her house. The mother interfered when she returned the child's telephone calls and allowed her to complain about life at father's rather than instructing her to discuss it with father, not her. . . . It is mother's own statement that Nathaniel did not want to go, but she was able to convince him to do so that particularly impressed the master and led to the conclusion that mother contributed to Ariel's refusal to visit with father.

It is . . . recommended that the parties address Ariel's expressed fear of her father . . . that is, to address whether the fear is within the normal range. . . . This clearly means that Ariel will have to engage in evaluation and possibly treatment with a trained professional. . . .

It is the recommendation of the master that Dr. Singer's involvement in this case cease . . . based largely on his testimony that he cannot work with these parties. . . .

Although the master finds the mother in contempt it does not rise to the level at this point that warrants sanctions. Continued failure to deal with Ariel's fear and obtain her compliance with the terms of the July, 18, 1988 Order of Court would be cause for sanctions. . . .

[Attached is a Proposed Order of Court.]

Carol S. Mills McCarthy, Esquire
Master

PROPOSED ORDER OF COURT

. . . After the Hearing on Plaintiff's Petition for Contempt, it is hereby ORDERED:

1. Mother is in contempt of the July 18, 1988 Order of Court to the extent that Ariel does not spend periods of partial custody with her father, as ordered.

2. Mother is not in contempt of the July 18, 1988 Order of Court for Ariel's failure to spend Friday after school until Sunday at 5 P.M. on the week one and week three or from Thursday after school until Friday morning in weeks two and four as the parties agreed to temporarily suspend the overnight time periods.

   Mother is in contempt of the modified provisions in that Ariel does not spend the agreed upon time on Saturday and Sunday in weeks one and three.

3. The July 18, 1988 Order of Court, as modified, shall be implemented by the parties.

4. Mother shall not pick Ariel or Nathaniel up at father's during his period of partial custody unless agreed upon by the parties.

5. Mother shall instruct Ariel or Nathaniel to discuss any displeasure during father's periods of partial custody with him.

6. Mother shall not allow Ariel to engage in any activities at her home during periods of father's partial custody, unless agreed upon by the parties, but shall insist upon

284 A FAMILY DIVIDED

Ariel returning to father's house should Ariel leave his residence during a period of partial custody.

7. Mother is to make Ariel and Nathaniel ready and available for the periods of partial custody in the July 18, 1988 Order of Court, as modified by the parties.

8. Father shall walk Ariel to his home from the school bus-stop and not walk her to mother's home, unless agreed upon by the parties.

9. Father is to allow Ariel access and egress from his house during periods of partial custody.

10. The parties, through counsel, shall immediately select an appropriate professional for the evaluation and treatment, if so required, of Ariel and Nathaniel, particularly as to the issue of Ariel's expressed fear of her father.

11. The parties shall address the issue of the resumption of the overnight time periods originally included in the July 18, 1988 Order of Court with the selected professional with the goal of the resumption of overnight time.

Michael was elated. The master had held Nancy accountable for disobeying the court order. But he strongly disagreed with many of her characterizations of himself and his ex-wife. He remained convinced that the court wasn't scrutinizing him and Nancy equally. It seemed to Michael that the mother was given the benefit of the doubt.

As for the specifics of the proposed order of court, Michael didn't object to any of the points, although he believed Nancy should have been found to have violated the court order in all its particulars. Aside from those concerns, Michael was overjoyed. Ariel would be with him again!

Michael and Paul Leventon didn't have time to savor the

victory. The child support hearing resumed less than twenty-four hours after the master released her report. Michael, scheduled to take the witness stand, expected that neither Nancy nor her attorney would be in a very good mood.

The proceedings picked up (once again in Jeanne Bingman's courtroom) with Nancy's attorney completing the case against her ex-husband.

PROCEEDINGS
[condensed]

Cynthia Dougan, Having Been First Duly Sworn, Was Examined and Testified as Follows:

DIRECT EXAMINATION BY MR. HOROHO:

OFFICER: [Mr. Horoho,] . . . why don't you go ahead and just summarize and have her affirm what you stated.

HOROHO: Cindy, you're employed by Pittsburgh Skin and Cancer. . . . You first began working there in 1978 when the business was formed. . . . You left that employment approximately 1981. . . . You returned in 1985. . . . Your job description there is essentially Office Manager.

DOUGAN: That is correct.

HOROHO: Okay. Mrs. Dougan's here to corroborate and indicate that from 1978 to 1981 while she was there, also from 1985 to 1986 prior to the separation, that Dr. Silverman and Dr. Michael Nieland continued to see approximately the same amount of patients, work the same amount of hours, . . . received the same amount of compensation, saw all types of patients. . . . Now, Cynthia Dougan is also here to testify that in 1987 that Dr. Michael Nieland made changes

to that arrangement . . . at or around the date of separation.
. . . He reduced his hours. . . . Nancy Nieland and [Alan Silverman] continued to work the same amount of hours that the parties, the three shareholders, agreed that they would work back in 1978. . . . Regarding the patients per hour, Cynthia Dougan's prepared to testify that, prior to 1987, the policy was that Alan Silverman and Michael Nieland both saw eight to ten patients per hour or approximately three per fifteen minutes. After 1986, beginning in 1987, . . . Michael Nieland saw no more than six patients per hour. Alan Silverman continued to see eight to ten. Also, an additional limitation that Michael Nieland indicated to Office Manager Cindy Dougan was that . . . he only wanted one new patient per fifteen-minute time slot. The office policy, prior to 1987, was that during the fifteen-minute time slot at some times two new patients would be scheduled. And—again, Alan Silverman and Nancy Nieland never made that same limitation. . . . Cynthia Dougan would also be prepared to testify if Dr. Michael Nieland would go back working nine to five . . . in her opinion more patients could be scheduled for him and, therefore, would result in additional income for Pittsburgh Skin and Cancer. . . . She's prepared to testify that the deposition statements that Dr. Michael Nieland gave . . . when he was asked, "Did you ever indicate to Cynthia Dougan that you do not want to see pediatric patients?" [and he answered], "I never stated that" . . . is false. He did inform her that he wanted no pediatric patients and . . . that began on August 6, 1987. . . . [As to] emergency patients prior to 1987, the office policy was that . . . all the doctors saw emergency patients. She's here to testify that contrary to what Dr. Nieland said in his deposition . . . he instructed her not to schedule emergency patients for him. And finally, with regard to vacations, the office policy was when a doctor was out of the office on vacation, the other doctors would cover. . . . [Michael] has changed that office policy. . . . When Dr. Silverman goes

away, Michael Nieland does not cover which obviously results in a reduction of the time that new . . . and old patients could be served. . . .

Now, Mrs. Dougan, you've heard the summary of your
testimony. . . . Is the testimony that you've given true and
correct to the best of your personal knowledge?

DOUGAN: Yes. It is.

HOROHO: Is there anything else you would like to add?

DOUGAN: No.

OFFICER: All right. Mr. Leventon, if you want to cross-examine—

LEVENTON: Sure.

CROSS-EXAMINATION BY MR. LEVENTON:

LEVENTON: Mrs. Dougan, are you familiar with Michael's
custody arrangement with the children? Yes or no.

DOUGAN: Yes.

LEVENTON: Now, is it not true that when he instructed you
to cut back his time at the clinic every other day, it was so
he could be available to pick up his children after school?

DOUGAN: Yes. That is true.

LEVENTON: What was the reason [Michael gave you for
wanting to see fewer patients per hour]?

DOUGAN: Because he needed time to catch up [on his work].

LEVENTON: And you testified that Dr. Nancy Nieland never
cut back on her hours at the clinic; is that correct?

DOUGAN: That is correct.

LEVENTON: . . . How many days a week does she come to the
clinic?

DOUGAN: One day a week.

LEVENTON: And—Alan Silverman obviously is not a party to this litigation. You don't know what his responsibilities are with his children; do you?

DOUGAN: No.

*   *   *

LEVENTON: What's the difference if Michael has a personal preference to cut back or not see pediatric patients and he's seeing in their stead adult patients?

DOUGAN: Because everyone saw them. . . .

LEVENTON: I'm asking you a question with respect to Michael's income. Did it impact on his income by not seeing pediatric patients if he was seeing adult patients?

DOUGAN: No. In that instance, no.

*   *   *

LEVENTON: Okay. And again, choosing or electing to cut back or not see "emergency" patients didn't impact on Michael's income to the best of your knowledge; did it?

DOUGAN: I would say yes. It did.

LEVENTON: Explain to the Court how?

DOUGAN: Because on a normal day we get anywhere from ten to twelve emergency phone calls. . . .

LEVENTON: Do you charge them more because they say it's an emergency?

DOUGAN: No.

LEVENTON: Is it not true that if there is a "true emergency" that the true emergency patient would likely take more than your allotted five minutes to treat?

DOUGAN: Sure. Oh, sure.

LEVENTON: So, in effect what you're telling this Court is that if Michael is working X number of hours seeing a patient list of, say, six patients per hour, that he is maximizing his income with those six patients versus minimizing because he would be spending more time with emergency patients. True or not?

DOUGAN: Yes. That is true.

*   *   *

LEVENTON: Now, you also said that—coming back to the number of patients per fifteen minutes— . . . you testified that you still do [schedule three patients every fifteen minutes] for Alan and Nancy because their practices haven't really changed?

DOUGAN: Okay, for Alan, it's two every fifteen minutes. For Nancy, it's now up to four every fifteen minutes.

LEVENTON: Oh! Alan now sees patients at the rate of two every fifteen minutes?

DOUGAN: That's correct.

LEVENTON: Which is the same for Michael; is it not so?

DOUGAN: For return patients for Dr. Michael—yes. For new patients, it's not true.

LEVENTON: Fine. Because he spends more time with new patients; is that not so?

DOUGAN: Sometimes, yes; sometimes, no. Depends on the condition.

LEVENTON: Of course it depends on the condition. This is not a factory; is it?

DOUGAN: No.

LEVENTON: Okay. Now, Nancy, on the other hand, . . . you're now telling the Court has you scheduling four patients every fifteen minutes?

DOUGAN: That is correct.

LEVENTON: . . . Why is she so fast? . . . Do Dr. Silverman and Dr. Michael Nieland . . . designate the responsibility to the staff the same way Nancy does?

DOUGAN: They do it the same way.

LEVENTON: Do Dr. Silverman and Dr. Michael Nieland spend more time with patients [than Dr. Nancy Nieland]?

DOUGAN: Sometimes. Yes.

LEVENTON: Do you have any personal knowledge how long it should take a dermatologist to examine and treat a patient?

DOUGAN: No.

LEVENTON: I have no more questions for this witness.

REDIRECT EXAMINATION BY MR. HOROHO:

HOROHO: . . . Prior to the [Nielands] having personal problems, Dr. Michael Nieland treated pediatric patients. He treated emergency patients and he worked and saw eight to ten patients per hour.

DOUGAN: That is correct.

RECROSS-EXAMINATION BY MR. LEVENTON:

LEVENTON: Mrs. Dougan, I show you a document and ask you if you can identify it?

DOUGAN: This is [last] Friday's schedule.

LEVENTON: Michael's last day in the office?

DOUGAN: Yes.

LEVENTON: Using this as an example, . . . [Michael saw] two emergencies and five new patients.

DOUGAN: That is correct.

LEVENTON: This is not a schedule that Michael prepared in anticipation of this litigation; is it?

DOUGAN: No.

LEVENTON: This is prepared by the office staff?

DOUGAN: This is correct.

LEVENTON: And it involves five new patients and two emergency patients?

DOUGAN: This is correct.

LEVENTON: And how many patients did Michael see on Friday, the day that he is supposed to pick up his kids at three o'clock . . . ?

DOUGAN: On this schedule he saw twenty-three people.

LEVENTON: Twenty-three people?

DOUGAN: Uh-huh.

LEVENTON: Twenty-three patients this day. Typical?

DOUGAN: Yes.

LEVENTON: Shirking his duty?

DOUGAN: I never said he was shirking his duty.

LEVENTON: Fine. Thank you very much. I move for the introduction of [Friday's schedule].

OFFICER: Any objection?

HOROHO: Is this the typical?—yeah—I do have an objection. ...I don't think she's testified that this is the usual schedule and occurs on a daily basis.

OFFICER: Well, to the extent that it does show and her testimony corroborates that he did see some emergency patients, I'll let it in to that extent, but not to the extent that it is a typical day.

FURTHER REDIRECT EXAMINATION BY MR. HOROHO:

HOROHO: Is your testimony still correct that Michael only wants to have scheduled six patients per hour or, if they're new patients, it's three?

DOUGAN: Yes.

HOROHO: So, [the schedule Mr. Leventon just showed you] is not a typical day ... ?

DOUGAN: No.

Michael couldn't believe Mrs. Dougan's last answer. Hadn't she just said moments prior that twenty-three patients in a day was typical?

HOROHO: There's no other questions. . . . Plaintiff rests, Your Honor.

Dr. Michael Louis Nieland, Having Been First Duly Sworn, Was Examined and Testified as Follows:

DIRECT EXAMINATION BY MR. LEVENTON:

LEVENTON: May it please the Court, with respect to the anticipated testimony of Michael Nieland in this case, it is suggested that the Hearing Officer ... determine two critical factors: number one—his net disposable income; [number two]—his reasonable living expenses. . . .

Michael will testify that his 1989 income, compared to the past five years, is reasonably constant within a 5 percent variation . . . despite the fact that Michael has, in fact, been compelled by the Custody Order in place to cut back his number of hours at the clinic. He will testify that his income from the laboratory, which is his primary source of income, and has always been his primary source of income, has increased—that he works many more hours there than he used to work because there he has the flexibility of working hours when he has free time, including weekends and evenings. . . . He will testify that with respect to the laboratory . . . that he and Dr. Silverman are partners there and the number of accessions has, over the past six years, gone from somewhere around 3,000 per year to over 16,000 over the past three years. . . . Accessions are . . . basically in a lay person's terminology . . . the slides that the dermatologists who use the lab send [there] for microscopic analysis. . . . Whatever decrease in income Michael has had at the clinic has been made up for by the income at the lab. . . .

He will testify as to the number of patients he is reasonably comfortable in seeing in fifteen-minute units. . . .

He will vigorously repudiate Nancy's suggestion that he is not earning to his earning capacity. And he will testify that there is a lot more to practicing medicine than just trying to run up as great an income as possible.

The second phase of his testimony will deal with his reasonable living expenses.

He will testify that he cannot compete with Nancy's style in buying the children's affection. That he believes her style is unreasonable, obscene, and destructive for the normal and natural growth of three children and that he refuses to be a party to it. . . . He will explain that to be forced to contribute additional moneys to the absurd spending habits of Nancy would be the equivalent of adding fuel to the fire.

He will also repudiate Nancy's testimony that, prior to separation, he had agreed with her for the perpetual baby-sitter or housekeeper style of raising these children. He will testify . . . he [complained] it was not the parents that were raising the children, but the babysitters . . . and [in regard to their marriage] that was one of the straws that broke the camel's back. . . .

OFFICER: Dr. Nieland . . . you heard the summarization by your counsel. . . . Is everything he stated on your behalf true and correct?

MICHAEL: Yes, Your Honor.

LEVENTON: Michael, there's been much to-do about your cutting back hours and your number of patients per hour at the clinic. First of all, tell the Hearing Officer how many days per week you work at the clinic.

MICHAEL: Your Honor, I work . . . three days a week at the Pittsburgh Skin and Cancer Clinic and I've always worked three days a week [there].

LEVENTON: And—the days that you don't work at the clinic—what do you do? Play golf like every other doctor?

MICHAEL: No. Every other day I am engaged full-time from nine in the morning until six or seven in the evening in the Pittsburgh Skin Pathology Laboratory in Shadyside [interpreting slides].

LEVENTON: Now, distinguish briefly for the judge the difference between the practices in the clinic and that of the lab.

MICHAEL: . . . Dermatopathology is the dermatologic subspecialty confined to pathology of the skin, tissue pathology of the skin, the microscopic pathology of the skin. It is a subspecialty which I brought to this city [Pittsburgh] . . . seventeen years ago. In the early 1970s this kind of work was done by general pathologists. I started a laboratory. . . .

LEVENTON: In other words, you say the emphasis in your dermatological practice is on . . . lab work, as contrasted with treating people with collagen or for pimples?

MICHAEL: It is. My approach to medicine has been a conscientious, responsible, careful approach to medical problems whether they are of a laboratory or investigative nature or whether they concern the practice of dermatopathology or whether it involves seeing patients. The main thrust of my career has always been investigative in nature.

LEVENTON: And how do you get the [lab] work? Is it fed to you at the lab from other dermatologists?

MICHAEL: We deal solely with other physicians. . . .

LEVENTON: Does Nieland & Francis feed you their specimens by happenstance?

MICHAEL: They have sent us specimens for years.

LEVENTON: And Dr. Silverman—your partner at the clinic— . . . he's also working now at Nancy's office [Nieland & Francis]?

MICHAEL: Yes.

*   *   *

LEVENTON: You heard the testimony of Mrs. Dougan with respect to you allegedly instructing her to cut back your hours during the alternate days that you're at the clinic. . . . Would you tell the Hearing Officer whether or not her categorization . . . was true or false.

MICHAEL: I told her to cut back my hours to a point where I could reasonably expect to get out of the office on time to go home and meet my children. . . .

LEVENTON: You also heard Mrs. Dougan testify with respect to you telling her to [schedule only six patients an hour].

MICHAEL: The instruction is accurate because it takes an hour to see six patients. . . . I give my patients my full attention. I am very methodical. I am very careful. I try to be very accurate. I try to be kind. I have many patients who are elderly who do not want to wait an hour or two in a waiting room for me. I have many executives who come to see me who do not want to wait an hour or two. I try to see my patients on time. And I find that if I see six patients an hour, then I can fairly reasonably stay on time and fulfill my responsibilities to my patients. . . .

LEVENTON: Did all of a sudden [in 1987] you decide that you couldn't service as many people or that your speed or production slowed down? Did you change?

MICHAEL: I essentially did not change. Her testimony is totally inaccurate that I was seeing eight to ten patients an hour because if you multiply that by an eight-hour day I would be seeing sixty-four to eighty patients a day! I have always, from the beginning of my practice, seen somewhere between twenty-five and forty patients a day. . . .

LEVENTON: Do you have an opinion as a specialist in dermatology what the minimum necessary time is to spend with a patient?

MICHAEL: I think it's practically unheard of to spend less than fifteen to twenty minutes with a new patient . . . or with a return patient at least five to ten minutes. . . .

LEVENTON: Do you believe that reduction in volume of patients [you have seen] is more attributable to the fact that you cut back your hours because of the Custody Order . . . as opposed to seeing fewer patients per hour . . . or a combination of both?

MICHAEL: It is solely attributable to my cutting back my hours so that I can finish early enough to get my children.

LEVENTON: With respect to your clinical practice, have you told anyone that you refuse to see emergency patients?

MICHAEL: I have never told anyone that I would refuse to see an emergency patient. I see emergency patients every day.

LEVENTON: Do you have preference as to not seeing pediatric patients?

MICHAEL: I see pediatric patients practically every week. . . . Perhaps other practices see more pediatric patients. The kind of patient who comes to a downtown office practice is not a pediatric patient. And I have never seen more than a very small number of pediatric patients during the week and still see a very limited number.

LEVENTON: Michael, do you believe that you are not working to your earning capacity at this time?

MICHAEL: I am working absolutely to my earning capacity. I couldn't possibly work any harder than I am now with all my responsibilities and two practices and as a parent to three children.

LEVENTON: If someone would choose to do nothing else or have no other responsibilities, could they work longer hours . . . and make more money?

MICHAEL: Yes. If . . . someone wanted to turn his children over to other people to take care of them, one could work theoretically all night long and all weekend long. But . . . it's not in the best interests of the children and it's certainly not in the best interests of being a balanced human being and parent.

LEVENTON: Thank you. I have nothing else.

CROSS-EXAMINATION BY MR. HOROHO:

HOROHO: . . . You're saying you're working as hard as Alan Silverman?

MICHAEL: Absolutely.

HOROHO: And you're saying, if your business records showed that Alan Silverman sees twice as many patients, the business records are inaccurate?

MICHAEL: The practice of medicine is not numbers.

HOROHO: I'm not asking you that question. Do you agree that your business records at Pittsburgh Skin and Cancer are accurate.

MICHAEL: Yes.

HOROHO: . . . You said your income has remained constant throughout the last couple years. That was your [testimony]. . . . In 1989, based upon the documents we received from Skin and Cancer—it is projected that you will receive $56,982 in 1989 . . . so you had a reduction from 1986— $93,360 to $56,982.

MICHAEL: I'll accept that. But—my total income has remained the same [because of increased hours and earnings at the laboratory].

HOROHO: Isn't it true, Dr. Nieland, that you have intentionally reduced your hours, patients, and workload beginning in 1987? . . . And you did that around the time that you and Nancy Nieland were having marital problems; correct?

MICHAEL: Approximately.

HOROHO: . . . Have you ever told anyone that you didn't need the amount of money that you previously earned?

MICHAEL: Absolutely not. . . .

HOROHO: . . . Have you ever told anyone that you could function on one-half your present income and pay your bills?

MICHAEL: Never. It would be impossible.

HOROHO: Have you ever told anyone that you do not need to go on practicing clinical dermatology . . . that you could practically run your lab from your home . . . that your lab can be run by remote control and your presence is not necessary?

MICHAEL: Absolutely not. . . .

Nancy's attorney apparently was referring to a comment Michael had made to his attorney in a May 10, 1987 letter— the time when Michael and Nancy were separated but both still living at the Inverness Avenue address. In this letter, which he believed had been opened and resealed prior to being mailed, Michael stated: "The laboratory I can run by remote control—my presence is not required but for a couple hours every other day." Horoho happened to omit the second half of the statement. All Michael was trying to make clear in that letter *to his attorney* was that he could, if necessary, be home more for his children by doing a significant amount of his laboratory work at his residence. He would just need a microscope, the slides to be interpreted, and a dictating machine.

HOROHO: Okay. Let me show you a letter dated May 10, 1987, addressed to your attorney. . . . Is that your handwriting?

MICHAEL: Yes.

LEVENTON: Do you have a copy? I don't know . . . what the letter is.

HOROHO: . . . It's not necessarily going to be used as an exhibit.

LEVENTON: Well, I'm still entitled to see it. . . .

HOROHO: I don't think you're entitled to see it unless I—

LEVENTON: Of course I am.

OFFICER: You're showing it to his client. I think he is entitled to see it.

HOROHO: Okay.

LEVENTON: I'd like to ask for the source of the letter. . . .

HOROHO: . . . It was at the marital residence prior to separation. This letter was written on May 10th of 1987.

*   *   *

MICHAEL: I can explain. This is a letter that Nancy took out of my briefcase. . . .

LEVENTON: I don't know what the privilege is on whether something is admissible. . . .

HOROHO: Your Honor, I could point out on the issue of intercepting communications, it's clear that he has waived that privilege and I can argue that. But at this time—

LEVENTON: Who has waived it?

HOROHO: Michael Nieland has waived that.

LEVENTON: Why? By having a communication stolen, he's waived it?

HOROHO: No.

LEVENTON: How has he waived it? . . .

HOROHO: Do you want me to introduce it into evidence or not? I'm only using it for impeachment purposes. . . .

OFFICER: If you want to put it in evidence, then you're definitely going to get into a problem. . . . Do you have any more questions?

HOROHO: Not on that letter. No. . . . During your marriage you and Nancy Nieland have always attempted to provide a very comfortable lifestyle for your children, correct?

MICHAEL: I've tried to provide a reasonable lifestyle. My former wife provided an extravagant, obscene number of items for the children.

HOROHO: And her spending habits continued during the marriage, right?

MICHAEL: They continued during the marriage and they probably always will. . . .

HOROHO: And you consented to that?

MICHAEL: Absolutely not! That's the whole reason I'm not married to her any more. . . .

HOROHO: . . . You never separated because of her spending habits prior to June of 1987? Yes or no.

MICHAEL: No.

HOROHO: And the household help that she has now—you and she both had prior to the separation; correct?

MICHAEL: She had. I tried to get all these people out of my house so I could spend time with my children. They were there morning, noon, and night seven days a week. It became a day-care center with the babysitters' children. This was another reason why I'm not married to her anymore. It's an insane way to live.

HOROHO: That insane way of living started in 1979 when you hired the housekeepers that she has now.

MICHAEL: She hired the housekeepers and I asked her to share taking care of the children with me on a reasonable basis, nights and weekends, so we wouldn't have these people around my house morning, noon, and night. . . . My children have to have a parent.

HOROHO: You can't continue to ramble on.

MICHAEL: I'm not rambling.

HOROHO: You haven't objected to Nancy Nieland's house care until after—

MICHAEL: Strenuously objected over and over and over again, and she wouldn't listen to me then any more than she does now.

OFFICER: Are you finished?

HOROHO: Yes. That's all the questions I have.

Just like that, the child support hearing ended. Perhaps the hearing officer had some other place to go. Michael noticed she kept looking at the clock throughout the morning's testimony. Now, after watching Mrs. Bingman rush off without first permitting either attorney to present a closing statement, Michael wondered if she fully understood what was at stake here: a child support order in the range of Nancy's "reasonable and necessary" expenses could very well force him to sell the family home and prevent him from being able to support the children during their time with him.

But, just as he had approached the two months of waiting for the petition for contempt ruling, Michael attempted to maintain a positive attitude. At least he could take solace in his belief that his attorney had successfully and forcefully presented his case, particularly concerning Nancy's primary claim that her ex-husband was not working up to his earning capacity.

It was time once more for Michael to resume what seemed to be a requirement for coping with the Family Division: waiting. Waiting for Judge Wettick to adopt the master's proposed order of court as the court's order. . . . Waiting for the hearing officer's ruling on child support. . . . Waiting for some movement on the personal property issue.

While Michael bided his time very little changed for him and the younger children: Nathaniel invariably stayed with his father, but Ariel rarely did. On a brighter note for Michael, Jennie now took his telephone calls and even accepted a few dinner invitations. Michael fervently hoped nothing—no one—interfered with this happy turn of events.

Meanwhile, Michael's attorney remained hard at work on the case. He didn't want any delay in the implementation of the master's ruling which meant point ten needed to be addressed right away: "The parties, through counsel, shall immediately select an appropriate professional for the evaluation and treatment, if so required, of Ariel and Nathaniel, particularly as to the issue of Ariel's expressed fear of her father."

Nancy's counsel was contacted to reach agreement on an appropriate professional. Gruener actually approved a selection process based on a pool of professionals recommended by Dr. Stephen Schachner. Leventon wasted no time in apprising Dr. Schachner of the need again for his services.

The groundwork seemed in place for getting the custody schedule back on track. But Nancy's attorney had more on his agenda than the custody schedule. Apparently, he was concerned for his client about the opprobrium associated with a finding of contempt. On August 10 he filed an appeal to Judge Wettick concerning the master's ruling: "The master erred in finding Defendant [Nancy] in contempt in that there was no evidence or finding of wrongful intent, . . . the acts of contempt found were not a violation of the specific language of the Order of July 18, 1988, . . . [and were] not supported by the evidence . . . [and were] against the weight of the testimony of Defendant, Dr. Singer, and lay witnesses, including

Ariel and the housekeepers . . . [and were] not in accordance with the law. . . ."

Michael wondered if the legal maneuverings in his case would ever end.

In the meantime, Dr. Schachner replied to Leventon (with a copy forwarded to Carol McCarthy) on August 10, 1989, concerning a recommendation for a mental health professional:

> Thank you for forwarding to me a copy of the master's Report and Proposed Order of Court in the matter of the Drs. Nieland. I understand that you would like me to recommend to you a number of names of mental health professionals. . . . I would be happy to do so. . . . The initial contact that is made with [the selected individual] should include identification of this office as the referral source with the suggestion to the therapist that they contact me. . . . I can recommend the following therapists: [Judith Carter M.D.; Ralph F. Wilps Jr., Ph.D.; Sylvia Mendelsohn, M.D.; Donna J. Zaffy, Ph.D.]. Dr. Mendelsohn is a psychiatrist who specializes in treating both children and adults and enjoys an excellent reputation in the community. . . .

Leventon forwarded the list to Gruener, and after conferring with their respective clients they agreed on Dr. Sylvia Mendelsohn. That bit of progress by no means erased Michael's anxiety. Weeks without Ariel kept passing—weeks which could never be replaced by a court order.

Michael's introductory session with Dr. Mendelsohn had a surprise. Michael had expected to spend the bulk of the meeting recapping the case history. He brought a copy of the master's proposed order of court and gave it to the psychiatrist so that she would be aware that Nancy had been found in contempt of the court order concerning the custody schedule and understand also what was to be her court-or-dered role: "the evaluation and treatment, if so required, of Ariel and Nathaniel, particularly as to the issue of Ariel's expressed fear of her father."

Dr. Mendelsohn thanked Michael for the background information. She informed him, though, that she was already familiar with the case based on conversations she had had with Drs. Singer and Schachner. She also indicated to Michael that she was agreeable to assume the role of court-ordered mental health professional in the case. She did reveal an initial concern—that she would be in charge of both evaluation and treatment—but she assured Michael she didn't expect that to be a problem.

Dr. Mendelsohn's comments were unsettling to Michael. He was particularly disturbed that she had discussed the case with Singer. He could only imagine what Singer might have said. He didn't object, however, because Mendelsohn came highly recommended by Schachner and she appeared to have an understanding of his plight. He hoped she would quickly put to rest the charge that Ariel had any fear of her father.

Before Mendelsohn could offer her analysis of the case, she stated that she must meet individually with him again and with Nancy and Ariel. Michael agreed. (After paying Singer thousands of dollars, what were a few more appointments, especially if it meant putting the fear issue to rest?) Nevertheless, more appointments meant more billing. Michael wondered how a divorced parent of more moderate means could persist or why any divorced person should be in this situation in the first place. Mendelsohn scheduled a meeting with Michael again on Thursday of the next week.

It was now September 1989; three months since the contempt hearing concluded and one month since the master issued her ruling. It was also one month since the child support hearing had ended and—just for the record—two years and nine months since Michael had filed for divorce from Nancy.

Michael pondered what might be taking so long for Judge Wettick to adopt the contempt finding by the master (whom he had appointed). In the hope of jump-starting the judge, Paul Leventon wrote him a letter asking about the status of his decision, but no immediate response was received.

But, alas, there was news on the child support front. On September 11, forty-one days after the proceedings had concluded with Court Officer Jeanne Bingman rushing out the door, she handed down her ruling on a one-page, handwritten form that had four sentences crossed out and one number written over another. Michael wondered just how many grueling hours she had put into this official document.

Regarding the decision, it wasn't what Michael wanted (zero child support payments) but it certainly wasn't what Nancy wanted, either: Michael was to pay $2,244 per month for the support of the parties' three children. The order was retroactive to September 15, 1987.

No mention was made concerning Kenneth Horoho's major accusation that Michael was not working up to his earning capacity. Perhaps the hearing officer determined it to be a nonissue?

Bingman had estimated a $6,600 monthly child expense, a far cry from Nancy's $13,308.30. For that, Michael again was relieved. However, it did not appear that Bingman paid any attention to his own expenses on behalf of the children. After all, they ate at his house, too. He also had a mortgage, taxes, and other monthly expenses which benefitted the children. He wondered just how she had arrived at $6,600 and his $2,244 share. She gave no details of her calculations on this lame-looking form. Forty-one days must not have been long enough to write out legibly a detailed explanation—or to check her facts.

At least her decision hadn't destroyed Michael financially. He couldn't claim victory, but it could have been much worse. Besides, if he could have only one clear-cut victory, he was pleased it occurred in the contempt hearing because he believed that the contempt finding (when it was finally handed down by Judge Wettick) might finally put an end to the undermining of the custody schedule.

But would it? Two days after the child support decision Judge Wettick's order of court arrived. Dated September 9, it was a photocopy of the typed, three-page proposed order of court with a few handwritten changes by Judge Wettick. The major changes involved crossing out all of points one and two. The contempt findings had been expunged! How could this have happened? Michael urged Paul Leventon to appeal Judge Wettick's decision to change the master's ruling, but Leventon told him it would do no good. All Judge Wettick would have to do is write an opinion in support of what he did. His order of court would stand.

Michael was in a state of shock at the potential ramifications. Nancy surely wouldn't change her behavior now that she had been found *not* in contempt of court. And, if she wasn't going to be held accountable for her actions, would Ariel ever spend time with him again? Did Judge Wettick realize that with those flicks of his pen he might have crossed out Ariel from her father's life forever?

Forever started the next day. It was September 14, 1989, Michael's custody day. He made the following entry in his daily log: "Met both Nathaniel and Ariel at the bus stop, but Ariel wouldn't come today (no reason). . . ."

7. Ethics Complaint

How could he? How could Judge Wettick overrule a master he himself had appointed? How could he evaluate the credibility of any of the testimony when he wasn't even there? Was he angry with Carol McCarthy because she bumped one of the regular and dependable court psychologists from the case? Or did he have an unwritten rule that a mother couldn't be in contempt of a court order? Whatever the reason I thought what he did was despicable. In fact, I thought Judge Wettick's comportment throughout my case had been deplorable. Those are strong words, I know, but his performance speaks for itself. Time and again it appeared to me that he looked the other way or acted contrary to long-standing Pennsylvania laws:

At the November 1987 conciliation he learned the court-appointed evaluator discussed my case with so-called ancillary contacts although neither my attorney nor I knew anything about these sessions. Such contacts clearly violate strictures in state law for psychologists concerning confidentiality. Did Judge Wettick throw Dr. Singer out of the case? No. In July 1988 he ap-

pointed him monitor of the custody order contrary to prohibitions in state law concerning dual relationships.

And then, after my attorney filed a motion for clarification in September 1988 to permit me to take my children to school he refused to make a judicial decision. Instead, he handed over interpretation of his own custody order (i.e., the law) *not to another judge, but to Singer, a psychologist!*

It became very clear to me that Judge Wettick, the administrative judge, the top banana in the Family Division, hadn't spent much time studying the rules and regulations in his area of responsibility. I discovered them during research for my complaint against Roland Singer. Basically, the Commonwealth's Code of Ethics for psychologists incorporates provisions of the American Psychological Association's Ethical Principles of Psychologists. *The state's mandate, all of three pages, could be read and digested in less time than it takes to go through the daily newspaper.*

I had always believed that judges are the ones who set the gold standard of behavior for everyone else in the judicial system. I never imagined under any circumstances that a judge could order others to act contrary to the law or ethical principles.

I'm aware Judge Wettick's crossing out the contempt verdict could be considered by some to be an exercise of his judicial discretion, but to me it seemed more like judicial abuse. After all, he did allow part of the master's ruling to stand. However, without a contempt finding the court order had lost its moral authority. Common sense dictates that if Nancy hadn't been abiding by the original court order—which the master believed to be the case— she wouldn't start following any court orders now. In addition, if her behavior made it necessary for me to file another petition for contempt with the court, she could defend herself now by saying something like, "My ex-husband's 'zeal to wrangle' is already legendary. We've been over this contempt charge before and it was found to be without merit. The truth of the matter is that despite my sincere efforts, the children can't stand Michael."

If Nancy were not to be held accountable for her actions, I had to hope the court and its appointees would be held responsible for their woeful performance. I realized proving their culpability would never give me back the years lost with Ariel, but at least it would expose the wrong done to my daughter and to me and, maybe, help the next family with the misfortune to end up in the Family Division.

I couldn't let this travesty of justice go unchallenged.
—*Michael L. Nieland, M.D.*
Crossed-Out Father

It was extremely disheartening to Michael that the contempt hearing was nothing more than a colossal waste of time, energy, and money. Perhaps he could claim a moral victory, but that was of little consolation. He didn't want victories. He wanted to be a part of Ariel's life.

In reviewing all of Judge Wettick's rulings in his family's case, Michael asked himself whether the judge could possibly harbor a grudge against him (even though Michael had never testified before him or had a conversation with him), or did Judge Wettick simply feel that mothers can do no wrong? Michael wasn't sure what motivated the judge, but he discovered while finishing his ethics complaint against Dr. Roland Singer that he was far from alone in his outrage over the judge's performance. He learned that many other divorced parents had initiated civil rights suits against Judge Wettick and also Judge Kaplan, who had appointed Dr. Singer in the first place. In fact, approximately twenty suits had been filed in federal court against both judges in the last decade. All were dismissed, though, because judges are cloaked with judicial immunity. Nevertheless, Michael believed Judge Wettick violated the canons of judicial ethics and if Michael could ever find the time he hoped to file a formal complaint against him, too.

In the meantime, Michael had dotted all the i's and crossed all the t's on his ethics complaint against Singer and he was ready to submit it to the appropriate psychological bodies and the state licensing bureau. Michael had decided to go this route initially, rather than initiate a civil suit, because, as with the judges, there is very little case law or precedent in this area and Michael certainly wasn't seeking (and couldn't afford) another lengthy legal battle. He simply wanted Singer to be confronted with what he had done—the sooner the better. By bringing an ethics complaint before Singer's peers and the state, there wouldn't be talk about case law. The question simply would be whether or not Singer had violated the *Ethical Principles of Psychologists* to which psychologists are bound. A malpractice suit could come later.

Accordingly, in early October 1989, Michael L. Nieland, M.D., formally filed an ethics complaint against Roland H. Singer, Ph.D., with the Greater Pittsburgh Psychological Association, the Pennsylvania Psychological Association, the American Psychological Association, and the Commonwealth of Pennsylvania's Bureau of Professional and Occupational Affairs. The following summary makes clear the premises of the case.

> This case concerns multiple violations of the *Ethical Principles of Psychologists* by a psychologist in a custody case. His behavior caused incalculable harm to me and my children. He demonstrated indifference to my fundamental rights and to his multiple conflicts of interest and he displayed irresponsibility, incompetence and ignorance of basic moral, ethical, and legal standards. . . .
>
> On January 12, 1987, I filed a Complaint in Divorce against Nancy S. Nieland, M.D., in the Family Division of the Court of Common Pleas of Allegheny County. As part of this action I sought the shared legal and physical custody of my children: Jennie, 15; Nathaniel, seven; and Ariel, six. Nancy Nieland resisted sharing the custody of the chil-

dren. On September 23, 1987, the Court appointed Roland H. Singer, Ph.D. "to conduct psychological evaluations of the parties and/or relevant persons, and to make recommendations to the Court regarding the parties' claims to custody and/or shared custody of the minor children."

Dr. Singer did not carry out his Court-ordered obligation competently or ethically: He did not conduct his evaluation in a timely fashion. He did not follow the usual and customary format for conducting a custody evaluation nor did he adhere to any recognizable standard of performance. He did not utilize any psychological testing. He did not restrict his interviews to relevant individuals. Instead, he tendentiously prolonged his involvement in the case and imposed himself on the parties in a therapeutic role in place of his mandated role and in violation of the *Ethical Principles of Psychologists*. By the time of the Custody Hearing Dr. Singer had logged 155 hours of interview time billable for a sum of $12,400. He spent almost no time with the children whom he was to evaluate and whose custody was at issue, Nathaniel and Ariel. While he performed no oral or written psychological testing of anyone he did spend many hours interviewing individuals with no standing in or relevance to the case, such as my former wife's exercise instructor, her companion-babysitter-housekeepers, and former neighbors, all of whom were her employees or patients. He concealed all these contacts from me although they were known to and arranged by my former spouse. He refused to reveal to me the substance of or reason for these dialogues. On the contrary, he claimed confidentiality in refusing to disclose to me the nature of the comments made to him by these persons despite their obvious relationship solely to my former spouse, their obvious severe conflicts of interest, and despite the fact that he should not have spoken with them in the first place. Principle Five of the *Ethical Principles* expressly prohibits him from discussing "information obtained in clinical or consulting relationships . . . with persons who are (not) clearly concerned with the case." Moreover, he denied me the opportunity to reply. His negligence and lack of instinct for fairness neither "preserved nor protected (my) fundamental human rights" [as dictated in the preamble].

Repeatedly, Dr. Singer urged my former spouse and me to "share" our problems with him. Otherwise, he said, he could not function effectively in our case. It was clear to me that, if either party declined to meet with Dr. Singer, there was a risk of not getting a "good report" to the Court. It was therefore impossible for me to resist Dr. Singer's ever-expanding involvement in and deepening therapeutic interest in our case. If I rejected him as therapist, I felt I might adversely affect his report to the Court concerning my fitness for the shared custody of my children. Dr. Singer's dual relationship, expressly forbidden to him by Principle Six, led to sheer exploitation . . . of his position and his records clearly show he milked the situation for all it was worth. Again and again, Dr. Singer assured me that he wanted only "to do what was best for the children," implying that if I were to reject his therapeutic role that it would indicate to him that I, their father, did not have the best interests of my children at heart. Over many months I had to spend an unreasonable amount of time in Dr. Singer's office away from my own professional activities and children. I had to respond endlessly to a multitude of trivial, bizarre complaints of my ex-wife transmitted to me through Dr. Singer. . . . I was induced to keep a massive handwritten log in order to respond to his obsessive scrutiny fueled continuously by my former spouse's complaints. . . . [She] endlessly interrogated the children every time they returned to her home concerning the time they spent with me and week after week she would present Dr. Singer with a new list of grossly inaccurate, inane, and bizarre complaints about me.

And so it went, month after month during the fall,

winter, and spring of 1987–1988 prior to the Custody Hearing of July 7, 1988. At the Hearing, Dr. Singer was the sole witness and his written report became Court Exhibit Number One. Although Dr. Singer had collected mountains of "data," the veracity of none of which he could vouch for, he had great difficulty understanding and assessing the motivations of my former spouse who had made every effort possible to keep my children from me. Instead of realizing that it was impossible for her to share the children and recommending that I be awarded sole legal and physical custody of the two younger children in order to substantially reduce the stress to which their mother subjected them, he recommended that "an equally shared custody arrangement should be attempted." Because he had for months done nothing but listen to hearsay and fabrication and had made no effort to establish any psychological truths about the individuals involved by performing any kind of psychological testing or evaluations of mental status, he was incapable of providing the Court with valid guidance. Unfortunately, and to his profound discredit, Dr. Singer had settled into a very comfortable and lucrative position.

During his testimony Dr. Singer revealed no discomfort with his dual role as Evaluator and Therapist. He repeatedly exaggerated the difficulty of the case, the acrimony between the parents (to which he was contributing fully) and the difficulties he had resolving issues. He insisted that the children had to continue to be carefully monitored. Instead of withdrawing from the case after 155 hours he sought and accepted continuing involvement. . . .

Th[e] transcript of the testimony leaves no doubt that Dr. Singer was indifferent to his dual role and gross conflict of interest. He did not demonstrate any understanding of the "consequences of his acts" nor did he make "every effort to ensure that (his) services were used appropriately" [as required by Principle One of the *Ethical Principles*].

Michael went on to detail how Singer subsequently demolished one provision of the court order after another. To his already multiple conflicts of interest as (1) evaluator, (2) therapist, and (3) monitor; Singer now added the role of (4) judge-surrogate as well, allowing his services to be misused by the court in a blatantly unethical manner. Michael quoted Principle 1(D) of the *Ethical Principles*, which states: "As members of governmental or other organizational bodies [infer: Court appointees], psychologists remain accountable as individuals to the highest standards of their profession." Michael pointed out that not only should Singer never have asked to be appointed "monitor"; he should have had the good sense not to accept this position even if the court had ordered him to do so, because Principle Six requires psychologists to "make every effort to avoid dual relationships that could impair their professional judgment or increase the risk of exploitation."

At my next to last meeting with Dr. Singer on January 31, 1989, he had no useful recommendations. Even at this late date he should have withdrawn from the case because his therapeutic intervention had achieved nothing but a worsening of the situation. [The Court Order had become virtually meaningless, as Nancy was not forced to adhere to it, and the relationship between Michael and Ariel had deteriorated so much that Ariel spent virtually no time in her father's custody.] (Principle Six: "Psychologists terminate a clinical or consulting relationship when it is reasonably clear that the consumer is not benefiting from it." *Ethical Principles*.) Dr. Singer was to have "monitored the children's progress" on the basis of adherence to a custody schedule, but he collaborated with my former spouse in dismantling the Court-ordered schedule. He had almost no contact with Ariel (or Nathaniel, for that matter) during these months, but relied solely on the mother's claims that she was doing everything possible to get Ariel to my house, but, she alleged, Ariel just refused to go. Later on, with Dr. Singer's knowledge and approval, the same ludicrous spectacle would repeat itself over and over again: My former wife would bring Ariel to my home in her car and five to ten minutes later return for her, ringing the doorbell incessantly to announce her return. But (vide infra) Dr. Singer felt that this "quality time" with me was better than no time at all!

At my last meeting with Dr. Singer on February 27, 1989, he again was unable to provide any useful recommendations to improve this disastrous state of affairs. He refused to recognize any possibility of a contribution to it by the child's mother or any dereliction on his part. I told him I doubted there was any psychological disturbance, other than manipulativeness, in my daughter. I told him that I felt his endless appeasement of my former spouse and his willingness to listen ad nauseam to her bizarre and unfounded complaints against me only encouraged her to ignore the custody schedule ordered by the Court and reinforced her in the belief that the most effective way to undermine the Court Order was to continue to make appointments with Dr. Singer. In this she had more than a willing and venal accomplice. I told Dr. Singer, not for the first time, that it was grossly inappropriate to permit a six-year-old to refuse to comply with a schedule established by adults and ordered by the Court. Dr. Singer became furious and jumped out of his chair. He began to shake uncontrollably and he turned purple with rage. I had never seen anyone so angry in my life. He said "you won't tell me what to do" and he tried to throw me out of his office. Astonished, I told him his behavior was rather inappropriate for a so-called mental health professional. I had never in my almost thirty years of medicine seen anyone behave in such a crude and abusive manner toward a patient. I told Dr. Singer that if he wouldn't voluntarily withdraw from the case, long overdue, that he was fired as far as I was concerned. It became impossible to communicate further with Dr. Singer because he was so agitated. As I left he . . . demand[ed] that I apologize to him!

At the conclusion of the Hearings on the issue of Contempt my former spouse was found in Contempt of the July 18, 1988 Order of Court by the master who heard all the evidence. In the narrative accompanying the Proposed Order of Court the master stated that Dr. Singer's involvement in the case should cease. . . .

The comments and responses on the part of Dr. Singer in regard to the issues of whether he adequately evaluated Ariel's "fear," whether he adequately monitored the children's progress, and whether he had justification for violating or acquiescing in the violation of a Court Order he was to monitor, raise serious questions about his competence. I believe it is clear beyond dispute that he is in violation of Principle Two: "The maintenance of high standards of competence is a responsibility shared by all psychologists in the interest of the public and the profession as a whole." He also has violated Principle 3(C): "In their professional roles, psychologists avoid any action that will violate or diminish the legal and civil rights of clients or of others who may be affected by their actions." In contributing to the violation of a Court Order, Dr. Singer willfully interfered with my legal and civil rights.

During the time Dr. Singer was acting as Evaluator and Monitor he billed the parties for $17,600. It would appear from Dr. Singer's own testimony that the actual time spent evaluating and monitoring was very limited. He was asked whether he had been using any of his time therapeutically. . . .

There cannot be any doubt that Dr. Singer was engaged in therapy despite his totally disingenuous and ludicrous responses. As much as Dr. Singer would prefer to conceal or obfuscate his therapeutic involvement he clearly was in violation of the prohibition against dual relationships spelled out in the *Ethical Principles*. Merely in consideration of the amount of time he spent in these sessions, 220 hours, one would have to alter the terminology in the field of psychology in order to avoid calling this length of involvement anything other than therapy. In fact, Dr. Singer was so busy therapeutically with the parents whose progress he was *not* assigned to monitor, so busy "mediating, problem solving" and "working through very serious problems in child management" that he totally ignored fundamental truths and principles established in his field: That one cannot assess any fear in children through comments verbalized by adults. That the only way to evaluate alleged fear in a child is to evaluate the child in a therapeutic setting, to spend time with the child. That one cannot relentlessly interrogate, investigate, or scrutinize only one of the parties in a child custody dispute. That it is essential to evaluate both adults to make certain that one of them is not exaggerating fear in a child to punish the other adult. That one parent cannot be allowed to control the availability of the child to the other parent thus permitting that parent to diminish the relationship of the child to the other parent. That the psychologist must generate his own psychological truths from his own observations and not rely on endless hearsay from the other parent. That the child may indeed be fearful of one or the other parent in intact families and that this is not at all unusual and may or may not require intervention or treatment of anyone. That an individual who conducts a psychological evaluation must be totally separate from the individual who facilitates, counsels, treats, or monitors the individuals involved.

Dr. Singer lost his ethical and moral compass so far back in this case that he never found his bearings again. He totally compromised himself, helped no one in the end, and, indeed, damaged every one of the principals in the case, including the children. The full extent of the psychological harm to all the children may not be apparent for years to come. Dr. Singer functioned throughout this case at an incredible level of mediocrity both in terms of professional competence and in terms of ethics and morals. His monumental obtuseness is illustrated by the fact that even after one of his own colleagues pointed out to him his ethical violations in a visit to him, he still declined to withdraw from the case. His surpassingly low capacity for even functioning in a humane manner is exemplified by his scurrilous personal assaults on me, a loving father, desperate to hold on to his children. . . .

I respectfully request the Ethics Committee to take whatever action it deems appropriate to redress the harm that has been done to me and my children and to ensure that no further harm is inflicted on other parents and children served by the Family Division of the Court of Common Pleas of Allegheny County due to the activities of Roland H. Singer, Ph.D. . . .

8. The End of the Beginning

Roland Singer's involvement in my case was a disaster for my entire family. I didn't have much doubt about that. I felt that the charges I leveled against him in my complaint were indisputable and I was confident a committee of his peers would agree. But no matter what the committee ultimately decided, nothing could restore the years lost to Ariel and me.

Even though I knew I couldn't retrieve that lost time, I had worked very hard on my complaint. For one thing, I thought I might be able to prevent other families from being torn apart when they entered the Family Division Twilight Zone.

I also had another, more personal motivation. It wasn't to punish Singer, though he certainly deserved it, and it wasn't to be awarded "triple punitive damages" in some future civil suit. I wanted to demonstrate that Roland Singer's "psychopathology" accusations against me came from a discredited source and were completely unfounded. No parent—or any individual for that matter—should be the victim of such an assault on his or her integrity. Just because Singer had been empowered by the judicial system to do a custody evaluation, he had no right to overstep his authority and—after our discordant parting—suddenly issue a spurious diagnosis of me that my former wife could and would use against me.

In order to minimize any damage Singer did to my standing in the community, I would have settled merely for a written apology from him admitting that his "evaluation" was grossly biased and that the accusations he made against me were false. I knew that anyone who knew me personally would never have believed Singer's so-called diagnosis anyway—but what about everyone else? I can only imagine the number of casual acquaintances, patients, and members of the medical community who had been hearing malicious gossip such as: "Michael Nieland broke his wife's arm,"* or "he verbally and physically abused his children" or "his children are afraid of him." Singer's accusations that I had a "severe personality disorder" and a "deeply rooted character disorder" might have led some to believe that these monstrous lies about me were plausible.

Am I overreacting? Not at all. I heard these stories repeatedly in the most unexpected places. For example, when I asked a neighbor to join me for dinner one evening, she declined. I asked her some time later why she turned me down. She replied, "I heard you were violent."

While Singer couldn't un-ring the bell for all the harm he did to my family, an apology would at least remove some of the hurt.
—Michael L. Nieland, M.D.
Maligned Citizen

Between Judge Wettick's crossing out the contempt finding on September 9, 1989, and Michael's filing the ethics complaint against Roland Singer nearly one month later, nothing

---

*Recall that, one night several years earlier, Nancy had attacked Michael in their bedroom while he was lying on the bed watching television. While still supine, he held up his arm to protect his head, and Nancy broke her arm while striking him. Although the Nielands told the hospital that Nancy had tripped, she subsequently told Dr. Corrado and others that Michael had broken her arm.

much had changed in regard to Ariel. Sometimes she followed the custody provisions of the court order; many more times she did not—as Michael noted in his daily log:

Mon., Sept. 18: Ariel wouldn't come with me from the school bus stop because of a ballet lesson that I knew nothing about. She told me not to tell her mother that she revealed this to me. Nancy told me later she "forgot" to tell me about the ballet lesson.

Wed., Sept. 20: . . . Ariel sat at the kitchen table with Jennie and me and chatted. . . . Jennie stayed until 5:10, but had to go back to Nancy's house for her guitar lesson.* Ariel went with her although I urged her to stay with me. . . . I called Ariel [around 6 P.M.], but she wouldn't come back. (I'm complying with the court order: I'm not preventing Ariel from leaving my home. Reciprocally, isn't Nancy obligated to send her back?)

Fri., Sept. 22: Met Ariel at her bus stop at 2:55. She insisted on leaving her school bag at Nancy's, but said she would come right away which she did. . . . At 3:50 Nancy came to my side door bringing Nathaniel's baseball and soccer clothes. Ariel saw her, went outside and said, "Can I come home now?" Nancy said, "If you want to. . . ." At 4:30 I went to Nancy's and Ariel was playing with a neighborhood friend. She wouldn't return.

Sat., Sept. 23: Went to get Ariel [at Nancy's]. Babysitter wouldn't bring her to the door. Later found out Ariel was at another babysitter's house. Babysitter said it was okay because "overnights were discontinued!" (Evidently, even the babysitters believe they can modify the court order.)

---

*As mentioned previously, Jennie had begun taking her father's phone calls and accepting some of his invitations a month prior to these log entries (i.e., in August 1989).

Michael had accurately foreseen continuing problems with Ariel the moment the contempt finding was extirpated from the court order. Without a doubt Michael faulted his former wife for what the master ruled to be her contempt of the court order in regard to Ariel's noncompliance, but he blamed Judge Wettick to an even greater extent because the judge let Nancy get away with it by finding her not in contempt.

Although the entire contempt hearing seemed to be an exercise in futility, Michael perceived one faint glimmer of hope—Singer was out; Mendelsohn was in on the basis of the July 31, 1989 proposed order of court. At last, what had become the "ultimate question" might be answered: Did Ariel fear her father? The answer came quickly. At Michael's October 4 appointment, Mendelsohn told him what he had known all along: Ariel wasn't the least bit afraid of him.

Mendelsohn explained to Michael that she was able to come to this conclusion after her very first session with Ariel. Prior to Ariel's September 27 appointment, Mendelsohn, as she told Michael at his first session, had consulted with Drs. Singer and Schachner. Based on those conversations and other materials she had gathered concerning the case she had fully expected to be meeting with a very timid, frightened child. Instead, she reported to Michael that Ariel was very playful and uninhibited. More importantly, Mendelsohn confirmed that at no time during her evaluation of Ariel did the youngster express or exhibit or otherwise indicate the slightest fear of her father.

But. . . .

But what? Michael wanted to know. Should he be doing something different as a father? Should he become a strict disciplinarian and tell Ariel she had better listen to him when she wouldn't go or stay with him? Absolutely not. Mendelsohn responded that there was no need for Michael to change anything. From all that she had learned and observed, she told Michael, he had been a competent, consistent, loving, attentive parent and he should continue doing everything he was already doing.

Then what was the problem? Ariel was his child. Why did she keep running away from him and refusing to spend time with him?

Dr. Mendelsohn explained to Michael the but: Ariel wouldn't accompany or stay with him because of her desire to please her mother and avoid her mother's wrath. The psychiatrist reassured Michael he was on the "right track" and that she would work with his former spouse in an effort to eliminate any interference with the relationships between all three children and their father.

Even though there was a but, Michael believed it was imperative that the attorneys be briefed immediately on Mendelsohn's crucial findings. Perhaps her analysis would accomplish what Michael had thought a contempt finding would do—get his relationship with Ariel back on track. Michael asked Mendelsohn when she would be available to discuss this matter with Harry Gruener and Paul Leventon. She replied that she couldn't meet with them. Why? Because, she informed Michael, "it's more complicated than that." The only way she believed she could help him, she reiterated, was "by helping Ariel resist her mother's pressure."

Michael found the psychiatrist's comments extremely disconcerting. What was so complicated? If Ariel was a happy little girl who was reacting in a normal way to intense pressure from her mother, why couldn't Mendelsohn complete her evaluation and report back to the lawyers or the court?

Furthermore, Michael didn't believe for one moment Ariel needed help. Since day one of the original 1988 court order he had been certain that the custody problems would disappear if only someone would stand up to Nancy's "subtle undermining" of Ariel's relationship with her father. Dr. Singer wouldn't. Judge Wettick wouldn't. And apparently Dr. Mendelsohn wouldn't either. What could Michael do? Could lightning really strike twice with court-ordered mental health professional number two?

Michael hoped for the best by reassuring himself that it would only take Mendelsohn a few weeks to accomplish with Ariel whatever it was she felt she must. However, even with this best-case scenario, Michael was clearly uneasy with the psychiatrist. First, she had spoken to Singer without first obtaining a signed release to do so. Michael never would have approved such a request out of concern that Singer would taint her objectivity. Now she refused to tender her evaluation to the attorneys. But, once again, Michael decided he had better not object. He must place his trust in Mendelsohn's professionalism.

Michael certainly had a lot on his mind. Every day when he checked the mail or his telephone messages he had no idea what he might find:

- word from Nancy or a babysitter that for one reason or another Ariel wouldn't be coming over during his custody time;
- a response to his ethics complaint against Roland Singer;
- an update from Paul Leventon about the child support ruling that both he and Nancy had appealed;
- news from Leventon regarding the resumption of talks on the personal property settlement and equitable distribution of marital assets; or perhaps
- recommendations from Leventon concerning Michael's downtown clinical practice with Alan Silverman and Nancy.

Michael had begun to entertain thoughts about leaving the downtown medical practice when it became apparent after the child support hearing that he couldn't count on any support from his partner, Alan Silverman. In order to preserve his working relationship with Alan in the downtown office, Michael dug out old office records to show him that Cynthia Dougan had misinformed the court. But his partner of more than a decade refused to acknowledge it.

Michael wondered if economic interests might have influenced Alan's decision not to support him. It couldn't be denied that Nieland & Francis, Nancy's other private practice, supplied anywhere from 15 to 20 percent of the volume of work to Michael and Alan's dermatopathology laboratory. Nancy had threatened to send her tissue specimens from her patients to another skin pathology laboratory, Alan told Michael. If Alan and Michael ended up losing their biggest contributor because of the divorce there would be significant cash flow repercussions for their practice. And, in addition to that financial relationship, Alan was supplementing his income by working part-time seeing patients at Nieland & Francis.

For all that, Michael found it hard to believe that Alan—with whom he had worked amicably for a dozen years—would succumb to such pressure. Perhaps that wasn't the case. Could it be that Alan had just overheard some ugly gossip? Whatever it was that eroded Silverman's loyalty, Michael knew it didn't make sense to stay in the downtown clinical practice.*

Fortunately, the Shadyside practice, the dermatopathol-

---

*The downtown clinical practice of which Nancy was a partner differed from the Shadyside dermatopathology lab (in which she did not participate) in that the clinical practice involved seeing patients. As Michael testified at the child support hearing, the dermatopathology lab did not see patients but instead focused on examining skin specimens (biopsies) through a microscope.

ogy lab shared with Alan, was another matter. There were no potential two-against-one type situations. He and Alan were equal partners. Together, they owned the Shadyside building that housed both the dermatopathology laboratory and an unutilized clinical office. Michael didn't foresee any reason for breaking up the thriving dermatopathology practice. He hoped, instead, that the strain in his relationship with Alan would pass once the ugliness of his divorce subsided.

There was little chance, though, of the tension dissipating at the downtown practice—not while Nancy was there. Michael decided it would be best if he departed and relocated his clinical practice to the unused clinical office at the Shadyside laboratory.

In the child support matter both sides had filed their appeals by the end of September (1989). In the exceptions filed on Michael's behalf Leventon contended that the hearing officer failed to take into account Michael's expenses when the children were in his custody. Therefore, he wanted the court to "reduce to zero (or at the very least to a more appropriate number) the amount of child support owing by Father to Mother."

Michael couldn't understand why the court hadn't long ago simply directed him and Nancy to support the children when they were in his or her respective custody without either parent sending money to the other. Such an edict seemed to make the most sense when two parents have substantial earnings, but Michael had found common sense or fairness to be a rare commodity in the Family Division.

It goes without saying that, as always, Nancy's attorneys had a different opinion. Kenneth Horoho, Gruener's associate, believed the hearing officer "clearly erred in her recommendation" because she failed to take into account that

Michael "willfully—and with a specific intent to avoid his child support obligation—reduced his earning capacity"; that "the children's monthly reasonable needs and expenses are substantially greater than $6,600"; and that the children are "in [Nancy's] custody" substantially more than "the limited amount of time that [they] spend with [Michael]."

Why did they even have a child support hearing? It seemed that every issue raised had surfaced again in the exceptions. Michael wanted closure on this issue—or on any issue for that matter! All of this litigation was getting to be *very* expensive. Perhaps there was frustration on both sides, since continuing talks finally began to bring about a negotiated end to the personal property and child support issues.

Michael fervently desired to put these issues behind him. He was dubious, however, that settling these matters would assuage what he saw as Nancy's rage against him, which he believed to be destroying his relationship with his younger daughter. To Michael this anger had no rational basis and he had no clue how to stop it. He wondered if Dr. Mendelsohn did.

The psychiatrist now saw Michael, Nancy, and Ariel regularly, but she didn't seem to be making any progress. (Nathaniel adamantly refused to see Sylvia or any other psychiatrist or psychologist.) By the end of 1989, Michael had noted what amounted to forty-eight alleged custody violations of the September 9 order of court in regard to Ariel, and another four alleged violations concerning his time with Nathaniel. However, there was some good news for Michael: Jennie had been acting like his daughter again!

She was with Michael almost every day and had been for the last few months of 1989. The change began when she asked her father for some advice regarding her college entrance applications. Michael jumped at the chance to do what dads do—maybe too eagerly. He ended up advising several of her friends, too. But—he wasn't complaining, or asking

Jennie questions about her past behavior, or blaming her for anything. He just loved being in her life again. And his teenage daughter seemed to enjoy hanging out with him (even if he was her father!). Michael looked forward to the day he and Ariel would share the same kind of loving father-daughter banter sitting at the kitchen table.

There was another development that made Michael feel slightly more upbeat about the future. Nancy was getting married. Perhaps now, with a new mate, an end would come to what Michael described in a note to his attorney as her "unfathomable, implacable, intense, unrelenting hostility toward me."

Michael didn't know much about Dick Fisher, the husband-to-be, except that he was a stockbroker and a divorced father himself. Michael had met him several times outside Nancy's front door when picking up the children or bringing them back. At those moments Fisher, called Fish or Dick by his friends, often was quite talkative. His favorite subject seemed to be his impending marriage. Michael recalls him rambling on about how he had all kinds of assets and Nancy had incredible cash flow so together they would make a dynamite combination. And, in an apparent mutual gesture of love, he revealed also that neither of them had insisted upon a prenuptial agreement. Michael never found Fisher's sentiments about his forthcoming union with Nancy particularly enthralling conversation. On one occasion, however, the husband-to-be did make a comment Michael found interesting. He said he would try to be helpful in putting an end to the acrimony. When Michael mentioned that passing remark to his attorney, Leventon suggested that this might be an opportunity to resolve some problems: "Look, Mike, you should use any avenue you can to try to settle some of these things. Why don't you meet with Dick?"

Michael followed his attorney's advice and met with the

stockbroker in his downtown office. Unfortunately, something or someone changed Dick's conciliatory attitude by the time the meeting took place. The conversation began pleasantly enough, but when they started to discuss the agenda of the meeting, the discussion took a rather ominous turn. Michael does not recall Fisher offering any helpful solutions. Instead, he told Michael that he and Nancy would budget whatever it took to outspend him if he continued to resist or litigate on the custody, property, or support matters. Michael tried to get across that he was not making unreasonable demands. All he wanted was to be with his kids and to get a few of his antiques back. But there was no softening Fisher's hardened stance.

Needless to say, Michael was less than impressed with the mediation efforts of Nancy's fiancé. Perhaps all was not lost, though. Maybe, just maybe, having a new husband would make Nancy anxious to end all the animosity with her second husband. Michael could dream, couldn't he?

Happy New Year. Three years had passed since Nancy and Michael formally separated. Three years without any resolution. Would 1990 at long last be the "Year of Agreements"?

The new year began with all of the post-divorce issues still unsettled. Michael decided to clean up what he could. He informed Nancy and colleague Alan Silverman he had definitely decided to leave the downtown practice. No objections were raised—not that Michael expected any. (Nevertheless, Michael was aggrieved it had come to this, particularly because it was his idea to start a practice downtown—which turned out to be a very successful location—and it was he who had done all the organizing, obtained the financing, rented the space, ordered all the equipment, and recruited the necessary personnel—including Alan.)

Leventon communicated with the attorney representing Alan and Nancy in order to lay the groundwork for a smooth transition and a fair buy-out in terms of Michael's share of the downtown practice. According to Leventon's calculations Michael, by late spring, should be able to relocate his clinical office practice to Shadyside.

Meanwhile, Nancy and Dick, as expected, had exchanged wedding vows. Their marriage on December 23, 1989, left quite an impact on Ariel. Dr. Mendelsohn related to Michael that Nancy's having a new love in her life made Ariel feel abandoned and uncertain of her relationship with her mother.

Michael believed now more than ever that his seven-year-old daughter needed to know that her father was devoted to her no matter what changes took place in her life. For Ariel's sake he couldn't give up the struggle to be with her. Someday it would all be worth it—for both of them. Until then, he must cherish the few instances when he and all his children were together. Such moments occurred occasionally as Michael documented in his daily log: "Mon., Jan. 22: . . . I went to meet Ariel [at the bus stop], who came home directly with me. I made her pizza and then went for Nathaniel. . . . Ariel played video games with Nathaniel and me. . . ."

But—many more of the entries read like that of January 18: ". . . Met Ariel [at the bus stop] who said she didn't want to come home. . . . Later, I went down [to Nancy's house] for Ariel—she wasn't there."

The new year was off to a much better start with Nathaniel and Jennie. Even though the college entrance applications were completed, Jennie continued to see or call her father nearly every day. And Nathaniel (except for a few instances) remained in full compliance with the custody schedule.

But, except for Jennie's change of heart, 1990 might as well have been 1989 or the end of 1988: Nothing was settled and Ariel spent very little time with her father. In the month of January alone Michael's daily log reflects eleven more alleged custody violations of the September 9 court order or, in father-daughter terms, eleven more days Ariel and her dad couldn't color together, play school, or build a snowman. By Michael's count, the grand total of violations since Judge Wettick had crossed out the contempt finding was fifty-nine —nearly one alleged violation for each of his custody days.

This intolerable situation brought Dr. Singer to mind. It had been three months since Michael had filed his ethics complaint. At last, the waiting ended with a telephone call from Arthur J. Van Cara, Ph.D., Chair of the Committee on Ethical Standards and Professional Conduct of the Greater Pittsburgh Psychological Association. He asked Michael if they could meet at Michael's home. Michael agreed. During the informal meeting Michael was pleased to hear that the committee was weighing his complaint very seriously. Dr. Van Cara believed that the accusations clearly had substance. When Michael asked him how a psychologist with Singer's experience could have allowed this disaster to happen, he was stunned by the candor of Van Cara's reply. In Dr. Van Cara's opinion she had seduced him. Then, Dr. Van Cara went on to relate the following anecdote:

Apparently, Nancy had invited the former court-appointed evaluator/monitor to her wedding and Singer told Van Cara he planned to attend. Even though Singer was no longer involved in the case, Van Cara told him that it wasn't a very good idea for him to be mingling socially with Nancy because it would give the appearance of impropriety. When Singer insisted on going, Van Cara made certain his colleague understood his position on the matter by stating: "Roland, you just can't go to this wedding." Van Cara told Michael that as a psychologist he was aghast that Singer could be so enamored of Nancy that he couldn't resist the inclination to attend her wedding.

Dr. Van Cara also had a few choice words concerning the judges in the Family Division. He informed Michael that despite his strenuous remonstrations with the judges, they simply had no understanding of or interest in the ethical strictures that apply to the psychologists they appoint. Michael had certainly found that to be the case.

At the end of the visit Dr. Van Cara asked Michael if he would be willing at some point to sit down with Singer to discuss an informal settlement. Michael replied that he would be willing to do so. Van Cara thanked Michael and mentioned to him that he would be kept apprised by correspondence of progress in the ethics investigation. (Michael never did find out whether or not Roland went to Nancy's wedding.)

A few weeks later Michael received a copy of a letter Dr. Van Cara had sent to Roland Singer:

February 17, 1990

Dear Roland,

As you know from our phone conversation, the Committee on Ethical Standards and Professional Conduct (CESPC) of the Greater Pittsburgh Psychological Association (GPPA) received [an] Ethics Complaint about you from Michael Nieland, M.D. According to the GPPA by-laws and the CESPC Operating Principles, the Committee is hereby opening an investigation of the allegations.... The by-laws and the Operating Principles allow for an informal settlement, if all parties are agreed. I have talked to Michael Nieland recently and he seems amenable to an informal solution if you will stipulate to several of the charges.... Barring that, an Ethics Panel will be constituted within sixty days of the postmark of this letter....

... You stated to me that if you committed any violations, they were done so innocently and with the mistaken notion that Court Orders took precedence over your ethical responsibilities. While Dr. Nieland feels that you may have innocently and naively erred ethically, he also felt that the process has been damaging to him and that you have perhaps been duped or complicit in siding with his wife.

Given those positions, as of the end of January, it seems that we may have the basis of an informal solution. To that end, a Subcommittee [of the CESPC] . . . proposes a meeting between the parties . . . to draft a Memorandum of Agreement between yourself and the complainant. . . . If you agree to such a meeting, I would like to hear from you in writing. . . . I am requesting that Dr. Nieland do the same. We are looking to an ethical and amicable solution to this distressing matter.

Sincerely,
Arthur J. Van Cara, Ph.D.
Chair, CESPC

Spring arrived with the one constant in the Nieland case: more alleged custody violations of the September 6 court order. The running total, according to Michael's daily log, through March 21, 1990, was seventy-five alleged violations concerning Ariel and four concerning Nathaniel.

Understandably, Michael's morale was deteriorating. Especially disheartening to him was the fact that he kept logging in the same kind of subtle actions day after day, month after month, year after year, as one day in February illustrates:

Tues., Feb. 13: Ariel had been at home with me, but then wanted to go back to her mother's house [during the time she was to be with me]. . . . Once inside her mother's house she apparently changed her mind and wanted to return home with me. Three times she tried to get out through the glass door [at the front of Nancy's house], but each time Nancy pulled her away after a struggle. On her fourth attempt Ariel succeeded in getting out the door and we walked home.

Where was Dr. Mendelsohn through all of this? Meeting with Ariel. And Nancy. And Michael. During Michael's sessions she offered him encouragement. She kept urging him to persevere because, she said, she had cautioned Nancy that, if she continued to try to alienate Ariel or Nathaniel from their father, her own relationship with the children would eventually deteriorate. Did Mendelsohn think this warning was all Nancy needed to change her behavior? Michael didn't believe the psychiatrist realized how serious the problem really was and that much stronger action was needed—perhaps even the threat of temporary loss of all custody rights for Nancy. But, Michael didn't argue with Mendelsohn. He couldn't. He wouldn't dare risk irritating yet another court-ordered mental health professional.

And, realistically, Michael couldn't go back to court, either. He could only imagine the overwhelming emotional and financial toll that would result from filing another petition for contempt against Nancy. Couldn't her attorney, Harry Gruener, portray Michael to the court as a chronic malcontent? Hadn't Gruener attempted to do this once before during the 1989 contempt hearing? And now, Gruener could add: "And Judge Wettick crossed out the contempt finding, didn't he?"

That might be all a judge needed to hear to decide that Michael was nothing more than a vindictive, crazed litigant with a "zeal to wrangle." Michael still remembered one of the master's comments during her questioning of Dr. Stephen Schachner at last year's contempt hearing that implied Michael may never be satisfied with any court-appointed mental health professional: "In other words, whenever we get to a crossroads in any form of therapy . . . if Dr. Michael Nieland flares up, becomes angry, he can just walk out of it and he has to start all over again which [causes another] delay [and can be] expensive."

Going back to court simply wasn't a viable alternative for

Michael. There was as much to lose as there was to gain. He convinced himself that if he waited just a little longer things would turn around. It did with Jennie; it would with Ariel, too.

While Michael bided his time, a historic moment occurred in the Nieland case: An agreement on something was reached between the two sides. After nearly three years, a tentative personal property settlement seemed imminent. Nancy would keep nearly everything she removed from the house that June weekend in 1987. Michael would get back his personal papers and files along with some of the antiques as soon as the logistics were worked out.

He didn't need to recall the independent appraisal to realize that he was getting the short end of the stick, but he just wanted to get on with his life and to have the freedom to be a father to Jennie, Nathaniel, and Ariel. So, when he approved the settlement, he added a plea that his attorney put some pressure on Gruener to get Nancy to comply with the custody schedule. Leventon notified Michael of Gruener's reaction, which was less than conciliatory. Gruener contended that neither the attorneys, nor the judges, nor Mendelsohn could compel Ariel to stay overnight with her father because she had steadfastly refused to stay overnight with him, running home to Nancy's whenever she chose. Leventon told Michael that it was Gruener's position that Nancy didn't undermine Ariel's time with Michael as evidenced by the fact that she didn't undermine Nathaniel's time with him.

Michael had expected such a response. What attorney would butt heads with his own client? Michael wondered, though, how well Gruener really knew Nancy. For instance, it is true that Michael's withdrawal from the clinic was progressing smoothly, but did Gruener even know (or care) about a disconcerting discovery Michael had made? Michael had learned during the buy-out negotiations that at least a year earlier, before Michael contemplated leaving the practice, Nancy and Dr. Silverman had taken out a $20,000 bank loan on behalf of the corporation for the purchase of a retiring dermatologist's practice. Now, Silverman and Nancy demanded that Michael pay his share of the loan that had been negotiated without his knowledge. Although the bank that had issued the loan had been satisified with the signatures of only two partners (Nancy and Silverman did, after all, constitute a majority), Michael found it appalling that he hadn't been consulted about such a large business expense. Nancy's behavior didn't surprise him. Would it surprise Gruener?

Michael decided not to protest the deal even though, as a partner, he bore responsibility for one-third of the loan from which he gained nothing. (It was later revealed to Michael that all of the appointments for the newly acquired patients had been scheduled with Alan or Nancy.) Michael knew that legally he didn't have a firm leg to stand on—it would be two partners against one—and, furthermore, the last thing he wanted to do at that point was delay his departure.

Besides, he had more important matters to occupy his attention. On April 1 he met with Dr. Singer and the members of the ethics subcommittee at Dr. Van Cara's home in order to try to arrive at an informal solution to his complaint. Michael and Singer were civil toward each other, but Michael noted that Singer didn't appear to be in a conciliatory mood. Every time Michael stated his position that Singer clearly violated the *Ethical Principles of Psychologists*, the therapist responded by saying, "Well, that's your opinion." At the meeting's end no agreements had been reached, although Van Cara expressed optimism that the subcommittee would be able to put something in writing that both Michael and Singer would find tolerable.

A few weeks later the subcommittee sent a proposed settlement to the parties:

MEMORANDUM OF AGREEMENT
Between
Roland Singer, Ph.D., Psychologist &
Michael Nieland, M.D., Complainant

History

... In a letter dated February 17, 1990, from the Committee on Ethical Standards and Professional Conduct (CESPC), Dr. Singer was informed of [Michael Nieland's Complaint]. ... Dr. Singer responded ... [that] his work with the Nielands was undertaken with good will, with the interests of the children at heart and with the belief that if he had committed any violations they were done innocently and with the mistaken notion that Court Orders took precedence over the American Psychological Association's (APA) Ethical Principles. ...

The Principles

Two points of ethics seemed clear from the outset. First, when doing a custody evaluation, written releases of information are necessary before talking to any and all parties contributing data to the evaluation and before releasing any information to either of the litigant's lawyers or the Court. In the case at hand, failure to follow procedures concerning confidentiality may have led to a biased sample of witnesses who were partial to one party. ...

Second, when a psychologist accepts a Court appointment to do a custody evaluation, his/her role must be limited to the evaluation. To accept a further Court Order to manage, monitor, mediate, or do family or individual psychotherapy in the case ... places the psychologist in a dual relationship, thereby risking impairing his or her judgment. ... This raises ... doubt about the evaluator's fairness or impartiality. CESPC took note of the fact that at the time of this custody evaluation, Dr. Singer was following the extant but mistaken practice of many local psychologists of accepting Court Orders to extend evaluations into case monitoring. . . .

The Agreement

1. Dr. Roland Singer acknowledges that he erred in accepting a Court Order (July 18, 1988) to extend his evaluation activities with Drs. Nancy and Michael Nieland. Through his experience with this case Dr. Singer has come to recognize the inevitable conflict of interest involved when a psychologist acting as an agent of the Court endeavors to attempt evaluation while concurrently working toward conciliation between parents. Even though the Court ordered Dr. Singer to participate further in this case, it was his ethical obligation to refuse the dual relationship of roles of mediating and/or monitoring in addition to his role as Custody Evaluator. He understands that one's judgment may be compromised and that clients may feel that in order to obtain a favorable evaluation, they have to remain involved beyond their desire to do so.

2. Dr. Singer realizes that subsequent to the initial evaluation of March 1988, that he was involved in a dual relationship, and he agrees to retract all documents pertaining to the Nielands. Within two weeks of the date of this Memorandum of Agreement, Dr. Singer will correspond with the concerned attorneys and the Court requesting return of original and copies of any reports or correspondence in the *Nieland* v. *Nieland* custody case subsequent to his report of March 1988. He will further request that any testimony he gave in the Contempt Hearing in 1989 not be used in determining custody arrangements for the Nielands with the explanation that they were developed in the context of a dual relationship and hence are of questionable validity.

3. Regarding confidentiality, Dr. Singer acknowledges that he should have obtained written consent from both the Nielands before receiving telephone information from out-

side parties. Dr. Singer recognizes that without the joint releases, he may not only have obtained a biased sample of witness reports which might have led to a flawed conclusion, but he did not allow Michael Nieland to counter with additional sources representing his perspective.

4. Although Dr. Singer believes that his services were both well intended and useful to Dr. Nieland, he acknowledges that his extended involvement in the case after the July 1988 Court Order placed him in a dual relationship impairing his utility to the Court and to the Nielands. He agrees to return to Dr. Michael Nieland all monies ($2,560) received from Michael Nieland after July 1988 and to forgive the complainant's balance of $1,000.

5. Dr. Singer agrees to participate in twenty hours of review and consultation with a psychologist familiar with custody evaluation, in order to consolidate what he has learned through the Nieland case. The psychologist will be selected by Dr. Singer and will be approved by and report to CESPC.

6. Within two weeks of the date of this Memorandum of Agreement, Michael Nieland will withdraw his Complaints filed with the Pennsylvania State Board of Psychology (SBP) and the Ethics Committees of the American Psychological Association (APA) and Pennsylvania Psychological Association (PPA) indicating that he is satisfied with this informal CESPC resolution. In addition, Michael Nieland agrees that he will not take further action against Dr. Singer for himself or on behalf of his children either in a court of law or with ethics bodies.

7. Dr. Singer agrees that he will continue to respect Dr. Michael Nieland's confidentiality.

8. Dr. Nieland agrees that he will refrain from making any pejorative comments about Dr. Singer in either professional or community circles.

[To be signed by:]
Michael Nieland, M.D.
Roland Singer, Ph.D.
C. Robert Eigenbrode, Ph.D., for the Subcommittee
Arthur J. Van Cara, Ph.D., Chair, CESPC

Michael respected Dr. Van Cara's efforts to attain an informal settlement of the ethics complaint against Dr. Singer.
The last thing Michael wanted or needed was one more pro-
tracted battle. But Michael would not accept a watered-down
acknowledgment that Dr. Singer may have botched the case.
He considered the proposed agreement to be unacceptable in
its current form.

However, Michael did regard the proposed agreement to
be a starting point. He planned to notify Dr. Van Cara of the
modifications he wanted in the final draft just as soon as he
could find the time to put his requirements on paper. Apparently, Michael wasn't the only one who wanted to alter the
document. Singer's attorney also had a few changes in mind
which he included in correspondence to Van Cara:

May 11, 1990

Dear Dr. Van Cara:
    . . . Dr. Singer has informed me that it is the desire and the
intention of the Subcommittee and the parties not to materi-
ally change the terms and conditions of the Memorandum of
Agreement. That approach is completely understandable in
view of the good faith exhibited by everyone on April 1, 1990,
to achieve an informal resolution of these disputes.
    However, Paragraph 2 [of the agreement] places Dr.
Singer in an extremely awkward position. Rule 251(c) of
the Local Rules of the Civil and Family Divisions . . . provides that "no records shall be withdrawn from the Pro-
thonotary Office without an Order of Court." . . . To suggest that Dr. Singer should nonetheless request that those

documents be returned to him would be an academic exercise in futility. . . .

[In addition], the language [in Paragraph 8 of the Agreement] does not restrain Dr. Nieland from publicly discussing the content of the Memorandum of Agreement. Obviously, the public dissemination of the content . . . would be contrary to the rehabilitative focus of the Subcommittee. Accordingly, I recommend the inclusion of Paragraph 9 below:

> Except as noted in Paragraphs 2, 5 and 6 above, Dr. Singer and Dr. Nieland hereby agree to keep confidential and not disclose the terms and conditions of this Memorandum of Agreement. . . .

Very truly yours,
William F. Ward

cc: Paul Leventon

Michael was delayed in composing his own response to the agreement because of his preoccupation with the continuing noncompliance of the court-ordered custody schedule in regard to Ariel, the completion of his withdrawal from the downtown medical practice, the stalemated child support issue, and the pending personal property settlement.

And if that weren't enough, there was a new active participant in the case: Dick Fisher, Nancy's new husband. Since his wedding Dick had become less and less cordial toward Michael during their infrequent encounters. Michael recorded several confrontations in his daily log: Dick yelling at him to get off his property, swearing at him, and at times behaving in a downright menacing fashion. Dick didn't seem to hold his fellow Harvard alum in high esteem. Michael couldn't say for sure why, but he had a pretty good guess. It was the same reason Ariel didn't follow the custody schedule, the same reason his partner and former office manager had turned against him, the same reason he long ago had lost contact with Brita and Sarah.

In the midst of these heightened tensions came final approval of the personal property settlement. Nancy had consented to the stipulations that she return to Michael his personal papers and files, two pieces of furniture, a few *objets d'art*, along with the division of a group of antique porcelain and pottery objects Michael and Nancy had accumulated over the years. Paul Leventon, in a memorandum, alerted Michael to Nancy's insistence regarding how the disposition shall take place:

> Nancy apparently is adamant that she does not want you physically in [her] residence; thus she proposes that she will box the collectibles and the alternating choice process [a flip of the coin will determine who goes first] will take place on her porch. She also suggests Sunday, June 17, 1990, as the date when same should take place.

Nancy's stipulation that the exchange occur on her porch was galling to Michael. He couldn't understand why they could not conduct the exchange inside her home in a more civilized and discreet manner. Did she think he was going to attack her in front of the attorneys, her husband, and the children? Or was it to intimate to the children that it was not safe to have Daddy in her house? The last thing Michael wanted, though, was yet more wrangling. He signed the thirteen-page marriage settlement agreement, as did Nancy, which included the following points:

> Whereas, it is the desire and intention of the parties, after long and careful consideration, to amicably adjust, compromise, and settle all property rights and all rights in, to, or against each other's property or estate . . . and to settle

all (except child and educational support) disputes existing between them. . . .

- Except [for the collectibles and Michael's personal papers and files], each shall retain ownership and possession of the personalty in his or her possession. . . .

- The issues of child support are currently pending before the Court. . . . The arrearages set by the Hearing Officer at $30,950.80 that accrued prior to the Hearing shall be canceled. . . .

- [Michael retains ownership of the family home; Nancy retains her pension fund.]

The signing of the agreement hardly initiated a new period of amity. The very next day Michael made the following entry in his daily log:

Tues., June 5: Went for Ariel and Nathaniel at 3:00. Ariel wouldn't come. Jennie told me later that Keri [one of Ariel's friends] was playing with her [at Nancy's house].
    . . . Nathaniel came home and we went to his cello lesson. . . . After his lesson we came home and I had him call his mother to ask if he could [come home an hour late] so he could go to the Pirates-Cubs baseball game for which Paul Leventon had given me tickets only that morning. She wanted to talk to me and was very nasty about letting him go. . . . We went to the game. . . .

It was painfully obvious to Michael that Nancy didn't plan to change her attitude toward him or toward the court order in the foreseeable future. He remained convinced that she continued to attempt to alienate the children from him. It was also very clear to him that Dr. Mendelsohn must have been having little, if any, success doing whatever she had said she would do so that Michael and Ariel would be reunited. Session after session, month after month, Michael kept telling the psychiatrist about Nancy's behavior and Mendelsohn nodded sympathetically and said that she would "take it up with Nancy." But nothing happened—just more appointments, more frustration for Michael, and more and more bills from Mendelsohn.

Leventon couldn't really provide any further insight. He had mentioned on one or two occasions that perhaps he and Gruener should consult with Mendelsohn, but such a meeting had not yet materialized. Leventon, like Michael, had probably hoped that it would be just a matter of time until Ariel was in full compliance with the custody schedule.

For Michael "just a matter of time" had gone from days to weeks to months. He dreaded the mere thought of that other option: going back to court with another petition for contempt against Nancy. He kept clinging to the fading possibility that the situation would change for the better if he just held out a little bit longer. He took some solace in the realization at least two issues had been settled. In the past few weeks he had successfully relocated his clinical practice, and both parties had signed the personal property settlement. Who knew? Maybe this truly was the beginning of the end? He would continue to be patient and let the professionals do their job.

Michael finally had more time to contemplate the proposed memorandum of agreement concerning Dr. Singer. On June 6, a noncustodial day, he penned his assessment on the subject to Dr. Van Cara:

June 6, 1990

Dear Art,
    . . . I believe that what has been composed thus far could serve as part of the resolution of my Complaint but it is not yet sufficient.
    First, the draft fails to make a clear connection between

violation of *any* ethical principles and what happened in my case. For example, the draft points out only that Dr. Singer's violation of certain ethical principles *may* have led to bias, *may* have compromised his judgment, and *may* have led to flawed conclusions on his part. In other words, maybe nothing bad happened at all! This is unacceptable.

Secondly, the Committee rendered opinion only in the areas of confidentiality and dual relationships to the exclusion of consideration of equally grave and obvious violations of the *Ethical Principles* in the areas of social responsibility, professional competence, and moral and legal standards. There is no indication, though, that Dr. Singer has even begun to understand the other ethical blunders he has made in this case, nor has he in any way acknowledged the harm he has done to me and my children.

Thirdly, the draft states that during his involvement in the case Dr. Singer was proceeding under the notion that Court Orders take precedence over (APA) ethical principles. This, by itself, is an appalling admission, but it does not make clear that Dr. Singer violated provisions of the Court Order that were not in conflict with any ethical principles. The Court Order did not separate me from my children. Dr. Singer separated me from my daughter. If only Dr. Singer had had respect for the Court Order! His sworn testimony was that he thought he had the right to repudiate provisions of the Court Order. . . . He made no effort to find out why my daughter kept running back to her mother's house. He simply accepted her mother's contention that Ariel was afraid of her father. He prevented me from taking both of my children to school. He disrupted the Court-ordered schedule of custody. "Quality time"—twenty minutes! There is much more to this case than issues of confidentiality and dual relationships. This is gross malpractice and total abrogation of moral and ethical standards.

Furthermore, could anyone who has lived during the middle of the twentieth century proceed for a single minute believing that governmental authority absolves one from

acting ethically? He was only following (Court) orders?
Where have we heard that before? An individual who functions at this level of morality shouldn't have a license to be a
dog-catcher. This degree of obtuseness is exactly what I described in my original Complaint to the various ethics committees. The draft comments that this was a "mistaken" notion. How horrible does the outcome have to be for such a
modus operandi to be more than merely a "mistake"? I have
now lost almost three years out of the life of my youngest
child, precious time that can never be restored to her or to me.

Fourth, the draft states that Dr. Singer was simply following the mistaken practice of many local psychologists
of accepting Court Orders to extend evaluations into case
monitoring, contrary to the *Ethical Principles*. However,
everyone wasn't doing it. Reputable psychologists in this
area were refusing to do this. Psychologists who did not
even have thirty years' experience were refusing to do this.
Ignorance of the law or the *Ethical Principles* is no excuse.
Even if others were doing this he should have known
better. The speeder stopped for driving 85 miles per hour
in a 55 mile per hour zone can't legitimately protest that the
cars in front and behind him were going even faster! The
Ethics Committee should not appear to condone this. In
our April 1, 1990 meeting Dr. Singer failed to acknowledge
that his errors were much more than technical violations of
rules of procedure. When I suggested to him that had he
followed the rules he might have arrived at a different formulation of the case, he would have none of it. Several
times he replied to me, "That's your opinion." The contu-
meliousness of Dr. Singer is beyond belief. Dr. Singer failed
to pay heed, to take care . . . and this led to a chain reaction
of blunders. But Dr. Singer still does not understand what
he did, or if he does, he won't acknowledge it, and I refuse
to accept his flouting decency and good sense.

Fifth, Dr. Singer insisted that the draft include a clause
stating that *I* will refrain from making "pejorative" remarks

about him as one of the stipulations of a settlement. I think I understand what pejorative means. In the letter Dr. Singer wrote to my attorney, a copy of which he sent to my former spouse's attorney, he stated that I was a "psychopath, an individual with a deeply rooted character disorder" and that I was "frightening" to my daughter. I think these are pejorative remarks. In fact these libelous characterizations have now been shown to many of my friends and colleagues. The draft states that Dr. Singer will retrieve the letter, but severe damage has been done to me. . . . I insist upon a retrieval of the letter, but also upon a specific retraction and an apology for these remarks. . . .

Sixth, Dr. Singer also insisted upon a stipulation that I will not take further action against him for myself or on behalf of my children in a court of law. But Dr. Singer has not expressed the slightest regret for the damage he did to me or the [children]. . . . If Dr. Singer wishes to avoid a suit and bring this matter to a prompt and equitable conclusion, he must provide the language which so far is missing from this document. I insist that in clear, unequivocal language he state the following:

1. That he realizes now with hindsight that his failure to follow the rules of procedure in regard to matters of confidentiality at the very earliest stage of his involvement in this case led to bias against me in his written and oral testimony to the Court, that he should not have spoken about me to individuals who had clear conflicts of interest, and that he should have recommended to the Court not only that I be awarded forthwith equal shared legal and physical custody of my younger children, but without any further need for monitoring by the Court or by him or any other equivocation related to alleged deficiencies in my child-rearing abilities or aspersions on my parental competence concerning which he had no firsthand knowledge.

2. That he should not have taken any action, directly or indirectly, or played any role in changing, circumventing,

undermining, or repudiating any provision of the Order of Court that would infringe upon my right to take my children to school or reside with me as stipulated in the Order of Court and that he regrets having done so.

3. That he retracts and repudiates the specific accusations in his April 14, 1989 letter that I am "frightening" to any of my children, and that I have a "severe personality disorder, psychopathology, a deeply rooted character disorder and personality problems," and that these charges are wholly false and he profoundly regrets having made them.

If there is any question at this point in Dr. Singer's mind as to what I require, I suggest he retain qualified legal counsel in order to communicate with my attorney, Paul J. Leventon, Esquire, with all deliberate speed.

Sincerely yours,
Michael

While Michael waited for Dr. Van Cara's response, the personal property issue returned to the forefront with the exchange of the collectibles. Michael eagerly awaited getting back a portion of the antique pieces he had collected over the years.

June 17, 1990, the date of the exchange, finally arrived. The festivities were to begin at noon on Nancy's porch. As it turned out, the younger children were in their father's custody that weekend and, as usual, Ariel spent Saturday night at Nancy's home. In order to spend some time with Ariel before the property exchange, Michael left Nathaniel (with his favorite chocolate doughnuts and the television remote control) and walked over to Nancy's home around 11 A.M. to pick up Ariel.

What happened during the next two hours, according to Michael's recollection, was anything but amicable:

As Michael neared Nancy's house on that sweltering day, he couldn't believe what he heard—banging, rattling, clattering. It couldn't be, could it? It was. Michael was hearing the sounds of the boxed-up collectibles being dropped from the hands of Dick Fisher onto the porch's wooden deck. When Fisher spotted Michael approaching, he yelled out, "It isn't noon yet. Are you here for property or some other reason?"

Michael barely heard the question. He immediately asked Fisher to please treat the century-old pieces with the care they required.

Nancy's husband responded by saying, "It looks like a flea market up here."

Just then Nancy walked onto the porch and announced, "Ariel's not ready yet, she'll be over in ten minutes."

"I'll wait here," Michael replied. He was afraid to leave Fisher unsupervised with the antiques.

Fisher ordered Michael to get off his property. Michael complied. He waited at the curb for Ariel, hoping his compliance would encourage Fisher to be more careful. He wasn't. Michael, incensed, decided he had better return temporarily to his house to cool off—in more ways than one.

At high noon, he returned with Nathaniel. Leventon had also arrived.

Michael's fears turned out to be true. Irreparable damage had been done to some of his most prized possessions. In just one instance, a beautiful porcelain tray, more than 100 years old, had a big chunk taken out of it. This particular museum-quality piece, probably worth a couple of thousand dollars, had lost all of its value—both aesthetically and monetarily. When Michael pointed out this particular breakage, Fisher replied, "Why, I don't see anything wrong with this. It's been sitting on my piano like that."

Michael was livid at the ruins before him, and asked Paul Leventon to do something. Like what? Leventon said that Gruener had told him everything was in good shape except for "normal wear and tear." Michael responded that this kind of destruction went way beyond minor chips or scratches. But

Michael or Paul could not argue that point with Harry Gruener, since he wasn't there. In his place was a junior associate from Harry's firm. The fill-in seemed to have little knowledge about the case. Leventon certainly had background knowledge about the case, but he had never previously examined Michael's and Nancy's possessions. Inasmuch as Leventon wasn't a collector himself, it must have seemed as though they were fighting over bric-a-brac. However, to Michael, it was appalling that valuable pieces so beautiful and so well preserved for generations had been disfigured.

The attorneys huddled.

Michael went back home and got his camera so he could photograph the remains of what had been promised to him. Upon his return, the attorneys talked with Dick, Nancy, and Michael. (Jennie looked on, as she had from the outset, while Ariel and Nathaniel were inside watching television.) An agreement was proposed that Michael receive a couple of replacement pieces for what was damaged. Nothing could be offered that would compare with what had been destroyed, but Michael realized he either had to accept the compromise or declare the agreement null and void and start negotiating a settlement all over again. With disgust, he gave his approval.

It was time to divide an antique French porcelain box collection. Both parties had agreed that the entire nineteenth-century collection would be on display. But it isn't, claimed Michael. It is, retorted Nancy. Out of the approximately sixteen high-quality pieces to be split evenly, per the agreement, Michael identified only five among the thirteen boxes present on the porch. He recognized four other boxes, but they weren't part of the collection. And, according to Michael, the remaining four were inexpensive dresser boxes, not antiques, that could have been purchased at any department store. Nancy denied Michael's accusation and insisted that this was the complete collection. Michael proposed they enter her home, confident that the missing boxes would be revealed one-by-one atop her shelves and mantles. The request was flatly denied.

Michael was furious. On the rare occasions Nancy or her babysitters had permitted him to wait for the children in her foyer over the past few years, he had noted many of the phantom pieces prominently featured in Nancy's living room. Jennie, too, seemed astonished at what was occurring, but she said nothing.

Once again, what could Michael do? He turned to his attorney, but law school had never prepared Leventon for this! There was another attorney huddle. Michael ended up with three of the five boxes he considered to be part of the original collection. In addition, he reluctantly agreed to take three of the disputed ones because he couldn't choose from among the boxes that Nancy said didn't exist.

With that, the friendly get-together was about over. Michael needed only the return of his files and other personal papers for the transfer to be complete. Fisher turned over the mass of papers—thrown into a huge plastic garbage bag. Jennie turned her back on the scene and reentered Nancy's house.

Michael also wanted to leave the porch. He asked Nancy to inform the younger children that it was time to go. Nathaniel came right out, Ariel didn't. She didn't want to go with her father. Michael still left with two children, however. Jennie had come out with Nathaniel. She planned to spend the afternoon with her dad.

When the three of them arrived home Michael sorted through the garbage bag. In keeping with the spirit of the day, he discovered to his dismay that many of the papers and files stipulated to be returned were missing. The list of non-returned items included, in part:

- income tax records;

- home mortgage documents and records of home repairs and renovations;
- office building documents;
- an autographed letter from Arthur Fiedler, conductor;
- a note from "one cellist to another" written by Nathaniel Rosen, renowned cellist to Nathaniel (just prior to his birth);
- an antique key that operated a fountain in Michael's home.

Jennie surely noticed her father's disappointment. Michael, though, had always refrained from criticizing Nancy in front of the children and that day was no different. He noted that Jennie was perturbed by her mother's behavior. He himself was appalled. It seemed unlikely that he would ever recall the events of June 17, 1990, with much nostalgia. Nonetheless, he wouldn't let what had just happened affect his time with his children, as his log entry attests:

Sun., June 17: ... When the property exchange was finished Jennie and I took Nathaniel to the Pirates-Mets baseball game. [Ariel remained at Nancy's house.] Home around 5:00 P.M. Jennie left and Nathaniel stayed until about 6:00 P.M. when I walked him back to Nancy's. ... Ariel later informed me that she had gone swimming with [one of the babysitter's daughters], but it was "after five."

Michael's civilized approach had an unexpected bonus. That evening Jennie returned to her father's house with a gift—some of the personal papers that were not in the trash bag. She told him that she had found them at the bottom of her mother's bedroom closet.

In every way the emotional day was typical of the unending strife: bitter antagonism, Nathaniel spending time with his dad, and Ariel not adhering to the custody schedule.

To top it off, the very next day Michael received a letter concerning Dr. Singer from Dr. Van Cara:

June 17, 1990

Dear Michael,

... Your requests seem to reopen several of the issues we thought were settled in our meeting of April 1, 1990.

It is important to reiterate that the Subcommittee of CESPC is not an adjudication panel and, as such, we do not have the power to investigate or remediate the grievances raised in your current letter. We do understand that you remain deeply upset about Dr. Singer's role in your custody litigation. The Subcommittee's work was to assist you and Dr. Singer in resolving your grievances. The arbitration is an attempt to seek a just resolution without going to a full Hearing Panel. CESPC felt that the [Memorandum of Agreement] approached this both in spirit and in content, and as such, we thought we were very close to achieving your goals.

In our view, the document provided a vehicle whereby the psychologist could be professionally educated regarding his errors. Dr. Singer stipulated to breaches of the *Ethical Principles* involving confidentiality and dual relationships. However, as we discussed earlier, issues of competence, social responsibility and moral and legal standards are beyond the scope of the Subcommittee because the evidentiary demands for proof [regarding these matters] are much more extensive. . . .

... Consistent with the Subcommittee's role, this [Memorandum of Agreement] cannot be languaged any stronger than that his behavior "may" have led to biases and flawed conclusions. It is not appropriate for the Subcommittee to draw ultimate conclusions regarding the effects of the actions involved. To test that hypothesis is up to a fully convened Ethics Panel. . . .

In summary then, it is the judgment of CESPC that most of the things you request in your letter of June 6th are

(1) either covered in the document as it stands, (2) are bound by the limits of the agreed upon subject of the document or (3) are outside the powers of the Subcommittee as an arbitration panel. . . . Our suggestion is that no changes be made on the basis of your letter. . . .

Sincerely,
Arthur J. Van Cara, Ph.D.
Chair, CESPC

Michael wasn't quite sure what to make of Dr. Van Cara's letter. Van Cara seemed to be suggesting that Michael should be satisfied with Dr. Singer's admitting to breaches of the *Ethical Principles of Psychologists* involving confidentiality and dual relationships and, in turn, Michael should forget about issues of competence, social responsibility, and moral and legal standards. Or—even an apology.

In a return letter to Dr. Van Cara, Michael politely let him know that he would not permit any part of his complaint against Roland Singer to be swept under the rug:

> . . . I am sure you understood from my letter of June 6, 1990, that I would accept the Memorandum of Agreement, as it now stands, with the additional three paragraphs [points 1, 2, and 3] to be added, not by the Subcommittee, but by Dr. Singer, should he choose to end the matter now. . . . Inasmuch as I want to give Dr. Singer every last opportunity to bring this case to a conclusion forthwith, would you please forward this letter and my June 6, 1990 letter to Dr. Singer. . . .

Michael's letter demonstrated he was still open to an informal settlement provided Singer acknowledged his grossly inadequate performance in the case and retracted his intemperate remarks.

Undoubtedly, upon receipt of Michael's letter, Van Cara

would inform Singer of Michael's position and then report back to the subcommittee before determining what would come next—perhaps a new agreement proposal, a fully convened ethics panel, or an apology from the therapist. Who knew how long it would take to arrive at such a decision? It had already been more than eight months since the complaint was first filed.

By now, Michael was used to the tedium of waiting. In fact, he had discovered that patience sometimes had its own rewards. A year ago Jennie had barely spoken to him. Now she lived with him!

Jennie's move began a few days after the porch drama, when she spent her first night at Michael's home since the divorce. One night became two. Two became three. As of mid-July, Jennie spent practically every night at Michael's home. Michael was elated at having his teenage daughter with him, especially because in a little more than a month she would be beginning her freshman year at the University of Pennsylvania in Philadelphia.

He didn't question her concerning her switch of addresses. He did not need to. Jennie had had a chance to observe the behavior of both of her parents during the previous three years. Perhaps the porch episode was the last straw for her. Whatever her reasons, Michael was not gloating. He made sure he did not dissuade his daughter from spending time at her mother's home. Michael wanted for Jennie what he wanted for all his children—to have a close relationship with both parents. Jennie's love for her father also served as a reminder to Michael why he must continue to fight for Ariel. He believed (or at least hoped) that, in time, children figure everything out.

As the first anniversary of Dr. Sylvia Mendelsohn's involvement in the case approached, Michael failed to note even a whit of progress in regard to her helping Ariel resist Nancy's pressures. Exasperated, Michael mulled over the one option he had not wanted to consider: going back to court with another petition for contempt against Nancy. After discussing this possibility with the psychiatrist, Michael wrote his attorney about her reaction: "Dr. Mendelsohn believes without reservation that Ariel must eventually abide by the court order. Dr. Mendelsohn told me to hold off going back to court to enforce it pending her efforts to get Nancy to cooperate."

Not wanting to lose Mendelsohn's support, he decided to abide by her wishes.

To complicate the custody circumstances further, Nancy was moving for the third time since she and Michael had separated. This time the destination was Shadyside, neighboring Squirrel Hill. Her new home was approximately one mile from Michael's residence. Now, it was no longer possible for Ariel to pick up suddenly and run back to Nancy's house. There were far too many busy intersections. Michael believed that was good news. Or was it? If Ariel knew she could not leave Michael's house on a whim, would she decide not to come at all? Michael would have to wait and see.

Meanwhile, patience on the child support issue apparently had waned on both sides. After several months, out-of-court settlement talks between the attorneys had led nowhere. On August 18, the court scheduled oral arguments for the defendant's exceptions and plaintiff's cross-exceptions to be held September 14, 1990.

Patience had evidently run out for Nancy's husband, also. He seemed to be getting tired of seeing Michael when he came for or brought back the children. They hadn't been the best of friends since the porch incident. Michael, in his daily log, recounted a specific incident in September:

Wed., Sept. 5: . . . I stayed downstairs with Ariel from the time we got home (3:30) until about 6:00 playing blocks. . . . About 6:15 Ariel announced she was going back to her mother's [new] house and she ran out the door. I ran after her. I pleaded with her to stay. She said, "My mother showed me the way home in case she couldn't come for me." I asked, "When did she say that?" and [Ariel] said, "Today," and started to go down the hill. . . . I followed her. . . . When I arrived at Nancy's house Ariel was waving at me from the back porch. I rang the doorbell and Nancy answered. I asked her to drive Ariel and me home because the Court Order required her to return Ariel to my custody. . . . She said, "Just a minute" and closed the door . . . then the door reopened and Dick came out and asked me if I'd like a ride home. I calmly replied I'd like him to drive Ariel and me home. He said, "She won't go with you!" and shoved me off his steps. I lost my balance and fell into the bushes. . . . I told him if he didn't take his hands off me I'd call the police. He immediately desisted and sat down on his steps and said, "Okay, let's call the police." I asked him again to drive Ariel and me home. He said, ". . . She's afraid of you; that's why we can't ever get her to go with you." I said, "Is that your final word?" and I walked down his walk. He said, "Yes." I yelled back, "See you in court." . . . I walked home. . . .

Michael filed harassment charges against Dick. He had to send a message to Dick that when it came to his children he would not be intimidated.

From one confrontation to the next. Three days prior to the September 14 oral arguments, Nancy's attorney Kenneth Horoho filed on her behalf a petition for contempt and request for college education expenses. The thirteen-page petition makes two basic points:

[1] Pursuant to the parties' Property Settlement Agreement dated June 4, 1990, the child support arrearages of

$30,950 were canceled. However, the issue of child support was not resolved and all arrearages that accrued subsequent to the initial Hearing were not canceled. . . . The filing of Exceptions does not cancel his child support obligation. Respondent [Michael] is currently in arrears. . . .

[2] Jennie Nieland joins in the within action against Respondent for her college support and signifies her agreement by her acknowledgment attached hereto:

ACKNOWLEDGMENT

I, JENNIE NIELAND, do hereby acknowledge that my mother, Nancy Nieland, is authorized to proceed on my behalf to seek the support to which I am entitled from my father, Michael L. Nieland, for my college education.

JENNIE NIELAND /s

The document presented to the court did not bear Jennie's signature or a photocopy of her signature, but, rather, an indication that the original document was properly signed.

Michael could not believe that Jennie had agreed to, let alone signed, such an acknowledgment. Since Jennie had just started her freshman year at Penn and lived in Philadelphia, Michael decided he wouldn't bring up the issue with her until she returned home for Thanksgiving break.

As for the rest of the petition, Michael realized that Dick Fisher was making good on his vow that he and Nancy would budget whatever it took to outspend him in the legal arena if he continued to oppose them. The judge had yet to rule on the exceptions concerning child support and Nancy had now initiated even more litigation on the matter. Michael's attorney advised him to counter her petition with his own. He did. Michael's petition for modification of a temporary support order basically made three arguments for reducing the child support figure:

(1) Jennie has become a full-time freshman at the University of Pennsylvania [and no longer lives at home full-time];

(2) Petitioner's [Michael's] net disposable income has decreased . . . as a result of his withdrawal from [the downtown] clinical dermatology practice;

(3) On or about December 23, 1989, [Nancy] married Mr. Richard E. Fisher. . . . Mr. Fisher's . . . earning capacity must now be considered in the allocation of certain child support costs and expenses such as home mortgage, real estate taxes, utilities, food, etc.

Judge Kaplan, who was back on the case, consolidated the petitions for a December 6, 1990 hearing and made his ruling—one month later.

ORDER OF COURT

AND NOW, on this 29th day of October 1990, upon consideration of the parties' Exceptions, Briefs in support thereof. . . . It is hereby ORDERED, ADJUDGED, AND DECREED that this matter is to be remanded to Hearing Officer Bingman for an explanation of her calculation of the children's needs. A Hearing may be held on that issue at her discretion. Upon Hearing Officer Bingman's submission of her explanation to the undersigned, the Court will then issue an appropriate order.

BY THE COURT:
Lawrence W. Kaplan

In other words, more waiting—this time for the hearing officer's explanation of her ruling concerning proceedings that ended more than a year ago.

One wait resumed. One wait ended. The harassment charges against Dick Fisher for the September 5 incident were thrown out at an October 30 hearing. The district magistrate considered the incident to be under the jurisdiction of the Family Division. Even though the magistrate refused to make a determination as to whether or not Fisher was guilty, Michael hoped Nancy's husband had gotten the message that all the pushing, shoving, name calling, threatening, and finger pointing wouldn't deter Michael from fighting for his children.

The fight was far from over. It had been more than a year since Judge Wettick crossed out the master's contempt finding, and in that time Michael asserted that Nancy (or her babysitters) violated at least one provision of the latest court order an incredible 162 times pertaining to Ariel—practically one violation for each of Michael's specified custody periods. (Nathaniel had consistently stayed with his dad and followed the custody schedule.)

Michael kept telling Mendelsohn about the problems with his daughter—Ariel arriving late, departing early, never staying overnight, and sometimes not being available at all during the days she was to be with her father. He asked the psychiatrist, yet again, what she was doing to put a stop to this. She insisted she was working hard with Nancy and with Ariel, but when he asked Mendelsohn what kind of progress she was making, the psychiatrist replied she couldn't violate her confidentiality with either Nancy or Ariel and urged Michael just to be patient.

On one occasion, though, Mendelsohn provided Michael with an example of what Ariel was up against. During that session, according to Michael's recollection, she explained that Ariel wouldn't go clothes shopping with him and also refused to return to her mother's house wearing any clothes purchased by her father because "she saw what happened to Nathaniel." Ariel apparently had witnessed several instances (some of which were mentioned during the contempt hearing) when Nathaniel returned to Nancy's house wearing clothes purchased by Michael. Nancy would insist he take off "Michael's clothes" immediately and within an hour or so she would leave them in a bag at Michael's side door.

What was Mendelsohn doing about these kinds of episodes? She kept repeating that she needed to continue her regular sessions with all the parties involved in order to end this kind of interference.

Dr. Mendelsohn, unlike Dr. Singer, seemed to comprehend the undermining going on, yet so far she had not prevented Ariel from being pulled away from her dad. She seemed incapable of taking a firm stand in regard to Nancy. Michael and Ariel were faced with the consequences. Clearly, Ariel loved her father and he loved his daughter, but one moment they might be playing together and the next moment Ariel might be running to her mother's house for no apparent reason whatsoever.

How could this still be happening after two years? Michael wondered how much longer he could survive this kind of life. To him, it wasn't living, it was chaos. At these times of discouragement he thought about his telephone conversations with Jennie. Invariably, she needed her dad's advice about a boy or a school paper or car problems. These moments made him realize he couldn't give up. His children needed him in their lives.

Michael needed all the inner strength he could muster. Nothing seemed to be going his way. Shortly after the charges against Fisher were thrown out Michael received from Dr. Van Cara a (lack of) progress report on the ethics complaint against Roland Singer:

> The Subcommittee and I have tried numerous ways to incorporate the changes that you requested. . . . We keep coming back to the same answer, namely, it is simply beyond our scope. . . . I need to clarify the Subcommittee's

role as arbiter. Our purpose is to reach an informal solution both to speed up the process and to reduce the amount of suffering on the part of both parties. This is usually done through the Memorandum of Agreement such as we were all seeking. When this is not possible a formal Ethics Panel is convened. . . . To forecast the outcome is not difficult and additional charges do not increase the chances of increased "punishment." The intent of professional ethics work is to strive for rehabilitation of the professional and remediation of the grievance. Professional societies can only at maximum remove one from membership and most ethics violations do not call for this extreme. In psychology, those circumstances are usually misconduct or commission and conviction of a felony. We are not in a position, given this mandate, to evaluate the degree of psychological harm caused by the violation. That is a matter of civil law. . . . We are turning the matter back to you and Dr. Singer. . . . If no informal solution is reached by January 4, 1991, the Committee on Ethical Standards and Professional Conduct (CESPC) will move to form a panel. . . .

The letter didn't please Michael, but he had no problems with having a formal ethics panel convened if that was the only way to proceed. Still, Michael would have preferred to get Singer out of his life sooner than later. In a November 15 letter to Paul Leventon, Michael wrote that he planned within the next few weeks to inform Dr. Singer's attorney that he would offer to withdraw the complaint, if Singer provided a retraction. Again, an apology is all Michael sought, provided it wasn't replete with "may have led" type phrases.

Thanksgiving arrived. Jennie came home from school. Michael and his three children had a mid-afternoon Thanksgiving dinner and later in the evening Jennie and Ariel joined their mother at her house. Nathaniel decided to stay with his dad (because it was Michael's custody period) and that night father and son watched a baseball movie.

Jennie, meanwhile, spent two nights at Michael's house and two nights at Nancy's house and then she returned to Penn, but not before first writing a very important note to Leventon with a copy to Gruener. She stated that she had seen the petition for contempt against her father and she wanted the court to know that she had had nothing to do with the preparation of it, nor did she want to be a party to it, nor had she signed any document that allegedly bore her signature.

This letter *was* signed by Jennie.

Michael knew in his heart that Jennie had never seen or approved, let alone signed any such acknowledgment as alleged by Nancy's lawyer. His paternal instinct had been right. With the truth now known Michael asked his attorney how Nancy's lawyers could have filed an unauthorized and therefore fabricated document. Leventon shook his head.

Michael and Leventon were not finished setting the record straight concerning Jennie. The day prior to a hearing on the dueling petitions to adjust the child support (in which the exceptions were still pending), Leventon sent the following memo to Kenneth Horoho:

December 5, 1990

In Re: *Nieland* v. *Nieland*, College Support

Dear Ken:

. . . Michael vigorously denies that he . . . has not properly contributed to Jennie's college education expenses.

In fact, Michael has voluntarily contributed in a proportion likely greater than that which the Court may determine to be his "fair share." . . .

Be further advised that Michael stands "ready, willing and able" to submit for the Court's determination on December 6, 1990, the issue of the allocation of Jennie's college education expenses. . . .

Very truly yours,
Paul

The lawyers did all the talking at the December 6 conciliation before Judge Kaplan. Nancy and Michael were instructed to wait outside. They did—but not on the same bench. At the conciliation's conclusion Paul told Michael it was nothing more than a shouting match. Needless to say, nothing had been resolved. Evidently, nothing could be resolved until Hearing Officer Bingman provided her explanation for calculating the "children's needs" so that Judge Kaplan could rule on both sides' exceptions. As fate would have it, Bingman's typewritten explanation was handed down the very next day (with only two words blotted out this time):

December 7, 1990

After reviewing the transcript and exhibits, it is the opinion of this Hearing Officer that no further Hearing is necessary. . . . While Plaintiff calculated her expenses at $11,467.23 and those of the children at $13,853.13, the numbers are clearly inflated. . . . While Plaintiff indicated that the child care arrangements had not changed since the separation, it does appear as though the child care expenses are far too high.

To conclude, it is this Hearing Officer's findings that the children's reasonable needs are in the neighborhood of $6,600 and that given the respective incomes and expenses, Defendant's [Michael's] share is calculated at 34 percent or $2,244. . . .

Jeanne J. Bingman
Hearing Officer

In a letter to Michael, his attorney shed further light on how the hearing officer concluded Michael was responsible for 34 percent of the expenses: "I believe the 34 percent is the approximate two-to-one ratio between Nancy's net disposable income and yours as calculated by the Hearing Officer . . . though she [Bingman] failed to input into her calculations your direct child support provided your children." While Michael was responsible for helping Nancy with expenses that included items such as food, clothing, transportation, child care, entertainment, gifts, vacations, cable television, dry cleaning, property taxes, residential utilities, and gardening, he, in turn, received absolutely no credit for providing the same kinds of necessities for his children at his residence. Had the hearing officer concluded that Jennie, Nathaniel, and Ariel didn't need a heated house when they were in Michael's custody approximately one-third of the time? The explanation made no sense to Michael.

It did to Judge Kaplan. His order of court, issued December 19, 1990, upheld the hearing officer's findings. Curiously, though, it made the order *retroactive* to September 15, 1987. Arrearages were set at $30,950.

Obviously, Judge Kaplan had failed to take the time to read the documents lying on his desk. In Nancy's September 11, 1990 petition to the court, one provision stated: "Pursuant to the parties' Property Settlement Agreement dated June 4, 1990, the child support arrearages of $30,950 were canceled." Additionally, Leventon had filed with the court on December 3, 1990, another document, namely an answer to Nancy's petition which agreed that the arrearages of $30,950 were canceled.

Both sides had clearly notified the court that the arrearages issue was settled. In addition, Leventon and Gruener had recently gone before Judge Kaplan to argue the child support issue on September 14, 1990, and December 6, 1990. Yet, Judge Kaplan's court order still contained this glaring error. Hadn't he even bothered to read or listen to what the attorneys presented?

368   A FAMILY DIVIDED

In a letter to Judge Kaplan, the two attorneys jointly informed him of his mistake:

January 3, 1991

Dear Judge Kaplan:

... Counsel for both parties agree that said Orders *should not* be retroactive to September 15, 1987, and that arrears *should not* have been set at $30,950 as of August 1, 1989.

The parties' Marriage Settlement Agreement dated June 4, 1990, specifically provides that, "The arrearages set by the Hearing Officer at $30,950 that accrued prior to the Hearing, shall be canceled. In the event that the Hearing Officer's Recommendations shall be modified upon Exceptions, any arrearages set for the period prior to the initial Hearing ... shall be canceled."

... It is respectfully requested by the undersigned counsel of record that you issue new Orders of Court consistent with the above.

Very truly yours,

Paul J. Leventon, attorney for Michael L. Nieland

Harry J. Gruener, attorney for Nancy S. Nieland

Judge Kaplan signed an amended order of court dated January 4, 1991, correcting his error.

Michael had had enough. He wanted his affairs out of the Family Division as soon as possible. He met with his attorney to formulate a child support settlement proposal which was submitted to Nancy on January 9, 1991. Nancy's side seemed receptive. They didn't accept the offer, but at least they offered a counterproposal. Perhaps Nancy was getting worn out, too.

Apparently though, Dr. Singer had no sense of urgency to resolve his differences with Michael. The January 4 deadline imposed by Dr. Van Cara for reaching an informal decision had been extended at the request of Singer's attorney,

William F. Ward. Nearly a month prior to the deadline, Michael had sent Ward his proposal for ending the matter:

December 12, 1990

Dear Mr. Ward,

. . . An immediate and amicable settlement of my Complaint against Dr. Singer is possible on the basis of the language I stipulated in my letter of June 6 to Dr. Van Cara. I agree with the comment you made in your May 11th letter to Dr. Van Cara that it would be futile to request return of Dr. Singer's April 14, 1989 letter. Dr. Singer must retract unequivocally the characterization of me contained in that letter. Dr. Singer must unequivocally disavow the role he played in undermining the Court Order in my case apart from the extenuations, euphemisms and circumlocutions contained in the remainder of the text of the draft memorandum and related correspondence.

This matter should be ended now. Scrutiny by the full Ethics Committee will only lead to findings of additional violations of the "Ethical Principles" and I am fully prepared to provide additional testimony. I believe, in addition, that the violations so far cited relating to confidentiality and dual relationships are not only transgressions of the *Ethical Principles,* but they are prohibited by the Pennsylvania Code as well.

I hope you will use your powers of persuasion to bring this case to a prompt and merciful conclusion. . . .

Please submit the draft memorandum to me with the necessary paragraphs provided by Dr. Singer. I will sign the document and as soon as it is returned to me with the signatures I will withdraw my complaint.

Sincerely yours,
Michael L. Nieland

As of January 3, one day prior to the deadline, Ward had not responded in any fashion to Michael's offer. Finally, with a few hours to spare, Singer's attorney decided to address the issue. He wrote to Van Cara, requesting an extension to January 17, 1991, due to his heavy mid-December schedule. In the interim he would continue to discuss the matter with Singer.

Mr. Ward requested a meeting with Michael on January 17, the final day of the extended deadline. Michael agreed. The meeting was cordial. No agreement was reached, though, as Ward informed Van Cara in a letter dated January 21, 1991.

More talking. More waiting.

But, lo and behold, an agreement was forthcoming on February 15, 1991, regarding child support. Michael would pay $1,125 a month for the support of Ariel and Nathaniel, in addition to half of their school tuitions. He would also be responsible for one-third of Jennie's college educational support.

Paul Leventon was very pleased with the settlement. Knowing the numbers could have been much worse for Michael, he considered this agreement to be a major victory for his client. Michael was not so sure. He still couldn't understand Bingman's and then Judge Kaplan's logic that he should be assisting Nancy with her household bills. She continued to outearn him. Furthermore, the children spent (or in Ariel's case were supposed to spend) substantial time with him, but Michael had received no credit at all for his expenses. But, as his attorney pointed out, Michael could take solace in the fact that the settlement meant at least he would not be crushed financially.

Unfortunately, the spirit of compromise on the child support issue had not, in Michael's estimation, lessened Nancy's hostility toward him. From Judge Wettick's September 9, 1989 crossing-out of the contempt finding and all through 1990, Michael recorded in his daily log 186 alleged instances in which Nancy (or her babysitters) had in some way interfered with the custody schedule of Ariel and another five times in regard to Nathaniel.

So far, 1991 had been no different. By the time of the support agreement signing, a mere forty-six days into the New Year, Michael believed Nancy had violated the intent of the court order another thirteen times with Ariel and once with Nathaniel.

Nancy's hostility apparently didn't end with the children. Without any explanation she had ceased sending her biopsies from her patients to Michael and Alan Silverman's laboratory for evaluation. On the one hand she had demanded and received child support from Michael, but on the other she had for all intents and purposes driven him out of his downtown office and had now taken away a large chunk of his dermatopathology practice and the income it provided. This came on the heels of last year's child support hearing when she had claimed Michael wasn't earning to his full income potential! Was she trying to make Michael unable to support their children?

Michael couldn't fathom Nancy's behavior toward him. He could not help but feel very alone.

He was not. He discovered that the Greater Pittsburgh Psychological Association (GPPA) had been besieged by grievances from other parents leveled against the conduct of judges and court appointees in the Allegheny County Family Division. These widespread complaints prompted the formulation of a GPPA Task Force to investigate the matter further and, in February 1991, the task force formally issued a sixty-one-page report entitled *Report of the Task Force on Child Custody Evaluation.* Michael found the report to be extraordinarily timely and significant. It addressed the very concerns he had raised in his ethics complaint against Dr. Roland Singer. He realized something else, also. There were a lot of Michael Nielands out there.

The task force document stated that grievances against psychologists involved in custody litigation were not new, but by 1988 they had reached "epidemic proportions." According to the task force, these types of complaints were part of a national pattern of grievances.

The task force commented that prior to the mid-1970s custody decisions were based on the "tender years" doctrine, which assumed that the child's mother was always the more appropriate parent during the child's formative years unless she was proven unfit. Later, judges began to appoint psychologists to assist them in making custody determinations concerning whether joint or sole custody was better for the child's development. It was commonly assumed then that the psychologist's main role was to give an opinion on custodial disposition. Yet, the task force maintained that when psychologists made such recommendations, they were engaging in a practice which was professionally and legally controversial.

It was the task force's position that the role of the psychologist in custody proceedings was not to make a decision, but rather to offer the judge data relevant to determining the child's best interests. The task force warned that the psychologist must make every effort to obtain equivalent information regarding each prospective custodian, obtain appropriate written releases, assess the credibility of the sources, and be aware of potential conflicts of interest or loyalties.

The task force contended that professional opinions on custody disposition must not be based upon the psychologist's personal values or "hunches." Furthermore, the task force urged psychologists to "make every effort to avoid dual relationships" that could compromise their professional judgment and their objectivity, as mandated by the APA Ethical Code.

Not only did the task force report offer further proof to Michael that his family has been damaged by the "ethical squalor" he and his children had encountered in the Family Division, it revealed to him for the first time the magnitude of the problem. The report identified complaints involving violations of the *Ethical Principles of Psychologists* to be "part of a larger pattern of grievances which had been cited on a national level." Michael had no doubts that behind every grievance lay a victimized family. He wondered why there should even be a contest to decide which of two parents should care for a child or have custody of a child after divorce. Divorce is between adults. Parents don't divorce their children.

He wondered, too, how many parent-child relationships had been destroyed over the years, how many of these devalued, demoralized parents had turned into Deadbeat Dads (or Moms) who fail to pay child support out of resentment toward their former spouse, how many of these children had been left to think they had been abandoned by their dad or their mom.

He wondered, too, if he and Ariel would end up as one more statistic.

9. A Matter of Principles

The task force report had to be polite. But I could read between the lines:

- *Family Division judges are indifferent to ethical considerations.*

- *Court-appointed psychologists ignore the ethical strictures of their profession.*

The judges demand psychologists do their work for them and the court appointees comply. At my family's July 7, 1988 custody hearing, Judge Wettick—in his very first statement to Dr. Singer —let it be known what was expected: "I want you to tell me what you think should be in a Court Order should a Court Order be entered today. That is my bottom line." Nobody was surprised when Judge Wettick's subsequent court order mirrored Dr. Singer's testimony—testimony based on data that was clearly gathered in violation of the Ethical Principles of Psychologists.

The task force stated that, "clinical psychology was not de-

signed nor clinical psychologists trained to assist in legal decisions nor interface with the courts." Moreover, "When practi-
tioners offer [custodial disposition] recommendations they should
be aware they are [in the opinion of many forensic psychologists]
overstepping their role as an expert." But who can prove that one
parent's love is more important to a child than the love of the
other? It is as ridiculous as attempting to demonstrate that either
the father's sperm or the woman's egg is more important in the
conception of a baby. It goes against nature. Even if court-appointed psychologists gather data in compliance with the Ethical
Principles of Psychologists (and the number of grievance filings reaching "epidemic proportions" suggests otherwise), by
giving recommendations they are demolishing families based on
nothing more than "hunches" which the task force unequivocally
declares "unethical."

Why do psychologists make such recommendations? Some
members of the psychological community are heavily dependent
on the Family Division for their livelihoods. Custody referrals
such as mine can be very profitable. Money-motivated psychologists realize if they don't give the judges recommendations they
won't be asked to participate in future court cases and that trans-
lates into a loss of income.

What's in it for the judges? Why do they ask the psychologists to violate the Ethical Principles? Because without psychologists' recommendations judges like Wettick and Kaplan
would be obligated to review the testimony and the history of the
cases before them, to read what is submitted by the attorneys, and
to be aware of current concepts in the field of psychology pertaining to custody matters—all before making an informed
ruling. If the judges gave even the slightest thought to what they
were doing they might figure out for themselves that children
need both parents—especially after divorce. Moreover, they
might realize the havoc they are wreaking on families and society.

—Michael L. Nieland, M.D.
Custody Reform Advocate

Sixteen months had passed since Michael filed the ethics complaint against Dr. Singer, yet it was still business as usual for the court-appointed psychologist, who was in no rush to apologize for his behavior in the Nieland case. Michael couldn't understand Singer's attitude. Did he believe he would be found not guilty of multiple violations of the *Ethical Principles*? Michael certainly assumed that would be the inevitable finding of a fully convened ethics panel.

Although Dr. Singer's alleged ethical violations involved issues (dual relationships; breaches of confidentiality, conflicts of interest) that are subtle, Michael had learned firsthand that these transgressions of the *Ethical Principles* were far from inconsequential. Michael's custody time with Ariel had been abbreviated for nearly two and a half years, and the consuming fight to retain his parental ties with Jennie, Nathaniel, and Ariel had cost him somewhere in the neighborhood of $200,000 (with the meter still running). For all of that, Michael blamed Dr. Singer, an ethically challenged judiciary, and the psychology profession. Nancy was certainly at fault, but in Michael's mind the entire system was more to blame because those in the judiciary as well as their appointees should have been wise to such behavior and eradicated rather than encouraged it.

It seems very clear that if reputable psychologists were appointed to the ethics panel, its members would have no choice but to condemn Dr. Singer for his actions. Nonetheless, Michael was willing to settle for an appropriate apology and withdraw the complaint so that he could get on with his life.

But the issue was out of Michael's hands now. When Van Cara turned the matter back to Michael and Singer in his November 11, 1990 letter he, in effect, put it in the domain of the attorneys. Michael had originally represented himself, but, because Singer had chosen to negotiate only through counsel, Michael had retained Paul Leventon in order to ensure a level playing field.

The attorneys met, for the first time, sixteen months after the filing of the ethics complaint. Afterward, Leventon informed Michael that William Ward, Dr. Singer's attorney, had suggested that Singer might be receptive to composing an apology to accompany the memorandum of agreement.

In the spirit of this good-faith negotiating Michael agreed to redefine the required content of the apology. On March 13, 1991, Leventon notified Mr. Ward (changes to the original apology request are in italics):

> 1. That he [Dr. Singer] realizes now with hindsight that his failure to follow rules of procedure in regard to matters of confidentiality at the very earliest stage of his involvement in this case led to bias against me [Michael] in his written and oral testimony to the Court, that he should not have spoken about me to individuals who had clear conflicts of interest, and that *but for his bias and breaches of confidentiality his recommendation to the Court could have been* not only that I be awarded forthwith equal shared legal and physical custody of my younger children, but without any further need for monitoring by the Court or by him or any other equivocation related to alleged deficiencies in my child-rearing abilities or aspersions on my parental competence concerning which he had no firsthand knowledge.
>
> 2. That he should not have taken any action, directly or indirectly, or played any role in changing, circumventing, undermining, or repudiating any provision of the Order of Court *which effectively* infringed upon my right to take my children to school, or reside with me as stipulated in the Order of Court; and that he regrets having done so.
>
> 3. That he retracts and repudiates the specific *statements* in his April 14, 1989 letter that I am "frightening" to any of my children, that I have a "severe personality disorder, psychopathology, a deeply rooted character disorder and personality problems," and that these *statements were inappropri-*

ately uttered, he profoundly regrets having made them, and apologizes to me and regrets any effect which they may have caused.

In my opinion, the above substantive changes satisfy the fundamental needs and concerns of both Drs. Nieland and Singer. From Michael's perspective, with the above language contained in a Memorandum of Understanding, the involvement of Dr. Singer is for all intents and purposes "neutralized" for use in any subsequent custody proceeding.

Michael explicitly agrees that a Nieland/Singer memorandum of understanding will not be employed by him "affirmatively" in any subsequent custody proceeding. . . .

The obvious flip side is that Michael needs to know that Dr. Singer's previously penned April 14, 1989 statements cannot continue to haunt him in any subsequent custody proceeding. . . . Should Nancy Nieland attempt to poison the Court by referencing Dr. Singer's April 14, 1989 letter, Michael then (and only then) would be entitled to introduce the Nieland/Singer Memorandum of Agreement in order to clear his name in the eyes of the Court.

I sincerely hope and trust that this letter serves as a catalyst to a final resolution of a very important . . . and percolating dispute.

Very truly yours,
Paul J. Leventon

The attorneys met again on March 14 . . . and again on March 18 . . . but no agreement was reached. Leventon remained optimistic. His client did not. As the months dragged on, it was becoming clearer to Michael that Dr. Singer had no intention of accepting an informal settlement that acknowledged his share of responsibility for the custody violations. In a March 19, 1991 letter to his attorney, Michael encapsulated his premonition: "Roland's main objective now is to save face and distribute his admissions of culpability in such a manner as to conceal it as much as possible."

Leventon didn't agree, and, although dubious, Michael gave his attorney the go-ahead to continue negotiating. He still believed, though, that Mr. Ward was stalling with the hope that his client's nemesis would disappear. Michael, however, was not going to fade away.

Michael especially wasn't enjoying the situation with Ariel. Nothing had changed. They had great times together, followed by no time together. Sylvia Mendelsohn continued to grimace appropriately when Michael related to her what was happening, but she seemed unable to do anything except schedule more appointments. Michael wondered if a breakthrough would ever occur. His entry in his daily log for April 17, 1991, didn't portray a breakthrough, but another go 'round with the same old problems:

I met Ariel at school at 2:30 and she requested we go to Wendy's for a plain cheeseburger, fries, and orange juice, plus cheese for her fries. . . . From there we went home. Nathaniel was waiting for us. . . . Ariel told me she had a piano lesson yesterday and went into the front room to play for me. I followed and listened. . . . Nathaniel asked to go to Frick Park (for his baseball game). . . . Ariel said she wanted to go to her mother's house, but she wouldn't tell me why. I offered her all kinds of incentives to stay with me. She said she would go with me to drop off Nathaniel, but then wanted me to take her to Nancy's house, which I did, arriving at 4:40. Nancy greeted her at the door. . . . I returned to Frick Park and stayed there until 7:15. In Nathaniel's B game he hit a triple with the bases loaded. The A game started around 6:45. He told me his mother knew he was playing in it [and had made arrangements for his transportation back to her house]. I told him I would deliver his stuff to Nancy's house. I drove directly to Nancy's house arriving at 7:22. I rang the bell and Dick and Nancy appeared in the doorway and I handed in Nathaniel's things. I asked to speak with Ariel because she left behind two sheets that looked as though they could be schoolwork. Nancy said, "I'll look for her" and closed the door on me. I waited a little while and then the door opened and Dick and Nancy reappeared with a young man, apparently a friend of Dick, who came out the door. I again asked Nancy where Ariel was. She said, "She's walking around the block with a friend." I said, "She's not supposed to be out with a friend during my custody time." . . . I pointed out to Nancy that I had arrived within my custody time to see Ariel and she should have been here. Then Dick said, "Well it's 7:30 now, get out of here, and he pushed open the glass door completely, came out, pushed me off the steps, and said again, "Get out of here" and pushed me again. I yelled, "Get your hands off me." He said, "If you don't get out of here I'll call the police." I started to walk away down his driveway and he yelled, ". . . get out of here." I said, "But I'm not on your property any more." He came up to me and put his face an inch from mine and said . . . , "You're an asshole." I waited a moment and then I asked him, "Are you sober?" He then backed off, uttered a sound sort of like disgust, and walked away. While all this was going on Nancy was standing on the lawn with a smirk on her face. When it was over she said to [her husband] loud enough for me to hear, "See, I told you he was psychotic." I then called to Nancy as I was getting into my car that she was violating the law by keeping Ariel from me because she wasn't supposed to be involved in "activities" during my time. . . . Then I drove off; I drove around the block looking for Ariel, but I couldn't find her and I went home.

The end result was two criminal complaints: (1) disorderly conduct and defiant trespass filed by Nancy against Michael; (2) harassment filed by Michael against Dick Fisher. District Justice Guido A. DeAngelis notified the parties that both cases would be heard on Wednesday, June 19.

In the meantime, Leventon had good news for his client. Mr. Ward, in an effort to reach agreement on an informal settlement concerning Michael's complaint against Dr. Singer, had indicated to Leventon that he had reworked the agreement so that it addressed Michael's concerns. Michael, somewhat surprised, was nevertheless elated. He and his counsel awaited the revised memorandum of agreement and accompanying apology. The agreement (but not the apology) subsequently arrived.

After reading the "final draft" Michael was anything but elated. Ward had implemented changes. The original memorandum of agreement—drawn up after an April 1, 1990 head-to-head meeting with Dr. Singer and Michael—contained eight provisions. The revamped final draft changes consisted essentially of an additional three provisions, all of which protected Singer from any further consequences. And still no apology. Not exactly the changes Michael had had in mind.

Michael, though, didn't want to waste time reworking the agreement once again. He told Leventon he would sign it, as he had agreed to sign the original agreement, provided Dr. Singer would simply write him the long-awaited apology incorporating the stipulations Leventon had mailed to Mr. Ward two months ago that asked Dr. Singer to admit he had made mistakes and take responsibility for his conduct. Leventon relayed the long-standing offer to Singer's attorney. Surprisingly, Mr. Ward seemed agreeable. He informed Leventon that Michael should soon expect an unsigned letter of apology from Dr. Singer which would then be signed along with the memorandum of agreement.

While there seemed to be some reason for optimism, Leventon filed against Singer in the Court of Common Pleas of Allegheny County a Praecipe for Writ of Summons in Civil Action. This filing insured that, should a settlement not be achieved and Michael decided to pursue a civil suit against Singer, the statute of limitations would not have expired.

While the wait for Dr. Singer's apology continued, Michael's June 19 court date with Nancy and Dick arrived. The morning went as Michael expected. Nancy and Dick Fisher were there with their attorney. Michael was there with his attorney. But there was no trial. The district justice stated one more time that "this properly belongs in the Family Division," he "wasn't going to deal with it," and "I don't ever want to see any of you in front of me again." That was fine with Michael; he had made his point once more: Shoving and offensive gestures would not be an effective means for the parties to communicate. If he and Nancy and Dick were going to interact with one another it would have to be in a civilized manner. Otherwise, there might be more wasted mornings at the courthouse for all concerned.

While Michael hoped this marked the end to his confrontations with Fisher, he remained greatly troubled by his custody schedule woes concerning Ariel. From his second run-in with Fisher to this court date, a span of sixteen days, Michael had documented in his daily log another eighteen violations of the custody schedule in regard to Ariel.

Michael couldn't take much more of this. If Dr. Mendelsohn couldn't establish full compliance with the custody schedule in the near future, he would have to initiate contempt proceedings against his former spouse a second time.

Should he feel forced to do so, Michael worried that the Family Division wouldn't be any more helpful than it was the first time and that the litigation would be just as expensive. This came at a time when he was still trying to recover financially from the changes in his medical practices—which entailed slowly rebuilding his relocated clinical practice and adjusting to the loss of Nancy's biopsies at the dermatopathology practice.

While Michael had been considering his limited options during the hours he had to wait around at his June 19 court appearance, Dr. Singer apparently had spent the day composing the apology that his attorney forwarded, unsigned, to Leventon.

In the draft letter, which was to supplement the memorandum of agreement that, according to Singer's counsel, he was ready to sign immediately, Singer stated that legal documents alone would do little to diminish the anxiety that he as well as Michael had endured in the case. He was ready to acknowledge further that his failure to follow strictly certain ethical principles had generated the conflict of interest detailed in the memorandum of agreement and that he might have obtained a biased sample of witnesses producing, thereby, a flawed conclusion. However, even if he disregarded the biased sample of witness reports and breaches of confidentiality, Singer still declined to speculate what his recommendation could have been.

Singer was prepared to admit that he should not have agreed to monitor the children's progress per the court order because it placed him in a dual relationship. If this apology letter were signed, he would also admit that it was inappropriate to state in an April 14, 1989 report to Leventon that he saw in Michael the symptomatology of a severe personality disorder.

This wouldn't do it. Singer had taken only a few bits and pieces from the language Paul Leventon had called for. Furthermore, the draft contained the kind of verbiage Michael had been objecting to for more than a year now: "I may have obtained a biased sample of witness reports which might have led to a flawed conclusion." (Why, Michael cannot understand, is it so hard to state that conclusions based on biased data are flawed?) In regard to Singer's infamous April 14 written observations concerning Michael, the psychologist apparently would admit that "it was inappropriate for me to make these statements to your lawyer," but Michael contends it was inappropriate for him to make them at all. Moreover, Singer had sent these inappropriate statements to Nancy's lawyer as well.

Possibly most irksome to Michael, however, was the phrase "the anxiety both of us have endured." Michael had been deprived of his daughter Ariel for years and perhaps forever. Dr. Singer, on the other hand, faced twenty hours of review and consultation with a psychologist whom he could select himself.

There would be no informal settlement. Michael informed his attorney that he would not accept this apology nor the proposed memorandum of agreement. Perhaps sensing Michael's despair, Leventon asked his client if he really wanted to pursue this matter any further. Michael was taken aback by the question. Did his own attorney not fully understand the subtle yet enormous impact Dr. Singer had had on Michael's family even though it had been Leventon who had urged Michael to get a second opinion from Dr. Stephen Schachner concerning Singer's handling of the Nieland case and, subsequently, it had been Leventon who supported Michael's filing an ethics complaint against the therapist?

Michael tossed and turned for the next few nights, grappling with why his lawyer would even question whether or not he wanted to go on. At last, Michael could hold back his thoughts and concerns no more. The weary father climbed out of bed and wrote a letter to his attorney, which concluded in part, "I'm not waiting any longer. This case screams out for justice and restitution and I'm sick of being diddled by Roland [Singer] and [his attorney]."

Leventon must have had no difficulty transmitting his client's position to Dr. Singer's attorney, as Mr. Ward responded that Singer's offer of settlement was withdrawn, although he was open to a new proposal from Michael, as long as it was received by June 28, 1991, 5:00 P.M. Ward informed Leventon that he would inform Dr. Van Cara that an informal resolution no longer seemed possible.

Mr. Ward shouldn't have bothered waiting by the telephone or the fax machine. There would be no counteroffer coming from Michael, who was appalled at Mr. Ward's assertions. How could anyone read the June 6, 1990 and March 13, 1991 letters, which suggested the wording for Singer's apology, and then state that Michael was "not acting in good faith," as Ward had? Michael and his attorney, from the very beginning, had let Singer know exactly and consistently what the content of the apology should include.

Leventon took Ward's accusations in stride. He was used to interminable negotiations. Michael was not. In medicine, doctors try to get patients well as rapidly as possible, but it seemed to Michael that in the field of law success is measured in terms of how long resolution of a dispute can be delayed. If enough time passed the plaintiff perhaps would lose interest or run out of money or become ill or die or have some other change in circumstance that would cause him or her to drop the case. Once again Michael surmised that the old adage "Justice delayed is Justice denied" must no longer be in vogue.

Michael wanted to make sure Dr. Van Cara realized that no informal agreement had been reached:

> ... Efforts to resolve amicably my Complaint against Dr. Singer have been unsuccessful. Mr. Ward and Mr. Leventon, my counsel, expended considerable time and effort on this matter to no avail and I wish to have my Complaint considered by the full Ethics Committee [of the Greater Pittsburgh Psychological Association]. . . .
>
> I will communicate also with the [Pennsylvania Psychological Association, American Psychological Association, and the State Bureau of Professional and Occupational Affairs] concerning the status of this case.

Michael needed to get away from it all. He was ready for some fun. This never-ending strife had put a serious crimp in his social life. After tending to his patients, his dermatopathology practice, and his children, he could barely find the time for his music or to arrange a date. Michael decided he must make some time for rest and recreation, so he attended a weekend antique show in Shadyside, not far from his office. Once there, he had no trouble unwinding in the tranquil atmosphere. He roamed around the various booths, admiring the many interesting and beautiful objects displayed.

But, when he approached the booth of an antiques dealer from Sewickley (a suburb about twenty miles northwest of Pittsburgh) he did a double-take. There, sitting on the shelf, were some French porcelain boxes that very much resembled those he had once owned. He walked closer. No wonder they looked familiar—they were his boxes, part of the collection that Nancy had claimed didn't exist when they exchanged property on her porch. Just to be sure, though he had no doubts, Michael flipped over the cards describing the objects (priced at $1,100, $850, and $750 respectively). The initials stared back at him: N. N.

The woman in the booth, who identified herself as Mrs. Bauer, the mother of the shop owner, explained that the three pieces were being sold on consignment for a Mrs. Nancy Nieland and that a fourth box had already been sold. Michael thanked her for the information, excused himself, and rushed outside to his car phone. He called his attorney and excitedly told him that he might not believe it, but Nancy had gone to Sewickley to peddle the phantom boxes and, by sheer luck, he had stumbled upon them in Shadyside. Leventon instructed Michael to return to the booth and explain to the proprietor that these objects were the subject of a personal property dispute and had to be withdrawn from sale immediately. Michael did so and Mrs. Bauer obliged. Her shop would retain possession of the three pieces until further instructions were received. Once again, it was time for the attorneys to talk. Paul Leventon contacted Nancy's lawyer, Harry Gruener, by letter:

> This weekend at the Pittsburgh Hunt Armory Antique show Michael found three collectibles which had been consigned by Nancy to Blair Bauer of Sewickley Traditions [a fourth box had sold earlier]; all four of which at the time of the personal property distribution Nancy claimed either did not exist or could not be located. . . .

So much for a calm weekend of getting away from it all! Michael spent the following weekend far away from Pittsburgh antique shows. He had convinced Ariel to go with him to visit Jennie in Philadelphia. (Nathaniel couldn't go because the trip conflicted with Little League baseball.)

Michael logged the trip's auspicious start:

> Sat., July 20: I went to Nancy's house at 2:30 to pick up Ariel, as I had indicated to Nancy by letter and conversation. Nancy answered the door, shut it in my face, and then after several minutes opened it again and Ariel came out carrying her suitcase. She announced she'd like to go straight to the airport which was my intention anyway. . . .

The trip got better. Ariel had her first Philly cheese steak, frolicked in the hotel swimming pool, and spent a day in Baltimore taking in a show at the National Aquarium. Michael, Ariel, and Jennie had great fun together. The three-day jaunt soon ended, however, and it was back to the real world.

The following weekend Michael took care of some unfinished business. He requested in letters to the Pennsylvania Psychological Association, the American Psychological Association, and the State Bureau of Professional and Occupational Affairs that they resume their independent investigations of Dr.

Roland Singer "because of the inability of the parties to achieve an amicable resolution of my complaint, and, in my opinion, in view of the wholesale violation of the *Ethical Principles of Psychologists* by Dr. Singer." Within days both associations and the state notified Michael that their investigations were underway.

Not much else was underway. As the third anniversary of the implementation of the original court order regarding custody approached, the schedule for Ariel remained as elusive as ever. And Nancy's attorney had yet to respond directly concerning the antique boxes. Leventon sent Gruener a wake-up call, reminding him that the personal property and custody issues would not just go away. Leventon implied that another contempt hearing could be initiated.

The correspondence got Gruener's attention. The attorneys met to discuss the custody situation. Neither one relished the thought of another contempt proceeding. Yet, clearly, something had to be done. Since the July 31, 1989 proposed order of court, Michael had documented a total of 251 alleged custody violations pertaining to Ariel and another six with Nathaniel, which amounted to an alleged violation of some sort for nearly every one of Michael's custody periods.

Who and/or what were to be believed? The attorneys decided it was time to turn to Dr. Sylvia Mendelsohn, in the words of Leventon's letter, to "discuss . . . the current status of the Nieland custody matter and to determine your views and opinion on the course of future custody counseling," and they requested an appointment.

Michael had little confidence left that Mendelsohn had the ability or willingness to improve the situation. She had been involved in the case for more than two years—longer than Singer had been—but Ariel had yet to be in compliance with the custody schedule. As distasteful as another petition for contempt once was to Michael, he now suggested to his attorney that it might well be the only recourse remaining, since the psychiatrist was reluctant to meet with the lawyers and seemingly unable to help Ariel deal with her mother.

The reply to the attorneys from Mendelsohn arrived on the same day Michael wrote to Leventon concerning the therapist's reluctance to grant the attorneys' wish to meet collectively.

Mendelsohn said she understood that the attorneys felt a meeting would be in the best interest of the Nielands, but that they had to realize that it was "impossible" for her "to wear the dual hats of custody evaluator and therapist." She also pointed out that she was as interested as they were in reducing the level of tension and conflict between the parents. However, she explained that given her previous experience with children whose parents are engaged in difficult custody disputes, she was concerned that such a meeting could backfire and "instead have a negative impact on her therapeutic work with Ariel and her parents."

Given those views, she concluded that she was unclear as to how she could be helpful if such a meeting took place. Before she would consider the proposal any further, she said it would be essential for her to learn more details about the exact purpose of the meeting and the specific information the attorneys would seek.

Michael found Dr. Mendelsohn's position more than a little confusing. She stated that "it is impossible to wear the dual hats of custody evaluator and therapist." Something didn't seem right. Michael put his recently acquired knowledge of ethical principles to use. He dug out his copy of the order of court stemming from the 1989 contempt proceedings and studied again Provisions 10 and 11:

10. The parties, through counsel, shall within twenty days select an appropriate professional for the evaluation and treatment, if so required, of Ariel and Nathaniel, particularly as to the issue of Ariel's expressed fear of her father.

11. The parties shall address the issue of the resumption of the overnight time periods originally included in the July 18, 1988 Order of Court with the selected professional with the goal of the resumption of overnight time.

It dawned on Michael what had happened. The court order was hopelessly flawed. Provisions 10 and 11 created all over again multiple roles of (1) evaluator (2) therapist and (3) monitor for an "appropriate professional" even though at the time of the contempt proceeding the master, Carol McCarthy (in her questioning of Dr. Stephen Schachner), had seemed to understand how the court could write an order avoiding dual (or triple) relationships.*

Questions abounded for Michael. Because Sylvia Mendelsohn had clearly stated in her letter to Paul that she must avoid "the dual hats of custody evaluator and therapist," why hadn't she objected two years earlier when she was selected as the "appropriate professional" given the dual hats requirement of the court order? Why, instead, had she agreed to provide evaluation and treatment (Provision 10) and to be essentially the monitor for the resumption of overnight time (Provision 11)?

Clearly, lightening had struck twice. The psychiatrist, per the court order, was wearing the dual hats she now claimed she had to avoid. This was just the kind of conflict of interest that Michael believed had made the Nieland family bait for financial and psychological exploitation: The longer Mendel-

---

*During those proceedings, McCarthy had specifically asked, in her examination of Schachner, "[I]f a Court-appointed specialist is asked to be in the role of evaluator, [then] there has to be someone else that does the treatment and the role [of evaluator] becomes coordinator of the treatment process?" Schachner agreed, further clarifying this by saying that the evaluator should monitor the treatment process "in the true sense of the word . . . regulating and watching."

sohn the evaluator refused to address "the issue of Ariel's expressed fear of her father," the longer Mendelsohn the therapist could provide Ariel (as well as Michael and Nancy) treatment. As the sessions (and billing) added up, Mendelsohn the monitor could pacify Michael by dangling before him resumption of Ariel's overnight time sometime in the future.

Michael was stunned. Again he wondered why Dr. Mendelsohn, suddenly so conversant with ethical considerations, hadn't rejected this obviously flawed court appointment from the beginning? Why, instead, had she apparently followed in the footsteps of Dr. Singer?

Michael wondered if any court-appointed mental health professional comprehended ethical strictures. The answer concerning one court appointee, Roland Singer, arrived in the mail from the Pennsylvania Psychological Association:

> . . . While the committee did not find evidence that you [Roland Singer] violated Principles 1, 2, or 3, it did find evidence that you violated Principles 5 (Preamble and Paragraph A), and 6 (Preamble and Paragraph A).
>
> First, with respect to the issue of Confidentiality, it is the Committee's opinion that . . . failure to follow these procedures concerning Confidentiality may well have led to a biased sample of witnesses who were partial to one party.
>
> Second, in terms of the issue of dual relationship, it is our opinion that when a psychologist accepts a Court appointment to perform a custody evaluation, his or her role must be limited to the evaluation. To accept a further Court Order to manage, monitor, mediate, or do family or individual psychotherapy in the case sets up a conflict of interest and automatically places the psychologist in a dual relationship, thereby risking impairing his or her clinical judgment, as well as casting doubt on the evaluator's fairness and impartiality. Although the Committee is aware that you may have been following the mistaken local practice of accepting

Court Orders to extend evaluations into case monitoring, . . . [this] in our judgment, does not exonerate you. . . .

The Committee unanimously decided to dispose of the above charges within the Committee and issue a Censure to you for violations of the above mentioned principles. For your information, a Censure may be issued when the Committee finds that "there has been deliberate or persistent behavior that could lead to substantial harm to the profession, although little harm may have actually occurred. Censure may also be applied to serious misconduct in which the psychologist shows an effort to modify behavior or strong potential for rehabilitation."

Because of the seriousness of this violation, the Committee also requires that you accept twenty-six hours of supervision. . . . We request that you provide us with the names and curricula vitae of up to three psychologists . . . (subject to our approval) who might provide you with such supervision. . . . [The supervisor will agree] that the emphasis of such supervision will be focused on the issue of avoiding dual relationships, particularly in child custody evaluations.

Thank you for your cooperation in this matter and I look forward to hearing from you soon.

Yours truly,
Vincent J. Rinella, J.D., M.A.
Case Manager,
Ethics and Standards Committee

[cc: Michael L. Nieland, M.D.]

Subsequently, Dr. Van Cara, Chair of the Committee on Ethical Standards and Professional Conduct (CESPC) of the Greater Pittsburgh Psychological Association (GPPA), reported to Michael that the "CESPC has been contacted by the Pennsylvania Psychological Association (PPA) [in regard to

the case, *Nieland* v. *Singer*]. The GPPA is in agreement with
the PPA's findings and their sanctions."

Then Michael received word from Betsy Ranslow, the Director of Investigations, Office of Ethics, for the American Psychological Association (APA), that "The APA Ethics Committee
found Dr. Singer in violation of General Principle 6 and Principle 6.a. of the *Ethical Principles of Psychologists* and, on that
basis, voted to Reprimand him and place him on Probation."

And finally, the State Bureau of Professional and Occupational Affairs informed Michael that Dr. Singer and his attorney had signed a consent agreement that acknowledged
he "unwittingly created Dual Relationships," and "agrees to
the placement of his [psychology] license on a six-month period of probation [that in part will include] twenty-six hours
of tutorial instruction [from an approved psychologist]."

All four adjudicative bodies that considered the ethics
complaint against Dr. Singer had found that the psychologist
had indeed violated the *Ethical Principles* of his profession.

At last, Michael had some sense of vindication. Clearly, he
was grateful. Still, he had some unanswered questions. If Dr.
Singer's performance, according to the PPA and GPPA, "may
well have led to a biased sample of witnesses," how could
they not conclude that Singer had violated the *Ethical Principle* entitled responsibility and competence? And, if they had
determined Singer's actions had "cast doubt on the Evaluator's fairness and impartiality," how could he not have violated the moral and legal standards principle? Moreover, had
the GPPA and the PPA really come to grips with Dr. Singer's
April 14, 1989 letter maligning Michael?

Despite these reservations, Michael, without a doubt, was
pleased he had exposed just a small part of the injustice he
and his family had faced within the Family Division. Would
it make a difference? He hoped so. He had great worries,
though, about what lay ahead for him and Ariel.

10. A Bottomless Pit

Although Dr. Singer had been severed from my family's case and censured for his role, his legacy lived on. More than two years after he had been removed from the case, violations of Ariel's custody schedule persisted. Now was the opportunity for Sylvia Mendelsohn to right this wrong, but she refused to speak with the attorneys or to communicate with the court.

It's not difficult to understand what happened. At the time Dr. Mendelsohn took over as the court-ordered mental health professional, I was distraught. My child was running away from me repeatedly. Mendelsohn offered me hope. She readily acknowledged that Ariel wasn't the least bit afraid of me, though she wouldn't tell that to the attorneys or to the judge. "It's more complicated than that," she insisted. I went along with her because I didn't think the court order gave me any other choice. Moreover, the therapist came highly recommended, she seemed competent, and—most importantly—she led me to believe that she would have Ariel in full compliance with the custody schedule in a reasonable period of time. That's all I wanted. I wasn't focusing then on ethical issues,

*so I accepted her approach. If compliance didn't occur, I fully ex-
pected Dr. Mendelsohn to so inform the court promptly—based on
the court order requiring an evaluation of Ariel's "fear"—that my
daughter was not the least bit afraid of me. However, she refused
to reveal to the attorneys or the court the basis for Ariel's behavior toward me and I believe the reason she didn't stems from
her conflicts of interest in the case.*

*Paul Leventon and I are not mental health professionals.
How could we have been expected to grasp what was happening
at the time? But, Sylvia Mendelsohn is a mental health professional who is supposed not only to understand but uphold the
ethical principles of her profession. Obviously, she understood
them as evidenced by her September 17, 1991 letter to my attorney, "I feel strongly that it is impossible to wear the dual hats
of custody evaluator and therapist." What I want to know is why
didn't she say that back in 1989—at the start of what would become $20,000 in fees?*

—Michael L. Nieland, M.D.
Billable Patient

Even with the censures and reprimands of Roland Singer,
Michael didn't feel much like a victor. Ariel still was in noncompliance with the custody schedule.

In the wake of the Singer decisions, Michael received a
follow-up telephone call from Dr. Van Cara, who passed
along an interesting bit of information that Michael sent to
Paul Leventon: "Art Van Cara told me that [yet another
court-appointed psychologist], Neil Rosenblum, had been
penalized with two years probation and fined $3,500 for [eth-
ical violations in custody cases] . . . and he had been one of
Judge Kaplan's favorite psychologists. . . ." Dr. Van Cara's remarks further reinforced Michael's increasing conviction that
the Family Division was mired in ethical squalor.

Michael learned some other very interesting facts about
the Family Division during a conversation with one of his

dermatology patients, a journalist. During her office visit they talked about raising children and she mentioned to him that the *Pittsburgh Press* had given a detailed report on the workings of the Family Division a couple of years earlier. Michael didn't recall reading or hearing about the story so she said she would bring him a copy of the article* at her next appointment. When Michael read it later he jotted down several comments in the margins for Leventon:

> Domestic relations officers settle about 75 percent of the cases, hearing officers about 20 percent and judges the remaining five percent, the often bitter and complex custody and property disputes.

It didn't sound as though the judges were overworked if they were handling only 5 percent of the cases and letting the likes of Singer and Rosenblum do most of the adjudicating.

> Frustrated in some way by the court system, some area residents have joined [organizations] that want to change or abolish the system. One such group, Access to Justice, recently has been seeking members in advertisements which ask:
> "VIOLATED/ABUSED—By Family Division courts?" More visible than the ads, though still small, are periodic demonstrations at the City-County Building.
> "What we hope to do is correct the injustices down at the family court. They are so blatant at violating people's rights," says Doug Martin, a 37-year-old chemist from Ingram who started Access to Justice. He says problems include "not being able to have a hearing in a timely fashion, deprival of due process, selectively hearing testimony."

---

*Lawrence Walsh and Bob Batz Jr., "Family Division Courts Are a War Zone with No Winners," *Pittsburgh Press*, October 29, 1989.

This sounded familiar.

> "There are a lot of horror stories," says James Clonan Jr., 41, of the North Side, who last year founded a local chapter of Fathers United for Equal Rights after becoming frustrated while seeking visitation and custody of his three children. He says the 50-member group's biggest complaint is that the system is biased against men. Common problems, he says, include unfair amounts of child support and lack of enforcement of visitation and custody orders.

This sounded even more familiar.

> Judge R. Stanton Wettick [who leads the division] and his colleagues deny the bias charge and say support is determined by Division guidelines which Pennsylvania has recently adopted. They also say fathers get primary custody about half the time—"if they persevere," Judge Gene Strassburger says. But the division doesn't keep statistics that would show that.

Persevere? Michael asked in his margin notes. How much longer do *I* have to "persevere," Judge Strassburger? And why, if the system were fair, should I have to "persevere" at all? Why shouldn't all loving, competent parents share equally in the custody of their children? Why should I be exploited at all by your court and its appointees?

The *Pittsburgh Press* article goes on to reveal several other facts concerning the operation of the Family Division as of 1988:

- recipient of more than $5 million in annual funding;

- comprised of 148 employees plus four judges;

- collected in 1988 more than $65 million in child support (up $40 million since 1980).

Evidently, the real thrust of the Family Division is not to keep parents and children together after divorce, but to support a very large industry devoted to creating misery. The justification for employing 148 individuals, not including countless attorneys and court-appointed professionals, seems to be to create and then collect vast amounts of money. What a cold-hearted business! . . .

Needless to say, Michael found the article most distressing. The Family Division's sole barometer for success seemed to be the amount of child support collected. Now Michael had a better understanding why he had been paying child support to a former spouse who earned substantially more income than he did while, at the same time, he had been tormented trying to maintain his ties to his children.

That particular month served as the latest example. Michael made his child support payment on time, as usual, despite the never-ending defiance of the court-ordered custody schedule. Just two days after receiving notification of Dr. Singer's censure, Michael made the following entry in his log:

> Fri., Sept. 27, 1991: I got Nathaniel up. . . . While he was getting dressed he said to me, "Did Ariel stay here last night?" I said, no and he responded, "She's using you." I asked what he meant and he explained that I was always getting her things and she didn't deserve them, that she never stays with me. I asked him if he understood why and he said that "Mom told Ariel if she doesn't want to stay with you she doesn't have to."

At least the news seemed better for Michael regarding the French porcelain boxes. Harry Gruener, in an apparent face-saving gesture for Nancy, had informed Paul Leventon that Nancy was willing to relinquish her claim to the three wayward boxes if Michael agreed to return *any* three *items* he received at the property settlement. Michael, weary of all the battles, told his attorney to accept the offer.

As for the real problem, noncompliance with Ariel's custody schedule and Dr. Mendelsohn's refusal to communicate with the attorneys, Michael was close to initiating a second petition for contempt. Once again, the attorneys put their heads together to determine if there were any other options. They decided to make another appeal to Mendelsohn. This time Gruener would compose the letter. Maybe he would have better luck than Leventon.

Gruener began by reminding Mendelsohn that he and Leventon were mindful of her position as "therapist." Indeed, he pointed out, the attorneys "were instrumental in her selection to function in that capacity." Gruener also gave his assurance that he and Leventon were respectful of her requirement that she not become involved in the adversary proceeding and do anything that would compromise her relationship with Ariel.

Having said that, Gruener reminded Mendelsohn that this case came to her after litigation that was expensive, time consuming, and seemingly unproductive. He went on to say that he and Leventon agreed that they were at a profound disadvantage in that they had not been part of Mendelsohn's work with the Nielands during the preceeding months.

In summary, Gruener stated that he believed Mendelsohn's suggestions, observations, and recommendations might be quite helpful at this juncture. The meeting, Gruener reiterated, was not designed to be adversarial. If it were, he pointed out, he and Leventon would not be writing to her together.

Therefore, concluded Gruener, he and Leventon believed Mendelsohn to be an important resource in the quest for an amicable resolution and both attorneys hoped that with her help the rancor between their clients might be reduced and, as a result, further litigation in this case would be avoided.

Gruener signed the letter and sent it to Mendelsohn with a copy to Leventon.

Harry's recapitulation of how Dr. Mendelsohn became involved in the case didn't seem quite accurate to Michael. Harry did remind her that the attorneys were instrumental in her selection as therapist. But the court order actually read: "The parties, through counsel, shall . . . select an appropriate professional for the *evaluation* and treatment, *if so required* . . ." (emphasis added).

Why hadn't Harry Gruener asked about the evaluation? Michael didn't ask Paul Leventon to object to the letter's contents, though, in the hope that Gruener's appeal would convince Mendelsohn to speak to the attorneys.

At Michael's next meeting with Dr. Mendelsohn, he implored the psychiatrist to help put an end to Nancy's subtle ongoing undermining. The therapist seemed receptive to Michael's plea. She would talk, but not with the attorneys. She wanted to meet with Nancy and Michael together in her office. Desperate for a resolution to his three years of anguish over Ariel, Michael accepted Dr. Mendelsohn's offer.

So did Nancy. On October 25 the meeting took place. Michael recorded his account of the meeting immediately after it concluded:

Notes from Meeting with
Dr. Mendelsohn, Nancy & [Michael]

1. Sylvia mentioned she told Ariel she was going to meet with us and asked Ariel if she could share what she had said with her parents. Ariel said absolutely not. Sylvia said this was very unusual for a child of her age [nine].

2. Sylvia . . . raised the issue of communication in general and I believe I spoke first concerning the terrible problems I had communicating with Nancy and the difficulties it raised for me and the children. . . . Nancy alleged all

kinds of issues about difficulties communicating with me.
. . . She bragged to Sylvia that she had been able to eliminate [al]most all interactions with me, leaving bags at my
side door, etc. I pointed out that we would have to communicate for the next fifteen years or more and that we had
had hundreds of peaceful interactions. Problems arose only
due to lack of communication.

2b. Sylvia asked both of us if we had noticed any
changes, improvements in Ariel's behavior. Nancy said she
had seen much improvement—less moodiness, etc. I responded that I never had any difficulties with Ariel four
years ago or now—only that [her stays with me were not]
in compliance with the two standing court orders.

3. I stated that the main issue for me was compliance
with the law, that there are two standing Court Orders [re-
garding custody] that have to be complied with, that I have
been patient and tolerant, that I have given Nancy more
rope than any one would have a right to expect, . . . that, if
I had to, I would go back to court.

4. Sylvia raised the possibility of joint sessions with her
to improve communication, etc. Nancy was initially unen-
thusiastic. I responded that I was agreeable to any sessions
to improve communication. . . . Nancy talked about [what
she thought] was in Ariel's best interest and that Sylvia was
to *monitor* Ariel's progress [regarding her "fear" of me], etc.
I responded that the fear issue was crap, that Ariel had
never been afraid of me, that she was caught in a terrible
vice because of Nancy's unrelenting [hatred] toward
me. . . . Sylvia was to find out if Ariel "feared" me and that,
if she did, she was to treat it and get her to spend time with
me. . . . This other stuff was smoke-screen. I pointed out
that we should not meet with Sylvia, but another professional, because of the risk of confusing Sylvia's role. . . .
Nancy flatly refused to meet with any other professional.

At the end Nancy started complaining that I had told the
children she "might go to jail" and that I told ten or eleven

people she "ought to be in jail," etc. I said the children ask me repeatedly if I hate their mother and I always respond no. They always reply, "Well, she sure hates you." ...

The meeting seemed to accomplish little and certainly didn't ease Michael's desperation. He was more concerned than ever that he and Ariel would never have the opportunity to have a normal, loving relationship.

While Mendelsohn contemplated her next step, Michael listed his concerns in a letter to his attorney. He related to Leventon his frustration with Mendelsohn and explained how Mendelsohn repeatedly told him that she couldn't change Nancy's behavior even if it was in violation of the court order. He recounted that Mendelsohn instead kept saying she was trying to strengthen Ariel's ability to withstand Nancy's pressure and that the psychiatrist hoped to convince Nancy that her behavior would eventually injure her relationship with Ariel.

In regard to his own behavior, Michael informed Leventon that the psychiatrist continually reassured him that he shouldn't be doing anything differently. He was a capable, loving father. Moreover, Michael stressed that, according to Mendelsohn, Ariel had never shown any sign that she had any fear of her father.

By the letter's end Michael indicated his exasperation: "Sylvia won't confront Nancy any more than Roland [Singer] would. Now Mendelsohn's rationalization for avoiding confrontation or telling the truth is that she doesn't want anyone to get mad at her and disrupt her therapeutic relationship with Ariel! What the hell am I suppose to do now?"

From the frustration apparent in Michael's letter, a second petition for contempt was imminent. Or so it must have seemed to Leventon—until he received his next letter from Michael, written the very next day, November, 6, 1991:

I met with Sylvia Mendelsohn this morning. In the last several days Dr. Mendelsohn also met with Nancy.

Dr. Mendelsohn told me that she had spoken with
Nancy concerning compliance with the Order of Court and
that she insists that starting immediately (tomorrow,
Thursday) Ariel comply with the overnights on alternate
Thursdays and by the weekend of January 24–26 fully
comply with the weekend schedule of overnights.

Dr. Mendelsohn strongly reiterated that she has never
told Nancy that Nancy did not have to comply with the
stipulation in the last Court Order that Ariel be returned to
my custody should she return to Nancy's house while she
was supposed to remain in my custody.

Dr. Mendelsohn also stated that in the event of noncompliance she would be willing to meet with the attorneys to affirm the above.

Could it be? Just like that—it was over? Apparently so.
Whatever Dr. Mendelsohn had said to Nancy worked. As of
November 6, 1991, approximately four years after Dr. Singer
had been appointed to do a custody evaluation, the entries in
Michael's log in regard to Ariel go into great detail about
games of tag, reading stories, and going to movies, but make
no mention whatsoever of any noncompliance with the custody schedule.

Michael was elated. And Ariel clearly seemed happy, too.
The only issue Michael didn't understand was why Mendelsohn had waited two years before she insisted that Nancy
follow the custody schedule. However, he didn't let that
issue ruin this new chapter in his relationship with his little
girl. Michael could hardly wait until the New Year when
Ariel commenced her weekend overnight stays.

The conclusion of 1991 did have a few kinks for Michael,
though. The porcelain box situation had yet to be resolved.
Nancy and/or her attorney hadn't bothered to address the

issue despite correspondence from Leventon to Gruener. And, on a professional note, Michael had a new crisis. The relocation of his downtown clinical practice to Shadyside over the past year had gone smoothly enough, but now an apparent rift had occurred in Michael's dermatopathology practice with Alan Silverman. The troubling situation arose when Michael, during a routine slide interpretation, requested a photocopy of a patient's original biopsy report from the patient's doctor. After an unusual delay, the photocopy finally arrived and Michael couldn't help but notice the letterhead—which bore the name of a new laboratory headed by Dr. Silverman!

Michael was incredulous that Dr. Silverman had established his own dermatopathology practice (in the same building, no less, as Nancy's clinical practice). It had long been hinted that he might start his own skin pathology practice for Nancy's biopsy specimens to offset the drop in income resulting from Nancy no longer sending her biopsies to his and Michael's laboratory. Michael never thought Silverman would follow through, though, in consideration of their amicable working relationship for more than fourteen years and, if nothing else, because it would seem to violate the spirit of an agreement the two had signed years earlier: *"Neither of the individual parties shall, without the written consent of the Corporation, engage in the practice of dermal pathology except on behalf of the Corporation."*

Michael felt totally betrayed by Silverman and told him so. His colleague didn't deny anything. He didn't have much of a defense.

After lengthy discussions between the doctors and then their attorneys, they concluded it was time to dissolve their partnership. Michael would purchase Silverman's shares in the Pittsburgh Skin Pathology Laboratory along with his half of their Shadyside office building (where Michael would continue both of his medical practices). It was not the friendliest of departures, as evidenced by Silverman's parting words: "And I hear your kids hate you, too." Michael didn't have any doubts as to where that had originated. Would the repercussions from the divorce ever end?

With the fifth New Year's Eve since the breakup of the Nielands at hand, attorney Leventon sent to Harry Gruener a note concerning the current state of affairs:

December 31, 1991

Dear Harry:

As another year passes and a number of matters remain unresolved, I feel compelled to bring to your attention . . .

1. That despite innumerable requests, Nancy has yet to effectuate the agreed-to transfer of the three French porcelain boxes. . . .

2. Michael still anxiously awaits receipt of the numerous "documents," . . . which Nancy has promised to transmit intact [per the] parties' Marriage Settlement Agreement. . . .

Another reminder that Dr. Mendelsohn has insisted that the existing Custody Order be implemented and strictly complied with in all respects by January 1992. It was upon this apparent agreement among the three of them (Sylvia, Nancy, and Michael) that no additional enforcement proceedings were initiated.

Wishing you and your family a happy and a healthy New Year. . . .

Very truly yours,
Paul

One month later, the letter drew a response from Nancy, who evidently instructed her attorney to pass it along to Michael's counsel. In Nancy's correspondence, dated January 31, 1992, she said she wanted to confirm that she did not possess any of the documents to which Michael referred. She stated that she had turned over to him all the papers he asked for, "except for one or two letters which Jennie found later and gave to him."

Regarding the custody order, Nancy wrote that Mendelsohn had seen Ariel on a weekly basis for more than two years and that Mendelsohn had also talked to Michael and her on a regular basis. Nancy commented further that Ariel's "visitation" with Michael had proceeded exactly as outlined by Mendelsohn.

As for the porcelain boxes which Michael requested, Nancy claimed that they had been inadvertently stored with Brita's wedding gifts, and, besides, Michael had taken several valuable antique jugs in exchange for those porcelain boxes. She offered, however, to exchange the boxes for three antique jugs which, she added, were in perfect condition when they were handed to him and would be subject to her inspection prior to her agreeing to the exchange. She concluded by instructing her attorney to let her know about the timing of any exchange.

Aside from the inevitable ugly encounters with Nancy during exchanges of the children (e.g., her repeatedly slamming the front door in his face and loudly locking the deadbolt while he waited for the children on her porch), everything proceeded as scheduled. Ariel had become very comfortable in her home on Inverness Avenue with her dad, her Inverness kitty, Ali, and her brother (though, like most preteen brothers and sisters, they were constantly at odds). The sudden departures had ended, but Michael continued to be very wary of ever reprimanding Ariel, or Nathaniel for that matter. He knew from past experiences that they would run to Nancy's house and most assuredly she would make Michael the bad guy. Nonetheless, Michael was thrilled to have his family together at last.

It appeared as if Leventon's overflowing Nieland file might be capped once the porcelain box dispute was resolved, although there was still no resolution in sight on this less-than-critical issue. Michael wanted to know what had happened to Nancy's original proposal to exchange the boxes for any three *items*? He reminded Leventon also that, contrary to Nancy's recollection that he had taken several valuable antique jugs in exchange for the porcelain boxes, there was nothing left of comparable value to take that day on the porch.

Leventon tried repeatedly to contact Gruener by telephone in order to pass along Michael's concerns. Gruener must have been very busy because he didn't return any of the telephone calls. Leventon resorted to sending him a note, dated February 11, stating "I have been unsuccessful in my attempts to reach you by phone in the past few weeks to remind you that the [box] exchange has yet to be completed. . . . *Please* . . . let me know when the appropriate exchange can take place."

Apparently, Gruener had lost his "zeal to wrangle" on this particular issue. He had delegated the negotiations to one of his legal assistants, who replied to Leventon's note, nearly two months later, with new and unanticipated (and somewhat strange) demands:

April 7, 1992

Dear Mr. Leventon:
    . . . I am enclosing a list of the items that . . . we are expecting in exchange for the three French porcelain boxes:
    1. One men's Polo Coat—coat belongs to the parties' daughter;
    2. One Chamberlin Whooster [sic] Cottage Jug;
    3. One Cottage Jug
    4. Capi-DiMonti [sic] Box
    5. Telephone answering machine with telephone (purchased from The Sharper Image by daughter).

Please contact me once you have received the appropriate items from Mr. [*sic*] Nieland to conclude the exchange. . . .

Very truly yours,
Rosemary A. Stein
Legal Assistant

Leventon forwarded the correspondence to Michael along with a note reading, "Why am I starting to feel like 'the spy who came in from the cold'?" After discussing the matter further with Michael, he sent a response to Gruener's legal assistant explaining that, although the coat and answering machine were not among the original items to be divided, Michael would return them.

> . . . Regarding the "three for three" other items, as you recall, the Capo-DiMonte box is apparently acceptable to Nancy.
>
> However, the second item you describe [a Chamberlains Worcester cottage jug] *does not exist*. Michael advises that he hasn't the vaguest idea what object Nancy is specifically referring to. . . .
>
> Finally, it is my recollection that when Harry and I discussed the "three for three personal property exchange" that the three items which Michael was to exchange were to be any three which he received inasmuch as the three boxes which he is to receive were originally to have been made available to him in the first instance. . . .
>
> Please, let's get this matter behind us.

Leventon concluded with another request that the rest of Michael's papers and files be returned.

Nine days later (on April 30, 1992) Rosemary Stein informed Michael's attorney by mail that "Dr. Nancy Nieland is in Florida until May 5, 1992. Upon her return, I will contact her and try to have this matter finally resolved."

Even though there seemed to be a lack of cooperation in

settling this property issue, adherence to the custody schedule continued to go remarkably well. Ariel had adapted very well to the complete resumption of overnights. She was sharing her schoolwork with Michael and she even surprised him one day with a valuable present—the long-lost antique key that operated the fountain in Michael's home. (Michael was to have received the key during the ill-fated property exchange, but it wasn't among the items Nancy had placed in the garbage bag or among the items that Jennie had discovered later.) Ariel came across the key in her mother's house. Michael was touched by what he perceived as his little girl's bravery in bringing it to him, hidden in her schoolbag.

Although the custody schedule was working now, there remained one problem, the tension that permeated the children's transitions from one home to the other. For everyone's sake, it needed to be lessened. Michael had an idea. He and his attorney concurred that a petition to modify custody should be filed. Paul Leventon did so on May 20.

Currently, Michael had custody of Nathaniel and Ariel at the following times as ordered by the court:

Weeks One & Three: Mon. and Wed. after school until 7:30 P.M.

Fri. after school until Sunday at 5:00 P.M.

Weeks Two & Four: Tues. after school until 7:30 P.M.

Thurs. after school until Friday morning when school begins.

Michael's petition stated: "The best interest of the children will be served by the Court modifying the initial Order so that Petitioner [Michael] does not have to return the children on school nights [Monday, Wednesday, and Sunday of weeks 1 & 3; Tuesday of weeks 2 & 4]."

The custody modification would effectively eliminate almost all of the painful interactions between Nancy and Michael during the transfer of the children by permitting Nathaniel and Ariel to spend the night at Michael's home, go to school the next day, and return at the end of the school day to Nancy's home.

The proposal made sense to Michael, but if Nancy hadn't as yet relinquished control of the three porcelain boxes Michael had discovered a year ago, what was the likelihood that she would agree to an inconsequential reduction of her time with the children? It was time for another discussion between the attorneys, after which Leventon related to Michael that Gruener had indicated to him (no great surprise) that Nancy would not support Michael's suggested changes in the custody schedule.

Both attorneys believed that the court appearance to discuss the petition to modify custody scheduled for July 22, 1992, would not result in any type of agreement, so Michael suggested to his lawyer that Dr. Mendelsohn speak with the domestic relations Officer (DRO), the person who would normally decide the modification issue. Leventon agreed. At Michael's next scheduled appointment with the psychiatrist, on June 15, he made his bid. He told her he was fully aware of her prior resistance to converse with anyone about the case, but he asked her only to tell the DRO what she had told him repeatedly during his two and a half years of counseling sessions—namely, that Ariel had never been afraid of him and that they had a normal, loving relationship. Since Dr. Mendelsohn seemed as reluctant as ever about revealing her evaluation, Michael pointed out that she wouldn't have to divulge any confidential information concerning Ariel or Nancy.

Michael's latest plea for Dr. Mendelsohn's cooperation fell on deaf ears. She declined to speak to a DRO, saying: "I just can't get involved in a custody dispute." Needless to say, Michael was very disappointed.

Just when he had given up on Dr. Mendelsohn's participation, he received some startling news from Leventon (based on information received from Gruener):

Dr. Mendelsohn was willing to speak to a court-approved mental health professional regarding the Nieland case. Both attorneys agreed with the suggestion, and would petition Judge Kaplan to appoint such a professional and then to make a ruling on the petition to modify custody based on that professional's recommendation.

Michael was confused. Why was the psychiatrist suddenly receptive to talking about the case with a court-appointed mental health professional, but still unwilling to speak directly to the attorneys, to a DRO, or to a judge? He wondered if it was because she wouldn't have to testify personally and wouldn't be subjected to cross-examination by the attorneys. Moreover, how did this *purported* change of position come about? Leventon had never spoken with Dr. Mendelsohn. Had Gruener spoken with her directly or was Mendelsohn's change of heart conveyed through Nancy? Why hadn't Mendelsohn discussed any of this with Michael?

Michael expressed these concerns to his attorney and suggested that he might be more comfortable going ahead with the July 22 hearing (the one both attornies believed would most likely be a waste of time) and sending a subpoena to Mendelsohn. That wasn't likely to be successful, Paul reminded his client, because Mendelsohn was unwilling to make a recommendation to the court directly. Michael would defer to his attorney's judgment. Besides, as long as the psychiatrist spoke the truth, what could go wrong? The court would finally learn what he had encountered in the post-Singer era. After considering the abrupt turn of events in that context, Michael remained hopeful. He permitted Leventon to pursue this new course of action involving a court-appointed mental health professional.

Hence, on June 25, Harry Gruener composed and submitted to Judge Kaplan at motions* and in Paul Leventon's presence a consent agreement entitled "Motion to Appoint Expert Mental Health Witness" (bearing both attorneys' signatures) that asked the court to "appoint a mental health professional to evaluate the situation, contact Dr. Mendelsohn, and to submit a recommendation to the court. By doing so, it is anticipated that litigation can be avoided. Both parties desire said appointment and are willing to share the cost."

Judge Kaplan immediately responded with a consent order that states:

> . . . On the pending matter of Defendant, Michael L. Nieland's Petition to Modify Custody, *Barbara Cymerman, Esq.*† is hereby appointed to confer with Dr. Sylvia Mendelsohn—and the parties' children, if necessary—within thirty days regarding recommendations on Defendant's *or Plaintiff's*† pending Petition to Modify custody and thereafter issue a report to the Court. . . . Costs of said evaluator shall be paid equally by the parties. . . . A conciliation before this member of the Court is scheduled for the 10th day of August 1992. (Disregard the Court's May 18, 1992 Order wherein a Conference/Hearing was scheduled for July 22, 1992.)
>
> BY THE COURT:
> Lawrence W. Kaplan

Michael was astonished to learn from his lawyer later that day that Judge Kaplan had appointed an attorney in response to their consent agreement calling for a mental health

---

*"Motions" refer to a procedure in a courtroom before a judge where attorneys present limited procedural or substantive questions for on-the-spot adjudication of many cases.

†handwritten in by the judge.

professional. Apparently, Cymerman's qualification for the role of mental health professional was that at the time the motion was presented she happened to be sitting in the first row of Judge Kaplan's courtroom, waiting her turn on another case. To the best of anyone's knowledge, she had no special training of any type as a psychologist or psychiatrist nor any degree(s) in lay, marriage, or pastoral counseling which would have given at least some credibility to her selection as a mental health professional.

The appointment made no sense to Michael whatsoever, but what could he do?

Nearly a week after Judge Kaplan's order, Michael had a brief conversation with Dr. Mendelsohn just prior to a scheduled visit for Ariel. She told him that Nancy had already informed her about Barbara Cymerman's appointment. The psychiatrist indicated that she had no hesitations or reservations about speaking with "Mental Health Professional" Cymerman. However, she explained that she would need Michael's written consent. He complied immediately (on her stationery). After all, the court had left him with no other choice and, anyway, as long as Mendelsohn told the truth her remarks would surely be helpful to Michael. And his encounter with the psychiatrist was so brief that Michael never had the opportunity to query her about her turnabout in terms of speaking to anyone about the case.

Michael had his scheduled meeting with Cymerman on July 6. At its conclusion he was confident he had stated clearly and concisely why the children would benefit from the slight modification he had proposed in the custody schedule. Cymerman seemed to understand his position, although Michael realized she still had to meet with Nancy, Mendelsohn, and, possibly, the children.

The day after Michael's session with Cymerman, his attorney received a letter from Harry Gruener. The correspondence explained why at motions on June 25 Gruener had asked Judge Kaplan to change the consent order to "Defendant's *or Plaintiff's* pending petition" (emphasis added to signify Gruener's change). Nancy, not to be outdone, had decided to file her own petition that contained some different ideas as to how the custody schedule should be modified. The following was submitted to the court by Harry Gruener on Nancy's behalf:

PETITION TO MODIFY CUSTODY

The July 18, 1988 Custody Order has been totally in place since January 1, 1992, including the overnight time. . . . Since the full implementation . . . under the auspices of Dr. Sylvia Mendelsohn, it has become apparent that a modification of the previous Order is in the best interest of the children. Petitioner [Nancy Nieland] believes and therefore avers that the best interest of the children would be served by modifying the time the children are in the physical custody of the natural father as follows:

a. Every other weekend from Friday at 3:00 P.M. or after school during the school year until Sunday at 5:00 P.M. when the children will be picked up by the Petitioner;

b. On the off weeks, after school on Thursday until 7:30 P.M. when the children will be picked up by the Petitioner.

The above modification is in the best interest of the children as the present schedule:

a. Is too disruptive and confusing to the children;

b. Is detrimental and counterproductive to their academic development during the school year;

c. Is a schedule lacking stability and continuity;

d. Does not work as the parents are unable to cooperate regarding the necessary changes in the schedule; and

e. Does not work in the [best interest of the children] during the school year as there is no structure in the time that they spend with the natural father and no limits are set while they are in his custody.

In other words, Nancy had seen an opportunity to further reduce Michael's time with the children, saying that the present schedule was "disruptive, detrimental, and unstable" because "the parents" were "unable to cooperate"—even though she was totally responsible, in Michael's view, for the lack of cooperation!

By now, Michael had learned to expect just about anything from Nancy. But—to him—this was beyond belief. Michael had simply asked for a few more overnights on evenings the children were already with him. Nancy's petition, on the other hand, would significantly reduce the time Nathaniel and Ariel would spend with their father.

Michael was depressed. Would the hostility ever end? This time Jennie wouldn't be able to call and cheer him up. She was studying in Italy during the summer.

Although it was too costly for Jennie to telephone her dad very often, she apparently had an urge to write him a long letter dated, appropriately enough, July 7, 1992 (the same day Gruener wrote to Leventon about Nancy's petition). Michael found the final paragraphs of the eight-page letter very therapeutic. Jennie wrote that she hoped her dad would stop worrying so much about everything and she acknowledged that certain people were trying to make his life miserable, but she pleaded with him not to forget how much she, Ariel, and Nathaniel loved him. Jennie described her family as a "great, close, happy, confident, smart foursome" and admitted that none of them was blind to the lunacy going on around them or the malicious acts directed at them by certain people. Don't worry, she repeated to her dad, his three children would stick together always in support of him.

Michael tried to take his daughter's advice as he anxiously awaited Barbara Cymerman's custody report. In the meantime, he received word from his attorney on the status of the other lingering matter—the wandering boxes:

Nancy would only exchange the three boxes for a white Enoch-Pratt jug and large, authentic Cottage jug, or, Nancy's other suggestion was for Michael to keep what he had and she would keep what she had and the matter would be resolved.

Michael had no idea what Nancy was demanding this time. They had never owned a "white Enoch-Pratt jug." For a moment, he thought that maybe he should advise Leventon to forget about the whole thing. (His legal bills were going to amount to more than the value of the boxes.) But he decided the matter must be pursued on principle, so he responded to his lawyer's query by reiterating that Nancy's actions had violated the signed property settlement and that she couldn't be allowed to get away with it. It was back to the negotiating table.

The moment of truth in regard to Barbara Cymerman finally arrived. Michael received from her an itemized invoice for services rendered, not as a mental health professional but rather as a domestic/intermediary for children (whatever that is). After 27.20 hours at $125 per hour, the total fee was $3,400, and Michael's share was $1,700.

Included among the itemized listings was ".20 hour telephone call to Michael Nieland—arranged to meet with him in my office." Or, in plain English, $25 for scheduling an appointment. Was she kidding? Apparently not.

Upon receipt of payment she sent her completed report to the attorneys. She didn't support either Michael's or Nancy's petition. Michael was disheartened by her recommendations and the report's overall tone—especially in regard to the comments and perceptions attributed to Sylvia Mendelsohn. Needless to say, at Michael's next scheduled visit with the psychiatrist he arrived with the report in hand so they could review it together.

REPORT ON NATHANIEL NIELAND AND ARIEL NIELAND

By: Barbara G. Cymerman, Esquire
Date: July 30, 1992

In her report, Barbara Cymerman first focused on summarizing the issue before her, namely that Michael was seeking to include overnight visits on the eight school nights a month that Nathaniel, eleven, and Ariel, ten, were in his custody. Nancy, on the other hand, had requested Michael's custody time with the children be reduced to two weekends a month, from Friday after school until Sunday at 5:00 P.M. and two Thursdays a month, from after school until 7:30 P.M.

Then, Cymerman described the individual sessions she had had with the Nieland family and Mendelsohn. When Michael and Mendelsohn went through those portions together, Michael made note of the psychiatrist's responses:

Conference with Dr. Sylvia Mendelsohn, Ariel's Therapist

I met with Dr. Mendelsohn . . . for approximately 1½ hours regarding this matter. Prior to our meeting, Dr. Mendelsohn had received a letter from mother indicating her cross-request for a change in the custody arrangement. This was my first notice of such request. Dr. Mendelsohn detailed mother's request to me and we discussed the history of the case.

Michael first inquired of Mendelsohn why she allowed herself to serve as Nancy's advocate by detailing Nancy's cross-request to Cymerman. The psychiatrist responded that she guessed Nancy had used her to present the cross-request because "Nancy hadn't had time to go through her attorney." Michael couldn't believe Mendelsohn did not realize how Cymerman might have been unduly influenced by learning about Nancy's custody petition through the psychiatrist involved in the case.

> Dr. Mendelsohn has never seen Nathaniel, but is informed of his status through her therapy with Ariel and her involvement with both parents. . . .
>   Dr. Mendelsohn relates a history of Ariel being resistant to spending time with her father.

Michael asked Mendelsohn if that was all she had to say on this subject. Didn't she tell Cymerman why Ariel always ran to her mother's house? Mendelsohn answered that she had touched upon this issue and she agreed that Cymerman's phraseology was indeed unfortunate.

> Gradually, through therapy and concerted effort on the part of the father, Ariel has spent the full amount of time set forth in the July 18, 1988 Custody Order with her father. It is, however, only since January 1992 that Ariel has fully complied with the times set forth in this . . . Order.

Michael found the implication of this statement infuriating—that it was *his* behavior which needed to be modified before Ariel would stay with him the required amount of time. Michael asked Mendelsohn if she remembered telling him that he need not change anything in his behavior toward Ariel, that all the custody problems stemmed from Nancy.

The psychiatrist nodded her head affirmatively, but said nothing. Michael could only shake his head in disgust.

> Ariel's progress in spending increased time with her father can be attributed in large part to the significant commitment of both parents to achieving this goal.

Was Barbara Cymerman kidding? He reminded Mendelsohn that for the last several years she had maintained that she was working diligently to prevent Nancy from interfering in Ariel's relationship with him. Had Mendelsohn not related to Cymerman at least a few of the painful episodes Michael had recounted during the past few years?

> This [commitment of both parents] seems a remarkable achievement in view of the demonstrated acrimony between the parties as well as their inability to agree on virtually any adjustments to the children's custody schedule. . . . Each has apparently cooperated with Dr. Mendelsohn's work in helping Ariel to attain the full extent of her custody time with her father.

"What a lie!" Michael asserted. Mendelsohn agreed with him that for Barbara Cymerman to imply that Nancy had cooperated in implementing the custody schedule was not accurate. Not accurate? To Michael it was patently absurd! He maintained that it was only when Mendelsohn had been confronted with his threat to file a second petition for contempt, in which case the psychiatrist might have been subpoenaed to testify in open court, that she insisted that Nancy comply with the court order regarding Ariel immediately. And Nancy did. Just like that!

> In this regard, the father has engaged in a successful course of behavior to "woo" Ariel to him.

Michael was aghast that Mendelsohn would describe his relationship with Ariel using a term loaded with sexual innuendo. Mendelsohn denied point-blank to Michael that she had ever used the word "woo" even though the term appears in quotes in the section of the report based on Mendelsohn's comments.

> The effect of this has been to allow Ariel to develop a good attachment and positive relationship with him. Mother has apparently cooperated with this course of wooing to encourage Ariel and to allow her to develop this good relationship with her father.

Cooperated?! That word again! Michael was irate that this "gross distortion of reality" appeared in the section of the report detailing discussions with Mendelsohn. Michael would find the following statement more accurate: "Nancy has done everything possible to destroy Michael's relationship with all his children."

Meeting with Michael Nieland

> I met with Dr. Nieland in my office . . . for approximately 2¾ hours. . . . Father claims that his request to extend his current weekday visits from 7:30 to overnight is something he wanted from the outset. He maintains that the . . . after-school schedules of the children are such that a 7:30 return to their mother is disruptive to their time together. Specifically, he claims that after the children arrive home from school, sometimes with friends with whom they play, and/or after their otherwise scheduled after-school activities have ended, and after homework, 7:30 P.M. has arrived and they have no real evening together. . . .
> Father believes that the extension of his midweek 7:30

P.M. visits to overnight visits would eliminate a substantial number of the painful interchanges between him and mother. . . . He wants to minimize the stress on the children and avoid having the children witness the hostility between him and mother. He sees this extension as something that will add continuity and calm to the children's lives and, therefore, help the children prosper. He sees his requested modification as a substantial improvement to the custody order and does not see any disadvantages. When I met with him, he had not yet received or even heard of mother's cross-petition for modification of the custody schedule. . . .

Meeting with Nancy R. S. Nieland

I met with Dr. Nancy Nieland in my office . . . for approximately 2½ hours. . . . She went into substantial detail about the history of the relationship between her and her former husband, a relationship which she claims was both physically and emotionally abusive.

Physically and emotionally abusive? To whom? In all seriousness, Michael pointed out to Mendelsohn that Nancy had continued to make these despicable allegations even though they were utterly false.

Mother maintains that she never liked the current custody arrangement and had previously discussed her concerns about its disruptiveness with Dr. Mendelsohn. Nevertheless, she stated that she has worked with Dr. Mendelsohn in implementing the prior schedule and did not move for a prior modification to avoid additional court proceedings, the uncertainty of a new court-ordered schedule, and its effect on the children. Dr. Mendelsohn substantiates this assertion.

Nancy "has worked with Dr. Mendelsohn in implementing the prior schedule"? "Dr. Mendelsohn substantiates this assertion"? Didn't Mendelsohn remember the incidents Michael recounted to her from his log over and over again that demonstrated how Nancy, contrary to Barbara Cymerman's characterization, had done everything possible to undermine the custody schedule? Mendelsohn indicated she too was puzzled over Cymerman's remarks.

> Mother believes that the current schedule . . . presents problems for the children . . . that when she gets the children at 7:30 P.M. on weekday and/or Sunday nights, Nathaniel has not finished his homework. . . .
>
> With regard to Ariel, mother claims that father has spent the last year "wooing" Ariel, who previously was afraid and/or would refuse to go to and/or stay at father's house. . . . Accordingly, father undertook to "woo" Ariel to spend time with him: he bought Ariel new bedroom furniture and redecorated her room and he bought her a cat, when according to mother, he hates cats.

Michael again protested the resurrection of the "fear issue" and to the repeated use of the word "woo." These characterizations denote, at least to him, something other than a healthy relationship with his daughter. He told Mendelsohn he hoped she wasn't going to permit these "lies" and "character assassinations" and this "trivialization of his relationships with his children" to go unchallenged. Wasn't she outraged too?

Meeting with Ariel

> I met with Ariel in my home . . . for approximately one hour. Ariel is a bright and articulate ten-year-old child who . . .

was wary of being put in the middle of this new custody battle. . . . Ariel confirmed that she now likes going to and staying over at her dad's house. . . . Ariel acknowledged that her dad spoils her badly, but that her mom will often do the same types of things—like bringing breakfast in bed—but says that her mom will find an excuse for doing so (like saying she [Ariel] is too tired to get up).

So, if Nathaniel and Ariel didn't have limits imposed upon them, as Nancy had charged, Michael was not solely responsible. Furthermore, Michael had noted, time and time again, if he placed limits on the children (e.g., "Sunday school this morning or no baseball this afternoon" or, "Do your homework before going out to play") they would seek refuge with their mother or the babysitters who certainly couldn't be counted upon to back up any type of discipline Michael had hoped to instill.

Ariel does not see a problem in staying overnight at either her mom's or her dad's house. She is not confused by the situation. She says she feels like she has two homes. . . . Homework for her has also not been a problem. . . . The only disadvantage she could cite to staying at her dad's house was that she missed her cat at her mom's.

When we spoke about bedtimes, . . . Ariel said that she went to bed as late as 10:30 or 11:00 P.M. at her mom's house. Comparing this to her dad's house, she said that . . . she went to sleep around the same time anyway. . . .

Ariel confirms that her parents do not get along at all. . . . She is extremely perceptive of their interaction, noticing such things as the fact that when either one of her parents picks her up from the other's house, they sometimes just don't talk to each other; and that her mother always calls her dad "Michael" and that her dad refers to her mother as "your mother."

Michael asked Mendelsohn how, after working with Ariel for three years, she had been unaware that the child's mother, when talking to her, didn't even acknowledge Michael as Ariel's father. It disturbed him that his little girl heard her father referred to by her mother as though he were a distant relative or neighbor. It was another example to Michael of Nancy's subtle but effective way of undermining him, of delegitimizing him in the eyes of their children. Mendelsohn responded by saying that she guessed she missed this particular habit of Nancy's because, when she met with Nancy alone, Nancy referred to Michael by his first name.

Ariel also knows that her mother does not want her to spend more time with her dad. All of this places an enormous and unfair pressure on Ariel to choose between her parents, both of whom she loves. Ariel would like to spend more time with her dad, particularly Sunday night until Monday morning, but she doesn't think it will work.

Meeting with Nathaniel

I met with Nathaniel on July 15, 1992, for approximately one hour. He claimed to be very tired. . . .

Michael pointed out to Mendelsohn that (because of some schedule juggling) Nathaniel had been in Nancy's custody for the five days right up to Cymerman's July 15 meeting with him. That alone should shed a different light on Nancy's assertion that the children were only exhausted when they returned from Michael's house.

Nathaniel is a perceptive child who will be twelve years old in October. His first reaction [about the current custody arrangement] was to indicate that all things are fine the

way they are, that nothing should change and that everything is handled evenly by his mom and dad. He does not
enjoy being in one house more than the other and likes all
things equally. He strives to maintain a position of neu-
trality with regard to his feelings. . . .

On the subject of school, . . . it appears to be Nathaniel's
position that both his mom and his dad help him with his
homework, both ask to see his homework, and both work
with him on his bigger projects. . . .

Like his sister, Nathaniel contradicted what Nancy had
told Cymerman.

Nathaniel believes that there are rules that he must abide
by at both his mom's and his dad's house. . . .

Again Nathaniel contradicted what Nancy had told
Cymerman.

Perhaps most interesting is Nathaniel's underlying knowledge that his dad will favor Ariel in certain matters af-
fecting planned activities such as where to go, etc. . . .
Nathaniel does not openly admit this favoritism. . . . That
this favoritism probably exists is supported by the systematic courtship behavior that father has engaged in to "woo"
Ariel into her visits with him.

"Outrageous!" declared Michael. He asked Mendelsohn
if she had been the one who coined the expression "systematic courtship behavior"? Was this even a psychiatric term or
could Cymerman have heard it while watching a National
Geographic Special on the mating habits of some frog or in-
sect? Mendelsohn assured Michael that she had never used
the terminology. Of greater concern to Michael was Cymerman's failure to understand why Nathaniel thought his dad

favored Ariel in certain instances. It should not have been too difficult to understand, Michael insisted. He explained that for several years Nathaniel had had his dad all to himself, but that wasn't true any more. Ariel was now at her dad's house as much as Nathaniel, which meant Michael had to give two children his full attention. Now, they couldn't always do what Nathaniel alone desired. Furthermore, Michael declared that Cymerman was hardly qualified to render such psychological interpretations.

Summary and Conclusion

> . . . It is apparent that both parties have invested considerable effort into having the children, especially Ariel, establish a good relationship and positive attachment with father. . . . Accordingly, presently it is not recommended that the father's time with the children be reduced.
>
> At the same time, the current schedule does seem to be presenting problems for both mother and father. The current every-other-day/every-other-week custody schedule requires constant interchanges of the children between the parents and presents problems in keeping track of the children's homework and clothes. In addition, although the children have not committed themselves to a preference, it is believed that the current schedule is also confusing for them.

Said who? Ariel stated unmistakably that she was "not confused by the situation" and Nathaniel concurred by remarking "things are fine the way they are." In fact, three years ago, at age nine, Nathaniel had testified during the contempt proceedings that the custody schedule wasn't at all confusing.

Mother and father agree, albeit for different reasons, that the current schedule is disruptive and detrimental to the children's academic work during the school year. . . . It is believed, however, that extending each of these visits into an overnight visit will only exacerbate the problems.

For these reasons, the following schedule is proposed:

1. In week (1) and week (3) of each four week period, the father shall have custody of the children from Thursday immediately after school until Monday morning when school begins.

2. In week (2) and (4) of each four-week period, the father shall have custody of the children from Thursday immediately after school until Friday morning when school begins.

It is believed that this proposed schedule will maximize father's time with the children. . . . The net effect of this proposal is to increase father's overnight time with the children from three overnights every two weeks to five overnight visits every two weeks. . . .

Michael strongly objects to the use of the word "visits." The choice of this word reveals the mindset that, in Michael's estimation, fosters the belittling of a father's role in the lives of his children.

. . . Finally, it is suggested that Ariel continue in therapy with Dr. Mendelsohn to continue to establish good relationships with both parents and to monitor any problems she may have in adjusting to the above schedule.

. . . It is also suggested that Nathaniel see a therapist of his own to work out his feelings about mother, father, and sister. . . .

After Michael and Dr. Mendelsohn finished reviewing the report, Michael expressed to her his indignation over Barbara

Cymerman's recommendations that evidently relied heavily on her discussions with the psychiatrist. Did Dr. Mendelsohn believe that Cymerman, an attorney by trade who, according to her own billing statement, had spent less than thirty hours on the case, had the training necessary to revise totally—not merely modify—a custody arrangement that had been in place for five years?

The psychiatrist's rejoinder was the same as her reply to most of Michael's comments and questions about the report—a feeble nod.

Michael couldn't believe Dr. Mendelsohn was not perturbed by the scope of Cymerman's recommendations. He explained further to her that, in effect, the Cymerman schedule would separate him from Nathaniel and Ariel for nearly a week at a time twice each month (from Friday morning until the following Thursday after school). With the modifications of the existing schedule that Michael had proposed, he would have seen his children at some point nearly every day and thereby stayed deeply involved in their lives on a continuing basis. His changes also would have ended the interactions between Michael and Nancy in the presence of the children during the school year. Again, the psychiatrist nodded indifferently.

In the hope of minimizing the damage from the Cymerman report, Michael requested that Mendelsohn immediately write a letter to Judge Kaplan and, at the least, correct the misstatements ascribed to her in the report. She declined to do so, saying to Michael once more that she "just can't get involved in a custody dispute." Michael responded, "How can you tell me you 'just can't get involved in a custody dispute' when you are already deeply immersed in it through your willingness to talk to Ms. Cymerman?" Dr. Mendelsohn had no rebuttal. Would she allow the apparent misconceptions and misquotes to stand?

Michael's main hopes seemed to rest with his attorney, who, two days before Michael's appointment with Dr. Mendelsohn, had filed exceptions to Barbara Cymerman's report:

> The schedule now in place has made it possible for [the] father to maintain a close involvement with the lives of his children . . . including school events, athletic events, social events, music lessons. . . . The proposed change in the custody schedule will twice every four weeks produce long stretches of time when Plaintiff [Michael] will not have contact with his children. Plaintiff feels that these long gaps are not in the best interest of the children and will damage his close relationship with them. . . . Father has scheduled his career [to] provide him with the flexibility needed to maximize his time with his children. Father, in order to comply with the proposed change in custody schedule, would now have to hire babysitters during his custody time *whereas previously he was with his children 100% of the time.* . . .
>
> Father categorically denies every assertion made by Mother. . . . Virtually all her assertions are groundless, irrelevant, or absurd. . . .
>
> Father additionally believes that the report errs in utilizing blatantly sexist and belittling language to describe Father's behavior with his daughter; specifically the word "wooing" [and the term] "systematic courtship behavior." To utilize this kind of language in order to trivialize Father's loving and affectionate relationship with his daughter is disgraceful!
>
> The report asserts as justification for changing the schedule now in place: ". . . it is believed that the current schedule is also confusing for them (the children)." However, Ariel stated flatly that "she is not confused by the situation." The present schedule works. Father only requested that his children remain with him overnight on the eight days each month they are already with him. There is

no justification for denying Father the additional time with his children.

Not unexpectedly, Harry Gruener filed an eleven-page response to Michael's exceptions on Nancy's behalf.

The proposed change in schedule does appear to have the endorsement of Dr. Mendelsohn. [Barbara Cymerman] indicated that the report was shown to Dr. Mendelsohn before release. . . . Further, Dr. Mendelsohn has stated to Mother that the present schedule is the worst she had seen. . . .

Father now resents having to alter his already flexible schedule to see his children. This from a man who boasted in letters and on the record that he could run his lab by "remote control."

His protest that he should never have to employ child care during his physical custody periods is unrealistic. Everyone has to employ child care from time to time in the real world. . . .

The Court-appointed psychologist . . . found that Mother has always been the primary caretaker of these children.

Gruener failed to mention that this evaluation was conducted by a court-appointed psychologist, Dr. Roland Singer, who had been censured and reprimanded in part because his actions had the effect of "casting doubt on the Evaluator's fairness and impartiality."

Father has recently attempted to overcompensate for his prior . . . behavior by "wooing" both children, being their buddy rather than their father and by refusing to set limits. . . .

Mother has several objections to the recommendation

of [Barbara Cymerman]: The Sunday overnight during the school year will seriously impair the academic performance of both children. . . . It is clear that the complete abandonment of rules and structure at Father's house will be harmful to [the children's] academic performance. . . . The weeks two and four Thursday overnights should also be eliminated as there are often exams and major papers and projects due on Friday. . . . Mother has no confidence that these will receive any attention by Father. . . .

Mother respectfully requests that either her petition be granted reducing the time with Father or that the recommendations of [Barbara Cymerman] be accepted as amended by the Mother's suggested changes [eliminate Sunday and Thursday overnights].

On the same day Paul Leventon filed Michael's exceptions, a conciliation took place involving the attorneys, Cymerman, and Judge Kaplan. Harry Gruener, according to Leventon, had reiterated to Judge Kaplan Sylvia Mendelsohn's statement to Attorney Cymerman that the existing custody schedule was "the worst (she) had ever seen" and, furthermore, Mendelsohn had read and approved Cymerman's report. Leventon reported to Michael that Cymerman didn't dissent from Gruener's comments.

Michael, after going over the Cymerman report at his August 12 visit with Dr. Mendelsohn, went on to ask her if she had, in fact, read the report prior to its issuance. She replied that she hadn't, but that Ms. Cymerman had read a few paragraphs to her over the telephone. When Michael informed her of her alleged statement that the custody schedule was "the worst (she) had ever seen," the psychiatrist was taken aback. She insisted to Michael that the only thing she had ever said to anyone about the custody schedule was that it was "interesting." She commented further that she didn't

make many of the remarks attributed to her in the Cymerman report, but she deflected Michael's repeated pleas to
correct these misconceptions presented to Judge Kaplan. Instead, she said she would think about it.

In any case, Judge Kaplan now had sitting on his desk
two petitions to modify custody, a report by Barbara Cymerman (a "said Evaluator" and/or self-styled "Domestic/In-
termediary for Children"), and two pending exceptions to
the report. Apparently, though, he needed more information.
He issued an order of court on August 12 that stated:

> . . . Following a conciliation with counsel and the Child Ad-
> vocate . . . it is hereby ordered . . . a hearing shall be sched-
> uled at 3 P.M. on August 28, 1992, for the purpose of taking
> brief testimony of each parent so that the Court may hear
> their respective views in this matter. Following the
> Hearing, the Court will issue an appropriate order revising
> the existing 1988 Order.
>
> By the Court:
> Lawrence W. Kaplan

Given the limitations imposed by Judge Kaplan, Leventon wouldn't have the opportunity to subpoena Dr.
Mendelsohn concerning the endless hearsay attributed to her
or to cross-examine Nancy or to call any other witnesses. So
much for due process.

Michael also noticed that Judge Kaplan had created further confusion in regard to Barbara Cymerman's appointment. Notwithstanding the fact that the qualification
"mental health professional" was a requirement in the motion originally agreed upon by both parties and *purportedly*
required by Sylvia Mendelsohn, and notwithstanding the
fact that Judge Kaplan referred to Cymerman as the "said
Evaluator" in his court order and she considered herself a

"Domestic/Intermediary for Children"—now, after the fact, Judge Kaplan designated her a "Child Advocate"!

Moreover, Michael fumed that Nathaniel and Ariel were taken to Cymerman's home for their interviews without Michael's knowledge or participation. Could Nathaniel's and Ariel's responses have been influenced by the presence of anyone other than Ms. Cymerman?

Several days prior to the August 28 hearing, Michael placed a telephone call to Dr. Mendelsohn and implored her to set the record straight. He read to her verbatim the statement in Nancy's exceptions that "Dr. Mendelsohn has stated to Mother that the present schedule is the worst she had seen." Again, Dr. Mendelsohn expressed her shock at the misrepresentation, but she refused to intervene, saying once more: "I just can't get involved in a custody dispute." She then added, "You and Nancy hired me only to be Ariel's therapist and I have no obligation to either of you to come to court. You didn't hire me to do a custody evaluation and the court didn't either."

Michael was appalled that the psychiatrist refused simply to correct this obvious misstatement, and he was stunned that for the first time she apparently refused to acknowledge that her involvement in the case stemmed directly from a court order requiring "the parties . . . [to] select an appropriate professional for the evaluation and treatment, if so required, of Ariel and Nathaniel."

There was no time, though, for Michael to dwell on Dr. Mendelsohn. He had to prepare as best he could for his moment in front of Judge Kaplan. Michael believed that if he stated his case effectively Judge Kaplan would understand the enormous injustice that has been done to him and his children over the years. This should ensure for Michael a just and equitable outcome at long last.

The big day arrived and he felt prepared. He was accompanied by his attorney; Nancy was accompanied by Harry Gruener. Judge Kaplan began the unprecedented proceeding:*

KAPLAN: . . . Both parties, I'm sure, are familiar with the recommendations that have been made by Barbara Cymerman and, also, both parties have [exceptions] communicated to the Court. . . . There will be no cross-examination. . . . We will start with our Plaintiff who is Dr. Michael Nieland and I guess we will ask you to take the stand since that's where your lawyer [indicates] he would like you to be. I don't know that it's any more comfortable and we do have a switch where we can turn the juice on [i.e., electric chair].

MICHAEL: Your Honor, . . . I brought this action never thinking that it would generate the kind of response that it has. . . . I requested this [the modification of the custody schedule] for several reasons. The children need more time to spend with me. . . . My children look forward to being with me. . . . They feel a sense of security with me . . . that their father is 100 percent involved with them. . . . When the children go back to their mother's house and there is an interaction between their mother and me, it is usually very uncomfortable for everyone concerned. . . . I think it makes the kids absolutely crazy to have to go through this.

I requested the children stay overnight so the next morning they simply go to school with me [and at the end of the school day] return to their mother's house. . . . I don't want to take any time away from their mother. I've never tried to take the children away from their mother. All I wanted to do is share these kids fifty-fifty because I think

---

*The hearing was unprecedented in that it did not permit witnesses to be called or the parties to be cross-examined. This court appearance violated the concept of substantive or procedural due process because the right to confront one's accusers guaranteed in the Constitution was nonexistent. (How does one cross-examine a report?) Without these necessary judicial ingredients, this should not have been called a "custody hearing."

for years I've been the parent who spent the time with them. . . . I don't have babysitters. Rarely have I ever had to hire somebody. I don't want to knock my ex-wife and get into a lot of this kind of angry stuff, but the fact of the matter is at her house there are nothing but babysitters morning, noon, and night, ninety-two hours a week. . . .

I have lived in the same house; my ex-wife has moved or lived in four different houses in the last five years. I think I represent continuity and reliability and emotional support to my children. . . .

I just enjoy being with my children. I've done everything that any parent does with a child. . . . [They] have never gone back to their mother's house without their homework being done. I've helped them endlessly with arithmetic, spelling tests. It is simply not true, as my ex-spouse has alleged, that these things are not taken care of when they go back to her house. The children have no problem with [the every other day, every other weekend schedule]. I think they need for their own emotional well-being to have support from one parent who is always, always there for them—morning, noon, and night.

As far as communication with my ex-spouse, I have tried endlessly to correspond with her. I've written innumerable letters to her. . . . She has never responded. . . . I wanted only—to me this was such a minor request—to have the children eight nights out of the month—when they are already with me—to stay with me. I'm telling you under oath that Dr. Mendelsohn, Ariel's psychiatrist, who spent three years with her, never said that this was the worst custody schedule she had ever seen. When I told her she had been quoted as saying that, she was shocked. She is not here today because she was not appointed by the Court or . . . employed by us to deal with custody issues. It was only to help Ariel deal with the tension. . . . Dr. Mendelsohn would [if she testified here today] deny that my little girl has ever been afraid of me. This was something that was induced in my daughter. I'm sure in all the years you have been on the bench you have seen what can happen between parents, how one parent can brainwash, can do horrible things to children to try to get them away from the other parent. . . .

For the year or so after the divorce I had no problem with my little girl. It was only when the psychologist involved in the case, Roland Singer, began to work with my ex-spouse in undermining the Court Order, disrupting everything. This man, you should know, has been [censured and reprimanded by professional associations]. . . . The fact that my little girl would run away or not stay with me has nothing to do with the fact that I didn't have the best possible relationship with her. It was due to this intense, incredible pressure that my ex-wife has put on her to keep her away from me. I don't know what fuels this antagonism. [There wasn't] anything that ever happened in our marriage that would fuel this kind of hatred and loathing. It's utterly inappropriate. The children love me . . . and I think it is absolutely reprehensible for my ex-spouse to continue to make efforts to keep my kids away from me. . . .

If the proposed schedule of Ms. Cymerman were put into effect, two weeks out of the month I [would] see my kids once. . . . I don't think that is in their interest. . . . I'm just as entitled as my ex-spouse is to have time with these kids. I'm a fully competent parent and I've demonstrated that. It would be, I think, cruel to disrupt this kind of relationship I have with my children. I've never wanted to take the kids away from their mother. I just want to share my children.

KAPLAN: Sounds good to me. We would be happy to hear from you now, Doctor [Nancy Nieland]. I know this is a very awkward situation, so I hope you will just relax and try to be yourself.

GRUENER: Your Honor, we are not going to rebut the attacks on Dr. Singer. I think that's just beyond the scope of why we are here today and that's a whole other history. . . . I would prefer she address the problems with the present schedule. . . .

NANCY: I just want to spend a little time initially answering some of the points that Michael raised during his time. . . . Number one, that he is always there. I just want to point out from the beginning I agreed with a much more limited schedule to have it tailor-made to Michael's work schedule. . . . Michael has not had to make the kind of tremendous juggling changes that I've had to make with my schedule in order to be with the children when they are home. [He says] he doesn't want to take time away from the mother. His proposed schedule, of course, would double the time he has and remove at least 35 percent of the time that I have with the children. [He says he] rarely has babysitters at his house. He is probably right, he doesn't, but he has been advised by Dr. Mendelsohn over and over again not to leave the children alone. He will take one out and leave the other [at home]. He says ninety-two hours a week for babysitters; . . . this is outrageous. When we lived together and I had five children and I was providing by far the bulk of the income for the family—and had no help whatsoever from their father, zero help—then I did have babysitters on weekends, late at night, and early in the morning. . . . [He mentioned] four different houses. I want to tell you this is a real aberration. . . . I turned [the marital residence] over completely to Michael, moved into a rental house for three months, . . . [then purchased a home and lived there] for three years, was remarried and [my husband and I] bought a house in Shadyside where we have lived now for two and a half years. So, I'm not moving every three months. As for never sending Nathaniel home without his homework completed—this is just outrageous. Can I tell you I don't believe there has ever been a single time when Nathaniel has been there when his homework has been completed. . . . [Regarding] the civil letters that Michael writes to me: it's true he has written letters because when we try to have any interchange there are these wild temper tantrums. I've resorted to having Dr. Mendelsohn act as the middleman in this thing. . . . If I write letters, it's not going to accomplish anything. . . .

The children already have a great deal of trouble dealing with two [weekend] nights at a stretch. To stretch this out to Friday, Saturday, Sunday—or for the child advocate's proposal to stretch it from Thursday, Friday, Saturday, Sunday, so that they would leave my house early on Thursday morning, not returning until Monday afternoon—it's already very difficult, very painful for them, very discombobulating. They are confused about which house they are supposed to be at. . . .

I want to say one thing about Dr. Singer: he received a very mild censure for acting in a dual role during the time he was seeing us and this is true with many psychologists, I understand, in the late 1980s until the guidelines were much more well-defined about whether they should deal with the parents and the children at the same time. So, it's not that he was found to have done anything terribly wrong. . . . All of this stuff happened, . . . to have him censured and so on, because he wrote a letter saying that Michael had a severe personality disorder that was unmasked only after he had visited with him many times. . . .

GRUENER: Let me ask you a question about Barbara Cymerman's report. She has suggested a certain change that would stop this every-other-day stuff. If you were able to tell Judge Kaplan how you would modify it, what would you tell him?

NANCY: First of all, I wanted for a long time to change this schedule. I was afraid to do it. I talked to Dr. Mendelsohn about it a great deal. She has told me it's like throwing a deck of cards in the air. That's her direct quote. This was one of the worst schedules she had ever seen—and she did say that. . . . I was afraid to go through all of this and then wind up on the other side not knowing what would happen. I did not do this until I was given this opening because Michael had asked for a modification. In general, I think her proposed schedule is far better than the one we have had. Far better for the children. . . . Much more structured.

GRUENER: How would you change her report?

NANCY: I'm terribly worried about the children being gone on Sunday evenings. A lot of major reports and exams are due on Mondays. . . . Nate [Nathaniel] is already exhausted and depressed when he comes home. Ariel is so tired she has to lie down. . . . It's exhausting for them emotionally and physically. They don't sleep; they don't bathe. They should not spend Sunday overnights away from home when they have school on Monday. It's terribly important to catch up on these things. . . . I would eliminate the Sunday overnights and eliminate Thursday overnights on weeks two and four. . . .

GRUENER: I think that's all I have about her criticisms of that schedule and how she would change it if she were the author.

KAPLAN: I appreciate your helping your client out. . . . Now, we will let Michael Nieland retake the stand for his five-minute time. . . . It's like a real debate here, isn't it?

MICHAEL: Your Honor, in medicine we call what you just heard confabulation. It has the ring of truth, it's spoken with great emotion—it's utterly false. . . .

LEVENTON: Michael, I'll ask you the same question that Mr. Gruener asked Nancy. If you had your druthers, how would you specifically modify the present schedule?

MICHAEL: Your Honor, I would just like the present schedule modified exactly as I requested. . . .

KAPLAN: All right.

GRUENER: We have no rebuttal.

KAPLAN: I must say that I feel for both of you that this kind of thing is going on, but most of all I feel for the kids. I really do because it just isn't right that this kind of attitude— I'm not putting blame on anyone—should exist and that the kids have to contend with that. . . . Somewhere along the line, even in this business, I see wounds heal, but all we are doing here is getting some very serious scarring; that is, things don't get better. And I must say you people are unique in that regard and that's the wrong kind of uniqueness to have. I can't put the blame one way or another. I haven't heard enough here to be able to do that and I wouldn't do it because I don't think that would help anyone. I just hope that some day this [hostility] doesn't get through any further to the kids and that there is someone out there that has a magic wand that can help you people solve this problem. I can't. The Court thanks you for coming in today and we will try to respond by issuing an Order here that is appropriate for the children.

Michael tried to be upbeat after the hearing. He believed he had sufficiently explained why his proposed modification of the custody schedule was more appropriate for Nathaniel and Ariel. It would eliminate a great deal of stress for all concerned and balance the children's time more equally between their mother and father. As for Nancy's claim that his petition would "remove at least 35 percent of the time that [she had] with the children," he could only shake his head at the absurdity of the calculation.

The custody schedule was in Judge Kaplan's hands. Michael hoped (unlike the child support proceedings) that the judge would actually read the documents before him that pertained to the case.

While everyone waited for Judge Kaplan's decision the invoices kept coming. Barbara Cymerman wanted another $100 each from Michael and Nancy for her role in the August 12 conciliation (including $37.50 for telephone calls to schedule the conciliation appointment). That brought her earnings in the case thus far to $3,600, billed evenly to Michael and Nancy.

Nearly one month after listening to the testimony of Michael and Nancy, Judge Kaplan issued his ruling:

ORDER OF COURT

... [I]t is hereby ordered, adjudged and decreed [on the 24th day of September, 1992]:

The report and recommendations of the child advocate, Barbara G. Cymerman, Esq., are attached hereto and are hereby adopted in their entirety and the objections of the parties thereto are hereby dismissed.

BY THE COURT:
Lawrence W. Kaplan

Michael had lost again. He was deeply disappointed. All he had sought was a slight modification of the existing custody schedule. Instead, the schedule was completely revised and he still had no more meaningful time with his children. Nancy didn't win either, but she didn't have to—the children were still with her most of the time, just as they had been for the past five years.

The new schedule began immediately. Michael decided to give it a chance. He had no other choice, for now. There was no question in his mind that being out of touch with his children for essentially two weeks a month was robbing them of the daily contact and the continuity that strengthens family bonds. This loss of day-to-day fathering could have been avoided, Michael was convinced, if Dr. Mendelsohn had only spoken up. Michael had certainly given her enough opportunities to do so.

Michael still held out hope, though, that Dr. Mendelsohn would write to Judge Kaplan correcting the misconceptions and misstatements he had pointed out to her in the Cymerman report. Then, Michael was sure he would be able to get a new hearing concerning the custody schedule. With that intention in mind he met with the psychiatrist. The October 13 session began with Michael expressing his profound disappointment in regard to what he perceived as Mendelsohn's moral failure to tell the truth. At the end of the session he asked one more time if she would write to Judge Kaplan to set the record straight for the sake of the children. Undoubtedly, Judge Kaplan's support for the Cymerman schedule was due in large part to the hearsay attributed to Dr. Mendelsohn. The psychiatrist replied that she would consider writing the judge. "I'm not saying that I won't do it," she stated to Michael. But first she insisted that he get some "second opinions" in regard to her ethical obligations. One of the professionals she suggested Michael consult was none other than Dr. Stephen Schachner, whom Michael had consulted during the Roland Singer era.

Michael met with Schachner on October 17 and again on October 22 to discuss once more suspected improprieties on the part of a mental health professional. After hearing Michael's exposition, Schachner said he, like Michael, was "appalled" that Judge Kaplan had appointed a lawyer to do a custody evaluation and, as a mental health professional, he was "disappointed" Dr. Mendelsohn had agreed to speak with Cymerman. Although he qualified his remarks as those of a psychologist and not a psychiatrist, Dr. Schachner thought it was a "gross deviation from standard medical practice" for Mendelsohn to have spoken with Cymerman—

a non-mental health professional. What Cymerman had done, he said, was "grossly incorrect" and her observations and conclusions concerning Nancy's degree of cooperation were clearly nothing more than "making nice."

Michael asked Schachner if he would put these observations into a report. The psychologist responded that he would try to help Michael, but there were things Michael should understand. Schachner confessed that Mendelsohn and he referred many patients to each other. In addition, he was a social friend of Cymerman and her husband, Steven Abramovitz, who was also an attorney and who did legal work for him in connection with his real estate interests. Moreover, he told Michael that Judge Kaplan referred cases to him. In conclusion, he recommended to Michael that he "put it all behind (him)" and work to obtain more time with his children "through legal channels."

Michael couldn't believe what he had just heard from the psychologist he had held in such high esteem.

Although Michael was still reeling from Judge Kaplan's decision, he didn't wallow in self-pity. His work continued at his medical practice and he resumed participating in his usual leisure activities, especially his music.

At one chamber music party he conversed with an old friend who was a psychiatrist and a fine pianist. Their conversation drifted to Dr. Mendelsohn. Michael gave him a brief overview of her involvement. His friend seemed surprised by the state of affairs and recommended that Michael consult with Dr. Loren Roth, a Pittsburgh psychiatrist who was said to be an authority in the areas of law, ethics, and psychiatry. Michael made an appointment with Dr. Roth the next day. And while he was thinking about unfinished business, he dropped a note to Paul Leventon asking about the status of the property/box issue.

Michael's attorney made a telephone call to Harry Gruener and followed that with a letter (November 5, 1992) informing Nancy's attorney that, "Despite the obvious cost ineffectiveness of proceeding, I have been directed by Michael to file the appropriate action to complete this transaction. In addition to the three 'boxes,' Michael does also require the return to him of all [personal papers and files] which were in Nancy's possession. . . ."

Michael met with Dr. Loren Roth on November 10 in his office at the Western Psychiatric Institute and Clinic (WPIC) on the University of Pittsburgh campus. Just minutes into Michael's description of the case—and before any names were mentioned—Dr. Roth broke into a grin and said to Michael, "You're talking about Sylvia Mendelsohn, aren't you?" But he didn't say much more. He just urged Michael to "forget about what has happened and put it all behind (him)." (Hadn't Michael heard this once before?)

Michael would not forget. How could he? How could any father? Furthermore, Michael wondered how Dr. Roth already knew about the case.

On November 12, just two days after his disappointing meeting with Dr. Roth, Michael had yet another scheduled appointment with Dr. Mendelsohn in response to her request that he get some "second opinions" about what she should do. His mood was somber. He refused to play any more polite games with her and, instead, told her what he was now hearing from Ariel—that she said, "it's a waste of time to see Dr. Mendelsohn" and that she wouldn't "tell [her] secrets" to Dr. Mendelsohn any more.

Mendelsohn replied that she could understand why Ariel felt this way. She admitted that Ariel had remarked to her that she was very upset her mom had found out that she said she had "two homes" and "would like to spend more time with her dad" (quotes from the Cymerman report). When asked by the psychiatrist why it upset her, Ariel had responded by saying it made her mom mad at her. As if that wasn't enough for a ten-year-old child, Dr. Mendelsohn also admitted that the drastic revamping of the custody schedule was "a huge change" and very upsetting to Ariel.

Even though the youngster felt she had been betrayed by having her confidences revealed in the Cymerman report, Dr. Mendelsohn assured Michael that she thought her sessions with Ariel were still beneficial. She also emphasized to Michael that she believed she had done nothing unethical. Michael asked Mendelsohn how she could make such a statement and she explained that she had been in touch with the American Psychiatric Association and, as a result of her conversation, she concluded that she "might have violated a legal duty had [she] not submitted to the interview [with Barbara Cymerman]." She also added that it was "*not* [her] duty to determine the competence of Barbara Cymerman." And, about the contents of the Cymerman report, Dr. Mendelsohn stated that, "It was not my job to correct misconceptions or misstatements. Someone else should do it."

Michael was amazed by what he heard. Dr. Mendelsohn talked about her "legal duty." But what about her legal, moral, and ethical duty to tell the truth? Once again, do court orders take precedence over ethical principles? Michael could see that Dr. Mendelsohn was not likely to write Judge Kaplan.

As Michael departed, the psychiatrist mentioned that he was behind in paying her bill. Michael explained that he had astronomical expenses resulting from his ongoing custody battle, including a bill approaching $800 from Dr. Schachner, whom Michael had consulted at Mendelsohn's urging. Consequently, Michael acknowledged he had fallen behind slightly in paying her. She said she understood and told him, "Just pay me whenever you can. I just wanted to be sure your bills weren't unpaid because you were angry with me."

Michael ended the session by saying that he would be in touch. In a letter dated November 24, 1992, after mentioning that Ariel no longer wished to see the psychiatrist and restating his disappointment that Dr. Mendelsohn would not correct the errors in Barbara Cymerman's report, Michael concluded: "The end result, unfortunately, is that I have come now to distrust you. Based upon the above and after much reflection I wish to inform you that by this letter you are discharged as therapist for my daughter, Ariel. Should you have any questions you may correspond with me directly."

Mendelsohn responded politely, but was careful to include her final bill, for $1,315. While Michael contemplated whether he should take any action against Dr. Mendelsohn, Paul Leventon informed Harry Gruener that he had taken legal action on behalf of Michael to secure the safe return of the orphaned boxes along with Michael's personal papers and files that remained in Nancy's possession.

The very same day Nancy initiated legal action against Michael concerning both his firing Dr. Mendelsohn and the money he still owed for her services.

Leventon immediately filed Michael's response with the court stating that Michael "fully believes that it is not in Ariel's best interest to continue to treat with Dr. Mendelsohn." Leventon restated Michael's belief that Mendelsohn had violated the *Principles of Medical Ethics* by "improperly delegat[ing] the exercise of her medical judgment to a nonmedical person." He closed his letter with the request that Nancy's motion be dismissed or an evidentiary hearing be held.

On December 15, Judge Kaplan directed Michael to continue to participate with Ariel in treatment by Dr. Mendelsohn. The judge, however, did leave the door open for Michael to petition to show cause why Dr. Mendelsohn should be discharged.

In other words, it was back to court to decide if Sylvia Mendelsohn should be fired as Ariel's therapist and if Michael should gain custody of the boxes. Michael wasn't shocked. Nothing shocked him any more. He was numb.

11. Boxed In

Why keep battling? Why not just give up? Why not be content with the limited custody time I have with Nathaniel and Ariel? Let Nancy keep the boxes. Forget about Dr. Mendelsohn, Ms. Cymerman, the judges.

I must admit, had I done so, my life would have been dramatically less complicated and I would have saved myself a fortune in legal fees and emotional energy. But then I think of the lesson it would have conveyed to my children: When they witness injustice, look the other way; when the going gets tough, forget about principles; when they are outnumbered, give up.

That isn't the kind of legacy I want to leave Nathaniel, Ariel, or Jennie. I had to continue on, no matter how great the odds against me.

—Michael L. Nieland, M.D.
Ethical Warrior

Nancy had been able to prevent by legal action, at least temporarily, the removal of Dr. Mendelsohn as Ariel's therapist.

Michael, for his part, decided to do what he could to put an end to the psychiatrist's grip on Ariel and his family. He never contemplated he would have to go down this road again, but for the second time he found himself composing an ethics complaint against a mental health professional, which was then sent to the State Bureau of Professional and Occupational Affairs and the American Psychiatric Association.

> ... I believe that Dr. Mendelsohn violated sections 2.19 (Unnecessary Services), 3.01 (Nonscientific Practitioners), 8.03 (Conflicts of Interest), 8.08 (Informed Consent), and 9.07 (Medical Testimony) of the *Code of Medical Ethics of the American Medical Association*; Sections 4-2, 4-7, 4-9, 5-4, and 6-1 of the *Principles of Medical Ethics with Annotations Especially Applicable to Psychiatry*; Sections II (Confidentiality), III (Consent), and IV (Honesty and Striving for Objectivity) of the *Ethical Guidelines for the Practice of Forensic Psychiatry of the American Academy of Psychiatry and the Law*; and Sections 16.61(a) 1, 2, 8, and 14 (Unprofessional and Immoral Conduct) of the *Rules and Regulations of the State Board of Medicine, Commonwealth of Pennsylvania*.

*   *   *

Discussion

Dr. Mendelsohn was well aware that her responsibility in this case from the outset was to evaluate Ariel's "expressed fear of her father" and to treat it, "*if so required*" (emphasis added), with the goal of resumption of overnight time with her father. Dr. Mendelsohn discovered immediately that Ariel wasn't the least bit afraid of me. During one of my earliest meetings with her, Dr. Mendelsohn said to me, "I expected to see a timid, frightened child on our first encounter—I found just the opposite." On several other occasions Dr. Mendelsohn reiterated to me that she found no evidence that Ariel "feared" me. On the contrary, what Dr.

Mendelsohn found was that Ariel was afraid of her mother or her mother's reaction should Ariel spend time with me, or express any positive comments about me, or relate to me in a normal fashion. . . .

After her initial evaluation Dr. Mendelsohn informed me that the only way she could help me would be to "try to make Ariel strong enough to resist her mother's pressure." I asked Dr. Mendelsohn repeatedly if there was something I should be doing differently and she always responded "No." Over and over again, Dr. Mendelsohn indicated to me that there was absolutely nothing I should change in my general approach to the children (or toward my former spouse, for that matter) in terms of behavior, activities, habits, or *modus operandi*. Nevertheless, she continued to make appointments with me. Never once in any session with me did Dr. Mendelsohn report to me any complaint, fear, or request from Ariel that I change anything about what I said or did when Ariel and I were together. More than once Dr. Mendelsohn pointed out to me how affectionately Ariel regarded me when she observed us together. Certainly, if there had been any useful advice from Dr. Mendelsohn concerning Ariel, it had nothing to do with reversing "fear" and, in any case, it is reasonable once in a while for a child to "fear" what a parent's reaction might be to a bad report card, for example, or bad behavior. However, Ariel is an A student, is her Class President and is the most wonderful child any parent could have. In terms of her instructions in the Court Order, Dr. Mendelsohn's evaluation revealed quickly that no treatment of Ariel for fear of her father was required because *there was no fear*. This was the only question Dr. Mendelsohn was required to answer.

At this point it was Dr. Mendelsohn's responsibility and capability to report her findings to the attorneys or to the Court. At the least, Dr. Mendelsohn should have bluntly and honestly told the truth to each parent. It would have been entirely reasonable (and probably indicated) for her to have recommended to Dr. Nancy Nieland that she see a separate therapist. Dr. Mendelsohn was well aware of the prior history in this case and Dr. Nancy Nieland's relationship with Dr. Singer. It certainly was beyond Dr. Mendelsohn's training, expertise, and experience to attempt to take on the task of modifying Dr. Nancy Nieland's behavior at the same time she was treating my daughter and counseling me. Indeed, if Dr. Mendelsohn deluded herself into believing that after three years she had succeeded in altering Dr. Nancy Nieland's behavior toward me, the mere fact that Dr. Nancy Nieland filed a Petition counter to my own in an effort to reduce the amount of time I spent with the children should have disabused her of the notion that she had made any progress in this regard.

Dr. Mendelsohn could have and should have taken steps early in this case to avoid the gross Conflicts of Interest that clouded her judgment and produced ethical conflicts which she handled poorly. It might have been reasonable for Dr. Mendelsohn to have referred me elsewhere for treatment of whatever defect of character that made me refuse to be separated from my children and for treatment of my own well-founded anxieties and fears of being detached from my children. After all, I had been victimized once already by the negligence of the Court, which appointed an unethical psychologist, Dr. Singer, who had done incalculable damage to me and my children. Instead of doing what would have been proper in terms of bringing about a reasonably prompt closure to this case in terms of her own involvement, Dr. Mendelsohn continued to see Ariel weekly, treated my anxieties monthly, and worked at a glacial pace in bringing Ariel['s time with me] into compliance with the Court-ordered schedule of custody, the only remaining task she was to accomplish.

After two years of "therapy" the Court Order was still far from implementation. Dr. Mendelsohn had succeeded only in getting Dr. Nancy Nieland to cease her interference so that I could bring Ariel to her appointments with Dr. Mendelsohn and take her home and Ariel started to stay overnight again at my home twice a month. However, Ariel was still far from full compliance with the Court Order. In the meantime, I had documented literally hundreds of continuing violations of the Custody Order on the part of Dr. Nancy Nieland. I told Dr. Mendelsohn that I had had enough of this abuse and I intended to go back to Court with another Petition for Contempt against Dr. Nancy Nieland. I asked Dr. Mendelsohn for help and requested that she testify, but she refused. From every point of view she had established a doctor-patient relationship with me and I felt I should have been able to call upon her for help. The American Medical Association *Code of Medical Ethics* states (Section 9.07) that "if a patient who has a legal claim requests a physician's assistance, the physician should furnish medical evidence, with the patient's consent, in order to secure the patient's legal rights." It was unreasonable for Dr. Mendelsohn to claim that testifying or merely talking to the attorneys might "have a negative impact on (her) therapeutic work with Ariel (letter, September 17, 1991)." It was disingenuous for Dr. Mendelsohn to state in that letter, "I feel strongly that it is impossible to wear the dual hats of Custody Evaluator and Therapist." No one asked Dr. Mendelsohn to perform a custody evaluation. My custody rights had already been set forth in two Orders of Court. Moreover, she had no right to claim that she had to treat a condition which did not exist, i.e., Ariel's "fear" of her father. Section 2.19 of the *Code of Medical Ethics* states that "Physicians should not provide, prescribe, or seek compensation for services that are known to be *unnecessary* (emphasis added) or worthless." The truth of the matter is, as Dr. Mendelsohn told me more than once: She feared that Dr. Nancy Nieland would disrupt or end her weekly sessions with Ariel if she, Dr. Mendelsohn, told the truth. The *Code of Medical Ethics* also states (Section 8.03) that "Under no circumstances may physicians place their own financial interests above the welfare of their patients." Whether Dr. Mendelsohn was interested in the considerable income this lucrative case was bringing her, or in the welfare of my daughter, I cannot say for sure. However, I began to feel exploited by Dr. Mendelsohn. That Dr. Mendelsohn had the leverage or ability to produce Ariel's compliance with the Court Order all along is clearly illustrated by the fact that, when pressed, Dr. Mendelsohn was able to accomplish this practically overnight. The obstacle to my daughter's compliance with the Court-ordered schedule could have been removed long before if Dr. Mendelsohn had chosen to act forthrightly instead of tendentiously and improperly prolonging her involvement in this case.

Dr. Mendelsohn's ethical and moral blunders thus far were only the beginnings of her negligence in this case. When I turned to the Court in May 1992 in order to increase my custody time with the children to the equally shared time originally recommended, I again called on Dr. Mendelsohn for help. Again she refused, this time telling me she "couldn't get involved in a custody dispute." I explained to her that I didn't need any recommendations from her about custody. I said to her, "All you have to tell the Court or the Domestic Relations Officer is that you never found any evidence that my daughter feared me and that I have a normal, loving relationship with her," but Dr. Mendelsohn absolutely refused. What made her change her mind and agree to talk to a "mental health professional" I do not know because she never discussed this matter with me nor did she obtain my truly informed consent in violation of Sections 8.08, 4-2, and III of the *Ethical Codes*. Perhaps she felt that if she spoke secretly with another psychiatrist or psychologist about the issues in this case she could avoid offending either of the parties and be able to continue seeing Ariel regularly. Perhaps she felt that she had irreconcilable Conflicts of Interest and her only way out was to finesse the problem altogether. Perhaps the entire case was ... much more complicated and problematical than I (or she) ever understood it to be and she needed the guidance of another mental health professional. In any event, the *Principles of Medical Ethics with Annotations Especially Applicable to Psychiatry* clearly state that a "physician should not delegate ... to any nonmedical person any matter requiring the exercise of professional medical judgment (Section 5-4)." Dr. Mendelsohn never indicated to me that she was ethically forbidden to talk to "mental health professional" attorney Barbara Cymerman, Esq., about this case when she asked me to give her a release to do so. Dr. Mendelsohn took advantage of the faith I had in her as her patient and exploited my trust to get me to agree to a procedure which she knew or should have known was ethically forbidden. That would be like a surgeon suggesting a questionable procedure to a trusting patient, obtaining the patient's consent, injuring the patient, and then saying, "Well, you gave me permission to do it!" I had previously asked Dr. Mendelsohn for truthful testimony in open Court only concerning myself which she repeatedly and unethically refused to do and then she turned around and gave secret testimony to someone incompetent to understand it, interpret it, or make appropriate recommendations based upon it. Dr. Mendelsohn's claim that she "might have violated a legal duty if she had not submitted to the interview" is preposterous. First of all, she herself had suggested this format or agreed to it with Dr. Nancy Nieland or her attorney because neither I nor my attorney had ever spoken to her about it. Secondly, Dr. Mendelsohn had no "duty" to respond to any Order which required her to do something unethical. She, unlike myself, was not a party to the action and not directly subject to the Court Order and, besides, her ethical and moral duty should be solely to her patients. Section 4-9 of the Code states, "when the psychiatrist is ordered by the Court to reveal confidences entrusted to him/her by patients, he/she may comply or he/she may ethically hold the right to dissent within the framework of the law." Her exculpatory comment to me that she "did not have to determine the competence of Barbara Cymerman" as a "mental health professional" is absurd and self-serving. If the judge had appointed a chiropractor as "mental health professional" would Dr. Mendelsohn have inquired about his/her credentials? Dr. Mendelsohn's comment that "it was not (her) job to correct misconceptions or misstatements made by Barbara Cymerman or Dr. Nancy Nieland. . . . Someone else should do it," is immoral and is a violation of Section IV of the *Ethical Guidelines for the Practice of Forensic Psychiatry*, which emphasizes Honesty and Objectivity. Dr. Mendelsohn was the only witness to the truth of statements attributed to her as direct quotations. How could she possibly permit absolute lies to go unrefuted? A further illustration of Dr. Mendelsohn's carelessness is the fact that she put herself in the position of advocate for Dr. Nancy Nieland in violation of Section 9.07 of the AMA Code which states that "The medical witness must not become an advocate or a partisan in the legal Proceeding." When Barbara Cymerman met with Dr. Mendelsohn for the first time Ms. Cymerman hadn't even seen or heard of Dr. Nancy Nieland's Counter-Petition to reduce my time with my children. She first heard about it, as her report clearly states, from Dr. Mendelsohn ("Dr. Mendelsohn detailed mother's cross-request to me."). No wonder she was confused as to Dr. Mendelsohn's stance on the issues.

Dr. Mendelsohn was not only indifferent to my rights, but she failed to protect my ten-year-old daughter's confidentiality. Sections 4-7 and 4-9 of the Code state that "Careful judgment must be exercised by the psychiatrist in order to include, when appropriate, the parents or guardian in the treatment of a minor. At the same time, the psychiatrist must assure the minor proper confidentiality and when the psychiatrist is in doubt, the right of the patient to confidentiality and, by extension, to unimpaired treatment, should be given priority." Because Dr. Mendelsohn did not look into Barbara Cymerman's total lack of training or experience in mental health she failed to protect Ariel from exposure by Barbara Cymerman to her mother's anger over statements which should have been kept from her mother. As a direct result, Ariel told me she did not want to share her "secrets" any more with [Dr. Mendelsohn]. Dr. Mendelsohn on her own commented to me on the violation of Ariel's Confidentiality but, revealingly, blamed Barbara Cymerman without acknowledging her own role in this grave error. Section IV of the *Forensic Psychiatry Ethical Guidelines* states also that "a treating psychiatrist should generally avoid agreeing to be an expert witness . . ." because "testimony may adversely affect the therapeutic relationship" and Section II states "The psychiatrist should take precautions to assure that none of the confidential information he receives falls into the hands of unauthorized persons." Dr. Mendelsohn never should have authorized Barbara Cymerman to take either of my children, one of whom was her patient, to Barbara Cymerman's home for unsupervised psychological evaluations. Dr. Mendelsohn completely abdicated her responsibility to my daughter.

In summary, Dr. Mendelsohn engaged simultaneously in the treatment and/or counseling of my ten-year-old daughter, Ariel, my former wife, Dr. Nancy Nieland, and me, but she failed to preserve the optimal conditions for a sound working relationship with all her patients, particularly with my daughter and me, and did not avoid obvious Conflicts of Interest. When called upon to furnish medical evidence on my behalf on two separate occasions Dr. Mendelsohn refused although she was ethically obligated to do so. In a later legal proceeding Dr. Mendelsohn requested my consent to speak with an unlicensed practitioner, Ms. Cymerman, without informing me that she was

ethically forbidden to do this. She aided and abetted an unlicensed person in the practice of medicine and delegated
to this nonmedical person matters requiring the exercise of
professional medical judgment. She violated my daughter's rights to Confidentiality and Unimpaired Treatment.
She did not adhere to Principles of Honesty and Objectivity
and refused to testify truthfully. She became an advocate in
a legal proceeding. In still another legal proceeding, because of her own pecuniary interest, Dr. Mendelsohn did
not take precautions to ensure that confidential information concerning me did not fall into the hands of unauthorized persons, namely, my ex-wife. Moreover, she became a
partisan in this legal proceeding also. As a result of Dr.
Mendelsohn's negligence, three years of expensive, time-
consuming effort to obtain compliance with a long-
standing custody schedule went down the drain and, as a
result, my younger children and I are separated for two
weeks out of every month, a painful and cruel outcome for
all of us. Although Dr. Mendelsohn had multiple opportunities to intervene and to prevent further harm to me and
my children and to correct faulty psychological assess-
ments and therapeutic recommendations made by an unqualified "mental health professional," she failed to do so.

I respectfully request from the State Board of Medicine,
the Prosecuting Attorney, and the Ethics Committees of the
American Psychiatric Association and Pennsylvania Psychiatry Society a clear response that Dr. Mendelsohn's performance represents unacceptable professional behavior. I
believe that Dr. Mendelsohn has violated not only numerous ethical precepts but also specific provisions of law,
namely the *Rules and Regulations of the State Board of Medicine, Commonwealth of Pennsylvania.* For one, she revealed
confidential information concerning me to my former
spouse which incited her to state falsely in a legal action
that I had "refused to pay the professional fees" that I owe
Dr. Mendelsohn. Section 16.61(a)1 prohibits revealing per-

sonally identifiable facts, obtained as the result of a physician-patient relationship, without the prior consent of the patient.

Secondly, Dr. Mendelsohn exhibited willful indifference to Sections 16.61(a)8 and 14 of the State Board's Rules and Regulations by conferring outside a courtroom setting with a lawyer posing as a mental health expert whose utter lack of qualifications and ill-conceived recommendations caused immeasurable harm to me and my children.

Thirdly, the *Rules and Regulations of the State Board of Medicine*, Section 16.61(a)2 impose a standard for the practice of medicine which may "be guided by adjudications of the Agency or Court which administers or enforces the standard." In this case the Pennsylvania Psychiatry Society (Psychiatric Physicians of Pennsylvania) which enforces the *Ethical Principles of the American Medical Association*, the American Psychiatric Association, and the American Academy of Psychiatry and the Law may provide guidance on all the other ethical violations cited in this Complaint not specifically cited in the *Rules and Regulations of the State Board of Medicine*.

Although the complaint against Mendelsohn had been mailed, Michael was not finished. He turned his attention to Barbara Cymerman and filed a nine-page ethics complaint against her with the state's Bureau of Professional and Occupational Affairs for "practicing psychology and/or medicine (psychiatry) without a license."

The complaints offered Michael some measure of satisfaction, but it was his time with the children that offered him his greatest reward. While Nancy still presented constant irritations (such as scheduling parties for the children during Michael's time without his knowledge or consent), he at last was having an opportunity to be a parent to his two younger children. Michael had even discontinued his daily log. He was too busy being a parent. He just wished that his modification to the custody schedule had been accepted so that he could have additional time and a more sensible schedule with the children.

As he waited for responses to his complaint filings, Michael assumed he would be hearing shortly from the common law arbitrator named by the court to resolve the box affair. Yet, Michael heard nothing.

Dr. Mendelsohn, meanwhile, continued as Ariel's therapist—a weekly occurrence—which distressed Michael. Since the Cymerman report, Ariel told her dad over and over again how much she objected to the sessions. He realized he couldn't wait for the complaints to run their course before attempting to have Mendelsohn removed.

While contemplating that distasteful chore, the last thing Michael wanted to do was send the therapist money. But he had no other choice, as Mendelsohn had informed both Gruener and Leventon that the $1,315 was now far overdue. It seems that when it came to her fees Dr. Mendelsohn had no reluctance communicating with the attorneys.

Michael made a payment on his outstanding bill because Judge Kaplan had agreed with the portion of Nancy's motion to compel compliance calling for Michael to "pay the professional fees that he owes to Dr. Mendelsohn." Nevertheless, it galled him that, after having been a patient of Mendelsohn for more than three years and paying her more than $10,000 in fees, his therapist evidently had no hesitation in sharing with Nancy the fact that he was two months behind in his payments.

Despite many unresolved issues, all was relatively quiet for the next two months, until at last there was some news to report. Michael received a response to one of the complaints he had filed against Mendelsohn. Dr. Morton Johan, the chair of the Ethics Committee of the Office of the Psychiatric Physicians of Pennsylvania (PPP), acknowledged receipt of the complaint and outlined the investigative process. Johan also indicated that the investigation "may well take a year or more to complete," and even if Mendelsohn were found to have violated the ethical principles, the process would not result in the suspension or revocation of her license to practice medicine, or restitution of fees to Michael.

Michael informed his attorney of this development and, in turn, his attorney informed him that a Daniel Butler had been named common law arbitrator in the matter of the boxes. Leventon wrote to Butler, but didn't receive a response. Consequently, on April 2, 1993, he sent Butler another letter to try to schedule the arbitration.

Concerning Dr. Mendelsohn's remaining Ariel's therapist, Leventon tried to ascertain from Harry Gruener if Nancy had also observed Ariel's unwillingness to see the therapist so as to avoid filing another petition. Harry's response came as no surprise: "[M]y client . . . believes that Ariel continues to benefit from the assistance of Dr. Mendelsohn. . . . It appears that the only reason to modify the present Order is because your client no longer wishes to pay for or have Ariel receive the benefit of Dr. Mendelsohn's counseling."

To court once more they went. At motions on April 12 Judge Kaplan scheduled a conciliation pertaining to the Dr. Mendelsohn matter for June 24. Another wait began.

There was still no word from Common Law Arbitrator Butler who, four months prior, had been appointed by the Court to resolve the porcelain box matter.

In the midst of this tension, Michael wanted to take Nathaniel to a Bar Mitzvah that fell on a day that Nathaniel was not in his father's custody. Placing a telephone call to Nancy to arrange this was not an option for Michael. Nancy hadn't spoken to him in years. He made his request in a letter, reminding Nancy of an instance about a month prior when he had allowed her to have the children on one of his weekends.

Nancy didn't deny Michael's request. She didn't grant it, either. She ignored it. Michael had no choice but to get the attorneys involved. Leventon wrote Gruener, requesting his immediate attention to the matter.

There was a breakthrough—Nancy's attorney informed Michael's attorney that Nancy was agreeable to the request.

So much for the breakthrough, however. As Leventon informed Gruener on May 26, 1993,

> ... It is Michael's belief that Nancy intentionally undermined [the weekend] by purportedly arranging a Friday night slumber party at her home with [two of] Nathaniel's friends.
>
> The three boys purportedly presented themselves at Michael's in jeans on Saturday morning and Nathaniel insisted on playing baseball with his friends rather than putting on his dress clothes and accompanying his father to the Bar Mitzvah.
>
> When Michael attempted to reason with Nathaniel, Nathaniel ran to Nancy's home.

Michael wondered if Gruener was finally getting a more complete picture of his client. If not, Michael mused, he would when the porcelain box proceedings took place (assuming that Mr. Butler eventually contacted someone).

Finally, nearly six months after being appointed by the court as the common law arbitrator to resolve the matter of the boxes and Michael's missing documents, Butler did contact Michael's attorney. A hearing date was scheduled for June 29, 1993, and, in a fax to both sides, Butler clarified what he obviously considered one of his most pressing concerns: "My fee is $125 an hour. I expect . . . that this case will not require more than five hours from presentation through decision. I would expect that payment would be split between the parties and available at the time of the hearing."

Five days prior to that hearing the June 24 conciliation regarding whether or not Dr. Mendelsohn should remain as Ariel's therapist took place. Again, there was no surprise outcome. In fact, there was no outcome. Judge Kaplan was going to think about it.

At last, though, one more wait was over. Nearly two years after three of the boxes that "didn't exist" had been found by Michael at an antique show, the hearing began for custody of the porcelain boxes and Michael's personal documents. The cast of characters included the regular foursome—Michael, Paul Leventon, Nancy, and Harry Gruener.

MICHAEL L. NIELAND VS. NANCY S. NIELAND
[condensed]

Michael Louis Nieland, Having Been First Duly Sworn, Was Examined and Testified as Follows:

EXAMINATION BY THE MASTER [DANIEL BUTLER]:

MASTER: Let me ask you a couple of questions to make sure I understand. First of all, on the day [of the property exchange when the porcelain boxes were to be divided equally] there were, in fact, thirteen items—thirteen of these porcelain boxes that were made available, of which [eight] were not valuable . . . ?

MICHAEL: That's correct. [Four had little value, four had modest value, and only five were a part of the collection of sixteen boxes to be divided.]

MASTER: You said you took only six [items], of which only three were what you considered to be valuable [a part of the collection]?

MICHAEL: That's correct.

MASTER: How do you explain the one-year gap before the next thing happened?

MICHAEL: . . . I think my ex-spouse felt she had gotten away with it and it was now safe to go peddling these items to various dealers. I have seen property that I owned all over East End antique shops. In fact, I bought some of my property back, including missing items that were never even included in the [1987 postseparation joint property appraisal —even though Nancy was under a Court Order at the time to have all the marital property she removed from the marital residence present for an on-site inspection by a qualified appraiser].

LEVENTON: Michael, excuse me, I don't think that's responsive to Mr. Butler's question.

MICHAEL: Perhaps I didn't understand the question.

MASTER: Why did you wait a year?

GRUENER: More than a year. . . .

MICHAEL: I think you have to understand, in this case there are so many issues going on, it's very hard to litigate intensively everything! . . .

MASTER: . . . Did you just never expect to see those things again?

MICHAEL: I thought I would never see them again.

*   *   *

EXAMINATION BY MR. LEVENTON:

LEVENTON: Were [all of the documents stipulated to be given back to you] made available to you for return?

MICHAEL: No. They were not. . . . Many income tax records, some very important files . . . and a number of other personal [mementos] were not given to me.

* * *

LEVENTON: . . . I would ask that if the Court finds in favor of Dr. Michael Nieland and orders [the return] of the three antique boxes and the documents that have not yet been returned, . . . that the Court also impose under Paragraph 17 of the Marriage Settlement Agreement, as specifically provided, reasonable counsel fees. . . .

MASTER: I just have one more question [for Michael]. Bottom line, what do you want?

MICHAEL: I want my documents back that should be returned to me and I want these boxes returned to me, these French porcelain boxes. . . .

* * *

CROSS-EXAMINATION BY MR. GRUENER:

GRUENER: I want to show you something that I think maybe you will agree with. . . .

MICHAEL: It's a renewal floater policy. . . . That policy had been in effect for at least eight or nine years. . . .

GRUENER: And you had no objections to those values and you were insuring [the three porcelain boxes in question today] with this policy; were you not?

MICHAEL: Everyone insures items for—you can't just keep going back year after year getting items re-appraised. It gets awfully expensive.

GRUENER: Let's take a look at [the three boxes in question as they are valued on the insurance policy]. A porcelain lidded French box—$185; another porcelain lidded French box—$85; and a third porcelain lidded box, French—$85.

MICHAEL: If these boxes are so valueless, why did your client steal them?

GRUENER: I object to that and ask that it be stricken from the record and I wonder if you [Special Master Butler] might admonish this witness—whom I have cross-examined many times before—to please stop with the innuendoes, the attacks.

MICHAEL: I am just telling the truth. This is a scam.

* * *

GRUENER: Mr. Butler, if you could please instruct the witness to please just answer my questions!

MICHAEL: I am trying to, but you keep shouting in my ear!

MASTER: This is his impassioned representation of why he is here.

GRUENER: I understand.

Nancy Selove Nieland, Having Been First Duly Sworn, Was Examined and Testified as Follows:

EXAMINATION BY MR. GRUENER:

GRUENER: It has been alleged in the petition that brings us here today that there were—specifically—four boxes that were not on your porch [on the day of the property exchange]. . . . Is that true?

NANCY: Yes.

GRUENER: Tell the Court why they were not on the porch.

NANCY: I moved out of the at-that-time marital residence quickly—upon the advice of my attorney and a psychiatrist I was seeing—because things were so awful. . . . I moved to a rental house taking my three young children at the time—who were four, six, and fifteen. . . . I resided in the rental house for about two months. Then I bought another house on Northumberland and moved there. . . .

GRUENER: Nancy, how long a time are we talking about in which you made two separate moves?

NANCY: Within eight weeks—and two weeks later my oldest daughter [Brita] was being married. . . . There was packing and unpacking going on, wedding gifts arriving. . . . Things were in a very confused state. [Brita]—who was in medical school at the time—was living in a small apartment, so all of the wedding gifts that arrived at our house were boxed up. . . .

GRUENER: So there was a lot of turmoil during that period?

NANCY: Yes—and a lot of packing and unpacking.

GRUENER: Now, when did you discover these four boxes?

NANCY: . . . Many of those boxes were not retrieved until [I] moved into a larger house in 1990 [after the property exchange]. . . . In some of the boxes [that I retrieved from storage] were these porcelain boxes that had been packed with my daughter's wedding gifts, things I hadn't used, and so on. . . .

GRUENER: Now you found the boxes and at that time did you want them?

NANCY: No. I did not.

GRUENER: What did you do with them?

NANCY: I gave them to an antique dealer to sell for me. . . . I didn't think there was any reason to contact Michael since he had been happy with the exchanges which he had made.

*   *   *

GRUENER: Nancy, let's go on for a moment to the documents. . . . Did you return to Michael Nieland any and all documents that you had in your possession now or at any other time?

NANCY: . . . I could not find some of the things that were on the list [at the time of the property exchange]. Later . . . some of these [missing documents were found] and these documents were given to my daughter Jennie who then gave them to Michael.

GRUENER: Who gave them to your daughter?

NANCY: I did. They were in my closet.

GRUENER: The implication in Michael's testimony was that Jennie found them and caught you [in an act of deceit]. But you gave them to Jennie?

NANCY: Yes.

GRUENER: And told her to give them to her dad?

NANCY: Yes.*

GRUENER: Do you have [any of the documents that Michael claims are still missing]?

NANCY: I do not have them now. I have not ever had anything that hasn't been returned to him. . . .

GRUENER: No further questions. . . .

---

*In a letter dated January 31, 1992, from Nancy to Harry Gruener (which he forwarded to Paul Leventon), Nancy stated: "I do not possess any documents [of Michael's]. . . . I turned over to him all the papers he asked for except for one or two letters which *Jennie found* later and gave to him . . ." (emphasis added).

After cross-examination by Leventon, the outing came to an end. Mr. Butler arrived at a decision more expediently than he did for simply scheduling the hearing date. But he notified both attorneys in writing of one minor detail before issuing his ruling: "You will note that [my] final [fee] figure is slightly higher than I had estimated. . . . Given the litigious history of the parties, I'm sure you understand that I am hesitant to become embroiled in their dispute further. For that reason, I must insist upon payment in full [of an additional $125 evenly divided between the parties] prior to releasing my decision."

Nancy and Michael got out their checkbooks once again. Mr. Butler, paid in full, rendered his decision (which, under the guidelines of Common Law Arbitration, could not be appealed):

> Now, therefore, it is ordered, adjudged, and decreed . . . that Defendant Dr. Nancy Nieland shall tender to Plaintiff Dr. Michael Nieland the three disputed porcelain boxes. . . . In exchange, therefore, she is entitled to the three items: the pitcher, Capo Di-Monte box, and the "other" porcelain box, which were offered by her ex-husband. This despite her having made it abundantly clear that she ascribes little or no value to the pitcher and the "other" box. . . .
>
> Any inequities which may appear to result from a disparity in value between items received by [Nancy] and items [Michael] is to be provided with, pursuant to the agreement, should be considered liquidated damages for the loss of [Michael's] papers which were also to have been provided him.
>
> In accordance with Paragraph 17 of the parties' [Marriage Settlement] Agreement, [Nancy] shall tender to [Michael] $2,000 as reasonable counsel fees incurred in pursuit of this matter. In addition, [Nancy] shall be required to pay the Arbitrator's fee totaling $750 of which each party has paid $375.

[Michael] shall be reimbursed for the portion he has already paid.

Daniel E. Butler, Arbitrator

Michael won. The boxes finally had a home.

But this episode was not just about boxes to Michael—this was about holding Nancy accountable to a signed agreement . . . about justice and fairness prevailing . . . about honesty and principles . . . and—perhaps most important to Michael—this was to demonstrate to his children that good guys don't always lose.

12. Obstruction of Justice, Cover-Up (i.e., Business as Usual)

As the porcelain box episode demonstrated, I've had my share of "victories" since my marriage came to an end. But, I'm hardly gloating. The price Jennie, Nathaniel, Ariel, and I have paid is far too high. Divorce should not be about winning or losing—particularly when it concerns children. Quite the contrary. All efforts should be expended to preserve, protect, even strengthen a child's relationship with both parents.

Unfortunately, judges and lawyers seem unable to understand an outcome that doesn't have winners or losers. Family Divisions seem to exist to create custodial parents and "monetary" parents—one parent keeps the kids and the other pays the bills. This system prospers because the more child support judges order, the more the public mistakenly believes the judges are doing their jobs correctly and the more federal matching funds are earmarked for Family Division courthouses. Accordingly, should children maintain close contact with both parents after divorce and both parents nurture and support the children everyone "wins," but the system would seem to have failed be-

471

cause such an arrangement cannot be quantified in financial terms so easily. Less money would change hands. The custody industry and those who profit from it know only one way to justify its existence—dollars and cents.

The terribly destructive adversary system that thrives on the creation of one-parent families should thoroughly alarm the public. It has no constructive role in family life. All it does is contribute to family destruction. Who could deny that the breakdown of the family has contributed significantly to the escalation of crime and violence in society?

What must be done then to promote "the best interests of the child" and the best interests of society? First, the adversary system as a means for determining custody should be abolished. The child's interests (and society's interests) are best served when children of divorce retain contact with both parents—free from the strife and guilt of having to favor one over the other and free from the devastation of losing contact with the "less important" parent. Legislators have already eliminated much of the destructiveness of divorce by creating "no-fault divorce." Now, they must enact "no-fault custody" to avoid the damage done to children, parents, and society by the inadequacies and failures of the present system. Legislators need to enact laws that not only encourage but mandate equally shared custody for divorced parents, and judges must not be permitted to thwart the intent of these statutes.

Such legislation would minimize the opportunity for either parent to undermine the other's custody rights because it would be a useless and profitless endeavor. Violations of custody orders would not be tolerated under any circumstances. (If there are accusations of child abuse, they should be adjudicated as a criminal offense, just as they are in any married, two-parent family.)

"No-fault custody" would also be cost-effective because it would significantly curtail litigation and its attendant expenses as well as the need for court-appointed advocates, evaluators, monitors, and therapists in Family Divisions. Surely, nothing would be lost in terms of "the best interests" of the child or society. Neither mental health professionals nor judges should make "ultimate de-

cisions" that impact children's and parents' lives forever based on a few days or weeks of observation or evaluation. Circumstances constantly change, the risk of error is far too great, and, most of all, children need both parents, especially after divorce.

Unfortunately, any reform of the system will come too late for my family. We've already experienced years of pain—with perhaps more to come: To put an end to what Ariel and I contended were unnecessary and coercive sessions with her psychiatrist, Sylvia Mendelsohn, I still had to "win" in court one more time.

—Michael L. Nieland, M.D.
No-Fault Custody Crusader

Michael believed that the best feature of the porcelain box episode was the absence of Judge Kaplan presiding over the proceedings. Michael had been less than impressed by the judge's attentiveness and sensitivity throughout his family's case—beginning with his appointment of Roland Singer. Unfortunately for Michael, he was still at the judge's mercy concerning Dr. Mendelsohn.

A few days after the porcelain box hearing Judge Kaplan, who had conducted a June 24 conciliation in regard to Michael's petition seeking Dr. Mendelsohn's removal as Ariel's psychiatrist, had decided how to proceed. He contacted Barbara Cymerman to meet with Ariel and determine the validity of the allegation that "Ariel absolutely no longer wishes to continue treatment with Dr. Sylvia Mendelsohn." Cymerman could then inform Judge Kaplan (via letter) of her opinion and he would decide the petition. Her time, of course, would be billed equally to Nancy and Michael.

Michael wondered if this was another example of Judge Kaplan's warped sense of humor. It was not. Apparently, the judge had no concerns about Barbara Cymerman in regard to her interviewing the children despite her lack of qualifications and experience in the field of mental health. Moreover, how could she be objective in view of the fact that Michael had filed a formal complaint against her six months earlier?

Judge Kaplan might not have had these concerns, but Michael did. So did his attorney. In what Michael deems a heroic act, Paul Leventon wrote directly to the judge:

> ... Very respectfully, be advised that my client, Michael L. Nieland, vigorously opposes any and all out-of-court communications, conferences, interviews, however identified, between Attorney Cymerman and Ariel or Nathaniel Nieland.
>
> Dr. Michael Nieland reminds me that both of his children are fully capable of speaking for themselves, as they ably did a few years ago, during a portion of a five-day bifurcated Contempt Proceeding. Ariel, now eleven, is able to testify either in open court or in your chambers with counsel present. ...
>
> Your attention is respectfully directed to the fact that in February of 1993, Michael L. Nieland filed a formal Complaint against Barbara G. Cymerman with the Commonwealth of Pennsylvania, Department of State, Bureau of Professional and Occupational Affairs. Enclosed herewith please find a notification form evidencing same.
>
> Is it possible that either Attorney Cymerman has not yet received notice of the filing of this formal Complaint or has failed to inform Your Honor of the initiation of same? I doubt that had Your Honor known of said filing that you would have issued your letter of June 29, 1993.
>
> Finally, in order to attempt to set the record straight, be advised that both of Michael's children independently informed him that they found their respective "interviews" by Ms. Cymerman to be ridiculous and disagreeable. Do you know of any other instances where children have been taken to the home of a non-mental health professional for purposes of being "interviewed"? Michael vigorously objects to any further unsupervised physical contact between At-

torney Cymerman and either of his children, with or without the acquiescence of their mother, Dr. Nancy Nieland.

Again, very respectfully, I suggest that your Honor conduct in camera* interviews with Ariel and Nathaniel Nieland, rather than having this judicial function usurped by an unqualified non-mental health professional.

Apparently, Barbara Cymerman didn't find Leventon's letter (of which she received a copy) quite so courageous. In an August 6, 1993 letter to Judge Kaplan, she claimed to be unaware of Michael's complaint against her, and "will not dignify with a response" the remarks Leventon had made regarding her previous meetings with the children—"unless the court so desires." Cymerman indicated that she would plan on proceeding as Kaplan had ordered, unless informed otherwise.

Judge Kaplan didn't bother to respond. In accordance with his wishes, Cymerman performed her "evaluation," billable to Michael and Nancy. She informed Kaplan that she would forward her recommendation immediately upon receipt of her $375 fee.

Cymerman shouldn't have expected prompt payment from Michael. He was seething. Didn't she or Judge Kaplan realize how many professional boundaries she had violated? In regard to Judge Kaplan, Michael could not fathom what moral, legal, or ethical world the judge inhabited. Didn't he have any sense of elemental fairness, of the limits of judicial prerogative or any understanding of professional responsibilities?

Evidently not. Almost simultaneously Michael received in the mail a psychology newsletter, which corroborated what Dr. Van Cara had told Michael previously about "one of Judge Kaplan's favorite psychologists." One Neil Rosen-

---

*Private interviews conducted in the judge's chambers (as opposed to those which occur in open court).

blum, Ph.D., was placed on two years' probation and fined for "having failed to value objectivity, engaged in a dual relationship, and committed unprofessional conduct in five child-custody cases." In addition, "the probation requires Rosenblum's custody-litigation related work to be supervised for a two-year period."*

If Michael had read the legal notice correctly, Neil Rosenblum was not prohibited from doing further custody evaluations for the court even though he had engaged in "unprofessional conduct" in five child-custody cases. Could this really be true? Out of curiosity, Michael asked Leventon to find out if Rosenblum or Dr. Singer still worked for the Family Division. His attorney, in turn, wrote the Family Division Custody Coordinator, Patricia A. Piercy, Ph.D., requesting the information. In her reply, she enclosed a list of court-appointed psychologists who did custody evaluations. Both Singer and Rosenblum were named.

Neither had missed a beat in his court-related psychology practices. While their penalties may not legally prevent court appointments, it was deplorable to Michael that the Family Division ordered families to work with these sanctioned, censured, and/or reprimanded individuals. Did the court owe a living to Singer, Rosenblum, and the other psychologists involved in what the task force report had classified as an "epidemic" of ethics complaints? Was the court, Michael wondered, totally indifferent to the suffering perpetrated upon children and parents by these people? Michael couldn't imagine why any psychiatrist or psychologist would want to be linked with Singer and Rosenblum by inclusion on the Family Division evaluator's list.

Because filing a formal complaint against the entire Family Division wasn't realistic Michael decided to do the

---

*"Disciplinary Actions," *Pennsylvania State Board of Psychology Newsletter* (Summer 1993): 7–9.

next best thing. He would file a complaint against the judges that were involved in his case—Kaplan and Wettick.

Just as he was about to embark on that task, Susan A. Groskin, the state's professional conduct investigator for the Law Enforcement Division of the Bureau of Professional and Occupational Affairs, contacted him regarding his complaints against Cymerman and Mendelsohn. Michael agreed to meet with Ms. Groskin at his home on August 10 to discuss his charges further. The day after their interview Michael sent her a photocopy of Cymerman's August 6 missive, which the investigator had not seen, along with a few follow-up comments concerning Cymerman's continuing involvement in the case: "I think Ms. Cymerman is totally out of control, is totally irresponsible, and is defiant of the law and plain common sense. Only someone bereft of any judgment would have attempted a psychological evaluation of my children given her level of training and her degree and would have persisted in this behavior. I hope you can put a stop to it."

Michael returned to preparing his complaint against Judges Wettick and Kaplan:

> ... I accuse both Judge Kaplan and Judge Wettick of unethical and negligent judicial conduct, judicial irresponsibility, and abuse of position. I believe the conclusion is inescapable that Judges Kaplan and Wettick have repeatedly violated Canons 1, 2, and 3 of the *Code of Judicial Conduct of the Commonwealth of Pennsylvania* which require a judge to "uphold the integrity of the Judiciary," to "avoid impropriety and the appearance of impropriety in all his activities," and "to perform the duties of his office impartially and diligently."
> ... Judge Kaplan and Judge Wettick have in my case and in many similar cases improperly and unethically misused psychologists, psychiatrists, and other professionals, including attorneys, in the performance of custody evalua-

tions. . . . My case represents just a glimpse into the ethical squalor of . . . the Allegheny County Family Division.

—At a conciliation [November 9, 1987] Judge Wettick was made aware of unauthorized interviews arranged by my former wife between Court-appointed Evaluator Dr. Roland Singer and numerous parties with no standing or relevance in the case. . . . Judge Wettick failed to take any action against Dr. Singer. . . .

—By [subsequently] appointing Roland Singer "Monitor" Judge Wettick violated Principle 6b of Section 41.61 (Code of Ethics) of the *Rules and Regulations of the State Board of Psychology,* which prohibits Dual Relationships. . . .

—[When I filed a Motion for Clarification], Judge Wettick neglected his judicial responsibilities . . . by ordering Roland Singer to decide this legal issue. . . .

—Furthermore, Judge Wettick overruled without cause a finding of Contempt made by a master he himself had appointed. . . .

—Judge Kaplan, instead of responding in an appropriate manner to a joint request that he appoint a mental health professional, chose a lawyer. . . . To my knowledge such an appointment is unparalleled in any Court and probably never occurred before even in the Allegheny County Family Division. . . .

What is perhaps even more extraordinary than anything so far recounted is the fact that Judge Kaplan and the other judges have reappointed censured and disgraced psychologists Roland Singer and Neil Rosenblum to the roster of psychologists whom the Court has approved as evaluators for custody cases. . . . The reinstatement of Rosenblum and Singer, at best, is unseemly and this goes to the root of the problem in the Allegheny County Family Division. The judges just don't care. I am not sure whether Judge Kaplan read the Task Force Report or if he understood it. . . . My case would seem to indicate that even if he read it, he couldn't comprehend it, or just didn't give a damn. . . . Judges who

appoint unethical psychologists out of indifference or ignorance are more culpable than inadequate psychologists because judges are supposed to know and uphold the law.

I hope that the Judicial Conduct Board will thoroughly
assess and weigh the accusations in this complaint and their
truthfulness, fully comprehend the magnitude of the problem in Allegheny County, consult with the state's licensing
boards, and . . . remove, severely reprimand, or otherwise
end the careers of the ethically corrupt judges, present and
former, in the Allegheny County Family Division. . . .

Had Michael waited another day or two to file his complaint, he might very well have charged Judge Kaplan with
one more impropriety. Evidently, the judge wasn't pleased
that one of his appointees, Barbara Cymerman, was being in-
vestigated for misconduct. As a result, he wrote a letter to
State Investigator Groskin, dated the same day as Michael's
complaint against him:

September 13, 1993

Dear Ms. Groskin:

As you know, I have appointed Barbara Cymerman, Esquire, to serve as the child advocate in the [*Nieland* v.
Nieland] custody matter. Ms. Cymerman has provided me
with a copy of your letter dated August 18, 1993, indicating
that a complaint has been filed against her before the State
Board of Medicine by Dr. Michael Nieland, the father in
this custody case. As a result, your bureau is conducting an
investigation. I consider this to be a direct interference in a
matter solely within the jurisdiction of the courts.

By copy of this letter to Ms. Cymerman and Zygmont
A. Pines, Esquire, Counsel to the Court Administrator of
the Commonwealth of Pennsylvania, I am advising Ms.
Cymerman not to respond to any correspondence and/or
interference by your office. Any further requests from your

office shall be presented by petition to the undersigned with notice to all appropriate parties.

Very truly yours,
Lawrence W. Kaplan
Judge

cc: Gene B. Strassburger III, Administrative Judge,
Family Division

Copies of the letter were also sent to both Michael's and Nancy's attorneys.

Michael was irked that Judge Kaplan seemed to be covering his tracks by misrepresenting the facts concerning Barbara Cymerman's role. Kaplan said in the letter that he originally appointed her "to serve as the Child Advocate" when he had done no such thing. He appointed her in vague terms a "said Evaluator," in response to the consent agreement before him entitled "Motion to Appoint Expert Mental Health Witness."

But, regardless of her role, did Judge Kaplan have the authority or the right to interfere with an investigation ordered by another government agency?

Michael hoped Judge Eugene Strassburger, the administrative judge ("Gene" to Judge Kaplan), would demand that Kaplan cease his interference with the state's investigation of Barbara Cymerman. No such order was forthcoming, however. Without a repeal of Judge Kaplan's letter, Michael feared the investigation of Cymerman had been compromised. Clearly, it would be difficult for John D. Kelly, the prosecuting attorney for the State's Bureau of Professional and Occupational Affairs, to pursue a case against Cymerman without Susan Groskin completing her investigation. Just in case Mr. Kelly wasn't aware of Judge Kaplan's latest action, Michael sent him a brief summary.

Kelly acknowledged Michael's letter, but the tone worried Michael. The prosecuting attorney didn't seem too concerned about what had been going on in the Allegheny County Family Division:

> I have received your letter regarding your complaint against Barbara Cymerman, Esquire. In response thereto, please accept my assurances that this office will review this matter . . . to ensure that any work of a psychological nature being conducted in the Commonwealth is conducted appropriately by qualified individuals. Please understand, however, that the Professional Psychologist Practice Act is obviously not the only law of the Commonwealth, and it therefore must be interpreted harmoniously with other laws of government as well. . . .

As the weeks passed, Michael had no more contact with Groskin or Kelly—not a good sign to Michael. All the while, Ariel continued to have "therapy" sessions with Sylvia Mendelsohn, though Ariel told her dad they didn't talk or do anything other than play board games or cards. Michael had no idea what Cymerman recommended to Judge Kaplan concerning the sessions because Michael refused to pay for what he considered a meaningless evaluation. He only hoped Mr. Kelly could grasp what was occurring in the Family Division. The answer came in the mail:

December 1, 1993
RE: Sylvia Mendelsohn and Barbara Cymerman
File # 93-49-00496   File # 93-63-00497

Dear Dr. Nieland:
    This is to advise you that this office has completed its investigation and review of the above referenced files. We have determined that your Complaints and the information that we obtained in our investigation do not provide us with sufficient grounds to bring formal disciplinary ac-

tion against either Dr. Mendelsohn or Ms. Cymerman. The basis for our decision is as follows:

Regarding Ms. Cymerman, it was our belief that none of the actions performed by her constituted the practice of psychology. . . .

The Professional Psychologists Practice Act does not make custody recommendations the exclusive province of licensed psychologists. Ms. Cymerman performed no psychological testing, conducted no therapy, and otherwise undertook no actions which were designed to affect the mental health of any member of your family.

Michael maintained that Cymerman, who flaunted descriptive terms such as "wooing" and "systematic courtship behavior," was practicing psychology and in this capacity she had most definitely affected the mental health of Ariel, in particular. Cymerman's Summary and Conclusion call for Ariel to continue therapy and Nathaniel to see a therapist. Was Kelly suggesting that prescribing therapy was not the practice of psychology or that undergoing therapy was not "designed to affect the mental health of an individual"? Reputable psychologists and psychiatrists would certainly agree that that is not the case, that unnecessary therapy can be injurious, and that an attorney is hardly qualified to determine the need for therapy!

As further evidence of Cymerman's adverse affect on the mental health of Ariel, Michael remembers his daughter stating, shortly after the issuance of the Cymerman report, that she wanted to end her three-year relationship with Dr. Mendelsohn. He also recalls Dr. Mendelsohn admitting to him that the change in the custody schedule recommended by Ms. Cymerman was "a huge change" and was very upsetting to Ariel.

Moreover, Michael found absurd Kelly's comment that "the Professional Psychologists Practice Act [PPPA] does not make custody recommendations the exclusive province of licensed psychologists." The PPPA, in fact, does state:

Nothing in this act shall be construed to prevent *qualified* members of other recognized professions, including, but not limited to, clergy, drug and alcohol abuse counselors, mental health counselors, social workers, marriage counselors, family counselors, crisis intervention counselors, pastoral counselors, rehabilitation counselors, and psychoanalysts, from doing work of a psychological nature consistent with the training and the code of ethics of their respective professions. [Emphasis added.]

As demonstrated by the numerous professions cited in the PPPA, any individual "doing work of a psychological nature" in the state of Pennsylvania must have the appropriate training. Could there be any dispute that custody evaluations are inquiries of a psychological nature? Why else was every individual on the Family Division's evaluator list a licensed psychologist or, in one instance, a psychiatrist? The PPPA makes no reference at all to custody evaluations because, Michael speculates, no one drafting the legislation ever would have thought that an attorney would be so presumptuous as to perform one.

Ms. Cymerman's communication with Dr. Mendelsohn, and repetition of her statement[s], do not constitute the practice of psychology; certainly anyone, including an attorney, can receive information and repeat it.

But, by Kelly's own account, Cymerman did more than "receive information and repeat it." She "reached a conclusion of her own" and "put this into a recommendation." In other words, she had collected facts about behavior and experience (hearsay from the legal point of view), then systematically organized these facts into a summary and conclusion, which contained recommendations that could influence the future behavior and mental health of the parties. Did this not constitute the practice of psychology?

As to Dr. Mendelsohn, from your lengthy Complaint, this office was able to glean five distinct areas about which you appear to be complaining: first, that Dr. Mendelsohn told you that from the first day she met your daughter, she did not detect fear of you but nevertheless Dr. Mendelsohn continued providing therapy to your daughter for two years; second, that Dr. Mendelsohn did not refuse to speak with Ms. Cymerman, since you did not believe Ms. Cymerman to be qualified to act as a Child Advocate; third, that Dr. Mendelsohn failed to clarify certain issues which you allege were inaccurate in Ms. Cymerman's report; fourth, that Dr. Mendelsohn had a duty to testify in Court for you since you were her patient; fifth, that Dr. Mendelsohn breached your confidentiality by informing the Court of your delinquency in payment of your half of your daughter's therapy bill.

I will address each of these issues in turn.

As to the first issue, Dr. Mendelsohn informed us that neither you nor your ex-wife had informed her when you contacted her for treatment of your daughter, that you were Court-ordered to do so.

Michael categorically denies this self-serving assertion by Mendelsohn. He alleges that if she did say this, it was a brazen lie and contradicted by abundant evidence to the contrary. He had handed her the proposed order of court at their very first meeting. Even Harry Gruener, Nancy's attorney, wrote at one point to Dr. Mendelsohn that the attorneys "were instrumental in your selection" in response to the proposed order of court stating that "the parties, through counsel, shall immediately select an appropriate professional for the evaluation and treatment, if so required."

Consequently, it was her intent from the outset to treat all of your daughter's emotional difficulties. As a result, Dr.

> Mendelsohn stated that, when you did inform her of the Court Order, she informed you that she would not only evaluate the alleged fear that your daughter had of you, but also all other problems that she may have had.

Not quite right, Mr. Kelly. First of all, Michael contends that Ariel had no emotional difficulties nor should Dr. Mendelsohn have begun with the intention to treat anything before first evaluating Ariel's alleged fear. Surely, a doctor must first make an evaluation (i.e., a diagnosis) before prescribing treatment (i.e., therapy).

Furthermore, if it had been Mendelsohn's intent from the outset to *treat* Ariel, how could she ethically accept the court-ordered role to *evaluate* Ariel? While it is true that in a noncoercive setting a doctor may do both, it certainly is not appropriate in a custody case. This is a dual relationship and it created the situation in which Dr. Mendelsohn, the therapist, probably did not want to hear from Dr. Mendelsohn, the evaluator, that Ariel didn't fear her father. Such an evaluation would have meant that Ariel did not need therapy, which would thereby end weekly fees (that would eventually amount to more than $20,000) for Dr. Mendelsohn, the therapist.

> Dr. Mendelsohn alleges that you consented to [her role(s)]. This is evident from the fact that you continued to take your daughter to see Dr. Mendelsohn.

Of course Michael continued to take Ariel to her sessions with Mendelsohn. He had had little choice. He and Nancy were required by a court order to provide evaluation and treatment for Ariel. In addition, it is Michael's clear recollection that Dr. Mendelsohn held out hope when his little girl was running away from him that she could help him only "by helping Ariel resist her mother's pressure." Michael doesn't consider the fact that he continued to take Ariel to see Mendelsohn any proof of consent—he was being encouraged to do so by someone he trusted.

> As to your second complaint, this office agrees with Dr. Mendelsohn that, pursuant to the Court Order and the releases signed by you and your wife, she had an ethical duty to speak with Ms. Cymerman.

Why is that? Dr. Mendelsohn had purportedly informed the parties that she would speak only with another mental health professional. And Kelly had failed to take into account that the *Principles of Medical Ethics with Annotations Especially Applicable to Psychiatry* state: "When the psychiatrist is ordered by the Court to reveal confidences entrusted to him/her by patients *he/she may comply or he/she may ethically hold the right to dissent* within the framework of the law." In addition, psychiatrists *"should not delegate . . . to any nonmedical person* any matter requiring professional medical judgment" (emphasis added). How could Kelly possibly have concluded that Mendelsohn did not violate these edicts in regard to Ariel?

And why did Kelly feel Mendelsohn had the right to pick and choose among court orders? Hadn't she had an equal duty to respond to the previous court order that called for the evaluation and treatment of Ariel and Nathaniel? Was the evaluation supposed to be kept a secret?

In regard to the issue of Michael's release, this was hardly truly informed consent because Mendelsohn never apprised him of the risks and consequences of permitting her to discuss the case with Barbara Cymerman.* She did not tell him that:

---

*According to the information included with the list of Family Division evaluators that Michael had received through his attorney, the methods used to gather information necessary for the evaluation of

1. She would not check Cymerman's credentials;

2. She would not correct or amend any distortions of her position by Cymerman;

3. She would not correct any misquotes attributed to her;

4. She might make observations that could be detrimental to Michael's custody rights.

Truly informed consent is a fundamental issue of malpractice—not just ethics. Such distinctions—consent versus truly informed consent, child advocate versus mental health professional—are apparently of little concern to Kelly. He even paraphrased one aspect of Michael's complaint as follows: "You did not believe Ms. Cymerman to be qualified to act as a child advocate." Not so. Michael never said or wrote any such thing. Ms. Cymerman wasn't ever appointed a child advocate, nor did she ever refer to herself as such. Michael took issue with her appointment in response to a consent agreement calling for a mental health professional.

> As to your [third allegation] that Dr. Mendelsohn has a professional duty to clarify for the Court the information from Ms. Cymerman's report which you allege to be inaccurate, this office does not perceive Dr. Mendelsohn's failure to do so as grounds to undertake formal disciplinary action. Dr. Mendelsohn quite appropriately stated that she does not believe in testifying in custody matters when she is the

---

"parental functioning and competence" and the assessment of "the developmental needs of the children involved" (the primary tasks of a court-appointed evaluator) would include "interviewing, standardized questionnaires, direct observations, and collateral data." However, the "Informed Consent" form that a parent had to sign offered no warning of what could go wrong: the individuals interviewed by the evaluator might be biased toward one parent, the "collateral data" might be skewed, or the recommendations might be inappropriate and/or unwarranted. The essence of truly informed consent is that it be voluntary and not coerced, but divorcing parents do not appear to have any real choice other than to sign the release once a judge has ordered an evaluation.

child's therapist. As you are well aware from the Singer case, it is inappropriate for a therapist to testify as an Evaluator. Again, since Dr. Mendelsohn was your daughter's therapist, it could have compromised the effectiveness of therapy for her to testify in Court.

It was Mr. Kelly who didn't seem to remember the Singer case at all. First, Singer was not supposed to be anyone's therapist—he was to be an evaluator only. Second, it is true that dual relationships are prohibited. But earlier in his letter, Kelly had stated flatly that it was Mendelsohn's intention to treat and then evaluate Ariel. Dual relationships are forbidden in any order.

As for Mendelsohn "quite appropriately" not testifying in custody matters, what exactly did Kelly think she was doing when she spoke to the court in the person of Ms. Cymerman? Even if Mendelsohn had been Ariel's therapist only, hadn't she spoken to the court in the person of Ms. Cymerman regarding custody matters?

Furthermore, you appear to complain that Dr. Mendelsohn failed to testify on your behalf, which you perceive to be required by the AMA *Ethical Principles*. However, you go on to complain that Dr. Mendelsohn essentially testified on behalf of your ex-wife by informing the Court that you were delinquent in your payment of her bills. Obviously, if it would be improper for Dr. Mendelsohn to testify for your ex-wife, it would be improper for her to testify for you.

Did Kelly learn this kind of logic in a law school?

First, the ethical principle that requires a doctor to testify, when asked, on behalf of a patient has nothing to do with the strictures against betraying confidences and voluntarily becoming a partisan in a legal dispute. Second, Kelly didn't directly address Michael's contention that Mendelsohn had improperly revealed information of a financial nature discussed with her in the context of their doctor-patient relationship. Michael had referred to Nancy's December 8, 1992 motion to compel compliance which stated: "Plaintiff [Michael to] pay the professional fees that he owes to Dr. Mendelsohn within ten days." Although Kelly skirted the issue, it seemed irrefutable that Mendelsohn involved herself as a partisan with Nancy in a legal dispute, thereby breaching the confidentiality of Michael's doctor-patient relationship with Dr. Mendelsohn.

> Again, it was for these reasons that these files were closed. This office does, however, thank you for having brought these matters to our attention.
>
> Sincerely,
> John D. Kelly

After digesting Kelly's rationale Michael wondered if Kelly, possibly as a result of Judge Kaplan's letter, feared locking horns with the Allegheny County judicial system. Or, perhaps he simply didn't understand the subtleties of custody determinations. After all, in the case of Roland Singer, Kelly had had no issues to decipher on his own. He already was aware that the psychologist had been censured and reprimanded by the American Psychological Association and its state and local branches. There were no prior decisions for the prosecuting attorney to lean on in his investigations of Michael's allegations against Barbara Cymerman and Sylvia Mendelsohn. Judging from his letter, Kelly understood little about the ethical aspects of custody cases.

Michael knew exactly what he was going to do about Kelly's decision: nothing. He could not take on the Commonwealth of Pennsylvania, too. Even Michael had his limits! Instead, he would hope for a better outcome from the

American Psychiatric Association concerning his ethics complaint against Sylvia Mendelsohn and from the State Judicial Conduct Board in regard to Judges Kaplan and Wettick.

There would be no more outcomes for Barbara Cymerman. She was off the hook. Michael wondered at what point she would stop sending him invoices for determining whether or not Ariel should continue her "treatment" with Sylvia Mendelsohn. Michael had absolutely no interest in whatever conclusions Cymerman might have drawn and he had no plans ever to send her the demanded $187.50 payment. He knew the truth from Ariel herself: She wanted nothing to do with Dr. Mendelsohn even though her mother kept making the appointments and the therapist kept accepting the fees.

Although Kelly's inaction disheartened Michael, he tried to keep it all in perspective. He had what he wanted most. In his life again were Ariel, eleven, who was following the Cymerman custody schedule, and Jennie, twenty-one, who was nearing her degree at the University of Pennsylvania. (Nathaniel, thirteen, had somehow avoided the separation from his father altogether.) These parental bonds with all his children, Michael realized, were far more important than the outcomes of his complaints.

With respect to the unresolved complaints, Michael had yet to hear anything from the State Judicial Conduct Board, but in the coming days he received a notification from the Psychiatric Physicians of Pennsylvania, an extension of the American Psychiatric Association, indicating that a hearing had been scheduled for January 15, 1994, regarding the charges levied against Sylvia Mendelsohn.

The news pleased Michael, though he was unhappy he would be excused prior to hearing Dr. Mendelsohn and her witnesses (who almost certainly would include Nancy) according to the procedures outlined in the letter. The stipulation also troubled Michael because it seemed to contradict the APA procedures: "The Complainant must be present at the Hearing unless excused by the Committee or Panel chair. The Complainant will be excused only when he/she has so requested and, in the judgment of the Chair, participation would be harmful to him/her." Why would participation be harmful to Michael? Nevertheless, he wouldn't object. He didn't want to run the risk of irritating the panel before the hearing took place.

Mendelsohn's "moment of truth" arrived on one of Pittsburgh's coldest winter days in years. The setting was the upper reaches of the Western Psychiatric Institute and Clinic. Present at the hearing were four panel members and a fifth nonvoting panel member, L. Alan Wright, M.D. (who had performed a preliminary investigation and decided the case had enough merit to warrant a formal hearing). Also present were Gwen Yackee, executive director of the PPP, and two attorneys advising the panel, Fred Speaker and David Lehman. And, of course, Michael was there, as were Mendelsohn and her attorney, C. Crady Swisher.

As Michael glanced around the room, he was surprised that one of the panel members was Mervin Stewart, a psychiatrist who resided in Pittsburgh. Michael recalled that both Dr. Stewart and his wife were Nancy's patients. If this was supposed to be a fair hearing how could Dr. Stewart participate as a panel member when Nancy probably would be one of Mendelsohn's key witnesses? But, once again, Michael chose not to protest because he didn't want to rile the panel members who would be adjudicating his case.

After the hearing Michael was filled with plenty of concerns. He felt more like the accused than the complainant. He contacted his attorney by telephone and proceeded to recount what had just occurred:

The hearing began with the chairperson, Dr. Morton Johan, questioning Michael, the complainant. Michael found the psychiatrist's interrogation of him as cold as the weather outside. There were no inquiries about Dr. Mendelsohn's behavior. Just one hostile question after another. Johan seemed determined to prove that Michael had no standing to bring an ethics complaint against Sylvia because he was never her patient. Apparently, Dr. Johan considered the thirty-seven regular sessions between Michael and Dr. Mendelsohn as nothing more than some sort of informative interaction. In an effort to prove this point, Johan asked Michael if he believed that, as a dermatopathologist, he had a doctor-patient relationship with a patient whose biopsy was sent to him by another doctor. Michael responded that he did have a duty of care to that patient, even if he had never met or examined the patient. Dr. Johan didn't seem to like Michael's answer.*

Michael then fielded some background questions from the second panel member, Dr. Sheila Judge, followed by more questioning from the third panel member, Dr. Richard Newman.

During the course of Dr. Newman's questioning, Michael recounted his consultation with Dr. Loren Roth. Michael related to the panel that Dr. Roth knew his case involved Sylvia Mendelsohn even before Michael had mentioned her name. Michael then commented to Newman something to the effect that "I knew then that the fix was in." If Mendelsohn hadn't done anything wrong, if she wasn't in jeopardy, why did Loren Roth know of the case?

Dr. Newman didn't seem to appreciate Michael's remark. He became visibly angry and asked Michael if he thought the conclusions of this committee were predetermined. Michael

---

*Although Dr. Johan was trying to show that some relationships are so tenuous that no doctor-patient relationship exists, he chose a bad example when he asked Michael about his role as a pathologist. Various court decisions have established that a pathologist examining a biopsy has a duty toward a patient identical to that of the treating physician.

replied that he hoped not, but Newman didn't seem to be listening.

Dr. Stewart, the fourth panel member, chose not to ask Michael any questions at all. Did he feel uncomfortable as a member of the panel because of his and his wife's relationship with Nancy?

With the panel's examination of Michael completed, Mr. Swisher, Dr. Mendelsohn's attorney, began to query Michael. Swisher immediately went on the attack. He tried to cast doubt on Michael's credibility, asking him if he ever said to anyone that Leventon's role was "to be my [Michael's] advocate and not the children's advocate," implying Michael didn't have the children's best interest at heart. Michael had no recollection of making such a remark, but he had, in a March 27, 1989 letter to his attorney.

Swisher then produced copies of an off-centered photocopy of the letter which he distributed around the table. Michael pointed out that the statement, nearly five years old, was not only taken totally out of context (Michael's recapitulation of a conversation in an elevator), but it had no bearing on the current proceeding, except to show that Mendelsohn in her defense would resort to using what had to be a stolen letter (that clearly was hurriedly copied). What did that say about her ethics? And who gave her yet another purloined letter written by Michael to his attorney?

Once the questioning returned to Mendelsohn's involvement in the case, Johan had a follow-up question: Why didn't Michael object when Judge Kaplan appointed Barbara Cymerman, an attorney, instead of a mental health professional? Michael responded that he wasn't present at motions when Judge Kaplan made the appointment. Only his attorney could accurately answer that question. It was Michael's understanding, though, that Leventon couldn't argue with the judge. Besides, Michael declared, it was Dr. Mendelsohn's responsibility to know the ethical principles of her profession and the responsibility of the judge to know the rules, too.

At a late-morning break in the hearing, Michael found himself having a cup of coffee in an adjoining room with Dr. Johan. After some small talk about the weather Johan asked Michael why he hadn't brought his attorney. Michael reminded him that Gwen Yackee, the executive director of the district branch of the APA, had written in her letter to Michael that bringing an attorney was not commonly done or required and she had told him, during a subsequent telephone conversation, that he need not do so. Michael then asked Johan if he had read the *Report of the Task Force on Child Custody Evaluation*. The psychiatrist responded that he hadn't read it, although he had "heard of it." Michael handed him a copy.

After the break Dr. Johan excused the complainant, but asked that he return mid-afternoon in case any of the panel members wished to question him further. When Michael returned a few hours later, he noticed Nancy sitting in an adjoining room waiting to testify. She never looked up.

Nancy went in to testify while Michael sat outside. Two other witnesses went in (Dr. Kenneth Stanko and Dr. Robert Wettstein, neither of whom had had any prior involvement in the Nieland case). Michael still sat outside. And that was how it ended—with Michael sitting in the corridor. The panel never asked him to return. He did not have an opportunity to hear or counter any of the testimony of Dr. Mendelsohn and her witnesses. Michael can only imagine what Nancy must have said about him. Did she wave Dr. Singer's diagnosis of him in front of the panel members?

Michael concluded to his attorney that the proceeding seemed to have nothing to do with Mendelsohn; it was more like hunting season and he was the attorney-less prey.

While yet another wait for a ruling began, Michael's thoughts returned often to what he had had to undergo that cold January morning. After a few weeks of pondering what should and should not have occurred that day, he decided to write the panel about his concerns:

1. The fact that he was told his attorney would be unnecessary, but then much time was devoted to legal matters;

2. That emphasis was placed on a stolen letter that had no bearing on the matter at hand (Michael characterized the extensive cross-examination regarding the letter as "sheer harassment");

3. The committee's failure to address the issue of the "coercion" of Ariel by Dr. Mendelsohn and Nancy to continue seeing the psychiatrist; and

4. The "ridicule of the legal steps I [Michael] took to comply with Dr. Mendelsohn's stipulations and requirements."

Dr. Johan responded to Michael's letter by assuring him that "Our handling of the case is reviewed, at that level, [by the Ethics Committee of the American Psychiatric Association (APA)] to ensure that we have properly followed the APA procedures," and that Michael would receive a response to his complaint once the APA had authorized it.

The wait continued both for the committee's decision on Mendelsohn and for any word at all from the State's Judicial Conduct Board concerning Judge Kaplan and Judge Wettick. At least these delays weren't nearly as frustrating to Michael as they used to be now that he finally had Nathaniel *and* Ariel with him on a consistent basis. Nancy's compliance with the Cymerman custody schedule didn't suggest, though, that there weren't still plenty of problems. Michael kept his attorney updated on the latest shenanigans, which had occurred in just one weekend. The following excerpt from a March 7, 1994 letter is typical:

1. Phone calls very late at night on Saturday, demanding to speak with Ariel. Hung up on me twice.

2. More phone calls on Sunday in the evening followed by a lengthy visit with the children at my side door, including taking Nathaniel in her car.

3. Snatching Nathaniel's gym bag from inside my side entrance.

4. Early morning phone calls on Monday followed shortly thereafter by her appearance at my side door in a rage state demanding "pictures of Nathaniel." Ariel was still asleep at 6:45 A.M.

5. Taking Nathaniel away in her car Monday morning without my permission.

6. Refusal yet again to inform me ahead of time of invitations to parties both children had received weeks earlier.

Michael had come to the realization that some things would never change. His life did move on, though—with his children, his practice, his music, and even a date or two.

However, his feelings of peace and contentment didn't last for long, as he received a letter from the ethics committee of the APA dated May 31, 1994, regarding Sylvia Mendelsohn: "We are . . . authorized to notify you that the Council of the Psychiatric Physicians of Pennsylvania, upon recommendation by its ethics committee, has found that Dr. Mendelsohn did not violate any of the *Principles of Medical Ethics with Annotations Especially Applicable to Psychiatry.* . . . The case is now closed."

The decision unleashed in Michael a variety of emotions, but mostly dejection and cynicism. Michael was hardly shocked that the local ethics committee panel had exonerated Dr. Mendelsohn, given the manner in which the hearing had been conducted. What infuriated him, though, was that, upon review, the ethics committee of the APA did not deduce that the hearing made a mockery of its own rules.

For the APA to call the *investigation* of Mendelsohn both *fair* and *comprehensive* was, in Michael's view, absolutely farcical. Had they simply decided to circle the wagons around one of their own kind? Could there have been some other influences as well?

Michael recalled Mervin Stewart's ties to Nancy—both he and his wife, Marcia, were Nancy's patients. He wondered if there were any other associations that could have slanted the panel's objectivity. There were. Michael discovered that Morton Johan's wife (who had recently passed away) had also been Nancy's patient for a number of years. And, there was more. After a little more investigating, Michael learned that Drs. Mendelsohn and Johan (and Loren Roth) had hospital appointments at "Western Psych" and that Drs. Mendelsohn, Johan, and Stewart (and Loren Roth) all had academic appointments at the University of Pittsburgh. For all Michael knew, the psychiatrists had regular coffee breaks together or friendships dating from training.

It is one thing, Michael reflected, to be judged by one's peers—it is quite another to be judged by one's friends and colleagues. Michael couldn't understand why Johan and Stewart had not disqualified themselves.

If that weren't enough, it also seemed to Michael that Dr. Johan, who had headed the panel, had no understanding of ethical issues as they pertain to custody cases. He had admitted to Michael that he had not even read the *Report of the Task Force on Child Custody Evaluation* (released some two years prior to the hearing) that addressed the ethical issues confronting those who participate in custody evaluations.

What now? Like Barbara Cymerman, was Dr. Mendelsohn off the hook, too? Not if Michael could help it. It was she who Michael held responsible for keeping Ariel apart from her father for more than two years. And it was she who had apparently endorsed the Cymerman report that led, in Michael's estimation, to a worse custody schedule than that which had existed. And it was Mendelsohn who, to this day, was still treating Ariel. Michael, new life and all, would not walk away from this battle.

Unfortunately for Michael, the APA guidelines didn't seem to leave the complainant with any recourse, but Leventon came up with an idea. Although no transcript of the hearing had been made, a tape recording did exist, and he would try to obtain a copy.

Michael was confident that the tape would confirm the outrageousness of the entire proceeding. He worried, though, that the APA might be hesitant to release what would be self-incriminating material.

In another five weeks, Michael's hunch proved to be correct. Gwen Yackee, the APA executive director, informed Paul Leventon that although the tapes were available should an accused physician wish to appeal, previously they had not been released to complainants (who have no right of appeal), and this case would be no exception. The letter concluded, "Please be advised . . . that this case is closed."

Nancy, who had been kept abreast of the proceedings, wasted no time seizing on the words "this case is closed." On August 17, Harry Gruener was back in court in order to file a petition for contempt that demanded Michael pay his share for Dr. Mendelsohn's "treatment" of Ariel ($3,875) as well as Nancy's "reasonable counsel fees" incurred in the contempt proceeding.

Judge Kaplan ordered a hearing for October 31, 1994.

Michael asked Paul Leventon if what he had just read could really be true: Judge Kaplan was going to continue to rule in this case even though his impartiality would clearly be in question? Surely, the judge must have been aware that Michael had a complaint pending against him with the State's Judicial Conduct Board. In addition, Michael's complaint against one of the judge's appointees, Barbara Cymerman, had clearly angered the judge, as indicated by his direct interference letter to State Investigator Groskin.

Acknowledging Michael's concern, Leventon informed his client that, if Judge Kaplan did not voluntarily remove himself from the case, he would file a motion to have the judge recuse himself. In the meantime, Leventon began working on an answer to Nancy's petition for contempt. Regarding Dr. Mendelsohn, Leventon mentioned to Michael that he and an associate, David Klett, Esq., were contemplating how best to proceed against her now that she had been exonerated by the American Psychiatric Association. He suggested that the three of them meet at Michael's home to discuss further Michael's legal options.

At the ensuing meeting, Leventon and Klett asked Michael to help them quantify the damage done by Dr. Mendelsohn. Michael responded by letter the next day:

> ... I do not believe that what I went through represents merely some degree of transient and trivial emotional distress. . . . Sylvia Mendelsohn's failure to tell the truth, her failure to cure the record, her intentional infliction of emotional distress was tied directly to my loss of time with the children. . . . Her malpractice was inextricably linked to deprivation of my parental rights, to my right to father my children. . . .

A cause of action was born. Leventon and Klett agreed that Michael's suit against Mendelsohn should be heard in federal court owing to the alleged violation of their client's "fundamental right to child custody, integrity of family, and enjoyment of child rearing." In other words, the suit alleged that Mendelsohn acted in concert with state authorities (via Cymerman) in an effort to deprive Michael of his civil liberties.

While Leventon and Klett prepared Michael's case, Ariel, clearly against her wishes, continued to see Mendelsohn (nearly two years after Michael had fired her). Michael made sure his attorneys didn't lose sight of this as the contempt hearing on Michael's failure to pay Mendelsohn's fees approached. The situation had degenerated to such a point that Ariel would not even leave the psychiatrist's waiting room and enter the office.

On October 17, 1994, Paul Leventon filed in federal court Michael's twenty-one-page civil rights action against Dr. Mendelsohn. The suit contained forty-nine separate allegations, concluding that "Dr. Sylvia Mendelsohn . . . committed egregious acts of medical malpractice."

The next day in the Family Division Leventon filed an answer to [Nancy's] petition for contempt, which states:

> . . . It is specifically denied that all Complaints filed [on behalf of Michael] against Dr. Sylvia R. Mendelsohn have been finally resolved. . . .
>
> By way of further answer, [Michael] vehemently avers that treatment prescribed and performed by [Dr. Mendelsohn] was not reasonable and necessary, constituted malpractice, and/or gave rise to Conflicts of Interest without the consent of the Parties involved, and/or was not in the best interests of the child involved, and/or contrary to the wishes of the Parties' daughter Ariel. . . .
>
> Accordingly, [Michael] respectfully requests [Judge Kaplan] issue an Order denying the within Petition for Contempt, and further, removing Dr. Mendelsohn as treating psychiatrist for the Parties' daughter, Ariel, in order to safeguard her interests.

Michael planned to call one witness at the October 31 hearing for contempt against him: Ariel. Michael related to Leventon that, at twelve years of age, she was more than capable of speaking for herself.

In all likelihood, Nancy wouldn't be enthusiastic to hear Ariel's testimony about Mendelsohn. Michael, for his part, was hardly pleased that Judge Kaplan might be the presiding judge. The attorneys conferred. An agreement was quickly reached: There would be no hearing. Michael would put into an escrow account approximately $2,500 representing the fees he supposedly owed Mendelsohn, less the legal fees Nancy still owed him as a result of the porcelain box decision.

With this agreement, the contempt hearing was continued indefinitely.

No formal agreement was reached concerning Dr. Mendelsohn remaining Ariel's therapist, but it would have been difficult for Nancy and the therapist to contend that the sessions were beneficial to Ariel: she wouldn't even enter Dr. Mendelsohn's office. Soon after the postponement of the contempt hearing, Michael learned from Ariel that her "therapy" had finally ended. Michael was relieved. At long last Mendelsohn's "therapeutic" relationship with Michael's family was over.

But, as always seemed to be the case, Michael had little time to savor this positive turn of events.

October 18, 1994

Dear Doctor Nieland:

This letter is in response to the Complaint you filed with the Judicial Conduct Board.

After considering the necessary inquiry and reviewing your Complaint, the Board has determined that there is no basis for further action. Therefore, the Complaint docketed to the above number [93-203A and 93-203B] has been dismissed.

Very truly yours,
Vincent J. Quinn
Chief Counsel, Judicial Conduct Board

After having received a nineteen-page complaint (accompanied by a stack of documents), was this the best the Commonwealth of Pennsylvania Judicial Conduct Board could do one year later—provide a three-sentence dismissal? Once again, what could Michael do? Judge Kaplan and Judge Wettick could walk away from the Nieland case thinking they did nothing wrong or improper.

So, after Judge Wettick, Roland Singer, Judge Kaplan, and Barbara Cymerman, it appeared that Michael's last bit of pending litigation concerned only Sylvia Mendelsohn. Despite the recent setbacks, and his own attorneys' observation that a civil rights suit against a psychiatrist in federal court on a custody case had probably never succeeded, Michael tried to be optimistic that justice would be served. Obviously, Dr. Mendelsohn had her own version of justice being served. On November 23, 1994, her attorney filed a seven-page motion to dismiss Michael's charges claiming that Michael's civil rights hadn't been violated and that the two-year statute of limitations had passed anyway.

Dr. Mendelsohn's attorney, Ray F. Middleman, also included a seventy-seven-page brief in support of motion to dismiss. U.S. Magistrate Judge Francis X. Caiazza ordered that "Plaintiff [Michael] be allowed until December 23, 1994, to file a brief in response to Defendant's Motion to Dismiss." Leventon and Klett started preparing their response while Michael examined the lengthy Mendelsohn brief. Among the attached documents was a five-page letter Michael had never previously seen. It was written to the Chair of the Ethics Committee of the American Psychiatric Association by Dr. Johan, Chair of the Psychiatric Physicians of Pennsylvania Ethics Committee. The March 1, 1994 correspondence proved once and for all to Michael that the panel had had to turn truth on its head to exonerate Mendelsohn:

In the letter, Johan surmised that Michael "accused Dr.

Mendelsohn of [seven] ethical violations." He broke down the panel's reasoning on the issues for each accusation:

1. Did Dr. Mendelsohn violate her confidentiality duty to her patient, Ariel, by talking with the Court-appointed Custody Evaluator? The Panel found that this action was not in violation for several reasons. The primary reason is that the Complainant, Dr. Nieland, gave his signed, informed consent allowing her to do so. He testified that he was very pleased at the time that she was willing to do this.

This was hardly truly informed consent. Michael had signed it because he had assumed that Mendelsohn would tell the truth and at last reveal to Cymerman what she had told him repeatedly—that Ariel was never afraid of him.

Moreover, Michael noted that Johan referred to Cymerman as "Custody Evaluator." Another title!

The committee also heard testimony from an expert in child psychiatry and custody matters that Dr. Mendelsohn's actions have been consistent with commonly accepted practices involving child psychiatrists treating patients whose custody arrangements are being evaluated by the courts. Those practices allow the therapist, with proper consent from the parents, to discuss clinical information with a Custody Evaluator appointed by the Court to bring an impartial perspective to custody decisions.

Nonsense. Michael had heard this line of reasoning in defense of Dr. Singer—everybody else does it this way, so it must be okay. The fact of the matter is that the one scholarly paper included in Mendelsohn's November 23, 1994 brief (as part of her defense), "The Therapist's Role in Child Custody Disputes,"*

---

*William Berent, "The Therapist's Role in Child Disputes," *Journal of the American Academy of Child Psychiatry* 22 (1983): 180–83.

makes clear that her actions are *not* accepted practices. "Usually the therapist will decide that it is best for the client and for the therapy if the therapist avoids active participation such as writing reports or testifying. The therapist may wish to become involved indirectly by sharing information with the independent psychiatrist who is performing the custody evaluation."

Obviously, Cymerman, an attorney, does not fit the description of a custody evaluator (i.e., independent psychiatrist).

> 2. Did Dr. Mendelsohn violate a confidentiality duty to the Complainant by speaking about Dr. Nieland to the Custody Evaluator? The Panel found that she did not. First, Dr. Nieland's signed consent form expressly permitted her to include information about him.

Dr. Johan's repeated reference to Cymerman as a custody evaluator only reinforced Michael's belief that Mendelsohn erred grossly by speaking with the court appointee. Barbara Cymerman is an attorney only. There were no attorneys on the Family Division's custody evaluator list—only licensed psychologists and, in one instance, a psychiatrist. So, apart from the issue of what constitutes truly informed consent, it seems incontrovertible that Mendelsohn was ethically forbidden to discuss the case with an attorney even if the attorney had been appointed custody evaluator. The onus was not on Michael to know with whom the psychiatrist could or could not consult. After all, in this setting she was the doctor; he was the patient.

> Secondly, the Evaluator's report does not indicate that any information about Dr. Nieland was conveyed other than that which related specifically to involvement with the daughter.

—Except for the fact that much of what the report conveyed was erroneous and misleading, according to Michael, and he had pointed this out to Mendelsohn during his August 12, 1992 session with her. Furthermore, the report did not provide an answer to the main question posed in the September 9, 1989 court order—did Ariel fear her father? It was this specific information Michael had thought would be disclosed to Cymerman when he signed the release, but it never appeared. Instead, there were statements such as "Father has engaged in a successful course of behavior to 'woo' Ariel to him." Dr. Mendelsohn, during a session with Michael, had denied making such a statement, but she refused to make the court aware of the inaccuracy. This was one of the major points of Michael's complaint that Johan was not addressing—that the information conveyed, merely from the legal point of view, was pure hearsay and that Mendelsohn refused to correct the record.

> Third, despite Dr. Nieland's contention that he was a patient of Dr. Mendelsohn's, the Panel found that they did not have a doctor-patient relationship. Dr. Mendelsohn did not treat Dr. Nieland. All the evidence indicated that their meetings were in regard to his role as the parent of a child in therapy, consistent with pertinent clinical practices and standards in such cases. She never made a diagnosis of Dr. Nieland, nor did she ever bill him as a patient.

Not true! Dr. Mendelsohn wrote to Leventon (concerning a meeting with the attorneys): "I am concerned that such a meeting could backfire and instead have a negative impact on *my therapeutic work with* Ariel and *her parents*" (emphasis added). Clearly, Mendelsohn had regarded Michael and Nancy as her patients. (Psychiatrists don't engage in therapeutic work with nonpatients!) Moreover, among the thirty-eight bills Michael received from Mendelsohn, twenty-nine began with the salutation "Dear Patient" (the others began "Dear Michael"). Each of the "Dear Patient" bills had been signed by her and she had also hand-addressed the envelopes.

As a matter of common sense, Michael declared that words would have to be deprived of their meaning to conclude that he hadn't been a patient of Dr. Mendelsohn. She repeatedly urged him to persevere, allayed his anxieties with repeated promises to take up with Nancy his allegations regarding her undermining the custody schedule, and led him on to believe she would help him by "helping Ariel resist her mother's pressure."

Concerning the absence of a diagnosis, Michael had asked Mendelsohn at the outset not to record a diagnosis (normally required by health insurance companies) because he feared that any psychiatric diagnosis, even "anxiety," could be used against him in the Family Division. (Consequently, Michael had never received any insurance reimbursement for his sessions with Mendelsohn.)

> 3. Did Dr. Mendelsohn violate her duty to properly include the parents in the daughter's treatment? No. . . .
>
> 4. Did Dr. Mendelsohn violate a confidentiality duty to the Complainant by reporting his failure to pay the therapy bill to his ex-wife? Again, the Panel found that she did not. Again, no patient-therapist relationship existed between them.

How could Dr. Johan continue to make this assertion when there was overwhelming evidence to the contrary? As further proof of a *patient-therapist relationship*, Michael had received a bill from Dr. Mendelsohn which specifically listed a "Therapy Session" for Michael on July 15, 1992.

Was Johan suggesting that therapy sessions were not direct evidence of a "patient-therapist relationship"? Perhaps most telling was that in that bill Mendelsohn took the time to differentiate her therapy sessions from meetings (e.g., with Barbara Cymerman). How could anyone with any common sense, based on Mendelsohn's own invoicing, not conclude that Michael had been involved in therapy? This constituted a monumental flaw in the panel's reasoning.

> Secondly, both Dr. Nieland and his ex-wife had engaged Dr. Mendelsohn's services, and the Panel found it was proper for Dr. Mendelsohn to discuss the payment situation with Dr. Nieland's ex-wife in that they had agreed to share the costs. When Dr. Nieland did not pay his share of the bill and the ex-wife desired the treatment to continue, it was necessary and proper for Dr. Mendelsohn to discuss payment issues with her.

Why? Michael and Nancy had always paid Mendelsohn's bills separately. If Dr. Mendelsohn believed Michael had withheld payment for reasonable and necessary medical services, her proper action should have been to initiate her own court proceedings, not share information with her patient's former wife and thereby become a participant and a partisan in Nancy's petition for contempt.

> 5. Did Dr. Mendelsohn commit an ethical violation by refusing to submit her own report to the Court or by refusing to testify on Dr. Michael Nieland's behalf when he sought legal action to change the custody arrangements? Both the PPP investigator and the Ethics Committee paid particular attention to this matter. They agreed that her refusal was proper, if she had been hired as Ariel's therapist, as Dr. Mendelsohn contended she was. Dr. Nieland, however, claimed that she had been hired specifically at the Court's direction to analyze whether or not Ariel ʾas afraid of him

and that she should have subsequently reported that Ariel was not afraid. Dr. Nieland testified several times that there was nothing wrong with his daughter and that the terms of Dr. Mendelsohn's engagement obligated her to testify to this on his behalf.

During the pre-Hearing investigation, the terms of Dr. Mendelsohn's engagement were not clear to the investigator [Dr. Wright] or the Ethics Committee members. At the Hearing, however, both Dr. Mendelsohn and Nancy Nieland-Fisher, the Complainant's former wife, testified that Dr. Mendelsohn was jointly engaged by both husband and wife to treat the daughter. They also testified that Dr. Mendelsohn was told at that time that the Court had ordered someone to evaluate Ariel, and they testified that Dr. Mendelsohn made her position very clear to all parties from the start—that she would be Ariel's therapist and would not act as a Court-appointed Evaluator. The testimony was substantiated by a copy of the actual Court Order in question. First, it was dated after the time of the first meeting which Dr. Mendelsohn had with the Nielands. The PPP investigator, who recommended we have a Hearing because of the dispute on this point, testified at the Hearing that at the time he wrote his report, he was unclear on the sequence of events. He further testified, however, and the documents show, that a Court Order had been proposed prior to the time of Dr. Mendelsohn's first meeting, but the actual Order occurred later.

Did Dr. Johan think twice about the plausibility of what he just stated? He acknowledged that the court "ordered someone to evaluate Ariel," and Mendelsohn and Nancy testified that "at that time . . . Dr. Mendelsohn made her position very clear to all parties from the start" that she would *not* "act as a Court-appointed Evaluator." Why then didn't Johan wonder why some other doctor was never brought in at that time to conduct an evaluation? Clearly, there had been no other doctor. Only Mendelsohn. Moreover, previous correspondence clearly demonstrates that Dr. Mendelsohn was hired in response to the proposed order of court.

> In the final analysis, however, the Panel members decided that the date of the Order was essentially irrelevant. Whether or not it had been signed before or after the Nielands first spoke with Dr. Mendelsohn does not matter because testimony and documents presented at the Hearing clearly established that Dr. Mendelsohn had made her position clear from the beginning: She would act only as a therapist hired by the parents and would not act as an agent of the Court.

What documents? What testimony? If Mendelsohn had stated that "she would *act only as a therapist*" then either she misinformed the panel or she misinformed Prosecuting Attorney Kelly who had written, "Dr. Mendelsohn stated that, when you [Michael] did inform her of the Court Order, she informed you that she would *not only evaluate* the alleged fear that your daughter had of you, but also other problems that she may have had" (emphasis added). Dr. Mendelsohn couldn't have it both ways.

> In addition, the records presented at the Hearing disproved Dr. Nieland's contention that Dr. Mendelson had only been hired to evaluate if Ariel was afraid of him and to write a report addressing this question. The actual Order states the following: "The parties [both parents], through counsel, shall immediately select an appropriate professional for the evaluation and treatment, if so required, of Ariel and Nathaniel, particularly as to the issue of Ariel's expressed fear of her father."

It is interesting and revealing that Dr. Johan quoted the proposed order of court and not the order of court itself. Moreover, the wording of the court order made it very clear that the specific focus of the evaluation was to be the fear issue and treatment of the fear, if so required. Why had Dr. Johan turned a hearing that was to be concerned with ethical violations into a case hinging on linguistics?

> Panel members agreed that the Order clearly called for treatment, not just evaluation, and that it clearly allowed for that activity in regard to matters other than Ariel's fear of her father.

But how could Dr. Mendelsohn have known that treatment of anything was required without first doing an evaluation? Through testimony and documentation (or the absence of it), the panel should have known that no other evaluator had been brought into the case and that Mendelsohn had plainly assumed both roles—even though she had known it was wrong: "I feel strongly," she had written to Paul Leventon and Harry Gruener, "that it is impossible to wear the dual hats of custody evaluator and therapist."

> Furthermore, nothing in that Order mentioned, much less required, the "appropriate professional" to do any reporting at all. Indeed, Dr. Nieland himself had offered sworn testimony in one legal Proceeding which contradicted his testimony on this point at the PPP Ethics Hearing. In explaining why Dr. Mendelsohn was not present for a particular Court Hearing, the Complainant had testified in Court that "she was not appointed by the Court or not employed by us to deal with custody issues. It was only to help Ariel deal with the tension."

Exactly!

This testimony concerned Nancy's assertio. that Dr. Mendelsohn stated that the custody schedule was the worst she had seen. Michael was trying to point out that Mendelsohn had not been brought into the case by the court to address the custody schedule or even to get involved in a custody dispute, but, rather, to perform an evaluation of Ariel's expressed fear of her father.

> 6. Did Dr. Mendelsohn delegate medical decisions to Barbara Cymerman, the lawyer who acted as a Custody Evaluator for the Court? Panel members found the evidence showed that she did not. She spoke of medical matters to Ms. Cymerman, with the Complainant's consent, but nothing in Ms. Cymerman's report indicates that the attorney made any decisions at all. Her report makes custody, rather than medical, decisions.

Did Dr. Johan really believe that Barbara Cymerman's determining whether or not an individual (e.g., Ariel) needs therapy was not a medical decision? Moreover, Mendelsohn had never evaluated, treated, or even met Nathaniel—yet, the summary and conclusion of Cymerman's report included the recommendation that Nathaniel see a therapist. It was incomprehensible that Johan and the panel regarded that as a custody—not a medical—decision.

> 7. Finally, did Dr. Mendelsohn breach the *Ethical Principles* by failing to make her relationship with the patient her most important consideration? The Panel answered no for two reasons. First, insofar as the allegation refers to Dr. Mendelsohn's failure to put her relationship with Dr. Nieland first (by not testifying as he wished her to do), the Panel reiterates its finding that he was not her patient.

—Even though the evidence overwhelmingly indicates other-wise!

> Secondly, insofar as the allegation refers to Dr. Mendelsohn's relationship with Ariel, the Panel notes that all evidence is that she continually strove to put that relationship first. Indeed, her insistence on doing so appears to have generated Dr. Nieland's filing of this Ethical Complaint. In deliberations the Panel members expressed surprise at Dr. Mendelsohn's ability under the circumstances to continue, to this day, a good therapeutic relationship with the daughter.

What?! If it had been such a "good therapeutic relationship" why did Ariel a few months *prior* to the hearing refuse to have anything to do with Mendelsohn other than play board games or cards with her to pass the time and then refuse even to enter her office? (And, of course, the "good therapeutic relationship" ultimately ended because of Ariel's utter refusal to participate in it any further.)

So, that was it?

It was amazing to Michael how easily the truth could be buried in order to obtain what he now believed was a preordained conclusion. His formal complaints against Mendelsohn, Kaplan, Wettick, and Cymerman had accomplished nothing. Yet, in retrospect, he was not surprised. How could any ruling body discover the truth when the statements and explanations of the accused were accepted without question, when the accused did not have to face cross-examination, and when the complainant was not even allowed to attend the hearing?

Michael may not ever have a transcript of the American Psychiatric Association proceedings, but at least now he could cite Dr. Johan's statements as indelible proof that the hearing had had nothing to do with fairness, that the presence of the panel's attorneys only gave the hearing a veneer of legitimacy, and that, unlike the psychologists who were able to bite the bullet and censure Dr. Singer, these psychiatrists had had no intention of sanctioning one of their own. To Michael, the panel's decision reeked of a blatant cover-up, topped off by the fact that two of the panel members (Johan and Stewart) had personal links to Nancy, who had indisputably tried to thwart Michael on a personal, professional, and paternal level for more years than he cared to remember.

Nancy certainly tried to come to the rescue of the psychiatrist. Michael discovered, in Mendelsohn's brief to dismiss civil rights action, an affidavit signed by Nancy that was evidently prepared in anticipation of her testifying on behalf of Dr. Mendelsohn at the January 1994 ethics hearing. Some of the major points of the document show that Nancy had some interesting recollections:

> In January 1987, Dr. Michael Nieland filed a divorce complaint against me. . . .
>
> Our divorce became final in the fall of 1988.

The foregoing statement is incorrect. The Nieland divorce became final January 7, 1988. The error may not seem significant, but in signing the affidavit Nancy had to swear to the truth of the facts contained in the document to an officer qualified to administer such an oath. How difficult could it have been for Nancy to ascertain the correct date?

> On September 23, 1987, the [Family Division] appointed Roland Singer, Ph.D., to evaluate Ariel and Nathaniel and to work with us as a family.

The September 23, 1987 order of court appointed Singer to "conduct psychological evaluations" *not* as Nancy states, "to work with us as a family." That is one of the reasons why Singer was censured.

> My [ex-husband] was initially pleased with Dr. Singer's work, especially his recommendation that the children spend a substantial portion of time with Michael.

The fact of the matter is that Michael had anxieties about Dr. Singer at the very outset of his September 23, 1987 appointment. These concerns only escalated after the November 9, 1987 conciliation when the psychologist revealed to Michael's attorney that he had met with "ancillary contacts" selected by Nancy. Though Singer recommended equally shared custody in his March 1988 psychological report, Michael was clearly unhappy with the interrogations leading up to the report, much of the content of the report itself, and with Singer's failure to recognize Nancy's apparent efforts to undermine Michael's parental rights.

> Michael became infuriated with Dr. Singer, however, when Dr. Singer recommended a decrease in the amount of time the children spent with him and further recommended that Ariel cease overnights with him, because of many problems related to Michael's handling of the children.

Michael would probably phrase this a little differently: "Michael became infuriated with Dr. Singer when the psychologist did nothing about (and in some instances aided and abetted) Nancy's undermining of the court-ordered custody schedule—all in an apparent effort to wound and punish her former spouse."

> In the summer of 1989, my ex-husband and I agreed that Ariel should be evaluated and, if necessary, receive therapy from a psychiatrist.

On the one hand, Michael was astonished at Nancy's use of the word "agreed" when they hadn't agreed on anything since their separation. On the other hand, Nancy (perhaps not realizing what she was confirming) stated that Ariel was taken to a psychiatrist to be evaluated and, if necessary, receive therapy.

> In August of 1989, my ex-husband provided a list of those psychiatrists he found acceptable and I chose Sylvia R. Mendelsohn, M.D., from his list.

Incorrect yet again. The only list ever provided was that offered in a letter by Stephen P. Schachner, Ph.D. In addition, Dr. Schachner had specifically referred to the proposed order of court in this correspondence and he also sent his letter to the master, Carol McCarthy, who authored the proposed order.

> After agreeing on Dr. Mendelsohn, each of us contacted her by telephone in August of 1989 and we hired her to evaluate and treat Ariel. . . .

Michael has no quarrel with this point insofar as he and Nancy (communicating through their attorneys) did contact Dr. Mendelsohn in August of 1989, per the master's proposed court order. But, less than four months after Nancy signed this affidavit, she had a different recollection (based on her testimony quoted by Dr. Johan): "Dr. Mendelsohn made her position very clear to all parties from the start—that she would be Ariel's therapist and would not act as a court-appointed evaluator." Which is it, Nancy? Was Dr. Mendelsohn only to be Ariel's therapist as Nancy was quoted as testifying at Dr. Mendelsohn's ethics hearing? Or was Dr. Mendelsohn hired to evaluate and treat Ariel as Nancy swore in the affidavit? This is the statement that is consistent with the proposed order of court, but it also in-criminates Dr. Mendelsohn.

That's not all.

John Kelly, in his December 1, 1993 letter to Michael ab-solving Mendelsohn of any wrongdoing as far as the Com-monwealth was concerned, commented that "Dr. Men-delsohn informed us that neither you nor your ex-wife had informed her when you contacted her for treatment of your daughter, that you were court ordered to do so." However, Dr. Johan's letter states that Dr. Mendelsohn said she "was told at that time that the court had ordered someone to eval-uate Ariel." Which version is the truth, Dr. Mendelsohn?

And, as for Johan's contention that the September 9, 1989 court order was dated *after* the first meeting Mendelsohn had with the Nielands—Nancy's affidavit helps prove his point is irrelevant and misleading because both parties considered the proposed order of court as binding and clearly responded to it as such.

It pains Michael that Dr. Mendelsohn never was required to respond to these discrepancies (through cross-examina-tion) before Dr. Johan's panel or (in a hearing) before the Commonwealth's Bureau of Professional and Occupational Affairs.

When we hired Dr. Mendelsohn, she made it clear that her customary practice was for both parents to be responsible for her fees and that she expected payment at the time of therapy. She suggested that the parent bringing Ariel to a session pay for that session. Because my ex-husband and I were not communicating well with each other, we decided Dr. Mendelsohn should bill each parent for one-half of Ariel's sessions and the full amount of his/my own meet-ings with her. Dr. Mendelsohn made it clear that if one parent defaulted, the other was responsible for full pay-ment of her fees.

Michael contends that no such billing stipulations were ever discussed. Dr. Mendelsohn had never asked for payment at the time of therapy (demonstrated by the regular invoices he received by mail from the psychiatrist) and she had never discussed with Michael what she would do if one parent defaulted.

> After a few sessions with Ariel, Dr. Mendelsohn was advised of the Court's September 9, 1989 Order [directing my ex-husband and myself to hire a psychiatrist to evaluate and treat our daughter]. At that time, Dr. Mendelsohn made it clear to me that she would not limit her treatment of Ariel to Ariel's relationship with her father, but would treat the broad spectrum of Ariel's emotional problems in accord with her best professional judgment. Dr. Mendelsohn further said she would not become involved in litigation between me and my ex-husband and would not, under any circumstances, testify in court. My ex-husband and I both agreed to the terms of Dr. Mendelsohn.

Once again, Nancy's formulation differs considerably from what Michael reported in his ethics complaint. Michael has no idea what was discussed between Nancy and Dr. Mendelsohn, but no such discussion and/or agreement of terms ever took place between him and Dr. Mendelsohn. Furthermore, Michael was never told by Dr. Mendelsohn—nor does he believe for one moment—that Ariel ever had a "broad spectrum of emotional problems."

> The foregoing statements of fact are true and correct to the best of my knowledge, information, and belief and are made subject to the provisions of 18 Pa.C.S.A. S4904 related to unsworn falsifications to authorities.
>   Nancy Nieland-Fisher, M.D.

Some facts!

The year 1995 dawned—eight years had passed since Michael and Nancy separated.

Michael's civil rights action against Sylvia Mendelsohn (filed on October 17, 1994) did not succeed in the local district court. The judge ruled that it had not been filed within the two-year statute of limitations which began with the September 24, 1992 adoption of the Cymerman report by the Family Division. Michael's attorneys disagreed because Sylvia had continued to meet with Michael through November 12, 1992, and during that time indicated to him that she might write Judge Kaplan concerning the misconceptions in the Cymerman report. Those representations, in the opinion of Michael's attorneys, constituted a continuing tort which was the basis for their client's appeal to the Third Circuit Court of Appeals.

While awaiting that ruling, a federal mediator, Mr. Jacob Hart, made strenuous efforts over many months to secure an apology from Mendelsohn that Michael would find satisfactory. Mr. Hart was unsuccessful and Michael was unsuccessful in his appeal. Case closed.

The litigation between Michael and Nancy seemed also to have run its course.

Nathaniel, fourteen, and Ariel, twelve, came and went, according to the 1992 custody schedule. When they were with their father, their days were filled with school, activities, and friends. Michael didn't object to their here-one-minute-gone-the-next schedules. He enjoyed watching them mature socially as well as educationally. And besides, there were plenty of opportunities to be a father—even with Barbara Cymerman's custody schedule. Nathaniel and Ariel knew they could count on their dad, whether it was for a ride to the movies, waking them up for school, or bantering with them while they all sat around the kitchen table.

Meanwhile, Jennie, twenty-three, had graduated with honors from the University of Pennsylvania (in three years) and had continued to live and work in Philadelphia. She talked to her father on the telephone frequently.

Unfortunately, problems still lingered in regard to Nancy. After all those years Michael still had difficulty contacting Nathaniel or Ariel when they were at their mother's home unless they were the ones to answer the telephone. In one instance, early in 1995, Michael had casually mentioned to Ariel that he had tried to call her the day before, but he was told by her mother that she was unavailable.

"Did she tell you I was in the shower?" Ariel responded.

"Why, yes," her dad answered. "How did you know?"

"I was standing right beside her when she said it."

Michael had reluctantly accepted the fact that some things probably would never change. But—change was coming.

A few weeks after Ariel's disclosure, Michael happened to call her again at her mother's house. This time Nathaniel answered the phone. (One hurdle overcome.) Michael asked him to track down Ariel so he could find out if she were going directly home (to Michael's house) after school the next day. Nathaniel knew that answer. She wouldn't be going to her dad's house at all.

"Why not?" Michael asked (it was his custody day).

"She's in New Jersey with my mom and Dick [Nancy's husband]."

Michael feared that he knew the reason for the sudden trip: They were visiting a boarding school.

The previous fall Ariel had told her dad that her mother suggested to her that she might want to consider attending boarding school the following school year. Since then, Ariel had mentioned that she liked the idea, although she wouldn't give her dad a specific reason why. Michael, in reply, had told her he would be very sad if she were to leave home at such a young age. He didn't object further because he didn't believe she was that serious. She would never leave her many friends, not to mention her family.

Evidently, he had been wrong.

When Michael hung up the telephone after his conversation with Nathaniel, he felt the way he did that June day in 1987 when he had returned home from a medical meeting and found his children had been moved out of the house by Nancy. Could it possibly be that after all the trials and tribulations he had gone through over his children, Nancy had found yet another way to take one of them away from him?

Upon her arrival home the next day, Michael heard the heartbreaking news from Ariel herself. She had applied to the Lawrenceville School, a private boarding school in New Jersey. She thought the experience would be good for her. Michael disagreed. He thought it was ridiculous for someone her age to leave home. But he was not going to argue with his daughter, who was not yet even a teenager, about what was best for her. Instead, he decided to appeal directly to the school. After an introductory telephone call, he sent a five-page handwritten letter to Robin Mamlet, the Dean of Admissions:

> My daughter, Ariel, age twelve and a seventh-grade student, has applied for admission to your fine school. On or about February 16 she visited your school in the company of her mother and, I believe, her mother's current husband. I had no notice prior to its occurrence that this visit was to take place although Ariel had indicated to me that she was thinking about going away to boarding school. I am sure that you found Ariel to be a very attractive applicant for many reasons and I am sure that she would complement your clearly select student body. This is precisely the

reason I am writing you. I am adamantly opposed to Ariel's leaving home to go to boarding school. . . .

. . . The issue in Ariel's case is whether she is going to be permitted to mature and develop normally from the psychologic point of view and cement, permanently, crucially important and loving relationships with members of her immediate family. I contend that in Ariel's case this is of paramount importance. Specifically, Ariel has to have the opportunity to form the very important bonds in her life with a father who adores her and the only other male in her family, her older brother, who is just a grade ahead of her in school and with whom she has just now, beyond the rivalries of childhood, started to develop an amicable relationship.

I have to bring to your attention the fact that Ariel has been the subject of a custody dispute that has been going on for eight years and has resulted in numerous court orders, three of which . . . implicitly establish that Ariel's mother and I have joint or shared legal and physical custody of our daughter. In fact, I have never sought anything other than to share custody and upbringing of all three children with their mother, who has fiercely resisted my efforts and right to have a normal paternal relationship with them. Perhaps because she is the youngest child, Ariel was less able to resist her mother's pressure and, for a period of several years, she was with me far less than the other children who have since made up for lost time and with whom I have very close relationships.

. . . Ariel and I are on the threshold of securing for her a normal and vital relationship with the first man in her life, her father. I am sure you understand the importance of this. I am sure you also understand how a child who has had the experience Ariel has had would want to get away from it all and escape the pressures to which she has been subjected. After all, she is almost a teenager with all that that implies. . . .

I am sure that a school as reputable and renowned as yours is cognizant of the issues I have raised in this letter and will not take any action to disrupt my family and influence adversely Ariel's growth and development. Ariel desperately needs to develop a secure and loving bond with at least one of her parents. I am bringing these matters to your attention because you could otherwise not know Ariel's background. There is a widespread belief that the most important moral and social issue facing our country is the issue of fatherhood and denigration of its importance resulting in family dysfunction, crime, violence, and all our social ills. I have tried to be a good father, in fact, the very best father to all my children, but it hasn't been easy. I hope that you and your school will do the right thing and not offer Ariel a place in your school. If I can provide you with any additional information I hope that you will not hesitate to call or write me. . . .

Five days later, Miss Mamlet sent Michael a photocopy of a letter mailed to Nancy, informing her that Ariel had not been accepted for admission to Lawrenceville.

Michael couldn't say definitively what impact his letter had had on the Lawrenceville School's decision not to enroll Ariel, but he had no doubts that she met the institution's academic criteria. Michael breathed one big sigh of relief, although it still distressed him how close he had come to losing his daughter.

But, the Lawrenceville School wasn't the only boarding school for twelve-year-old girls. Ariel told her dad that her mom had a directory of boarding schools and had sent in her application to yet another school. Michael, on May 2, sent essentially a duplicate of his Lawrenceville School letter to the Fay School in Southborough, Massachusetts—an elementary day school and boarding school for the sixth through the ninth grades. Once again, Michael hoped that a school previously unaware of the custody battle over Ariel now would consider his wishes and not disrupt his relationship with his daughter. His answer came in the mail a few weeks later:

May 18, 1995

Dear Dr. Nieland:

I am writing to let you know what has transpired with respect to Ariel's application to Fay School. Once we received the application and once Ariel had visited Fay for an interview, I sought legal opinion to determine what action the school should take. After reviewing the documents you forwarded to me with our lawyer, we took the position that there was no legal reason why Fay should not act on this application. It is our understanding that Ariel's mother is within her rights to seek admission to another school, including a boarding school.

While I am very sensitive to your concerns and point of view, we needed to consider all sides of the situation. It is our opinion that Ariel would like to attend a boarding school, her mother filed the application, and there is nothing to prohibit us in taking action. Therefore, today, I authorized the Admission Office to act on their recommendation that Ariel be accepted. . . .

Sincerely,
Stephen C. White
Headmaster

Michael, crestfallen, considered his options.

If he did nothing, Ariel would attend Fay for the next two years (eighth and ninth grades), then most likely would transfer to yet another boarding school for her remaining three high school years. (Michael had discovered she already had an application pending in at least one such school.) And in the summer, if the past few summers were an indication, she would probably be off to camp somewhere far away.

(That summer it was Colorado.) Consequently, by the time she graduated from high school she would already have been away from home for five years. By then, she would barely know her father. Or her brother. Or her mother. Or her childhood friends. Could this be in the best interest of the child? Could a father's wishes be totally ignored?

On the other hand, what if Michael fought this in the Family Division? Would it be another colossal waste of time and money? Or, if, by chance, he prevailed, would Ariel resent it and cut him out of her life?

Michael's indecision didn't last long. He apprised the Fay School headmaster of his intentions:

> In my telephone conversation with you and in my May 2nd letter I appealed to you in terms of my daughter's best interests from the educational, social, psychological, and emotional point of view. You responded as though this were purely a legal matter and, clearly, you felt that you could act with impunity because you are beyond my legal reach. You have done precisely what you wrote you would not do, namely, "interfere with family dynamics or custody situations." . . .
>
> Your action in accepting Ariel will cause the uprooting of long-term relationships with teachers and the abandonment of friends in school and in her community. Even more importantly, you have severed her ties to her brother and father. These are all precious bonds which should be nurtured. . . .
>
> You have, in effect, robbed me of my daughter and stolen my daughter's childhood from her. I assure you that I will do everything possible to reverse the consequences of your decision and prevent you and your school from taking my daughter from me.

In the end, it was not a hard decision for Michael to go back to court one more time. He had to fight on. He didn't want his daughter ever to think that he had given up on her. The last eight years had made him a realist, however. He knew that even though it was his right and his duty to be a father every day to his children, the Family Division would never let that happen.

There had to be a better way.

Postlogue

If you shut up truth and bury it under the ground, it will but grow, and gather to itself such explosive power that the day it bursts through it will blow up everything in its way.

—Émile Zola, *J'accuse*

Millions of parents nationwide, especially fathers, will recognize the torment that my family has endured in the Family Division as not unlike their own experience. Divorce should never be undertaken lightly and it certainly does not create the ideal conditions for raising children, but it is not something that merits retribution from the courts or society, either.

The fact of the matter is that many times there is no viable alternative. How could any husband or wife—perhaps faced with a spouse's infidelities or gross financial irresponsibility or simply confronted by irreconcilable differences—be expected to continue in an incompatible union? I know in my case I could no longer sustain a marriage engulfed in interminable tension and turmoil and I couldn't make it better.

When I concluded that I had to divorce my wife I was convinced that I would at least be able to develop stronger bonds with my children. It never occurred to me to do anything other than share custody of my children with my former wife.

Enter the Family Division. The name seemed at first like a harmless designation—even user-friendly. As far as I was concerned, the name could have been Family Department or Family Section or Family Bureau. Very quickly I learned there was more significance to the title "Family Division" than I had originally thought. To my utter dismay, I came to realize that it meant exactly what it said: family *division*—the place where they divide families, parents from children.

It could have been so simple for us. Two one-parent homes for Jennie, Nathaniel, and Ariel. Not as good as everyone living under one roof, but better than any other alternative. This common-sense arrangement would have meant no Roland Singer, no Sylvia Mendelsohn, no Barbara Cymerman—just a mother and father rearing their children. All Judge Kaplan or Judge Wettick had to do, way back in 1987, was order Nancy and me into a room to work out a custody schedule with only one stipulation—that custody time between the parents be equal. No exceptions, unless both parents agreed to them. If it turned out that one of the children didn't want to adhere to the schedule, too bad. There are lots of things little boys and girls don't want to do (brush their teeth, eat their dinner, go to bed), but they are told to do these things because they are good for them. And what can be better or more important for a child than love, nurturing, and guidance from both a mother and a father?

Unfortunately, neither Judge Wettick nor Judge Kaplan ever issued any such order. They did what they probably do in nearly all contested custody cases, what their colleagues throughout the country do under the guise of the "best interests of the child" (and before that under the "tender years" doctrine which assumed that the mother was always the more appropriate parent to have custody during a child's formative years)—they diminish the role of one of the parents in the lives of their children, almost always that of the father. No-fault divorce may have put an end to judging the behavior of husband and wife during the marriage, but the system has no qualms about pretending to identify a more important parent—a primary parent—even though there is no such thing.

A mother may spend more time with the children so that the father can be the principal breadwinner, even in the age of dual parent incomes. But does the child then love or need one parent any more or less? And does that mean, if circumstances suddenly changed (e.g., divorce), that the breadwinner parent would be incapable of organizing a carpool or scheduling a dentist appointment or preparing a school lunch? Why is a parent penalized for providing for his or her family?

The notion that a child would function better psychologically in the custody of one parent rather than with both parents is as preposterous as the concept that "consistency" or "continuity" provided by one home is more important after divorce than strong ties to both parents in two homes. Why is it so difficult for judges and court-appointed psychologists and psychiatrists to understand that when parents divorce they still have something very important to offer *their* children? Children must not be divided between capable, loving parents! But that was exactly what the Family Division did to me—separated me from my children (Ariel in particular).

I am a competent parent. So, if this could happen to me, a caring, responsible father with adequate financial resources, this could happen to anyone. And it does. In my county alone the local psychological association documented an "epidemic" of complaints and parental losses. Undoubtedly, this "epidemic" is just the tip of the iceberg. Surely, most parents and children do not comprehend how brutally their rights have been trampled upon. How many court-appointed psychologists and psychiatrists (let alone the judges and the attorneys) care about or even understand ethical issues such as dual relationships and conflicts of interest?

Doctors are supposed to treat patients ethically based upon a diagnosis (i.e., an evaluation) and try to restore health and well-being as quickly as possible. Patients can seek a second opinion or decline the treatment. Those choices don't exist in the Family Division. In my case, Dr. Roland Singer and Dr. Sylvia Mendelsohn called for ongoing (and unending) monitoring and/or therapy, which meant paycheck after paycheck for them. With my family in the clutches of the Family Division, I could not refuse. Ethical principles for psychologists and psychiatrists are supposed to prevent this kind of exploitation. Sadly, there appears to be little adherence to these principles. The judges and the mental health professionals are indefatigable in their misguided efforts to choose a so-called primary (i.e., more important) parent and make the other parent merely a "visitor" in the lives of his or her children.

By choosing between mothers and fathers, Family Divisions inevitably drive away "less important" parents. This outrage must stop for everyone's sake, particularly for the million or so children of divorce every year. It is a disaster for them and for society. Increasingly, studies indicate that the unraveling of the family is the major cause of the escalation of crime and violence nationwide. The importance of mothers and fathers (as nurturers, educators, and role models) to their children knows no social or racial borders. Children want and need *both* parents whenever possible to teach them the differences between right and wrong and good and evil—whether the youngsters live in housing projects or in affluent communities. Family Divisions are creating emotional and social chaos, destroying families that could have easily been preserved by simply establishing two one-parent households.

The deleterious effects of divorce on society have been endlessly discussed in the media, but divorce is not the problem. The problem is our judicial system, our adversarial legal system, which destroys the family after divorce. Prior to my divorce I would never have thought that a significant cause of family and social breakdown and criminality in the United States would be the judicial system itself. It sounds implausible, but it is true.

I have come to this conclusion after witnessing and experiencing for nine years (and counting) the emotional and financial disaster that befalls families arriving at the gates of the custody industry. Women and children to the left, fathers and checkbooks to the right as Family Divisions process an endless stream of victims. It is this enterprise which plays the largest role in creating the Fatherless America of our generation. The boys and girls of divorce who then grow up without adequate ties to their fathers are deprived of one of their two most important role models. These youngsters never have a chance to observe that masculinity and fatherhood are not about having sex with partner after partner, or doing drugs, or carrying a gun, or running away from responsibility.

In my opinion, judges, attorneys, mental health professionals, and the rest of their ilk bear much of the responsibility for the modern calamities of rampant drug use, domestic abuse, violent crime, and white-collar crime. The seeds are sown in Family Divisions throughout the country. Daily the judiciary and its minions destroy thousands of families by:

- ignoring constitutional protections such as due process;
- creating "less important," disposable parents;
- arbitrarily tearing away the "less important" parents from their offspring;
- stimulating huge child-support demands in order to justify the need for Family Divisions and misleading the public with the notion that Family Divisions are doing something worthwhile.

Let us hope that it is just a matter of time before the public realizes that the real Criminal Divisions are the Family Divisions. Americans clamor for immediate results, though, especially when it comes to crime. The public wants more gun control, more prisons, more police officers, tougher laws, even the abandonment of individual rights. In the meantime, the latest preschool victims of the Family Divisions are growing up in stress-filled and dysfunctional homes, often to become tomorrow's angry, disturbed, violent adults . . . tomorrow's gang leaders, embezzlers, and murderers. Clearly, the way to solve the crime problem isn't just more gun control, prisons, police officers, and laws—just as the cure for polio was not more iron lungs. One major source of the problem must be eradicated. Family Divisions, Family Courts, in their present state, must go.

The current system—even correcting for the ethical corruption I encountered—doesn't work, can't work, and won't ever work because it is structured on the false premises of "primary" parents and "less important" parents. The judicial system must no longer be permitted to judge what cannot be judged. The "best interests of children" are unimpeded and continuing access to both parents. Fathers and mothers must continue to take care of their children after divorce—not abandon them and not be shoved out of their children's lives.

Lamentably, my family will never know true justice. Al-

Postlogue 533

though I hold the system responsible for our immeasurable pain and suffering, I do not in any way pardon the "ethical" conduct of those who could have made a difference.

The judges in particular, who more than anyone else are expected to uphold the law, failed to follow the rules as they apply to the judiciary. Then, they ordered their appointees to violate the ethical strictures of their professions. The ancient Middle Eastern proverb is indeed apt: A fish begins to stink at the head.

"But I sure as heck am going to do everything I can to see what I can do to save the kids," said Judge Kaplan sanctimoniously at a 1992 public forum on "Strengthening Marriage and Family Life." Save them from what, Judge Kaplan—a loving parent? By appointing and reappointing unethical psychologists? Judge Kaplan went on to assert that he is an "advocate of mediation as a way of helping people solve their problems. That's a negotiation between folks using an independent, neutral party who will assist them to come to an arrangement." Sounds good. Mediation has a nice soft sound. It seems to subsume middle ground, mean, median, remediation. Yet, how can mediation be fair when both sides are aware that, if the case goes back to court, the "primary" parent will win and the "less important" parent will lose? In other words, the "less important" parent—generally the father—had better be happy just to have his children every other weekend or he'll run the risk of losing them altogether at the hands of a Family Division judge. Mediation isn't an opportunity for reaching a fair arrangement—it is more like court-sanctioned blackmail, not to mention an opportunity to reduce the court's workload and make money for mediators.

Judge Kaplan himself, in an article he wrote for a quarterly publication called *Family Advocate*, minced no words about the pitfalls of taking up his time by litigating in the Family Division. The article's title: "Stay Out of Court."*

Family Advocate 13, no. 1 (Summer 1990): 8–10.

What a deplorable philosophy for a judge! Is the citizenry supposed to fear the judicial system? Shouldn't the public be able to depend on the courts to stand for fairness, due process, and equal protection under the law?

Bradley Plowman couldn't stay out of Judge Kaplan's court. When he and his wife, Diane Plowman, divorced in 1988, she was awarded primary physical custody of their only child and Bradley settled for partial physical custody. Less than a year later, Diane decided to move out of state with their son. Bradley immediately petitioned the court to prevent her from moving. Judge Kaplan denied the father's petition without even holding a full evidentiary hearing. Two years later, the Superior Court of Pennsylvania ruled:

"This was *error*. . . . However, we cannot redress this error by eliminating all the proceedings that have occurred until this point. Our review must be based on the best interests of the child at the time of the present hearing. . . . We cannot ignore the last two years of the child's life as though they never occurred. Therefore, we find . . . that it would be useless to pass judgment on the prior decision" (emphasis added).*

Bradley Plowman had to fight on for two years before being vindicated in the State's Appellate Court, but he still didn't get his child back. Assuredly, there are other parents who have had the same injustices perpetrated on their families, but who are probably too drained emotionally and financially to resist or even compose a complaint or a petition. How can anyone survive the Family Division gulag and then return to tell about what goes on there? The damage to society that Kaplan, Wettick, and their fellow judges perpetrate by dividing families (sometimes based on the recommendations of censured psychologists) is nothing short of barbarous.

Diane Plowman v. Bradley Plowman, Appellant, in the Superior Court of Pennsylvania No. 01290 Pittsburgh 1990.

I know that the damage my children and I have suffered at the hands of the Family Division is not as severe as the misfortunes of others. I have heard stories far more ghastly than my own from divorced parents who, through no fault of their own, have forever lost all contact with their sons and daughters. These traumatic tales undeniably serve as a warning for other parents who think they may have the wherewithal to fight for their children. Word gets around and many attorneys representing the "less important" parents no doubt advise them that, if they wish to spend more than every other weekend with their children, they had better have plenty of money, be prepared for the long haul, and be prepared ultimately to lose.

If good parents with significant financial resources have, at best, limited success in Family Divisions when they are opposed by adversarial former spouses who have been dubbed the "primary" parent, where then does that leave good parents of limited financial means: the school teacher, the insurance salesperson, the truck driver, the laid-off worker? It leaves them shut out of their children's lives without any hope. Their children are as important to them and to society as mine are to me. Could these brokenhearted, devastated parents be the so-called Deadbeat Dads and Moms?

The vast amount of child support that changes hands in this country is unconscionable. The total, in the billions of dollars, should not be regarded as a benchmark of success for the system, but more as a measure of failure, a measure of the loss of love and emotional support of countless children, and a measure of the bitterness of countless parents deprived of their children (but not their bills). If Family Divisions made sure divorced parents independently housed and nurtured their children, there would not be the need to force the transfers of these huge sums of money and I believe there would not be the exploding trend of one-parent families, almost all of which are headed by mothers. The absence of fathers has nothing to do with any ambivalence, irresponsibility, or inadequacy regarding men toward fatherhood. It reflects the end result of the prejudice against "less important" parents, invariably fathers. Many of these "less important" parents eventually disappear from their families because it is impossible to fight this dreadful system and it is too painful to endure the loss of a child. Could anyone have really blamed me had I chosen at some point to give up, cut my losses, and walk away from the relentless assault on my fatherhood?

For the good of the nation the American people must get the judicial system out of family life following divorce. I have sacrificed my family's anonymity because I want my children to live in a safe and just society. Family Divisions must stop dividing families. In other words, unless one parent voluntarily relinquishes his or her rights, custody should always be joint (shared). (Even in such a case, however, the parent relinquishing rights should be urged to do otherwise for the sake of the child.) Divorcing parents don't suddenly forget how to be mothers or fathers. They still love their children. They just can't live with their spouses any longer. No matter what their income level or social status, children need both parents, even more so after divorce.

Changes have to be made:

- I call for state legislatures to mandate no-fault shared custody and to guarantee a presumption of equality between the sexes following divorce. The best interests of children are served when they have continuing, unimpeded access to both parents. They don't need the judicial system trying to determine if one parent is more capable than the other. To a child there is no such thing. (Even if there were such a being as a "primary parent," what my case illustrates is that the judicial system would never figure out who it is!) Custody should be equal for each parent unless otherwise agreed upon. Detractors of joint custody claim that if former spouses don't get along, joint custody isn't the answer because of the effects of continuing acrimony on the children. But why reward either parent with sole or primary custody for being uncooperative? With mandated joint custody both parents will have to live reasonably close to each other. Out-of-state moves with the children for economic or personal reasons will not be tolerated unless the other parent gives his or her consent. Moreover, parents will understand from the start that they had better abide by the law and cooperate with the other parent or face the loss of all custody rights. (Maybe some parents then will decide to stay married.)

In regard to cases involving alleged child abuse, such charges should be adjudicated in a criminal court because child abuse is much more than a custody issue. It is against the law. Guilty parents should be sentenced accordingly, as should parents making bogus charges.

• I call for child support to be fairly apportioned so that each parent can afford to provide a home for his and her children. It may mean more fiscal restraints for the parents and the children, but what is more important to a child, his accommodations or a continuing relationship with both parents? In my case, the court paid no attention to the expenses I incurred to support my children (e.g., clothing, food, maintaining my family home).

- I call for all divorced mothers and fathers to recognize the obligation to continue to take care of and nurture their children. Child support is not just financial support. It is emotional support and psychological support—from both parents.

- I call for all married (and engaged) couples to sign a (pre)nuptial agreement which states: In the event of divorce, we agree to equally shared joint custody and agree that neither of us will interfere with the other's custody rights and obligations to any and all children from our marriage and that this is in the best interests of our children now and always. Again, if abuse is a possible issue, it should be handled by the criminal courts. A prenuptial agreement would certainly not provide a loophole in that instance.

- I call for mandatory continuing education on ethical issues for all Family Division judges, attorneys, court appointees, and all other appropriate professionals.

- I call for state legislatures to put an end to the flagrant abuse of constitutional guarantees and the reign of error in family courts. Citizens must no longer lose their children and property through the lack of proper hearings, the inability to confront one's accusers, and, in general, the total lack of due process.

- I call for psychologists and psychiatrists to get out of the business of splitting up families and desist from participating in court-ordered custody evaluations and becoming the tools of the courts. There is no way to truly determine an "unfit parent" (barring instances of abuse), and such a creature may not even exist. Who would determine the criteria for deciding who is unfit?

- I call for attorneys to stop acting as "hired guns" for their clients. The legal profession and society must refrain from characterizing men (or any group) as spousal abusers, child abusers, child molesters, and all the rest when there is no credible evidence to support these claims. This demonization of men ultimately prods Family Division judges to exclude even more fathers from their families, thereby creating more angry, maladjusted children who, in their maturity, are even more likely to become dysfunctional or even violent. Keeping men away from their children does not make women and children safe—it makes all of us less safe.

- I call for the media to cover Family Divisions with the same attention reserved for criminal courts. If families are forced into a public forum, then what occurs there should be subject to public scrutiny. In the same vein, related reports and studies that have far-reaching implications for the general population (such as the task force report) must no longer go unreported in the press.

- I call for an end to the election of judges as if they were politicians. Selection for judgeship should depend on more than an identifiable name, a clever campaign slogan, and a political war chest. Judges should be nominated by independent panels and the nominees should then have to pass examinations of competency (dealing not only with legal, but with ethical issues). A law diploma alone is not a sufficient credential for a judgeship. (In order to be a specialist in dermatology and in dermatopathology I had to take two competency examinations, years beyond medical school.) Many elected judges demonstrate no objective measures of competence and they are more than capable of causing horrific damage to individuals and society.

- I call for the formation of judicial conduct boards that have sufficient staffs and resources to adjudicate complaints in a comprehensive and timely manner. It took more than a year for a decision to be reached concerning my complaints against Judges Wettick and Kaplan. During that time period the judicial conduct board had no full-time prosecuting attorney and only one investigator. I don't even know if any kind of formal investigation or hearing took place. The decision made available to me was all of four lines long.

- I call for State Bureaus of Professional and Occupational Affairs to pay as much attention to complaints of ethical violations in custody cases as they do (at least by newspaper accounts) to cases of sexual exploitation and drug addiction.

- I call for the members of the American Psychiatric Association to reevaluate how they adjudicate ethics complaints against their members and to pay more attention to protecting patients than psychiatrists. Procedures currently in place favor the accused member: the complainant is not permitted to hear the testimony of the accused, there is no cross-examination of the accused, no opportunity for any rebuttal by the complainant, no venue for closing arguments. It was painfully obvious at the Sylvia Mendelsohn ethics hearing that the lawyers present as "resource people" were merely there for window dressing and that the panel members themselves did not have any understanding of the ethical issues. Perhaps the creation of independent bodies including citizens completely unbiased toward the profession would be the best way for arbitration to proceed.

- I call for the federal judicial system to respond to civil rights suits in family matters when so much is at stake for parents, children, and society. (Unfortunately, my suit against Dr. Sylvia Mendelsohn was dismissed prior to a trial on the grounds that the statute of limitations had expired before the suit was filed. My attorneys appealed the decision with the firm belief that the judge had erred in his decision, but the appeal was denied. Perhaps the federal court took the easy way out because my case could have opened a Pandora's box. Innumerable other divorced parents have suffered the same kinds of civil rights violations, but are totally unaware of the ethical violations which led to the loss of their children.)

And, of course . . .

- I call for the return to me of my daughter, Ariel, who at the age of thirteen has been taken from me by the Family Division. My appeals concerning her attending an out-of-state boarding school have been for naught.

At an August 11, 1995 emergency hearing concerning my petition to prevent Ariel from being enrolled in boarding school, Judge Kaplan heard Ariel testify in his chambers. In response to questions from the judge and the attorneys in the case, she made the following statements:

My mom suggested the idea of going to boarding school. . . . I disagreed at first. I didn't want to go, but I thought about it more and more and then . . . I told her that I was thinking about it. . . . So we started to look at them. . . .

I told [my dad] I was thinking about going to boarding school. He said, "Over my dead body." . . . I think . . . he thinks that a child should be brought up with the family and that they shouldn't be taken away from those relationships. I think going away to boarding school, especially this boarding school, . . . would give me a chance to learn new things. . . . And there's also so many more things I can do there because it's a much bigger school, . . . more sports and probably more clubs. And I also think it would better the relationship I have with my parents because now that I am home all the time and I see them all the time, I argue with them a lot and going away—I mean communicating with them through letters and over the phone, I think, would make it easier. There wouldn't be arguments. . . . I think going away to boarding school is the best for myself. . . . This [conflict with my parents] is definitely part of why I want to go away. It's my school mostly, but also that . . . some of the things that go on [conflict between my parents] really bother me, but . . . it's not constant worry.

Judge Kaplan then heard me, in open court, give the following replies to the questioning by Paul Leventon and by Harry Gruener:

. . . Ariel has been deprived of a great deal of contact with her father over the last few years and I think it is terribly important that she be given the opportunity . . . to, at long last, develop a very, very close bond with her father. . . . Ariel is an incredible child. I think she is beautiful, smart, articulate. She's certainly no shrinking violet or wallflower. She speaks her mind and I think it is terrific that she thinks she is competent to go off to boarding school and lead her own life and make decisions on her own. But—she is only thirteen years old and that is what parents are for. . . . Adults make the decisions and, if we choose between a child's opinion and the one parent who wants to take care of her, I submit that it is the father's opinion that ought to hold sway and not that of a thirteen-year-old. . . . I think

Ariel's [desire] in going to boarding school is of interest, but I don't think it is the overriding factor. . . . Ariel needs me more than she realizes at this stage and anybody who has ever studied [these things knows that] what gives [children] the best chance of growing up and doing well in life is having two parents available to them. You can't have surrogate parents at a boarding school. You have to have your own parents, and that is what is going to give her the best chance in life. . . . If Ariel feels conflicted [between my former wife and me], I am as much a victim as Ariel. . . . Her mother has moved mountains to try to keep my daughter away from me . . . so to lose Ariel at this point in her life not only victimizes Ariel because it deprives her of both parents, it victimizes me because I have been the one who is suffering the loss of my daughter all these years. We have three standing Court Orders that say Ariel is supposed to be with me every week of the year and I am not the one who has violated these three standing hard-fought Court Orders and sent my daughter off 500 miles away. And being 500 miles away is not going to solve Ariel's problem about being conflicted between two homes. The intense, incredible . . . animosity . . . that emanates from her mother is not going to be solved by sending her 500 miles away. It's not going to solve any of Ariel's problems. You don't solve problems by running away from them. It's better for Ariel to have stress and parents than to go off to school and have perhaps no stress and no parents or have different kinds of stress at school and no parents. . . . [Should we discount the reasons Ariel reportedly gave in Judge Kaplan's chambers this morning as to why she wants to go to boarding school?] Yes. I think you have to understand where Ariel is coming from. . . . She knows what answers to give. She also knows whatever she says is going to be reported to both parents. Ariel was horribly burned when her words were betrayed by the psychiatrist [Sylvia Mendelsohn] she was forced to see. . . . Ariel has been extremely careful not to say things that are going to alienate either of her parents. . . . The issue is not the [boarding] schools' quality. I am sure [they] are fine schools, but they are no better than schools that are available to my daughter in Pittsburgh. . . . I love my daughter . . . and I will take care of her and make sure she gets a good education and is prepared for the rest of her life. . . .

Though present, Nancy never spoke. Her attorney did by way of closing argument. First, however, Paul Leventon reiterated my views:

This is the Proceeding where Michael Nieland felt he had to draw the line. . . . Despite his attempts to cooperate and make things well or as well as they can be between him and his children and his former wife, it never happened. The one thing that was constant in this case, there was always contact on a weekly basis between all of the minor children and both parents. . . . We are not talking about what she wants to do. . . . To be sent away to boarding school—and no doubt she wants that right now—I think is adverse to this child's best interests at this time. . . . Michael Nieland is willing to run the risk of having his daughter angry at him because he knows what he is doing is in her long-term best interests. And I think that is the critical, fundamental, underlying fact that the Court has to decide today.

Harry Gruener then gave his summation:

Your Honor, I would like to bring us back to where I think we are procedurally. There has been a petition in this case for emergency relief. The Court has heard from the child and heard from the only other witness [Michael] that the moving party in this case plans to present. And, therefore, we are evaluating at this stage without having my client or any of my witnesses testify because I think the burden of proof rests with the Petitioner [Michael]. The question, therefore, on the threshold is whether or not that burden has been met. . . . Your Honor, . . . who can initially make this educational decision? This educational decision has now been characterized to you [by the Plaintiff] as a decision that has been made by a thirteen-year-old. In fact, that decision is supported by that thirteen-year-old's mother who, . . . approximately 70 percent of the time, [has] physical custody [of Ariel]. . . . My client . . . was certainly within her rights to listen to her daughter and to either take an affirmative or a negative position. . . . I think it is presumptuous and incredible that her father would get up on the stand and tell you that nothing she [Ariel] says should be given any credence. Nothing she says means anything. Nothing she says is worth anything. . . . Dr. Nieland characterized . . . boarding schools as bad for his child. . . . There is simply an absolute closed, steel-trap mind. There is no alternative. If the kid doesn't stay here, nothing is any better for her. . . . I don't think that kind of testimony sheds light on anything. . . . With all due respect, Dr. Nieland is entitled as a parent to come in and offer his opinion on what is in the best interests of his child. But—this Court has been in the habit of meeting your burden of proof in this case to require a little more than that. . . . If Ariel is going to be forever traumatized and psychologically damaged, he better come in here with some evidence of that. There are no other witnesses. There is no other corroboration. There is no other substantiation. This is an extraordinarily angry man. . . . This is a man who is absolutely obsessed with the notion that this child is his and belongs here with him under his tutelage. . . . There is no reasoning with the Plaintiff. . . . I think that the Court, unlike Dr. Michael Nieland, will not disregard everything the child says. . . . Therefore, Your Honor, in closing, . . . I think that the burden of proof required under the Petition has not been met and for that reason . . . I would ask at this point that the Court deny the relief sought.

After the attorneys concluded their comments, Judge Kaplan made his unsurprising ruling:

> I must say that I found [Ariel] to be quite impressive and, obviously, this child inherited something good and I have to assume that it came from both sides of the family. . . . In fact, I think that everyone agrees that she is quite remarkable. . . . The Supreme Court has made it clear that the child's preference is certainly not binding on the Court—that a preference, however, is a factor to be given weight. . . . Now, I understand the father's concern, . . . presented rather passionately, that you just can't let a kid have his or her own way on something as important as this. But the thing that I find really disturbing was the inability of the father to accept anything that Ariel might express by way of complaints or concerns or desires and that all of her feelings in this regard should be discounted. I think this is a cruel and insulting attitude to take toward a child that obviously has as much competence and maybe even brilliance as this young woman. . . . I think we have a young person who has reached a point in her life where she is crying out to be heard. That, if we don't recognize her feelings in this regard, we could be doing some harm to her. . . . To think that going away to school is writing her off as a child, I think, also belittles her as an individual and her capabilities. I would see perhaps in this new chapter in her life a new appreciation, in fact, coming from her for her family. . . . So, I feel, based upon the evidence that we have received in this case, that the request of the father for an injunction to prevent Ariel from being enrolled in boarding school, that the evidence does not support that and on that basis, having not met the burden which I feel would be required, I think it is appropriate to dismiss the Petition with the understanding, therefore, that Ariel would be in a position to enroll in the school as she has planned and we will enter an Order consistent with that.

Aside from the fact that it was up to me, *her father*, to meet a burden of proof to keep my daughter from leaving me, there are no words to express my outrage when I heard Judge Kaplan call me "cruel and insulting" because of my "inability ... to accept anything that Ariel might express by way of complaints or concerns or desires and that all of her feelings in this regard should be discounted."

Wasn't Judge Kaplan listening when I testified: "I think it is terrific that she thinks she is competent to go off to boarding school and lead her own life and make decisions on her own. But—she is only thirteen years old and that is what parents are for"? Or, when I said that Ariel's desire to go to boarding school "is of interest, but I don't think it is the over-riding factor"?

I guess not. After eight years in this man's courtroom I didn't think anything he said or did could offend me any more. I was wrong. He placed 500 miles between my daughter and me and mocked me to boot.

All that was left was for Ariel to leave for school, which she did on September 7, 1995. Nancy had won again. But all of us lost.

—Michael L. Nieland